TOWN AND COUNTRYSIDE
IN WESTERN BERKSHIRE, c.1327–c.1600

Town and Countryside in Western Berkshire, c. 1327–c. 1600

Social and economic change

Margaret Yates

THE BOYDELL PRESS

First published 2007
The Boydell Press, Woodbridge

ISBN 978-1-84383-328-4

The Boydell Press is an imprint of Boydell & Brewer Ltd
PO Box 9, Woodbridge, Suffolk IP12 3DF, UK
and of Boydell & Brewer Inc.
668 Mt Hope Avenue, Rochester, NY 14620, USA
website: www.boydellandbrewer.com

A catalogue record of this publication is available
from the British Library

This publication is printed on acid-free paper

Typeset by Carnegie Book Production, Lancaster
Printed in Great Britain by Biddles Ltd., King's Lynn, Norfolk

For Nick

Contents

List of tables, figures and maps

Tables

Figures

Maps

Acknowledgements

The research for this book began as my DPhil thesis, was expanded during a post-doctoral fellowship at Birmingham and continued after my return to Reading. Over the years I have received a multitude of kindnesses and incurred many debts and it gives me great pleasure to record my gratitude and appreciation.

I am delighted to begin by thanking Barbara Harvey and Richard Smith for their unstinting generosity of time and expertise that continues to the present and this book. I had the great good fortune of having two supervisors whose personal and professional qualities complemented each other to my advantage. The examiners of my thesis have also played a part in my achievements, the late Rees Davies, and Richard Britnell who continues to exert an 'invisible hand' in gently guiding and supporting me and for which I am extremely grateful. His detailed reading and recommendations improved this book considerably and prevented several pitfalls. It is a pleasure to record my thanks to Chris Dyer who provided me with two stimulating years at Birmingham, expanded my intellectual horizons, and has been a meticulous and very generous mentor. Jim Bolton ensured my time at the IHR was stimulating and enjoyable. The thesis and fellowship were both funded by the ESRC (R000237829 and R00429334393) and I was the fortunate recipient of a Yorkist History Trust Fellowship to finance my final year. I am grateful to both for their generosity.

Over the years friends and colleagues have made research a real pleasure and have been willing to debate, affirm and challenge my ideas and assumptions and generous in sharing their insights and references. There are too many to cite here and many will be found in the footnotes and bibliography but I must thank Rowenna Archer, Ian Blanchard, Paul Brand, Bruce Campbell, Anne Curry, Joan Dils, Ralph Evans, Ross Faith, John Hare, John Hatcher, Ralph Houlbrooke, Stuart Jenks, Hannes Kleineke, Ro Leamon, John Lee, Mavis Mate, the late Thora Morrish, Avner Offer, Zvi Razi, Phillipp Schofield, David Stone, Anne Sutton, Robert Swanson and my colleagues at Reading. I would like to single out Jane Whittle and Richard Hoyle in appreciation of their particular friendships.

The documentary research undertaken would not have been possible without the assistance and advice from the staff at various archives who I would like to thank: the Berkshire Record Office, the National Archives, New College Oxford, Winchester College, the British Library, Shakespeare Birthplace Trust, St George's Chapel Windsor, Southampton City Archive, Surrey History Centre, Hampshire Record Office, the Bodleian Library, West Berkshire Museum, the Mercers' Company, the Guildhall in London, and to Mr Eyston for allowing me to consult his family archive. I am particularly grateful to Caroline Dalton, Peter Durrant, Eileen Scarff, and members of the MEMRIS team for their guidance. Amanda Loaring at West Berkshire Museum has been generous in permitting the use of the image of Shaw House.

A special thanks are due to Caroline Palmer at Boydell and Brewer who was instrumental in ensuring the book would be published.

It is a pleasure to acknowledge the loving support I have received from my children and their tolerance of growing up in 'thesis country'. Finally, and above all, my thanks are to Nick for the many and varied, often silent and unseen, ways in which he has encouraged and enabled me to achieve my aspirations. It is with love that the book is dedicated to him.

Lammas Day, 2007

Abbreviations

AgHRev	*Agricultural History Review*
BIHR	*Bulletin of the Institute of Historical Research*
BL	British Library
BRO	Berkshire Record Office
Cal. Close Rolls	*Calendar of Close Rolls* (HMSO, London, 1892–)
CPR	*Calendar of Patent Rolls* (HMSO, London, 1891–)
CUHB	D. M. Palliser (ed.), *The Cambridge Urban History, of Britain: Volume I, 600–1540* (Cambridge, 2000)
EcHRev	*Economic History Review*
EETS	Early English Text Society
EHR	*English Historical Review*
JBS	*Journal of British Studies*
JEH	*Journal of Economic History*
L&P Henry VIII	*Letters and Papers Foreign and Domestic, of the Reign of Henry VIII* (London, 1862–).
Miller, *Agrarian History* III	E. Miller (ed.), *The Agrarian History of England and Wales, III, 1348–1500* (Cambridge, 1991)
NCA	New College Archive
SBT	Shakespeare Birthplace Trust
SHC	Surrey History Centre
Thirsk, *Agrarian History* IV	J. Thirsk (ed.), *The Agrarian History of England and Wales: IV, 1500–1640* (Cambridge, 1967)
TNA	The National Archives
TRHS	*Transactions of the Royal Historical Society*
VCH Berkshire	Ditchfield, P. H., and W. Page (eds), *The Victoria History of the Counties of England: Berkshire*, 4 vols (London, 1907)
WCM	Winchester College Muniments

Sums of money

Monetary values are cited in pre-decimal sterling (pounds, shillings and pence), in which:

12 old pence (styled as 12d.)	= 1 shilling (1s.)	= 5 new pence (5p); and
20 shillings (20s.)	= £1	
Thus £1 6s. 8d.	= £1.34	
A mark was 13s. 4d.		

CHAPTER 1

The end of the Middle Ages?

A powerful concept has developed in the minds of historians and the history-reading public alike that society and the economy of the sixteenth century were fundamentally different from what had gone before.[1] A historical fault line of seismic proportions lies at the end of the fifteenth century. It has been re-enforced by the institutional and academic divisions within the discipline into 'periods' of history as medieval, early modern and modern which have led to segregation into specialisms and a fragmentation of research into chronologically discrete agendas.[2] This notion is now challenged by medievalists who argue that core structures and important changes were already under way before 1400 and many had their roots in an earlier period.[3] The purpose of this book is consciously to bridge the historical divide at the end of the middle ages through a case study of western Berkshire that identifies evidence for the nature and pace of change in town and countryside from the fourteenth century and continues through the sixteenth century. In doing so it addresses key historical questions of what changed, when and why in a period that has become characterised as one of transition.

To understand how the idea of an end to the middle ages developed we need to begin with the Italian Renaissance. In the conditions of rapid social and cultural change scholars wanted to create a direct link between themselves and the period of classical antiquity, and in doing so to distance themselves from the more recent past which they regarded as significantly different from their own time.[4] The division into medieval and modern history in England

---

[1] It is explicit in the work of K. Wrightson, see particularly *Earthly Necessities. Economic Lives in Early Modern Britain* (New Haven, 2000), 22–4.

[2] This concept is not confined to the discipline of history as it also acts as a constraint in archaeology. D. Gaimster and P. Stamper (eds), *The Age of Transition. The Archaeology of English Culture, 1400–1600* (Oxford, 1997), ix–xiii.

[3] Most notably R. H. Britnell, 'The English Economy and the Government, 1450–1550', in J. L. Watts (ed.), *The End of the Middle Ages? England in the Fifteenth and Sixteenth Centuries* (Stroud, 1998), 89–116.

[4] During the seventeenth century the notion of three historical periods – antiquity, the middle ages, and modern times – was being employed academically in historical

was reinforced at the moment when the subject was becoming recognised as a professional discipline, usually regarded as the appointment of William Stubbs to the Regius Chair of Modern History at Oxford in 1866.[5] In his lectures delivered in 1880 'On the characteristic differences between medieval and modern history' the medieval period ended with the conclusion of the Wars of the Roses and the advent of strong monarchical government.[6] History as conceived by Stubbs and his followers was almost entirely political and constitutional and there was an assumption that economic changes would follow.[7] Indeed, William Cunningham accepted, as a matter of convenience, the chronological periods of political and social history as the divisions for economic history.[8]

A strong and recurring theme in the writings of economic historians of the late nineteenth and twentieth centuries was their perception of the rapid and revolutionary changes of the fifteenth and sixteenth centuries. They sought to identify the cause and foundations of the English Industrial Revolution and so were particularly interested in the features of the agrarian revolution such as the conversion of arable to pasture and an increase in the amount of enclosure; and also the expansion in the manufacture of cloth with changes in the organisation from that based on the independent family unit to the capitalist clothier or merchant who controlled the various processes of production. These features were seen in association with the expansion of trade and markets following the voyages of discovery. And all were taking place in the context of the cultural and religious changes of the Renaissance and Reformation.[9] Their

instruction. These began with Cellarius' manuals for the classroom that were in use in 1675. W. K. Ferguson, *The Renaissance in Historical Thought* (Cambridge, Massachusetts, 1948), 1–77. A. Marwick, *The Nature of History*, 3rd edn (Basingstoke, 1989), 273.

[5] N. B. Harte (ed.), *The Study of Economic History: Collected Inaugural Lectures* (London, 1971), xviii.

[6] W. Stubbs, *Seventeen Lectures on the Study of Medieval and Modern History and Kindred Subjects*, 3rd edn (Oxford, 1900), 238–76.

[7] Harte, *Economic History*, xix.

[8] W. Cunningham, *The Growth of English Industry and Commerce during the Early and Middle Ages* (Cambridge, 1882; 4th edn 1905), 20–1.

[9] There is a huge literature and what follows is just an illustrative outline. Cunningham, *Growth of English industry and commerce*, 473ff, where the preliminary survey of the Tudor period begins with a section 'The age of discovery' that covers the voyages and new trade routes. W. J. Ashley, *An Introduction to English Economic History and Theory: Part II, The End of the Middle Ages* (London, 1893; 8th impression 1914), 219–58 within chapter 3 'The woollen industry' and also in chapter 4 'The agrarian revolution'. G. Unwin, *Industrial Organization in the Sixteenth and Seventeenth Centuries* (London, 1904; new impression 1963), 19, describes the process from the fourteenth to the sixteenth century by which the economic independence of the medieval craftsman gave way before the widening of the market and increasing employment of capital, although more emphasis is placed on the mercantile activities of the London liveried companies. R. H. Tawney,

writings have had a strong and protracted influence on our perception of the period as one of significant change.[10]

A common influence in shaping these ideas were the writings of sixteenth-century commentators, men such as Thomas More, Henry Brinklow, Thomas Starkey, and William Harrison who wrote vigorously, and usually in condemnation of the rapid changes they were observing. We should be cautious, however, in accepting their comments literally as many had reasons to exaggerate the conditions of the time.[11] Nevertheless, their comments continue to exert a powerful influence over our interpretation of this as a period of significant change.[12]

The fifteenth and sixteenth centuries have been regarded as the birthplace of the modern economy and society in many of the theoretical explanations for change. Adam Smith traced England's economic progress from the time of Henry VIII and its prosperity from the reign of Elizabeth which, he argued, was a feature that continued until his own day.[13] For Marx the conditions that laid the foundations for the capitalist means of production were to be found in rural England in the last third of the fifteenth century and first few decades of the sixteenth century, which he called the period of primitive accumulation.[14] He dated the capitalist era from the sixteenth century,[15] although the removal of the peasantry from the land was a longer process which was not

The Agrarian Problem in the Sixteenth Century (London, 1912), 184–230 where he argued for the primacy of landownership, the emergence of a new breed of farmer, and the expropriation of the peasantry in the century and a half after 1485, subsequently known as 'Tawney's century'. E. Lipson, *The Economic History of England: Volume 1 The Middle Ages* (London, 1915; 11th edn 1956), chapter IV, 'The agrarian revolution'. J. Clapham, *A Concise Economic History of Britain. From the earliest times to 1750* (Cambridge, 1949; reprinted 1966), 185ff, emphasises the significance of the sixteenth century before his preferred turning point at 1750. W. G. Hoskins, *The Age of Plunder* (London, 1976), a rather later contribution whose title refers to the effects of the re-distribution of land following the Dissolution of the Monasteries.

[10] For example in the work of Wallerstein who emphasises formative events such as the discovery of the Americas, the influx of bullion, the opening up of new markets and the general expansion of trade as revolutionary features of the late fifteenth and particularly of the sixteenth century. I. Wallerstein, *The Modern World-System: Capitalist Agriculture and the Origins of the European World-Economy in the Sixteenth Century* (London, 1974), especially 128.

[11] Lipson, *Economic History of England*, 179–84. M. Yates, 'Between Fact and Fiction: Henry Brinklow's *Complaynt* Against Rapacious Landlords', AgHRev, 54 (2006), 24–44, where Brinklow's comments do not find support in the economic and tenurial conditions at Kintbury in Berkshire where members of his family lived.

[12] Wrightson, *Earthly Necessities*, 3–4.

[13] Adam Smith, *The Wealth of Nations*, Books I–III (Harmondsworth, 1997), Book I p. 192, Book III pp. 517–18.

[14] Karl Marx, *Capital*, vol. I (Harmondsworth, 1990), 873–95, specifically 878.

[15] *Ibid.*, 876.

completed until the end of the eighteenth century.[16] These interpretations have had a lasting impact; for example, Brenner fully accepted Marx's chronology of events.[17] As an early modern historian, Wrightson identified a quickening in the pace of change from the second quarter of the sixteenth century that required major adaptations on the part of contemporary society.[18]

A recurring challenge for historians has been in explaining the dismantling of feudal institutions and the protracted process of transformation into capitalism that has become known in the literature as the 'great transition'. That is, from the system of feudalism where social organisation was not commercial but based on personal loyalty that enabled landlords to extract labour and rent from their dependent peasants in return for land. To a society that understood the concept of profit, production was primarily for the market, where the ownership of land was concentrated in the hands of entrepreneurs who responded to commercial opportunities, whilst the peasantry were no longer tied to the land and increasingly obtained income from wage labour.[19] Nevertheless, it should be noted that many of these characteristics were not new features of the sixteenth century but had their roots in a much earlier period. Recently both Dyer and Wrigley have argued for a protracted period of transition which stretched from 1300, following the rapid structural changes of the twelfth and thirteenth centuries, until at least 1800 when the economy remained 'organic' at the end of half a millennium.[20]

Medieval historians emphasise the significance of the changes that occurred during the two centuries before 1300 of population increase, rapid urbanisation, a greater proportion of the population dependent on the market for essential foodstuffs and waged earning, and they place less importance on the events of the fifteenth and sixteenth centuries.[21] Indeed, from Britnell's

---

[16] *Ibid.*, 883.

[17] T. H. Aston and C. H. E Philpin (eds), *The Brenner Debate. Agrarian Class Structure and Economic Development in Pre-Industrial Europe* (Cambridge, 1985), 46–54.

[18] Wrightson, *Earthly Necessities*, 22–5, 115.

[19] This is an extreme simplification of a vast and complex subject. Important explanations of feudalism and capitalism can be found in C. Dyer, 'Were there any Capitalists in Fifteenth-century England?', in J. Kermode (ed.), *Enterprise and Individuals in Fifteenth-century England* (Stroud, 1991), 1–24. R. H. Hilton, 'Capitalism – What's in a name?', in *idem, The Transition from Feudalism to Capitalism* (London, 1976), 145–58.

[20] C. Dyer, *An Age of Transition?* (Oxford, 2005), 246. E. A. Wrigley, 'The Transition to an Advanced Organic Economy: Half a Millennium of English Agriculture', *EcHRev*, 59 (2006), 435–80.

[21] R. H. Britnell, *The Commercialisation of English Society, 1000–1500* (Cambridge, 1993). *Idem,* 'Commerce and Capitalism in Late Medieval England: Problems of Description and Theory', *Journal of Historical Sociology* 6 (1993), 359–76. *Idem,* 'Specialisation in Work in England, 1100–1300', *EcHRev*, 54 (2001), 1–16. C. Dyer, *Making a Living in the Middle Ages. The People of Britain, 850–1520* (New Haven, 2002), 363–5. E. Miller and

detailed study of the years 1450 to 1550 he was unable to identify any unprecedented development of commerce and regarded the century as one of 'exceptionally gradual and unremarkable economic change in England'.[22] He found strong intellectual and social continuity between 1471 and 1529 that 'defied all attempts at identifying fundamental change'.[23] Campbell, rather differently, characterised the later middle ages as a period of contraction in which a protracted process of rationalisation and restructuring was under way after the achievements of the twelfth and thirteenth centuries. This realignment produced the framework on which the new order of the early modern period was founded.[24] Dyer also identified the roots of many of the tendencies of the end of the middle ages in the period before 1300 and argued for a remodelling of social structures and methods of production in the 'long fifteenth century (1350–1520)'.[25]

A framework of events

What were the characteristic features and trends of the period whose interpretation can be the subject of such disagreement? This is a difficult question to answer as there were very few clear trends and many differences of experience that occurred without any unifying force. An attempt will be made here to describe them which will create a framework in which to place the evidence from Berkshire in the following chapters.

We will begin by identifying those elements where continuity was the strongest characteristic; nevertheless even here there were aspects that were modified and developed over the period. The main institutions of the country and social structures were in place before 1400, even 1349 (another favourite watershed), and they would continue after 1600.[26] England was ruled by a monarchy, although subject to usurpations and depositions and an unsettled

---

J. Hatcher, *Medieval England. Rural Society and Economic Change, 1086–1348* (London, 1978), 249–51.

[22] Britnell, 'English Economy and Government', 116.

[23] R. H. Britnell, *The Closing of the Middle Ages? England, 1471–1529* (Oxford, 1997), 254.

[24] B. M. S. Campbell, 'People and Land in the Middle Ages, 1066–1500', in R. A. Dodgshon and R. A. Butlin (eds), *An Historical Geography of England and Wales* (London, 1990), 69–70, 102–13, and reiterated in *idem*, 'England: Land and People', in S. H. Rigby (ed.), *A Companion to Britain in the Later Middle Ages* (Oxford, 2003), 23.

[25] C. Dyer, *An Age of Transition?* (Oxford, 2005), 1–3.

[26] This is another enormous subject and for an excellent summary in a British context see R. H. Britnell, *Britain and Ireland, 1050–1530. Economy and Society* (Oxford, 2004), especially the conclusion.

period of civil war in the middle of the fifteenth century.[27] Monarchs had the ability to disrupt the general trend of economic growth by engaging in foreign wars and imposing the costs on the population through various forms of taxation.[28] Many of the financial and legal institutions that were to continue into the modern period were also in place. Parliament had gained control of taxation, was developing areas in which it could place limitations on the power of kings, and was capable of regulating property rights and labour contracts in the formation and passing of statutes. These were enforced in the king's courts, within the common law, and through developments in the concept of equity, such as the cases before Chancery.[29] One of the outcomes of these developments in the legal system was the facility to curb the arbitrary power of lords.

Throughout the period under study the majority of people lived in the countryside, with about 20 per cent of the population living in towns.[30] Agricultural production dominated the economy. There was little technological change in either agriculture or industry between the fourteenth and sixteenth centuries. The population and economy remained susceptible to changes in the weather and diseases of animals and humans which were seen especially during the harvest failures of 1314–17 and 1438–39, and the arrival of plague in 1348. At the heart of society the family continued to function as the primary social unit.

It is more difficult, however, to identify the precise economic characteristics and defining features of the period as they remain relatively unclear. Many events were episodic and we are aware of the transitory nature of change, especially when we think we can glimpse characteristic features of the future, such as large peasant composite holdings or entrepreneurial industrialists, but find that they were not sustained. It was also a period of contradictory tendencies. Most importantly, there were strong regional differences in the rate of, and reasons for, change. Events in East Anglia were very different from those occurring in the north of England, or indeed, in the Midlands.[31] These

---

[27] There is also a long historiography associated with either supporting or refuting the notion of the 'new monarchy' of the Tudors that is usefully reviewed in J. L. Watts (ed.), *The End of the Middle Ages?* (Stroud, 1998), 1–22.

[28] This was a particular feature of the reigns of Edward I and Edward III. For the negative impact of taxation on the economy of the Tudor period see R. W. Hoyle, 'War and Public Finance', in D. MacCulloch (ed.), *The Reign of Henry VIII* (Basingstoke, 1995), 75–99.

[29] Later developments included the courts of Requests and Star Chamber. See below for implementation at local level.

[30] C. Dyer, 'How Urbanized Was Medieval England?', in J. M. Duvosquel and E. Thoen (eds), *Peasants and Townsmen in Medieval Europe* (Gent, 1995), 169–83.

[31] The regional differences are covered by the relevant chapters in E. Miller (ed.), *The Agrarian History of England and Wales, III, 1348–1500* (Cambridge, 1991) hereafter Miller, *Agrarian History* III, and J. Thirsk (ed.), *The Agrarian History of England and Wales,*

differences can be identified in the rate of population growth, the level of commercialisation, effects of fluctuations in export markets, political upheavals, wars, and raids by the Scots on the North. Within agriculture there were slumps in arable cultivation at the same time as dynamism in pastoral farming. Industrial activity was scattered: it was dominated by the manufacture of cloth that varied in size of operation and level of specialisation,[32] whilst other forms of industrial activity, such as mining, always remained very localised, although capable of long-distance trade.[33] There was no unifying economic force or 'engine' driving economic change as has been argued for the modern period.[34] Subsequent chapters will demonstrate how, even within one region, there were significant differences of experience.

Having acknowledged these difficulties we need to make an attempt to overcome them and describe long-term trends, albeit with caution and caveats, to provide a framework for the detailed study. Changes in the total size of the population have provided important elements within various explanations of this period such as the growth of the economy, urbanisation and market demand. It is important, therefore, to quantify population and understand those influences that shaped demographic change. There are, however, significant methodological difficulties encountered when estimating population in an era without national census data.[35] Prior to this, and especially before 1538, all figures are the result of informed 'best guess' calculations.[36] They reveal a great cycle of expansion, then protracted decline, before a swing back to growth again. Estimates for the size of the population around its medieval

---

IV, 1500–1640 (Cambridge, 1967) hereafter Thirsk, Agrarian History IV. For a detailed comparison of western Berkshire with north-east Norfolk see J. Whittle and M. Yates, '"Pays Réel or Pays Légal"? Contrasting Patterns of Land Tenure and Social Structure in Eastern Norfolk and Western Berkshire, 1450–1600', AgHRev, 48 (2000), 1–26.

[32] M. Zell, Industry in the Countryside. Wealden Society in the Sixteenth Century (Cambridge, 1994). A. R. Bridbury, Medieval English Clothmaking (London, 1982). P. J. Bowden, The Wool Trade in Tudor and Stuart England (London, 1971). E. Carus-Wilson and O. Coleman, England's Export Trade, 1275–1547 (Oxford, 1963). E. Carus-Wilson, Medieval Merchant Venturers (London, 1954).

[33] J. Hatcher, The History of the British Coal Industry. Volume 1, Before 1700: Towards the Age of Coal (Oxford, 1993). I. Blanchard, 'Labour Productivity and Work Psychology in the English Mining Industry, 1400–1600', EcHRev, 31 (1978), 1–24.

[34] F. J. Fisher, 'London as an "Engine of Economic Growth"', in London and the English Economy, 1500–1700 (London, 1990), 185–98.

[35] These are allayed somewhat from 1538 with the introduction of parish registers and the requirement that all incidents of baptism, marriage and burial be recorded. E. A. Wrigley and R. S. Schofield, The Population History of England (Cambridge, 1981), 1–7, 15–32.

[36] A useful review of the evidence for the medieval period remains J. Hatcher, Plague, Population and the English Economy, 1348–1530 (Basingstoke, 1977).

peak in 1300 can range from 4 to 6.5 million.[37] The moment when population levels began to fall remains unclear, it was certainly cut back by the famine of 1314–17.[38] It is widely accepted that the Black Death of 1348–49 and subsequent outbreaks of plague reduced the population by as much as one-third or even a half, and the population in 1377 may have been between 2.25 and 3.25 million.[39] Stagnation or even continued decline in the population for the late medieval period is currently accepted,[40] and could have continued into the 1520s when the population may have been less than 2 million.[41] Whether the failure of the population to recover was due to continuing high levels of mortality or changes in fertility such as a late age of marriage, are a matter of some debate.[42] We

[37] Smith argued for a figure of c.5.5 to c.6.5 million based on back projection from the Poll Tax. On the other hand, Campbell argued for between 4 and 4.25 million from calculations of food supply. R. M. Smith 'Plagues and Peoples', in P. Slack and R. Ward (eds), *The Peopling of Britain. The Shaping of the Human Landscape* (Oxford, 2002), 177–216 and especially 180–1. B. M. S. Campbell, *English Seigniorial Agriculture, 1250–1450* (Cambridge, 2000), 386–410, and 403 for the table of data on size of population. Also see Smith's detailed review of the subject in 'Demographic Developments in Rural England, 1300–48: a Survey', in B. M. S. Campbell, *Before the Black Death* (Manchester, 1991), 25–77.

[38] B. F. Harvey, 'The Population Trend in England between 1300 and 1348', *TRHS*, 16 (1966), 23–42. B. M. S. Campbell, 'The Agrarian Problem in the Early Fourteenth Century', *Past and Present*, 188 (2005), 3–70. C. Dyer, 'Did the Peasants Really Starve in Medieval England?', in M. Carlin and J. T. Rosenthal (eds), *Food and Eating in Medieval Europe* (London, 1998), 53–72.

[39] Smith argued that the population had fallen by at least 50 per cent, whilst Campbell calculated 2.25 to 2.5 million for 1377. References as above.

[40] Mortality levels were certainly high among the monks of Canterbury and Westminster. J. Hatcher, 'Mortality in the Fifteenth Century: Some New Evidence', *EcHRev*, 39 (1986), 19–38. B. Harvey, *Living and Dying in England, 1100–1540: The Monastic Experience* (Oxford, 1993), 112–45. The evidence is reviewed in J. Bolton, '"The World Upside Down". Plague as an Agent of Economic and Social Change', in M. Ormrod, and P. Lindley (eds), *The Black Death in England* (Stamford, 1996), 17–40. See also M. Bailey, 'Demographic Decline in Late Medieval England: Some Thoughts on Recent Research', *EcHRev*, 49 (1996), 1–19.

[41] Figures from B. M. S. Campbell, 'England: Land and People', in S. H. Rigby (ed.), *A Companion to Britain in the Later Middle Ages* (Oxford, 2003), 3–25, especially 9. Previous attempts to estimate the population in the 1520s include Wrigley and Schofield, *Population History*, 566–8. J. Cornwall, 'English Population in the Early Sixteenth Century', *EcHRev*, 23 (1970), 32–44. B. M. S. Campbell, 'The Population of Early Tudor England: A Re-evaluation of the 1522 Muster Returns and 1524 and 1525 Lay Subsidies', *Journal of Historical Geography*, 7 (1981), 145–54. Urban figures can be found in A. Dyer, '"Urban Decline" in England 1377–1525', in T. R. Slater (ed.), *Towns in Decline AD 100–1600* (Aldershort, 2000), 266–88.

[42] For a recent general discussion, and one that emphasises the high levels of mortality in the fifteenth and early sixteenth centuries, see J. Hatcher, 'Understanding the Population History of England 1450–1750', *Past and Present*, 180 (2003), 83–130. This has been

remain unclear about the moment when the population began to expand, and also on the rate of growth;[43] by the 1540s it may have been between 2.8 and 3.1 million.[44] Mortality rates were also high in the 1540s and 1550s, and population did not grow rapidly until the third quarter of the sixteenth century, reaching a figure of 4.1 million in 1601.[45] In addition, we are becoming increasingly aware of the impact of migration in those areas where we can discern early signs of demographic recovery.[46] We should be cautious, therefore, in employing population growth as an explanation for change until late in the sixteenth century.

In the older accounts of the period the opening up of new markets and the general expansion of trade were all perceived as revolutionary features of the late fifteenth and particularly of the sixteenth century.[47] This observation is based upon an assumption that English society was commercialising more rapidly at this time than during earlier centuries, and that considerations of profit were beginning to dominate. Wrightson has argued that medieval economic culture lacked the concept of a market order as a self-regulating system of economic relationships; instead it had been one that was hostile to the notions of individual freedom in economic affairs that he was able to identify in early modern England.[48] The subject of marketing activity should therefore concern us. A traditional method of charting change over an extended period of time has been to examine the movement of prices and exports.[49] This is a

countered by a re-assertion of the importance of economic constraints on marriage to be placed alongside mortality in determining the size of the late medieval population in P. Nightingale, 'Some New Evidence of Crises and Trends in Mortality in Late Medieval England', *Past and Present*, 187 (2005), 33–68.

[43] Hatcher, 'Understanding the Population History' for a summary of the evidence. Ian Blanchard had argued for a continuation of the late medieval pattern until the 1520s in I. Blanchard, 'Population Change, Enclosure and the Early Tudor Economy', *EcHRev*, 23 (1970), 427–45, especially 435, 441–2. Local variation can be seen in Essex where the population of Birchanger was still in decline until 1540 when there was evidence elsewhere of demographic growth in L. Poos, *A Rural Society After the Black Death: Essex, 1350–1525* (Cambridge, 1991), 109.

[44] Wrigley and Schofield, *Population History*, 563–9, especially 566.

[45] Smith 'Plagues and Peoples', 183. Wrigley and Schofield, *Population History*, 528. The evidence for the mortality of the 1550s is summarised in the debate between J. S. Moore and M. Zell in *EcHRev*, 47 (1994), 354–61

[46] M. Yates, 'Change and Continuities in Rural Society from the Later Middle Ages to the Sixteenth Century: The Contribution of West Berkshire', *EcHRev*, 52 (1999), 617–37. And see below, chapter 2.

[47] See references above although the idea has continued, see Wallerstein, *The Modern World-System*, 128.

[48] Wrightson, *Earthly Necessities*, 29.

[49] The following summary is largely drawn from Miller, *Agrarian History* III. Thirsk, *Agrarian History* IV. N. J. Mayhew, 'Population, Money Supply, and the Velocity of

powerful but dangerously simple procedure as the data do not reflect regional differences, the diversity of experience in both rural and urban areas, variations between the different commodities, or changes in patterns of consumption. The importance given to the movement of prices and exports rests on an assumption that the majority of the population were engaged in some form of marketing and trading of commodities, and thus fluctuations in prices and exports will have had an effect on the general well-being of society. Exports are the easiest to quantify, and the main feature was the replacement of wool with manufactured woollen cloth. Continuing alongside, moreover, were the exports of metals such as lead, tin and pewter. Nevertheless it was the quantifiable rise in the export of woollen cloth that underpins the notion of the rapid expansion of trade and manufacture at this time.[50] The total number of cloths exported each year rose from 4,422 in 1348 to 14,445 in 1380 and 38,872 in 1400, followed by a slow-down from 1402 to 1421, and then rising again, to 59,830 in 1440.[51] This was followed by decline during the mid-fifteenth century due to the constraints on trade by political action associated with disputes with the Hansards and Burgundians so that cloth exports reached a new low of 19,957 in 1465.[52] Recovery was quickly achieved, and in 1478 55,968 cloths were exported;[53] thereafter increases were rapid and in 1500 75,890 cloths and in 1544 137,223 cloths were exported. Expansion was disrupted with the breakdown in political alliances from 1563 which led eventually to the collapse of the market at Antwerp and subsequent re-orientation of England's major export industry. There is, however, an assumption here that growth in exports indicates growth in the economy generally; and yet the manufacture of cloth and other industrial processes were scattered and often associated with individual entrepreneurial activity, as will demonstrated in chapter 3. London's dominance of the export

Circulation in England, 1300–1700', *EcHRev*, 48 (1995), 238–57. C. G. A. Clay, *Economic Expansion and Social Change: England, 1500–1700*, 2 vols (Cambridge, 1984). E. M. Carus-Wilson and O. Coleman, *England's Export Trade, 1275–1547* (Oxford, 1963).

[50] Lipson, *Economic History of England*, chapter 9. It is also identifiable in the rapidly expanding centres of cloth production such as Newbury discussed in chapter 3.

[51] Data on number of cloths exported from A. R. Bridbury, *Medieval English Clothmaking* (London, 1982), 118–22 where data supplied by O. Coleman as the figures from the graphs in E. M. Carus-Wilson and O. Coleman, *England's Export Trade, 1275–1547* (Oxford, 1963), 138–9.

[52] But note this was not a cessation as there were always merchants who were prepared to trade, see A. F. Sutton, *The Mercery of London. Trade, Goods and People, 1130–1578* (Aldershot, 2005), chapters 9 and 10.

[53] English recovery was associated with developments in trade, manufacture and the supply of silver that were taking place in Europe in the 1460s: see J. H. Munro, 'The 'New Institutional Economics' and the Changing Fortunes of Fairs in Medieval and Early Modern Europe: the Textile Trades, Warfare and Transaction Costs', *Vierteljahrschrift fur Sozial- und Wirtschaftsgeschichte* 88 (2001), 1–47.

trade from a 50 per cent share in 1450 to 90 per cent in 1550 will also have to be considered as having a distorting effect on these general trends.[54]

. The domestic market is more difficult to quantify, but probably more representative of economic activity. Following the expansion of the early period there was a decline in the use of formal marketing structures in the fifteenth century as part of a wider trend in falling numbers of markets functioning after the Black Death and lower aggregate activity.[55] Indeed, all forms of marketing activity appear to have reached a nadir in the middle of the fifteenth century and it was exports that reveal the first signs of recovery, albeit with marked regional differences in the moment when signs of recovery are discernible.[56] Marketing activity increased over the sixteenth century with a more rapid expansion associated with market towns from 1570.[57] There was also a tendency for markets to specialise and concentrate in regional centres.[58] Nevertheless, the number of markets did not expand proportionately,[59] even though there was a smaller proportion of the population who were self-sufficient in food.[60] It would appear, therefore, that the structure of marketing did not undergo any fundamental alteration in this period, and we might conclude perhaps,

---

[54] Britnell, 'The English Economy', 95.

[55] Evidence is drawn from receipts of market tolls and rents. Britnell, *Commercialisation of English Society*, 157–60. *Idem*, 'Urban Demand in the English Economy, 1300–1600', in J. A. Galloway (ed.), *Trade, Urban Hinterlands and Market Integration, c.1300–1600* (London, 2000), 1–21.

[56] J. Hatcher, 'The Great Slump of the Mid-Fifteenth Century', in R. H. Britnell and J. Hatcher (eds), *Progress and Problems in Medieval England* (Cambridge, 1996), 237–72. R. H. Britnell, 'The Economic Context', in A. J. Pollard (ed.), *The Wars of the Roses* (Basingstoke, 1995), 43–56; and in his *Commercialisation*, 184 he describes the depression in terms of a conjunction of events. A. J. Pollard, *North-eastern England During the Wars of the Roses* (Oxford, 1990), 78–9 provides a rather different timing for economic slump in the north east of England. J. Hare, 'Growth and Recession in the Fifteenth-century Economy. The Wiltshire Textile Industry and the Countryside', *EcHRev*, 52 (1999), 1–26. M. Mate, *Trade and Economic Developments, 1450–1550. The Experience of Kent, Surrey and Sussex* (Woodbridge, 2006) provides detailed evidence of the impact of the slump in this region.

[57] Everitt noted a sudden leap forward in the volume, organisation and impact of agricultural trading in the English economy in the seventy years leading up to 1640. A. Everitt, 'The Marketing of Agricultural Produce', in Thirsk, *Agrarian History* IV, 502, 587.

[58] J. A. Yelling, 'Agriculture 1500–1730', in R. A. Dodgshon and R. A. Butlin (eds), *An Historical Geography of England and Wales* (London, 1978), 161–4.

[59] Everitt 'Marketing', 475–7, where he identified only a few examples of new foundations.

[60] *Ibid.*, 564.

that those changes that were taking place were doing so within the existing system.[61]

Table 1 *Indices of prices, 1450–1600 (1450–99 = 100)*

Decade	Grain	Livestock	Wool	Industrial products
1450–59	98	97	82	99
1460–69	99	102	109	103
1470–79	93	98	99	100
1480–89	114	105	113	103
1490–99	97	99	96	97
1500–09	112	111	93	98
1510–19	115	117	119	102
1520–29	154	138	111	110
1530–39	161	143	122	110
1540–49	187	185	153	127
1550–59	348	259	206	186
1560–69	316	281	205	218
1570–79	370	336	234	223
1580–89	454	352	225	230
1590–99	590	414	315	238

Source: Data taken from P. Bowden, 'Statistical appendix', in Thirsk, *Agrarian History* IV, 860–2.

To function smoothly markets required a steady supply of coin. In addition, changes to the amount of money in circulation would have an impact on everything that had been given a monetary value. The trend for the substitution of cash for goods and labour, especially in transactions between lords and peasants, would increase the impact and effects of changes in the currency. There is, moreover, a potential negative impact as dependence on money for commerce can be restrictive. We need to be aware therefore of the chief monetary features of this period which were the decline in *specie*, particularly in the middle of the fifteenth century, and the rise in the velocity of the circulating medium in the sixteenth century.[62] The depth of the fifteenth-century recession and the extent to which this was the result of a shortage of

[61] A point made by C. Dyer, 'Trade, Urban Hinterlands and Market Integration, 1300–1600: a summing up', in J. Galloway (ed.), *'Trade, Urban Hinterlands and Market Integration, 1300–1600* (London, 2000), 109.
[62] This is a grave over-simplification of the monetarists' arguments made here for economies of time and space. P. Spufford, *Money and its Use in Medieval Europe* (Cambridge, 1988), part III. C. E. Challis (ed.), *A New History of the Royal Mint* (Cambridge, 1992), appendix 1, for the amount of coin minted. J. Day, *The Medieval Market Economy* (Oxford, 1987). Mayhew, 'Population, Money Supply, and the Velocity

coin is a matter of some debate.[63] The discovery of the Americas and influx of bullion did have an inflationary impact on the economy of Europe. The causes of the rapid inflation of the sixteenth century in England, however, remain controversial and we must also consider whether the effects of deflationary forces have obscured the full extent of the rise.[64] Nevertheless, we can observe a rise in arable and livestock prices from the 1520s, with marked inflation during debasements between 1542 and 1551. The relative differences in prices between the commodities in Table 1, and the corresponding impact that this had on those who supplied the market should be noted. Thereafter prices continued to rise with peaks associated with years of harvest failure. That association was a consistent feature throughout the period under examination. From 1380 there was stability in the level of prices that continued until the years of almost national harvest failures of 1437–39 associated with bad weather and wet summers, particularly in 1438, when the prices of various types of commodities rose. Harvest failures returned after another period of stability and the years 1482–84, 1555–56, 1586, and 1595–97, stand out as being particularly harsh over large areas of the country.[65] The effect of the general rise in prices in the second half of the sixteenth century will be a recurring feature of subsequent chapters. In particular, it had a detrimental effect on those whose income was largely derived from wages which did not keep pace with inflation.

It is generally agreed that towns were an essential and integrated part of the country's trading network, particularly when acting as centres of exchange.[66] The changing fortunes of towns, however, remain a controversial topic. Vast quantities of ink have been expended on the debates surrounding urban decline, and diversity of experience appears to be the key to any form of unifying description.[67] Why did places such as Salisbury and Newbury grow compared

---

of Circulation in England', 238–57, especially 241, and his debate with Miskimin in *EcHRev*, 49 (1996), 358–61.

[63] P. Nightingale, 'England and the European Depression of the Mid-Fifteenth Century', *The Journal of European Economic History* 26 (1997), 631–56.

[64] R. B. Outhwaite, *Inflation in Tudor and Early Stuart England* (Basingstoke, 1969). J. R. Wordie, 'Deflationary Factors in the Tudor Price Rise', *Past and Present*, 154 (1997), 32–70.

[65] Figures for the fifteenth century taken from Miller, *Agrarian History* III, 434, and for the sixteenth century from D. C. Coleman, *The Economy of England, 1450–1750* (Oxford, 1977), 46. W. G. Hoskins, 'Harvest Fluctuations and English Economic History, 1480–1619', *AgHRev*, 12 (1964), 28–46.

[66] See chapter 3 for a discussion of towns, urban hierarchies and spheres of influence.

[67] The general debate on urban decline is summarised in A. Dyer, *Decline and Growth in English Towns, 1400–1640* (Basingstoke, 1991). Another important summary is D. M. Palliser, 'Urban Decay Revisited', in J. A. F. Thomson (ed.), *Towns and Townspeople in the Fifteenth Century* (Stroud, 1988), 1–21. Nevertheless, see Britnell's suggestions for a unifying framework of the conditions of demand and supply to explain the general

to older centres such as Winchester and Oxford that were in decline? The controversy has centred on which was the more typical urban experience: those towns in decline or those that were expanding.[68] Indeed, Britnell found that it was difficult to generalise with any assurance about the performance of late medieval urban economies.[69] This case study allows us to examine an example of the significant urban category of a town that was expanding due to the manufacture of cloth.[70] Towns were not isolated entities, and we should avoid separating the more specifically urban phenomena from the general economic trends of the period. Meanwhile London was exceptional in the size of its population and its control of trade, both features which expanded throughout the period of this study.[71] London appears to have been unique in its dominance of the export market, shown above, which occurred at the expense of places such as Southampton, and also in maintaining a growing population at a time of more generalised demographic contraction, with migration as an important contributing factor.[72] The effects of London's growth had repercussions both for those ports that lost trade, and for the city's hinterland which provisioned the capital. There is yet another part of the debate which is concerned with the

features of urban decay in the late medieval period in R. H. Britnell, 'The Economy of British Towns, 1300–1540', *CUHB*, 330–1.

[68] The importance of country market towns as places of growth at a time of more generalised urban decline, a theme that will be returned to later in the book, is argued in C. Phythian-Adams, 'Urban Decay in Late Medieval England', in P. Abrams and E. A. Wrigley (eds), *Towns in Societies* (Cambridge, 1978), 159–85 and especially 166–73.

[69] Britnell, 'The Economy of British Towns', 313.

[70] This is an important category of towns that includes places such as Lavenham and Stroud, but there are few published case studies. E. M. Carus-Wilson, 'The Woollen Industry before 1550', in E. Crittall (ed.), *A History of the County of Wiltshire*, vol. 4 (Oxford, 1959), 115–47. D. Dymond and A. Betterton, *Lavenham: 700 Years of Textile Making* (Woodbridge, 1982).

[71] A total population of as many as 80,000 to 100,000 at its peak around 1300 and before the decline of late medieval period. C. Barron, 'London, 1300–1540', *CUHB*, 395–440 and references below. For a judicious assessment of London's population over the medieval period see C. Barron, *London in the Later Middle Ages* (Oxford, 2004), 237–42. For the role of the Merchant Adventurers in the expansion of London's control of trade see Sutton, *The Mercery of London*.

[72] P. Nightingale, 'The Growth of London in the Medieval English Economy', in R. Britnell and J. Hatcher (eds), *Progress and Problems in Medieval England* (Cambridge, 1996), 89–106. B. M. S. Campbell, J. A. Galloway, D. Keene and M. Murphy, *A Medieval Capital and its Grain Supply: Agrarian Production and Distribution in the London Region c.1300* (Historical Geography Research Series, 30, 1993). D. Keene, 'Medieval London and its Region', *London Journal*, 14 (1989), pp. 99–111. A. A. Ruddock, *Italian Merchants and Shipping in Southampton, 1270–1600* (Southampton, 1951), 262–9. The wider implications of London's growth were discussed by Fisher, 'London as an "Engine of Economic Growth"'.

point at which sustained urban growth can be identified. The earlier pessimism of Slack and Clark is now contested, and the preferred interpretation is of a general and substantial, if unspectacular, progress, particularly after 1570.[73] Yet towns and their regions were more integrated in their economic and social exchanges than these urban studies would imply, and the readjustment of the urban hierarchy should be viewed within the wider economic trends and regional characteristics of the time.[74]

As we have already noted, agricultural output remained the dominant form of economic activity throughout the period of study.[75] The early economic historians, however, had observed an 'agrarian revolution' during the fifteenth and sixteenth centuries characterised by the rise in number of large leasehold properties farmed for profit by a new breed of landowner, especially members of the gentry and entrepreneurs, and an increasing amount of land enclosed for private use, predominantly for pasture. The result, they argued, was increased agricultural productivity.[76] These features, however, had a longer history than was implied. Moreover, they did result in structural change in two key areas; the units of production and the layout of fields.[77] At the beginning of the fourteenth century there were two main forms of agricultural unit: demesne and peasant. The former were large units, managed directly for lords, and worked by waged labour augmented by the labour services of peasants. Peasant units were smaller and varied in size, were held under different tenurial conditions, and tended to be worked by family labour.[78] Change can be observed before the fourteenth century in the gradual leasing of the demesne lands accompanied by a decreased use of customary labour. The result was a continuation of large farms but now held by lessees and peasants and, from the later fourteenth

[73] P. Clark and P. Slack, *Crisis and Order in English Towns, 1500–1700* (London, 1972), and again in *English Towns in Transition, 1500–1700* (Oxford, 1976). Dyer, *Decline and Growth*, 53. Goose argues that the period of growth in provincial towns lay in the later sixteenth and early seventeenth centuries N. R. Goose, 'In Search of the Urban Variable: Towns and the English Economy, 1500–1650', *EcHRev*, 39 (1986), 165–85, especially 184.

[74] Britnell, 'Economy of British Towns', 320, 330–1. *Idem*, 'Urban Demand in the English Economy, 1300–1600', 9–21.

[75] The key works on agricultural output for the medieval and early modern periods are Campbell, *English Seigniorial Agriculture* and M. Overton, *Agricultural Revolution in England* (Cambridge, 1996).

[76] According to Overton's more modern figures agricultural output did increase at the latter end and between 1520 and 1600, Overton, *Agricultural Revolution*, 85.

[77] See chapter 4 for bibliographical references and details of agricultural units, the different proportions of lands held as demesne, free and customary, and changes in tenure.

[78] See Dyer, *Making a Living*, 160–78, 357–62 for details of differences and an emphasis on the impact of the cumulative productivity of peasant units and their engagement in the market.

century, the rural economy was more peasant-based, with a greater proportion of land held by peasants with family efforts augmented by hired labour. A larger proportion of land and labour was now held on an increasingly contractual basis. Serfdom did not survive under these changed agrarian and tenurial conditions, and by the late fifteenth century was only found in small, isolated pockets. The situation from the late fourteenth to early sixteenth centuries of low population pressure on land, improved tenurial conditions, increased opportunities for waged employment and freedom from the worst of seigniorial impositions combined to produce optimal conditions and a 'golden age' for the English peasantry.[79] But this change was transitory. Large agricultural units continued during the sixteenth century but a greater proportion were leased by yeomen and gentry. Enclosed lands did not revert under pressure from an increasing population. The result was a larger proportion of the population living as cottagers or smallholders and increasingly dependent on income from wages. Government concerns over rising unemployment, vagrancy and social unrest were more appropriate in the conditions towards the end of the sixteenth century than they had been at the beginning.

The second agrarian structural change was in the layout of fields and was the result of several different but complementary factors. First, there was the general period of crisis in the agrarian economy in the early fourteenth century with retreat from marginal lands in the context of climate change.[80] Second there was a shift in emphasis in land use from the late fourteenth century from arable to pasture driven by decline in the market for grain to feed a reduced population and associated changes in diet, and the additional demand for wool for export and in the manufacture of woollen cloth. Third, enclosure, rather than being viewed as an innovation of the fifteenth and sixteenth centuries associated with the increase in pasture, is now regarded as a feature of specific regions and landscapes and a continuation of an ongoing process. Allied to these features is the notion that in periods of reduced demand for arable we can observe agricultural diversification as in the cultivation of saffron, rabbits and flax.[81] Furthermore, the shift in emphasis during the sixteenth century to increased agricultural productivity, seen in the publication of practical manuals

[79] Thorold Rogers coined this expression based on his study of prices and wages. J. E. Thorold Rogers, *A History of Agriculture and Prices in England, 1259-1793*, 8 vols (Oxford, 1866-1902), vol. IV, 23.

[80] Campbell, 'Agrarian Problem in the Early Fourteenth Century', 3-70. Recent evidence from dendrochronology suggests severe disruption in the first half of the fourteenth century associated with climate change, the possible effects of volcanic activity, and plague. M. G. L. Baillie, *A Slice through Time: Dendrochronology and Precision Dating* (London, 1995), 128-30.

[81] J. Thirsk, *Alternative Agriculture: A History from the Black Death to the Present Day* (Oxford, 1997), chapter 1.

on husbandry, was not new but a development based on earlier treatises such as that by Walter of Henley in the thirteenth century. The combined outcome of changes in land use was to be found in the physically altered layout of fields, a process that had taken place over several hundred years and was not complete by 1600.

The regulation of local society reveals another pattern of change whereby existing medieval institutions and informal strategies were adapted, re-shaped and formalised through the increasing intrusion of Tudor governance.[82] Medieval solutions were effective. Minor misdemeanours and petty crimes were dealt with in the lord's manor court, as was the regulation of communal concerns such as common field agriculture, and the jurors and other local officials were elected from among the tenants of the manor.[83] McIntosh has identified the use of a variety of local courts and systems, such as the passing of bye-laws, employed for maintaining the peace in local society.[84] Churchwardens were parochial officers who were elected from the middling ranks of lay society and brought a variety of secular experience in fulfilling their responsibilities and varied duties, including the management of parish income and expenditure.[85] Dyer has shown how local communities arranged for the collection and payment of their fiscal subsidies, and also the provision they made for poor relief.[86] These were all local and often *ad hoc* responses to maintain the peaceful working of local society and fulfil communal responsibilities. Change came with the increase in governance by the Tudor state that bound centre to locality more closely and developed and expanded the role of existing institutions and officials, such as commissions of the peace, assize justices and justices of the peace.[87] Government became intrusive in local institutions, especially the parish, which was turned into a local government unit and adapted for secular administration with an associated decline in the use of manorial jurisdiction.[88] What had functioned outside the state system now became a closely monitored part of its local government structure. This

---

[82] For an excellent summary see S. Hindle, 'County Government in England', in R. Titler and N. Jones (eds), *A Companion to Tudor Britain* (Oxford, 2004), 98–115.

[83] P. D. A. Harvey, *Manorial Records* (London, 1984). M. Bailey, *The English Manor c.1200–c.1500* (Manchester, 2002).

[84] M. McIntosh, *Controlling Misbehaviour in England, 1370–1600* (Cambridge, 1998).

[85] B. Kümin, *The Shaping of a Community* (Aldershot, 1996), 22–52.

[86] C. Dyer, 'The Political Life of the Fifteenth-century English Village', in L. Clark and C. Carpenter (eds), *The Fifteenth Century IV. Political Culture in Late Medieval Britain* (Woodbridge, 2004), 135–57. *Idem*, 'Taxation and Communities in Late Medieval England', in R. Britnell and J. Hatcher (eds), *Progress and Problems in Medieval England* (Cambridge, 1996), 168–90.

[87] S. Hindle, *The State and Social Change in Early Modern England, 1550–1640* (Basingstoke, 2002).

[88] Kümin, *Shaping of a Community*, 241–59.

process can be observed in the passing of various acts such as that of 1555 for the repair of highways, the 1536 regulations over vagabonds, and especially the various legislative measures that culminated in the Elizabethan poor law of 1598 and 1601.[89] The relative autonomy of the medieval parish ended with statutory communal responsibilities, the 'voluntary' dimension of parish budgets declined, and lay control, especially by the middling group, expanded to unprecedented levels.[90]

The Reformation provided another important break with the past in the older accounts of the end of the middle ages. The changes in religion, however, are not covered in detail in this study of social and economic change; nevertheless, they cannot be ignored as their impact extended into all aspects of life.[91] The result was the infiltration of the state in the worship of the parish. Furthermore the Dissolution of Monasteries from 1536 resulted in a massive transfer of land into predominantly secular hands. This change of landowner, often after a long period of stability as in the case of Abingdon Abbey, had the potential to introduce a different style of management and administration of the income from the estates that might have had a detrimental effect for the tenants and their conditions of tenure.[92] The Dissolution of the Monasteries brought a shift in the role of the Church in the countryside from varied and sometimes secular concerns to a more concentrated focus on religious provision for parishioners and their spiritual welfare.

Until now the emphasis has been on continuity and, it has been argued, when changes did occur they were the result of a long period of development. It is important therefore to draw together and focus attention on those medieval features that did not survive. The first was the decline of serfdom whose incidence had largely ceased by the sixteenth century. Second, there were the developments that occurred in agriculture in the units of production and organisation of fields. Other features that have been mentioned were the loss of the monasteries as one of the country's major landowners, the infiltration of government into parish worship and the local community, and the increased use of the parish as a unit of administration, with a decline in influence of

[89] Kümin, *Shaping of a Community*, 247–9. Hindle, 'County Government in England', 107. A. L. Beier, *The Problem of the Poor in Tudor and Early Stuart England* (London, 1983). P. Slack, *Poverty and Policy in Tudor and Stuart England* (London, 1988).

[90] Kümin, *Shaping of a Community*, 258. S. Hindle, 'A Sense of Place? Becoming and Belonging in the Rural Parish, 1550–1645', in A. Shepard and P. Withington (eds), *Communities in Early Modern England* (Manchester, 2000), 96–114.

[91] For recent comprehensive coverage of the subject see F. Heal, *Reformation in Britain and Ireland* (Oxford, 2003).

[92] A point that is developed more fully in chapter 4. The transfer of lands at the Dissolution and the new breed of landowners were viewed as important forces that created a fundamental break with the past during the sixteenth century, see for example in Tawney, *The Agrarian Problem in the Sixteenth Century*.

the manor. These were all major and irreversible changes and their significance should not be overlooked as they represent a significant break with the past.

Proposed approach

We must not forget, however, that national trends and data series tend to flatten the variety of experience across the country that was a real feature of this period. Regions differed, and their examination, although providing us with detailed evidence, can create the impression of a series of isolated units functioning independently from a national context. To overcome this we will employ the combined approach of a detailed local study that maintains a national perspective. Thus local events are not isolated episodes but are integrated aspects within a wider historical framework. Furthermore, there is a need for detailed regional studies such as the present one, which go from the fourteenth century into the second half of the sixteenth century, and which avoid the fragmentation of earlier studies that tended to end around 1530, or to begin in 1550.[93] There are, however, methodological difficulties that need to be overcome as few documentary sources span the two centuries.[94] Indeed, the production of various new types of record implied institutional and administrative change that enhanced the sense of a break with the past.

We have already observed various general influences at work that affected the pace of change in an area and which might act as a constraint or provide opportunities for change. Events at the local level were affected by these influences when they operated within the general social and economic conditions of the period. In addition, there were factors that shaped change in a particular locality which could have a significant impact. They included: the underlying ecological structure that largely shaped the pre-modern economy; the administrative policies of landlords that modified the opportunities for tenants to react to the social and economic changes of the time; a symbiotic relationship between town and surrounding countryside; and finally, the presence of individuals within the local community who were prepared to take risks and to innovate. It was the combined influence of these four factors that are shown through this study to provide an important explanation for the variety of experience of change in these centuries. Nevertheless, we cannot explain what happened in a predictive manner; rather we should describe what is happening and the influences that we can observe at work.

[93] The pioneering work of Marjorie McIntosh has been very influential in this respect. M. K. McIntosh, *Autonomy and Community: The Royal Manor of Havering, 1200–1500* (Cambridge, 1986) with her *A Community Transformed: The Manor and Liberty of Havering, 1500–1620* (Cambridge, 1991) and her later publications continue to bridge the chronological divide.

[94] See appendices for chapters 2 and 4 for an evaluation of the documentary sources.

We need to define criteria and identify indices which are robust enough to measure change during this period. Those that have been developed for this study fall into three main areas; landlords' revenue, tenant society, and trade. The first are the payments that could be demanded for properties in the form of rents, entry fines, and heriots. Revenue from these sources was influenced by the style of seigniorial administration, level of occupancy of tenancies that depended on the conditions of tenure and size of the population, and additionally, the tenants having the coin to pay their dues. Changes that occurred within tenant society are measured in terms of the distribution of wealth, size of landholdings, availability of wage labour and the degree of violence and disorder within the communities. The criteria for measuring trade are seen in the context of urban–rural relationships and include a study of patterns of debt in both town and countryside, data from import and export accounts, the erection of market stalls, and manufacture for local and export markets. In addition, it is important to consider more qualitative evidence for shifts in perceptions and attitudes to authority, consumption and the poor. The examination of these different criteria will provide the basis for our exploration of this transitional period.

Western Berkshire has been chosen as the site for investigation as it remains a largely under-explored area in central southern England and provides useful evidence for comparisons with the data derived from elsewhere. The area of western Berkshire is defined for the purposes of this book by the survival of the nominal returns of the 1381 Poll Tax and 1522 Military Survey.[95] These provide the framework of data – for both intra-regional and national comparisons between the fourteenth and sixteenth centuries – of the population, economy and society, and create a context for the more detailed analysis of individual communities that lie at the heart of this study, and are the source of the majority of the quantitative and qualitative evidence.[96] The choice of area to investigate was, of necessity, arbitrary. Nevertheless, it contained three distinctive regions, of vale, downland, and wood-pasture, that were important for understanding local diversity; and the town of Newbury that was expanding through the manufacture of cloth. Town and countryside were bound together through symbiotic and functional ties of marketing, manufacture and social intercourse, and it is essential to integrate their experiences when examining features of

[95] Although West Berkshire has existed as a unitary authority since April 1998 it is a political construct and is not employed in this study. Rather, western Berkshire comprises those places where the documentary evidence survives of both the nominal returns of the 1381 Poll Tax and the 1522 Military Survey. TNA, 1381 poll tax, E179/73/41–43, 46, 48–55, 62. 1522 Military Survey, E315/464. See Maps 1 and 2.
[96] Detailed case studies of: Buckland and West Hanney in the Vale; Ashbury and Woolstone in the Downs; Kintbury and Shaw in the Kennet; and the town of Newbury. They are shaded on Map 2.

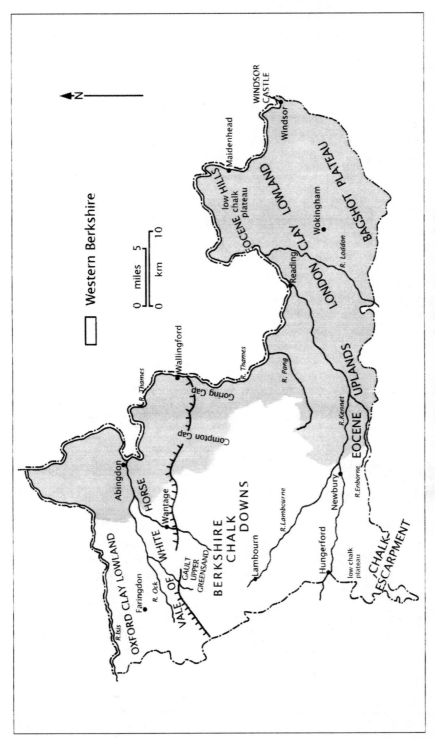

Map 1 The topography of Berkshire (western Berkshire unshaded)

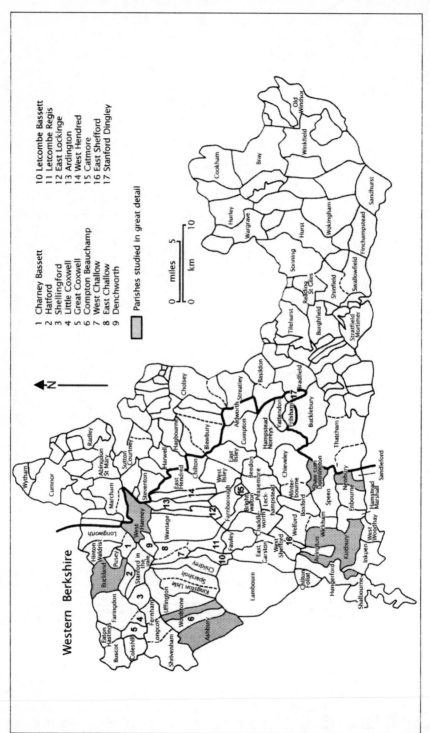

Map 2 The parishes of Berkshire (case studies shaded)

social and economic change, although few detailed studies have been able to achieve this effectively, and certainly not for the period of this study.[97] There is also a paucity of studies of cloth-producing centres which were significant, along with London's hinterland, as the areas where early economic recovery was identifiable.

In the remainder of the book the data from western Berkshire are employed to identify the nature, pace and reasons for change. Chapter 2 describes the various local economies and societies of western Berkshire in detail and demonstrates how they changed between the fourteenth and sixteenth centuries in the relative size of their population, and distribution of wealth and land. Distinctive sub-regional variations are revealed and explaining these differences is the purpose of the next three chapters. Chapters 3 and 4, 'Town and country relations' and 'Estate management and profitability', investigate these two major influences on the rate of change. Tenant society is the focus of chapter 5 and we examine their actions both in response to the changing conditions of the period, and in shaping their own lives. The final chapter draws together those events that have chronological significance and locates the experience of western Berkshire firmly within its national context.

It will be argued that by 1400 the process of change that would shape the economy and society of the future was already under way and had developed out of what had gone before in the preceding centuries. The fifteenth century saw little that was decisive or unprecedented. People would continue responding and adapting to changing circumstances, their environment, and often unexpected forces such as disease, climate and religion. The elements of choice and chance are unpredictable and cannot be factored into a causal explanation. The pace of change in certain aspects of the economy and society would escalate in the second half of the sixteenth century, but it would be insufficiently rapid to identify a specific moment that constitutes a break with the past and the end of the middle ages, or share sufficient common characteristics to describe a particular transitional period. Rather, it was one phase in a discontinuous process which continues to this day. Yet it is undeniable that fundamental change had occurred by 1600. As a result of this study we will have a clearer understanding of what changed, the reasons behind variations in pace, and the specific chronological characteristics of this period.

---

[97] The notable exceptions are J. Lee, *Cambridge and its Economic Region, 1450–1560* (Hatfield, 2005), and C. M. Newman, *Late Medieval Northallerton: A Small Market Town and its Hinterland, c.1470–1540* (Stamford, 1999). Urban studies that contain investigations of the hinterland include: R. H. Britnell, *Growth and Decline in Colchester, 1300–1525* (Cambridge, 1986); M. Kowaleski, *Local Markets and Regional Trade in Medieval Exeter* (Cambridge, 1995); J. Goodacre, *The Transformation of a Peasant Economy. Townspeople and Villagers in the Lutterworth Area, 1500–1700* (Aldershot, 1994).

CHAPTER 2

Landscapes, population and wealth in western Berkshire from the fourteenth to the sixteenth century

Introduction

It is worth stating again that the different landscapes, economies and societies of the regions of rural England affected the pace of change in their various localities. The pre-modern rural economy was heavily influenced by the geological and topographical structure of its regions. Whether we divide England into highland and lowland regions, or into champion and woodland areas, or by dispersed and nucleated settlement patterns, the regional differences across the country are clear. It is widely accepted that these underlying features account for one of the most fundamental explanations for regional variations in the economy. How landscape shaped the local economy in the pre-industrial period is an important factor in explaining past economies and has been described in detail by other historians and geographers.[1] What is less widely discussed, particularly for the late medieval period, is how the different societies within these regions varied, and in turn had an impact on the shape of change in the locality.[2] It is the purpose of this chapter to describe the landscape and rural

---

[1] Perhaps the most consistent advocate has been Joan Thirsk, see especially her *England's Agricultural Regions and Agrarian History, 1500–1750* (Basingstoke, 1987), and as editor of *The English Rural Landscape* (Oxford, 2000).

[2] This is a subject that more actively engages archaeologists and early modern historians than those investigating the late medieval period; nevertheless see R. Hopcroft, 'The Social Origins of Agrarian Change in Late Medieval England' *American Journal of Sociology* 99 (1994), 1559–95, where she stresses the social organisation of agriculture in this context. T. Williamson, *Shaping Medieval Landscapes: Settlement, Society, Environment* (Macclesfield, 2003). For a review of the constituent elements see N. Davie, 'Chalk and Cheese? 'Fielden' and 'Forest' Communities in Early Modern England' *Journal of Historical Sociology* 4 (1991), 1–31. The classic studies of the early modern period are M. Spufford, *Contrasting Communities, English Villagers in the Sixteenth and Seventeenth*

economies of western Berkshire, and then to chart shifts in the distribution of population and wealth between the fourteenth and sixteenth centuries. This will reveal broad patterns of both continuity and change, whilst explaining these differences will be the purpose of the following three chapters.

Landscape and rural economy in western Berkshire

It is essential to begin by describing the landscape and local economies of western Berkshire as they form the context for the subsequent detailed analysis. This part of Berkshire has been defined as an area of mixed farming containing corn and stock in various combinations.[3] It can be further divided into three main regions: the Vale of the White Horse to the north, the Berkshire Downs, and the valley of the River Kennet in the south.[4]

The Vale of the White Horse is the general term used to describe northern Berkshire,[5] although, more precisely, the clay vale is only the flat area of gault and then kimmeridge clays that run in successive bands from west to east.[6] To the north lies the corallian ridge that faces the river Thames and the Oxfordshire plain, and to the south there is a band of fertile upper greensand of varying width that nestles below the chalk slopes of the Berkshire Downs. The whole area was suitable for arable cultivation, particularly the fertile upper greensand, but with rather more emphasis on pastoral husbandry from Buckland and Denchworth westwards.[7] The clay vale was watered by the river Ock and its tributaries which joined the Thames at Abingdon, and was liable to flooding. Settlement in this area is found on small elevations with characteristic names ending in -ey such as Hanney and Childrey.[8] Otherwise settlement by the time of the Domesday survey was along the elevated areas of the corallian

---

Centuries (Cambridge, 1974), and D. Underdown, *Revel, Riot, and Rebellion: Popular Politics and Culture in England, 1603–1660* (Oxford, 1985). In both cases a correlation was made with religious nonconformity, and Underdown also makes an association with political allegiances. But see the criticisms of Underdown in J. Morrill, 'The Ecology of Allegiance in the English Revolution' *JBS*, 26 (1987), 451–67.

[3] Thirsk, *England's Agricultural Regions*, 28.

[4] See maps 1 and 2.

[5] This northern area of Berkshire was taken into Oxfordshire in 1974.

[6] These generalised landscape divisions are based on W. Mavor, *General View of the Agriculture of Berkshire* (London, 1809) which was cited as an authority in J. Stephenson, *The Land of Britain: The Report of the Land Utilisation Survey of Britain, Part 78, Berkshire* (London, 1936).

[7] J. Cottis, 'Agrarian Change in the Vale of the White Horse, 1660–1760', Ph.D. thesis, Reading (1984), 12–13.

[8] P. H. Ditchfield and W. Page (eds), *The Victoria History of the Counties of England: Berkshire* (hereafter *VCH Berkshire*) vol. II (London, 1907), 167.

ridge and the upper greensand.[9] The small market town of Farringdon lies in the west of the Vale. Beyond the region, but still exerting an influence, was the town of Abingdon, which together with Farringdon and Wantage, acted as market centres for the region.

The Vale of the White Horse is typical of other lowland vale areas.[10] By the late medieval period it was characterised by nucleated villages, each usually with two or three large common fields,[11] and there was an emphasis on arable husbandry, particularly in the east. Fields were farmed in a rotation of grain, fallow, and beans and peas were grown as livestock fodder. Wheat and barley dominated arable cultivation and, travelling through Berkshire in 1542, John Leland was impressed by the 'fruteful vale of White Horse' and remarked on the abundance of corn at Hanney.[12] The organisation of the common fields was characterised by strips and furlongs whereby the strips of the tenants of the different manors were intermingled within the various furlongs.[13] The majority of holdings in this area were measured in virgates that varied in size around a modal value of 30 acres depending on the manor.[14] Virgates, or yardlands as they were sometimes called, may have been a relic of an earlier division of land.[15] Pasture rights were allocated in proportion to the arable contained in

[9] E. M. J. Campbell, 'Berkshire', in H. C. Darby and E. M. J. Campbell (eds), *The Domesday Geography of South-East England* (Cambridge, 1962), 246.

[10] C. Dyer, D. Hey and J. Thirsk, 'Lowland Vales', in J. Thirsk (ed.), *The English Rural Landscape* (Oxford, 2000), 78–91.

[11] *VCH Berkshire*, II, 169–70. H. L. Gray, *English Field Systems* (Cambridge, 1915), 60–1, 63.

[12] L. T. Smith (ed.), *Leland's Itinerary in England and Wales* (London, 1964), vol. I p. 120, vol. V p. 78.

[13] For example, at West Hanney a holding of a messuage and half virgate of land were described more fully as consisting of: an acre of arable land lying in Cotman field in ledebroke furlong between the land of William Robyns to the north and the land of Robert Felse to the south and abutting upon the ledebroke ditch at the eastern end, and another acre lying in the same field and furlong between the land of William Dunnseden on the north and the land of Henry Nevell on the south, and another acre lying in the same field and furlong between the land of William Palmer on the north and the land of Henry Nevell on the south, and the entry continued in the same way for the remaining arable lands of the half virgate. NCA, 4060 court of 2 June 1502. The description of the glebe lands of the parish in 1634 reveals the continuation of this distribution of strips in the common fields. I. Mortimer (ed.), *Berkshire Glebe Terriers, 1634* (Berkshire Record Society, 2, 1995), 69–70. In the south of the region the arable lands of the manors of Beenham Valence and Beenham Lovell were also intermingled. *VCH Berkshire*, II, 202.

[14] For example at West Hanney the size of the virgate varied between 20 and 32 acres, whilst at Shaw it was specified as either 24, 36, 40 or 48 customary acres. M. Yates, 'Continuity and Change, in Rural Society, c.1400–1600: West Hanney and Shaw (Berkshire) and their region', D.Phil. thesis, Oxford (1997), 319 for a more detailed discussion of the size of the virgate.

[15] J. Blair, *Early Medieval Surrey* (Stroud, 1991), 71–4.

these virgates and the 'stints', or numbers of animals allowed to pasture on the various manors, were jealously guarded. Dairying was important in the more pastoral areas of the west and along the banks of the river Thames, and large numbers of cheeses were produced. Sheep were also reared and several large flocks were kept by tenants throughout the study period in places such as Buckland.[16] The whole agricultural system of the region was regulated through the individual manorial courts, particularly where the strips in the fields were held of several manors, and the passing of agricultural bye-laws was an increasing feature of this period.[17] The amount of early enclosure in this area of Berkshire was relatively small, dispersed, and piecemeal, and often varied according to the policies of the different manorial lords, a theme that will be developed in chapter 4. Mixed farming dominated the local economy, and the absence of other forms of economic activity was noticeable and noteworthy, particularly in the sixteenth century. We will see how this was a consistently prosperous sub-region throughout the period of study.[18] The lands were cultivated by affluent tenants in a region of fairly large landholdings, and there was little evidence of wage labour. The more general changes in agriculture, such as a shift in emphasis from arable to pasture,[19] were not found in this region; indeed, there appears to have been an increase in arable cultivation in the Vale. The pull of London as a market for agricultural produce was felt here.[20] In 1300 the demesnes devoted a high proportion of their acreage to wheat.[21] Malt was produced in significant amounts in the Vale and many of the sixteenth-century probate inventories contained quantities of malt in the various stages of production.[22]

The chalk downlands, like those elsewhere in southern England, are smoothly contoured hills. The underlying chalk is starkly revealed in the famous carving of the White Horse at Uffington which gives its name to the northern region. The summit of the Downs ranges in altitude from 260 metres at White Horse Hill in the hillfort of Uffington Castle, to 170 metres north of East Ilsley, and along the whole escarpment runs the routeway of the

---

[16] For the size of flocks of sheep see below, chapter 5.

[17] On the regulation of local society see below, chapter 5.

[18] Below, Table 3, pp. 36–7.

[19] C. Dyer, 'Warwickshire Farming, 1349–c.1520', Dugdale Society Occasional Papers 27 (1981).

[20] Berkshire forms the western part of the study area in B. M. S. Campbell, J. A. Galloway, D. Keene and M. Murphy, A Medieval Capital and its Grain Supply: Agrarian Production and Distribution in the London Region c.1300 (Historical Geography Research Series, 30, 1993). F. J. Fisher, London and the English Economy, 1500–1700 (London, 1990), 65.

[21] Campbell et al., A Medieval Capital, 124–5.

[22] Indeed, in 1573 the Vale supplied 12–18 per cent of the malt consumed and stocked by London brewers. I would like to record my thanks to Professor D. Keene for the data on malt and the London brewers.

prehistoric Ridgeway. The chalk forms a steep scarp at White Horse Hill that becomes gentler towards the east. To the south the whole dipslope is gently sloping and dissected by dry valleys leading to the Lambourn valley.[23] By 1086 the high downland was largely empty of habitation and the settlements that faced northwards were clustered along, or slightly below, the spring-lines that emerged at the base of the escarpment between the lower chalk and upper greensand.[24] To the south settlements were concentrated in the river valleys, particularly the river Lambourn. The ancient town of Wantage lies within this region and, along with Lambourn, provided the market functions for the locality. As in other areas of chalk downlands arable cultivation was practised on the gentle slopes of the downs, whilst the upper and steeper slopes were used for grazing sheep.[25] There is evidence in later estate surveys for the survival of strips of old ridge and furrow, which implies that the upper downs may have been cultivated with arable during the Middle Ages.[26] The arable on the lower slopes was cultivated on a two-field system whereby half was left fallow and fertility restored by dung from the sheepfold. The great tithe barn belonging to Beaulieu Abbey at Great Coxwell on the edge of the Downs is evidence of the success of this system of agriculture. The whole area of the Downs was noted for its large flocks of sheep held by both lords and tenants.[27] There were a number of wealthy sheep farmers on the Downs in the fourteenth century, and the marked differences between their wealth and that of the smaller tenants is a subject that will be returned to later in this chapter. Berkshire wool was of short staple and good quality, typical of that found in other chalkland regions. A price schedule of 1454 graded Berkshire wool in the seventh group (7 marks) out of 51 grades and later in the century it had risen in rank order, and presumably quality, to third out of 35 grades (16.5 marks).[28] Berkshire wool was important for the manufacture of cloth and was used in the expanding industries of Reading and Newbury. In fact, as the sixteenth century progressed Berkshire clothiers had to buy additional wool from elsewhere as the local product was being sold for export and for use in the West Country cloth industry.[29] In the fourteenth century an additional

[23] M. G. Jarvis, *Soils of Wantage and Abingdon District* (Harpenden, 1973), 9.

[24] Campbell, 'Berkshire', 246; D. Hooke, 'Anglo-Saxon Estates in the Vale of the White Horse', *Oxoniensia*, 52 (1987), 138.

[25] J. Bettey, 'Downlands', in J. Thirsk (ed.), *The English Rural Landscape* (Oxford, 2000), 27–49.

[26] Hooke, 'Anglo-Saxon Estates', 135. BRO, D/EC E13, P12–13.

[27] Below p. 197; R. Faith, 'Berkshire: Fourteenth and Fifteenth Centuries', in P. D. A. Harvey (ed.), *The Peasant Land Market in Medieval England* (Oxford, 1984), 167–73.

[28] E. Power and M. M. Postan (eds), *Studies in English Trade in the Fifteenth Century* (London, 1933), 49.

[29] C. Jackson, 'The Berkshire Woollen Industry, 1500–1650', Ph.D. thesis, Reading (1993), 45.

economic activity in this region was the rural cloth industry centred on Hendred and the surrounding parishes that subsequently declined.[30]

Lying between the Vale and the Downs are a distinctive group of linear parishes that include features of both areas. They are the remnants of an Anglo-Saxon estate system whereby each unit contained arable, meadow and downland pasture.[31] They are characteristically long and narrow, running from high downland to clay vale, ensuring that each parish (or smaller estate) had meadow land on the valley bottom, arable land and downland grazing. In the subsequent analysis of fiscal records these have been grouped together as 'Mixed Parishes' and form a distinctive sub-section. Nevertheless, the largest proportion of the land of these parishes lay on the scarp slope of the Downs. Their economies were dominated by the raising of sheep; in subsequent analysis, therefore, they are grouped together with other parishes in the Downs region. It is important to distinguish them here as a distinctive region, but we will have to conclude that there were no significant distinguishing features in the pattern of change over time, except perhaps of more fluctuations than elsewhere.

The final, southern, sub-region within western Berkshire is that of the valley of the river Kennet. It is a broad low-lying alluvial tract bordered by gently sloping terraces; settlement was gathered along the gravel by the time of the Domesday survey.[32] To the north the land rises by gentle or moderate slopes towards the Downs dipslope. To the south the bordering slopes are moderate or steep to the gravel-capped eocene uplands, or to the low chalk plateau west of Kintbury that forms the south-west corner of Berkshire. From here the land then rises to Berkshire's highest point of 297 metres at Walbury Hill within the earthworks of the other famous Iron Age hillfort of the area. To the south of Newbury is an area of heathland. The Kennet valley was once heavily wooded and by the medieval period was an area of woodland pasture, that is, an area with a mixture of pasture, wood, arable and heath.[33] It was an area of dispersed settlement where large villages were often associated with smaller hamlets. The fields associated with these settlements were also distinctive. They included areas of open fields, but were more restricted in area than those of the clay vale and included many enclosed parcels of land in closes and crofts which were visible by the fourteenth century. Arable cultivation on the fertile loam soil to the north of the river was profitable, although not to the same extent as that in the Vale of the White Horse. The size of agricultural

---

[30] See chapter 3, pp. 82–3.
[31] Hooke, 'Anglo-Saxon Estates', 129–43.
[32] Campbell, 'Berkshire', 246.
[33] Although the Kennet area was not included, it does contain the characteristic features of this type of landscape described by C. Dyer, 'Woodlands and Wood-Pasture in Western England', in J. Thirsk (ed.), *The English Rural Landscape* (Oxford, 2001), 97–121.

holdings varied and this region contained a larger number of smaller units than elsewhere that were viable due to the availability of alternative and additional sources of income. In addition, by the sixteenth century several large farms had been created, whose tenants were wealthy individuals. There was a greater emphasis on pastoral husbandry in this region than in the Vale. The inhabitants of the Kennet valley were able to graze animals on the commons and to collect fuel in the woods. The woodland was intensively managed and provided an important source of manorial income for the lord, and alternative means of employment for the tenants to that of agriculture, such as hurdle making and charcoal burning. The Kennet region, along with other areas of wood pasture in England, is characterised by economic diversity and by the fifteenth century tanning was a flourishing trade. The extraction of clay and chalk were also important economic activities, and bricks were made in the region.[34] These various forms of economic activity became eclipsed with the expansion of the manufacture of cloth. This was centred on the town of Newbury, but Hungerford was also producing cloth, and the surrounding villages contained outworkers for the industry. The rivers Kennet and Lambourn supported several fulling mills, as well as tanning mills and a large number of corn mills.[35] Both Newbury and Hungerford acted as the market centres for this region of western Berkshire.

Thus even within the relatively small area of western Berkshire there were three distinctive regions of vale, downland, and woodland pasture. Landscape helped to shape the local economies so that the Vale was an area of mixed farming with an emphasis on arable cultivation, the raising of sheep on the Downs dominated economic activity there, and the Kennet valley was distinguished by the diversified elements within its economy that exploited the woodland and other natural resources of the region in addition to those of agriculture. It was also affected by the growth of the clothing town of Newbury.

Linking the various sub-regions of western Berkshire and uniting the whole area with the rest of the country were the roads and rivers. These formed the routes of communication and the arteries for conducting people and goods. Rivers provided an important method of transportation, particularly of heavy goods prior to the construction of the railway, and, although the rivers Thames and Kennet were not fully navigable at all times of the year, they formed an essential means of communication between Berkshire and the rest

---

[34] For example at Shaw, a brickman, was making bricks in a brick-kiln in 1451. TNA, SC2/154/53 court of 15 May 1451.
[35] Discussed in more detail in chapter 5. See also M. Yates, 'Watermills in the Local Economy of a Late Medieval Manor in Berkshire', in T. Thornton (ed.), *Social Attitudes and Political Structures in the Fifteenth Century* (Stroud, 2000), 184–201.

of England.[36] Prior to 1723, when the Kennet between Reading and Newbury was made fully navigable, the extent to which that river could provide a means of transport for heavy goods, and the effects of seasonal variations remains unknown, although the active markets of the two towns would suggest that it was important.[37] The major roads across the study area from west to east included the ancient Ridgeway along the top of the Downs, the Icknield Way to the north and then the road from London to Bath in the south. The road from London to Gloucester had been diverted in 1416, when a new bridge was built over the Thames, from Wallingford to Abingdon.[38] The route from Oxford to Southampton via Newbury ran north–south through western Berkshire, and archaeological deposits suggest that it was frequently used for trade. Another important route from the north of the region ran eastwards to Henley, an important grain entrepot, and from there gained access to the Thames and London.[39] The importance of road transport is strengthened by the evidence from the Southampton brokage accounts that record a steady traffic of carts travelling between the port and Newbury.[40]

Changes in the distribution of people and wealth in rural western Berkshire

We turn now to consider relative change in the distribution of population and wealth within these distinctive areas of western Berkshire. It is generally accepted that there was a wide variety of experience between the different regions of England, and this was the case even within the relatively small area of western Berkshire. The task now is to create a general framework of developments within the population and economy of western Berkshire between the fourteenth and sixteenth centuries, and this will reveal marked differences in the experiences of continuity and change between the sub-regions.[41]

The following is a quantitative analysis of data that are largely drawn from fiscal records which were created at a national level and are therefore suitable for comparisons over a wide geographical area. There is an established historiography for this type of exercise. Schofield's methodological approach and use of statistical analysis have been extremely influential, and numerous

---

[36] R. B. Peberdy, 'Navigation of the River Thames between London and Oxford in the Late Middle Ages: a Reconsideration', *Oxoniensia*, 61 (1996), 311–40.
[37] K. R. Clew, *The Kennet and Avon Canal* (London, 1985), 25.
[38] *VCH Berkshire*, IV, 435.
[39] Peberdy, 'Navigation', 323.
[40] See chapter 3.
[41] See Appendix I for a detailed discussion of the documents employed in this chapter, the methodological approach adopted, and the full data.

other studies have followed.[42] Individuals have taken specific taxes whilst others have combined their data.[43] There are now a large number of published county editions of the various taxes.[44] It is unfortunate that there are no suitable records for the fifteenth century, and we have to rely on comparisons of data compiled in the fourteenth and sixteenth centuries. The result is a broad picture of regional variations across the country in the distribution of wealth and the pace of change with a marked north–south divide and a broad band of increasing wealth across southern England.[45] There is a noticeable correlation between those areas of growth and those involved in the manufacture of cloth, often associated with the residence of wealthy clothiers such as the Spring family of Lavenham.

Although regional variations in the pace of change are now generally accepted, there remains the need to examine more closely those within a specific area comprising a variety of different landscapes and economies to refine the conclusions of the broader analysis. This is achieved by examining the Berkshire data, first in its national context, and second through a more detailed analysis that will reveal subtle shifts that underlie the broad patterns described by others.[46] Schofield's analysis of the distribution of assessed wealth ranked Berkshire as one of the wealthiest counties in both 1334 and 1515.[47] In 1334 it was ranked fifth out of 38 counties, and classified in the group of wealthier than average counties (ranks 1–12). In 1515 the range of assessed wealth was very much wider than 1334. Again Berkshire was firmly located, at rank 10, within the band of wealthiest counties. Berkshire was not, however, in the group that experienced outstanding increases in assessed wealth between

[42] R. S. Schofield, 'The Geographical Distribution of Wealth in England, 1334–1649', EcHRev, 18 (1965), 483–510.

[43] R. E. Glasscock (ed.), The Lay Subsidy of 1334 (Oxford, 1975). C. C. Fenwick (ed.), The Poll Taxes of 1377, 1379 and 1381, 3 vols (The British Academy, 1998, 2001, 2005). J. Sheail, 'The Distribution of Taxable Population and Wealth in England During the Early Sixteenth Century', Transactions of the Institute of British Geographers, 55 (1972), 111–26, and his thesis which has been published as J. Sheail (ed.), The Regional Distribution of Wealth in England as Indicated in the 1524–25 Lay Subsidy Returns (List and Index Society Special Series, vol. 28, 1998). H. C. Darby, R. E. Glasscock, J. Sheail and G. R. Versey, 'The Changing Geographical Distribution of Wealth in England: 1086–1334–1525', Journal of Historical Geography, 5 (1979), 247–62.

[44] For example, P. Franklin (ed.), The Taxpayers of Medieval Gloucestershire (Stroud, 1993). A. C. Chibnall (ed.), The Certificate of Musters for Buckinghamshire in 1522 (RCHM, vol. 18, 1973). R. W. Hoyle (ed.), The Military Survey of Gloucestershire (Gloucester Record Series, 6, 1993). J. Pound (ed.), The Military Survey of 1522 for Babergh Hundred (Suffolk Records Society, 28, 1986).

[45] Conclusions drawn from Schofield and Darby above.

[46] This paragraph is based on an examination of the whole county of Berkshire, rather than the specific area of western Berkshire.

[47] Schofield, 'The Geographical Distribution of Wealth in England', 503–10.

the fourteenth and early sixteenth centuries. Berkshire's growth ratio of 2.77 (rank 18) was typical of the region of the south midlands (which experienced an average increase of between two- and threefold).[48] In the analysis by Darby and others, which was not based on county units, growth in Berkshire between 1334 and 1525 had a regional dimension.[49] The area from Newbury to Reading was classified in the highest category of growth in the country, the most north-western part of the county was placed in the lowest category, whilst the area between was classified as 'intermediate' in the rate of growth from 1334 to 1525. Subsequent analysis will largely confirm these findings and demonstrate in detail that there were marked sub-regional differences in the experience of change, with growth in the area around Newbury in the early sixteenth century and economic stability in the Vale of the White Horse.

The distribution of people and assessed wealth in fourteenth-century western Berkshire

The purpose of this section is to establish the relative distribution of the rural population and its assessments of wealth within western Berkshire during the fourteenth century. The results provide a benchmark against which to assess the changes or continuities that had occurred subsequently, and by the sixteenth century. The fourteenth century was a momentous period in terms of severe levels of mortality with the arrival of plague in 1348–49, and the more general crisis in the agrarian economy that preceded the Black Death.[50] We need to establish the impact that these events had on the relative distributions within western Berkshire. That is, were some areas more adversely affected in comparison with others, and are regional differences in the pace of change discernible in the fourteenth century? This cannot be a demographic investigation, as the evidence from the documentary sources is not strong enough; instead, we are interested in measuring relative change between the regions, with the data analysed by rank order. Comparisons are confined to totals of men due to the inconsistent recording of women in the documentation.

---

[48] *Ibid.*

[49] Darby, Glasscock, Sheail and Versey, 'The Changing Geographical Distribution of Wealth in England', especially map on page 258.

[50] Examined in the collection of articles in B. M. S. Campbell (ed.), *Before the Black Death: Studies in the 'Crisis' of the Early Fourteenth Century* (Manchester, 1991).

Table 2 *Changes in the male taxpaying population*

Rural region	Acres	Men in 1327	Idem per 100 acres	Rank	Men in 1381	Idem per 100 acres	Rank	Resident men in 1522	Idem per 100 acres	Rank
Downs	44100	226	0.051	4	466	0.106	4	574	0.130	4
Kennet	27167	220	0.810	3	374	1.377	3	518	1.907	1
Mixed	25001	294	1.176	2	503	2.012	2	365	1.460	3
White Horse	41340	661	1.599	1	995	2.407	1	777	1.880	2

Towns	Acres	Men in 1327	All taxpayers in 1381	Men in 1381	Resident men in 1522
Hungerford	3346	53	183	110	141
Newbury	1242	69	289		243
Wantage	4387	63	300	165	127

Notes:

Rural region
Nominal data are only compared from those parishes that have surviving documentation
for 1327, 1381 and 1522. The parishes are:

Downs: Beedon, Chievley, East Garston, Frilsham, Hamstead Norris, Lambourn,
Leckhampstead, Peasemore, Welford, Yattendon.

Kennet: Avington, Enborne, Hamstead Marshall, Inkpen, Kintbury, Shalbourne, Shaw
Cum Donnington, Speen, West Woodhay.

Mixed: Ardington, Ashbury, Childrey, Lockinge East and West, Hendred East and
West, Kingston Lisle, Sparsholt.

White Horse: Balking, Buckland, Charney Bassett, Coxwell Great, Denchworth,
Challow East and West, Farringdon, Grove, Hanney East, Hanney West, Hatford,
Hinton Waldrist, Longworth, Pusey, Shellingford, Shrivenham, Stanford In The Vale.

Towns
Hungerford includes the vills of Calcot, Hidden, Leverton and Sandon Fee.
Wantage includes the vills of Charlton and Circourt

Sources: TNA, E179/73/6; E179/73/41, 42, 43, 46, 48, 49, 50, 51, 52, 53, 54, 55, 62; E315/464.
There appears to have been a membrane missing from the nominal returns of 1381 for
Newbury and only total figures are obtainable. C. C. Fenwick (ed.), *The Poll Taxes of 1377,
1379 and 1381* (The British Academy, 1998), 15. Appendix 1 has full data.

The 1327 Lay Subsidy can be employed as an indicator of the number of
male taxpayers resident in western Berkshire before the Black Death. As a
consequence of the tax threshold, this cannot be regarded as a complete picture
of the population, but it does provide a measure of the relative distribution
of the taxable male population across the region. Due to the varying sizes of
the different areas of western Berkshire, and the nature of their terrains, it is

necessary to make the comparisons in units of 100 acres. The data presented in Table 2 reveal that the Vale of the White Horse was the most heavily settled region of western Berkshire, with the Kennet valley having significantly fewer people living there. As one would expect, the Downs were sparsely populated, a feature largely determined by their landscape.

It is widely accepted that the arrival of the plague in England had a catastrophic impact.[51] Plague appears to have arrived in Berkshire as part of the dissemination of the disease from west to east, from Bristol into Oxfordshire, Berkshire and Buckinghamshire, in 1348–49.[52] The effects that the Black Death had on the population of Berkshire, however, are only discernible from indirect and fragmentary evidence. For example, at Brightwalton twelve deaths were recorded in April 1349 among the more substantial tenants of the manor.[53] An Inquisition of 17 July 1349 for Buckland recorded that all the villeins and cottars of the manor were dead of the pestilence.[54] At Woolstone the effects of the fall in the tenant population were felt on the receipts of the manor in 1352, by which time several lands were also in the lord's hands due to the pestilence.[55] A tanning mill in the town of Newbury was valueless on account of the plague there.[56] The desertion of Seacourt, Hodcott and Whitley probably occurred in the wake of the Black Death, as perhaps did the migrations at Basildon and Cholsey and the shrinkage of Farnborough.[57] Despite the fragmentary nature of these references, the impression gained is one of initial dislocation caused by plague; nevertheless, some partial recovery may have come quite quickly afterwards.

A comparison with the relative distribution of population in 1381, and after the initial outbreaks of plague, reveals remarkable stability.[58] The impact of plague may have been devastating, but it had not altered the relative distribution of the taxable population. The Vale of the White Horse remained the most densely settled area and the Downs the most lightly populated. The underlying structures in the distribution of population in western Berkshire appear to have remained largely unchanged during the fourteenth century.

---

[51] R. Horrox, *The Black Death* (Manchester, 1994). M. Ormrod and P. Lindley (eds), *The Black Death in England* (Stamford, 1996).

[52] P. Ziegler, *The Black Death* (London, 1969), 142.

[53] Faith, 'Berkshire', 131.

[54] TNA, C135/103 piece 46.

[55] Faith, Berkshire', 122, 124.

[56] *VCH Berkshire*, IV, 137.

[57] J. Brooks, 'The Deserted Medieval Villages of North Berkshire', in J. Dils (ed.), *An Historical Atlas of Berkshire* (Reading, 1998), 40.

[58] The different types of tax and thresholds account for the marked increase in the total numbers between the two dates. Nevertheless, the rank orders remain unchanged. See Appendix 1 for a discussion of the limitations of the sources.

The towns are briefly mentioned here, although they are considered in greater detail in chapter 3. Nevertheless they cannot be entirely omitted from the discussion due to the symbiotic relationship between towns and the countryside. In this chapter only Newbury, Wantage and Hungerford are discussed.[59] The chief feature to note is the similarity in size of the towns of Newbury and Wantage in the fourteenth century; indeed Newbury may have been in decline in the late fourteenth century.[60]

Table 3 *Summary data of change in the relative distribution of taxable wealth*

1327	Acres	Total tax paid by men	Idem per 100 acres	Rank
Downs	75233	£85 7s. 8¾d.	27.24d.	4
Kennet	32126	£41 4s. 8d.	30.80d.	3
Mixed	36389	£56 9s. 8¼d.	37.25d.	2
White Horse	49329	£110 0s. 1¼d.	53.52d.	1

1334	Acres	Total assessment	Idem per 100 acres	Rank
Downs	75233	£125 8s. 9¼d.	40.02d.	4
Kennet	29731	£62 1s. 6¾d.	50.11d.	2
Mixed	40131	£80 5s. 9¼d.	48.02d.	3
White Horse	50682	£174 13s. 0d.	82.70d.	1

1381	Acres	Total tax paid by men	Idem per 100 acres	Rank
Downs	44100	£22 7s. 6½d.	12.18d.	4
Kennet	27167	£16 14s. 1d.	14.76d.	3
Mixed	25001	£24 4s. 6½d.	23.26d.	2
White Horse	43081	£90 10s. 10d.	27.26d.	1

1522	Acres	Total assessment on resident men	Idem per 100 acres	Rank
Downs	74523	£5390 14s. 8¾d.	1736.08d.	4
Kennet	29731	£2586 2s. 3d.	2087.61d.	2
Mixed	37253	£3021 1s. 4d.	1946.30d.	3
White Horse	49714	£5096 4s. 2d.	2460.25d.	1

1546	Acres	Total assessment	Idem per 100 acres	Rank
Downs	68445	£96 19s. 8d.	34.01d.	4
Kennet	27167	£44 14s. 8d.	39.52d.	3

[59] The small towns of Lambourn and Faringdon are included in the rural distributions of this chapter because of the large areas of their parishes. Their urban centres are singled out for examination in the next chapter.

[60] See chapter 3.

Mixed	29637	£58 2s. 7d.	47.07d.	1
White Horse	33093	£63 0s. 1d.	45.69d.	2

Towns	Acres	Total tax paid by men in 1327	Total assessment in 1334	Total tax paid by men in 1381	Total assessment on resident men in 1522	Total assessment on men in 1546
Hungerford	3346	£9 7s. 1d.	fifteenth £15 1s. 6d.	£8 16s. 1d.	£759 15s. 7½d.	£9 3s. 0d.
Newbury	1242	£19 6s. 8d.	fifteenth £27 9s. 6d.	£14 9s. 0d.	£2431 7s. 4d.	£44 3s. 8d.
Wantage	4387	£8 4s. 4¾d.	tenth £10 19s. 0¼d.	£14 10s. 2d.	£779 16s. 0d.	Illegible

Notes:
Acreage varies depending on number of parishes with surviving data.
Hungerford includes the vills of Calcot, Hidden, Leverton and Sandon Fee.
Wantage includes the vills of Charlton and Circourt.

Sources: TNA, E179/73/6; R. Glasscock (ed.), *The Lay Subsidy of 1334* (London, 1975), 6–14; TNA, E179/73/41, 42, 43, 46, 48, 49, 50, 51, 52, 53, 54, 55, 62; E315/464; E179/74/178, 181. Appendix 1 has the full data.

We turn now to an analysis of the distribution of assessed wealth of those resident within western Berkshire in the fourteenth century where a similar, but not identical, pattern emerges. Once again the emphasis is on relative change between the rural sub-regions. There is, moreover, a strong statistical correlation between size and assessed wealth in the parishes, the largest being the wealthiest and the area of the Downs will always be affected by the nature of its terrain and settlement.[61] Several significant patterns emerge from Table 3. The first is the persistent affluence of the Vale of the White Horse and its dominance of the distributions throughout the century. This area consistently ranked highest of the four in assessed wealth per 100 acres. The second is the relative prominence of the Downs, in terms of total assessments, although the average wealth per acre in this area was lower than elsewhere. Large assessments of tax could be made despite the dispersed nature of the population. The third is the fortunes of the Kennet valley which lagged significantly behind the other regions in the total assessments.

Nevertheless some change had occurred in the intervening period. There were areas of western Berkshire that appear to have been experiencing

[61] The Pearson Product Moment Correlation Coefficient between acreage and wealth in 1334 is 0.611 and the Spearman Rank Order Correlation Coefficient is 0.746, both significant at the 0.001 level with 68 degrees of freedom. This level of significance was also obtained in 1381 and 1522 for the association between acreage and wealth.

economic hardship before the Black Death. A comparison of the returns of the Taxation of Pope Nicholas IV in 1291 and the Inquisition of the Ninth 1340–42 confirm the pre-eminent wealth of the Vale of the White Horse, but also describe an area in the Downs and Kennet region that was encountering hardship.[62] The taxation of Pope Nicholas IV was considered by contemporaries as a true valuation; nevertheless, there is evidence that its assessments were low, and thus those parishes with a lower valuation in 1342 may have been experiencing a very hard time.[63] There were a group of parishes, particularly in the southern Downs and centred on Chievely, whose valuations fell, and there was a significant amount of special pleading from this group.[64] The types of complaint varied from soil exhaustion to severe winters, a lack of seed corn and a reduced number of sheep available for assessment. Although these parishes may be characterised by their propensity to offer special pleading, there may have been underlying economic reasons for their complaints, especially in the context of the distributions of Table 3.

A brief analysis of the towns of western Berkshire reveals the continued prosperity of the ancient town of Wantage, the only town in the study region to be taxed at one tenth in 1334. Its parity with Newbury in 1381 may be evidence of the relative decline in the latter's fortunes after the Black Death.

Until now the discussion has concentrated on aggregate trends between the regions. The danger with this approach, however, is that it obscures the people living in the region who comprised these totals. It was the assessments of their wealth that we are considering. Therefore we need to examine the social distribution of assessed wealth of the inhabitants of western Berkshire in the fourteenth century. It is possible to identify the wealthy members of society in 1381 as the commons had decreed that:

> ... for the sum total reckoned on each township the sufficient shall (according to their means) aid the lesser provided that the most wealthy do not pay more than sixty groats for themselves and their wives ...[65]

---

[62] *Taxatio Ecclesiastica Angliae et Walliae Auctoritate Pope Nicholai IV circa AD 1291* (Record Commission, 1831). *Nonarum Inquisitiones in Curia Scaccarii Temp Regis Edwardi III* (Record Commission, 1807). Additional data from TNA, E179/73/16.

[63] B. Harvey, *Westminster Abbey and its Estates* (Oxford, 1977), 57–60. A. H. R. Baker, 'Evidence in the "Nonarum Inquisitiones" of Contracting Arable Lands in England during the Early Fourteenth Century', *EcHRev*, 19 (1966), 518–32. R. Graham, *English Ecclesiastical Studies* (London, 1929), 271–301.

[64] Parishes whose valuations fell included: Aldworth, Avington, Brightwalton, Chievley, Chilton, Compton, Compton Beauchamp, Coxwell, Enborne, Frilsham, Hamstead Marshall, Hatford, Hinton Waldrist, East and West Ilsley, Kintbury, Lambourn, Peasemore, Sparsholt, Speen, Stanford Dingley, Stanford in the Vale, Yattendon.

[65] C. C. Fenwick, 'The English Poll Taxes of 1377, 1379 and 1381: A Critical Examination of the Returns', Ph.D. thesis, London School of Economics (1983), 155.

Some of the payments in the Berkshire sample of 1381 were very large. The highest sum paid was 16s., by Edward Danvers of Winterborne, who came from the Downs region, as did John Estbury of Eastbury who paid 13s. 4d., and there were ten other people who paid more than 5s. from this region. In the Kennet area Almeric de St Amand of West Woodhay paid 13s. 4d., and there were two other men who paid more than 5s. In the Vale there were nine men who paid between 5s. and 10s. 4d. In the area of Mixed Parishes six men paid sums of between 5s. and 8s. These were all exceptional payments of sums far greater than the rest of the population. Fenwick has argued that they do not reflect the real wealth of the individuals, just their ability to pay the larger sum.[66] Their distribution does suggest that in 1381 there were a larger number of wealthy individuals in the Downs than elsewhere in western Berkshire and is perhaps a reflection of the success of wool growing in the region.[67] Those resident in the three towns of the region did not pay the exceptional sums of 5s. or more. The wealthy individuals of western Berkshire in 1381 were rural inhabitants. The situation in Newbury was to change dramatically by the early sixteenth century.

Nevertheless, the wealthy only comprised a small proportion of the total population of an area. The nature of the graduated poll tax does not allow us to determine the number who were poor, but a statistical examination of the relative inequality of the assessments for the poll tax can be undertaken.[68] The results show that wealth was not equitably divided among the population in the fourteenth century, and they do reveal regional contrasts in the distribution of inequalities of wealth. In particular, the Downs had the greatest level of inequality of wealth whilst the Vale of the White Horse had the least; in other words wealth was most equitably distributed in the latter region.

The presence in a vill of those who obtained their livelihood from wages as servants or labourers may account for some of the inequality and offer an opportunity to identify the poorer members of local society. Some assessors of the poll tax recorded the occupations along with the names of those being taxed.[69] The recording of servants in 1381 may present us with an opportunity to

---

[66] *Ibid.*

[67] See below, p. 88.

[68] Gini coefficients are a statistical measure of inequality and the results lie within the range of the gini index that goes from 0.0 perfect equality to 1.0 perfect inequality. The wealth bands that were chosen for the calculations were: 4d.–6d., 7d.–12d., 13d.–18d., 19d.–24d., and 25d. and over. Results Gini coefficients: Berkshire Downs 0.296; Kennet Valley 0.244; Mixed 0.191; Vale of White Horse 0.162.

[69] Where this was undertaken in a consistent manner it does provide invaluable data on the occupational structure of an area. See the works of R. H. Hilton, *The English Peasantry in the Later Middle Ages* (Oxford, 1975). P. J. P. Goldberg, 'Urban Identity and the Poll Taxes of 1377, 1379 and 1381', *EcHRev*, 43 (1990), 194–216 and *idem, Women, Work, and Life Cycle in a Medieval Economy: Women in York and Yorkshire c.1300–*

assess the presence of this social group with relatively low levels of remuneration. In western Berkshire, however, their recording was very inconsistent and only allows their presence to be established.[70] Male servants comprised 10.63 per cent of the total male population, although this figure conceals a wide variety of experience.[71] While servants are visible in the Berkshire returns of the poll tax the inconsistent manner in which they were recorded makes it difficult to establish their significance in the work force at this time.[72]

It has been possible to demonstrate that in fourteenth-century western Berkshire the impact of demographic change was a fairly uniform experience across the regions, with the Vale remaining the most densely settled area, and the Downs having the most dispersed population. The distribution of assessed wealth of the taxable population suggests that the Vale was consistently the wealthiest region, and, whilst there were several wealthy individuals living the Downs region, due to its large area and low density of population, it was ranked the lowest in terms of rank order of wealth. There does appear to have been continuity alongside decline in the distribution of wealth in western Berkshire over the course of the century. Continuity was strong in the Vale, which remained the wealthiest region. In comparison, in the Downs there were places that suffered hardship before the arrival of plague and the Kennet region may have experienced some decline after the Black Death. Wealth in fourteenth-century western Berkshire, when it could be identified, was found in the rural areas as there were no wealthy individuals taxed in the towns at this time.

The distribution of people and assessed wealth in sixteenth-century western Berkshire

Having established the relative distribution of people and wealth in the fourteenth century we now turn to a comparison with the situation in the sixteenth century to identify the patterns of both continuity and change. In this way we can make a contribution to the discussions concerning when the population of England began to rise again after its decline and continued

1520 (Oxford, 1992). L. R. Poos, *A Rural Society after the Black Death: Essex, 1350–1525* (Cambridge, 1991).

[70] The terminology employed to describe them also presented difficulties for analysis as 350 were listed as *serviens*, 18 as *famulus*, and only one *laborator* was recorded.

[71] As a percentage of the male population they could range from 22.99 per cent in West Hendred to 1.3 per cent in Hinton Waldrest with a mean of 8.1 per cent and a median of 6.8 per cent. Yates, thesis, 96–7.

[72] A discussion of the social implications and impact of changes in the use of non-familial types of labour can be found below and in chapter 5.

stagnation in the fifteenth century.[73] Our first opportunity to identify change in the size of the population of western Berkshire after 1381 is in 1522. In Table 2, comparing only those parishes with data for 1381 and 1522, and only men resident in the parishes, there were 2,338 men living in the region and paying tax in 1381, and 2,234 men in 1522. These figures are very close and confirm the hypothesis of stagnation, or even fall in the size of the late medieval population, and slow or perhaps no recovery by the early sixteenth century. This is particularly the case if we accept that there was widespread evasion of the tax in 1381 and comprehensive coverage in 1522.[74] This conclusion, however, misses the local variation in the population between the regions.

It is only through detailed local studies such as this one that relative changes can be discerned. It is the movements of people within a population that are considered here to have been an important factor in explaining apparent changes in the size of the population. By 1522 there were 23 parishes in which the number of men had risen since 1381, and in 21 parishes the numbers had fallen. There was a strong regional dimension to their distribution, as revealed in Table 2. The populations of the Downs and Kennet regions had grown, while those of the White Horse and Mixed regions had fallen. Change in the relative size of the populations of the towns in western Berkshire can also be discerned and the most significant feature was the proportionate rise in the size of Newbury compared with decline at Wantage.[75] The trend of rise in the rural area of the Kennet region was mirrored in the experience of its town. An important feature drawn from a comparison of relative change in the population across the period of study was the shift in pre-eminence from the Vale of the White Horse to the Kennet region. Explaining this shift within the population of western Berkshire will form a recurring theme in subsequent chapters. Rather than changes in the fertility or mortality regimes of the population, it was perhaps the migration of people that played the key role in the variations in the size of the population and regional differences in the rate of change across the country.

Determining when the population began to expand has implications for associated economic features where demand is an important factor, such as agricultural produce, opportunities for employment and the availability of landholdings. It is possible to continue the current analysis further into the sixteenth century by employing data derived from parish registers, and six parishes within the study area had suitable documentation.[76] These reveal

---

[73] See references in chapter 1.
[74] See Appendix for the discussion of the limitations of the documentation.
[75] For towns see below, Tables 2, 3 and 7.
[76] Chaddleworth, Hamstead Norris, Hatford, Letcombe Regis, Peasemore, Stanford Dingley. Respectively BRO, D/P32/1/1, D/P62/1/1, D/P65/1/1, D/P81/1/1, D/P92/1/1, D/P117/1/1.

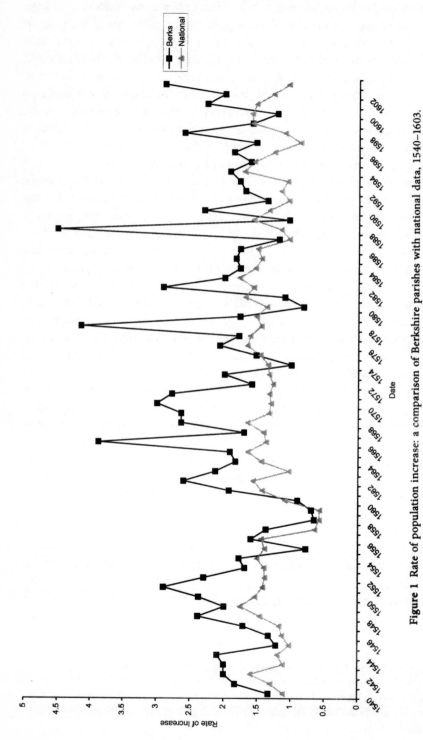

Figure 1 Rate of population increase: a comparison of Berkshire parishes with national data, 1540–1603.

Sources: BRO, D/P32/1/1, D/P62/1/1, D/P65/1/1, D/P81/1/1, D/P92/1/1, D/P17/1/1. Wrigley and Schofield. *Population History*, 496.

an underlying trend of growth in the population, but with significant short term fluctuations. Figure 1 presents the data of the crude rate of increase of the Berkshire parishes and that derived from the national data published in *The Population History of England*.[77] It demonstrates that Berkshire's rate of population increase was consistently higher than that of the rest of England. The underlying trends in the graph are similar, but the Berkshire data peak in 1566, 1578 and 1588.

A very tenuous attempt can be made at calculating population totals for the rural areas. If we assume that, in 1522, 37 per cent of the population were under the age of sixteen, and there were an equal number of women to men, then the Military Survey figures can be converted into population totals.[78] These can then be compared with those derived from parish registers employing the method developed by Poos.[79] The results from an aggregate of the six parishes with suitable documentation were: 1522 population of 506.69 compared with 1546 population of 570.57. The differences between the two figures might be accounted for by the rate of population increase that had occurred since 1522 which is calculated as 0.49 per cent *per annum* and would suggest a buoyant pre-industrial rural population. Should there have been no increase in the population between the two dates then the Military Survey was accounting for 88.8 per cent of the population. Although these figures are very tentative, and based on a number of assumptions, they do suggest that the population of western Berkshire was increasing naturally in the first half of the sixteenth century rather than just through migration. Nevertheless, these are aggregate figures and may hide the variety of experience that has already been identified for the earlier period.

The 1550s was a period of high mortality both in western Berkshire and more generally.[80] The data from the parish registers confirms this statement

[77] Derived by calculating the aggregate baptismal and burial entries for each calendar year beginning in January, and then dividing the baptismal totals by the burial totals, and finally producing an aggregate of the western Berkshire figures. These were then compared with those obtained from Wrigley and Schofield, *Population History*, 496.

[78] Wrigley and Schofield, *Population History*, 568. Thus the total number of men in 1522 in the rural parishes shown in Table 2 of 2,234 will produce a population figure of 7,092.

[79] L. Poos, 'The Rural Population of Essex in the Later Middle Ages', *EcHRev*, 38 (1985), 527. That is to take the quinquennial burial rates for the six Berkshire parishes and inflate by 1000/D, where D is the national Crude Death Rate calculated for England for each of the corresponding years as given in Wrigley and Schofield, *Population History*, 531. This method is, however, vulnerable to volatile mortality in the short or medium term and is therefore inappropriate for the late 1550s when there were high levels of mortality in Berkshire along with the rest of the country.

[80] Above, p. 9. The evidence is summarised in the debate between J. S. Moore and M. Zell in *EcHRev*, 47 (1994), 354–61.

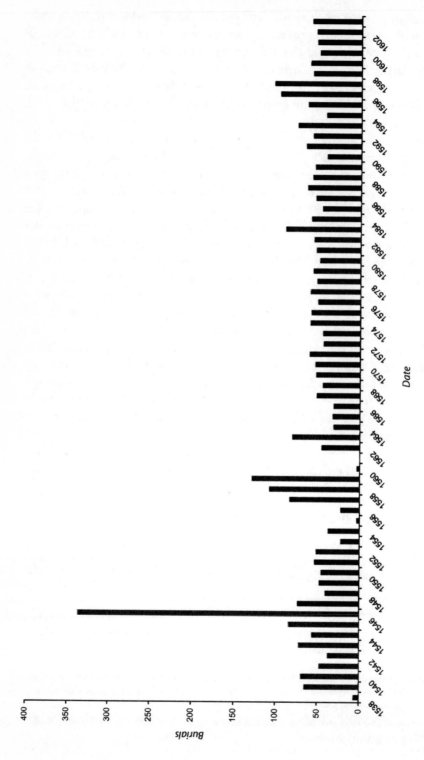

Figure 2 Newbury burials.
Source: BRO, D/P89/1/1.

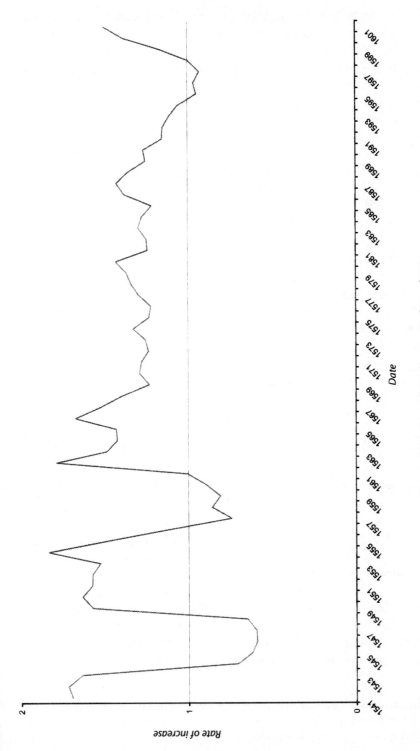

Figure 3 Newbury rate of increase of population.

Source: BRO, D/P89/1/1.

and can be substantiated by indirect evidence from the manorial court rolls of an increase in the number of *post mortem* transfers of land. Moreover, the town of Newbury experienced crisis mortality in 1546, as shown in Figure 2. The burials were concentrated in the late summer and autumn; that is, of the 336 people who died in 1546 there were 79 burials in July, 85 in August, 70 in September, and 41 in October. The seasonality of this mortality suggests that death was due to plague, although the cause of death was never specified. Newbury was also affected by the general high mortality of 1558 and 1559 with an increase in the total number of burials, although not on the same scale as the mortality of 1546. The graph presented as Figure 3 demonstrates that the population of the town was having difficulties in reproducing itself in the sixteenth century. The increase in size identified in Table 2 must have been partially fuelled by immigration. The impact that this had on the rural hinterland has to be acknowledged, particularly acting as a force for depletion of the rural population. At the same time, the rural population of western Berkshire in the middle of the sixteenth century was also suffering from periods of high mortality.[81]

Turning now to changes in the relative distribution of assessed wealth in the sixteenth century, as set out in Table 3, the most significant feature to notice is the rise in the fortunes of the Kennet region by the early sixteenth century. In 1522 the Vale of the White Horse remained the most affluent region in terms of the assessments per 100 acres, although in total taxable wealth the Downs had the largest sum. The Kennet region had increased its position in relative terms in relation to size. By the early sixteenth century there were a number of wealthy farmers living in the region and cultivating large holdings.[82] Moreover, the growing prosperity of this area was closely linked to the town of Newbury, which was expanding rapidly by the sixteenth century. Wealth was largely concentrated in the hands of the clothiers and merchants of the town in 1522 and reveals a marked contrast to the situation in 1381, and a significant change from the pattern of the medieval period. By the middle of the sixteenth century the earlier rise of the Kennet region was not maintained, that had to wait for another decade for stability to return after the rapid changes of landholding in the 1540s described below. The pre-eminence of the Vale region was lost to that of the Mixed area, whilst the Downs continued to pay the largest amount of the subsidy. We must note here the experience of change of those parishes classified as Mixed, whose pattern of change was characteristically that of fluctuations with no other distinguishing features. It has been useful to examine these parishes as a separate group, but in subsequent analysis they

---

[81] Sufficient to make calculations of population totals employing Poos' method invalid. See note above.

[82] Below, chapter 5, Table 18 and p. 191.

will be included with the Downs region as the majority of their lands lay on the north scarp of the Downs.[83]

The towns of western Berkshire also experienced relative change between the fourteenth and sixteenth centuries. The nominal returns of 1381 portrayed Wantage as a thriving urban centre bustling with commercial activity. The town's subsequent decline in the proportion of tax paid by the sixteenth century had parallels with the fortunes of Abingdon and Wallingford in the eastern Vale. In contrast, Newbury was growing rapidly by the early sixteenth century. This was due to the expanding cloth industry of the town and the presence of wealthy clothiers and merchants, especially John Winchcombe II. He is discussed in more detail in the next chapter, but it is important to point out the effect that wealthy individuals had on the rank order of English towns in the early sixteenth century. Places such as Newbury and Witney owed their prosperity, in terms of rank order in the national hierarchy, to the presence of individuals whose assessment of wealth was disproportionately large.[84] Hungerford was also prospering in the sixteenth century and producing cloth, but never on the scale of Newbury, and without the presence of very wealthy individuals. By 1546 John Winchcombe II was assessed with the commissioners of the Subsidy and his exceptional wealth was not recorded in the town.

Before turning to an examination of the distribution of assessed wealth within the population in the sixteenth century it is worth digressing a little to consider an additional source of evidence that supports these general observations regarding the regional nature of change. That is, we can study the dates of alteration and embellishment of the parish churches of western Berkshire (excluding their chancels, which were not the responsibility of the parishioners). The parish church was an important focus for the community as the physical representation of their spiritual life. Until the middle of the sixteenth century bequests of money were regularly left for its maintenance, repairs and new building works.[85] Together with masses for the dead and elaborate funerals, these benefactions illustrate a form of conspicuous consumption that declined

---

[83] This does have the disadvantage of making the area of the Downs region very large compared with the other regions, but is considered to be more representative of the landscape and rural economy of the area.

[84] J. L. Bolton, and M. M. Maslen (eds), *Calendar of the Court Books of the Borough of Witney, 1538–1610* (Oxfordshire Record Society, 54, 1985), liv, Richard Wenman paid four-fifths of Witney's tax in 1524.

[85] These varied in date between the different parishes studied. At Newbury regular bequests were made up to 1550 and only isolated cases thereafter; at Kintbury payments were regular until 1559; at Hanney only two instances were found in 1558 and 1566. On the other hand, at Buckland repairs to the church and its maintenance were associated with the wealthy of the parish in 1494, 1497, 1544, 1546, 1557, 1559, and then small sums in 1590 and 1593. For a study of the whole country see B. Kümin, *The Shaping of a Community* (Aldershot, 1996).

and eventually ceased after the Reformation. A study of surviving architectural features of the parish churches of western Berkshire revealed the full extent of these legacies.[86] The majority had some form of alteration and embellishment made to the church in the fourteenth or fifteenth centuries, whilst there was markedly less work of the sixteenth century.[87] The distribution of some form of embellishment in the fifteenth century was fairly uniform throughout the study area, with a significant number of towers being either built or extended. However, work of the fourteenth century was predominantly found in the northern half of the region.[88] This can be seen as a physical expression of the wealth of these communities. A few major projects were related to wealthy individuals, such as the rebuilding of St Nicholas' church in Newbury largely due to the benefaction of John Winchcombe I; John Norreys rebuilt Yattendon church in 1450; and East Shefford church received a large benefaction in the will of John Fettiplace in 1464. In addition, several chapels or chantries were established, such as those by John Wormstall (d. 1469) at Newbury and John Eastbury in Lambourn (d. 1372). These forms of conspicuous consumption declined over the course of the sixteenth century and reflect a real shift in the concerns and perceptions of this society.

The focus of this section now shifts to an examination of the social distribution of assessed wealth within the population of western Berkshire in 1522.[89] In doing so we can engage with those who describe a widening of the gap between the wealthy and the poorer sections of society as one of the novel features of social change. Certainly there were many forms of publicly expressed fears about the increasing numbers of the poor in the sixteenth century.[90] One method of investigating the validity of these concerns is to take a quantifiable approach to the distribution of taxable wealth. In particular, to consider any differences in the distribution of assessed wealth among the various social groups, especially at the two polar ends of society.

---

[86] Based on an analysis of the architectural features described in *VCH Berkshire*, IV, for the parishes of the study area.

[87] From the 74 parish churches surveyed there were 67 that had alterations made in the fourteenth or fifteenth centuries, excluding their chancels. Sixteenth-century work was identified on only eleven churches. Newbury was completely rebuilt between 1485 and 1533.

[88] Fourteenth-century work was identified in the north on 23 churches and in the south on 6 churches.

[89] This date is chosen due to the comprehensive nature of the documentation that has no equivalent later in the century.

[90] A. L. Beier, *The Problem of the Poor in Tudor and Early Stuart England* (London, 1983). P. Slack, *Poverty and Policy in Tudor and Stuart England* (London, 1988), 114–22. S. Hindle, 'A Sense of Place? Becoming and Belonging in the Rural Parish, 1550–1650', in A. Shepard and P. Withington (eds), *Communities in Early Modern England* (Manchester, 2000), 96–114.

The place of residence of wealthy individuals in western Berkshire in 1522[91] had altered since 1381; indeed the distribution was fairly uniform across the rural study area, with rather more in the enlarged Downs region than elsewhere.[92] The wealthiest rural inhabitant was found in the Vale: Thomas Snodenham of Stanford in the Vale, and a merchant of the Staple, was assessed at £400.[93] The next in affluence were two men in the Berkshire Downs who were valued at £200 each. There were no men assessed at over £100 in the Kennet region. As stated earlier, the wealthy of this region were resident in Newbury in 1522. In Wantage and Hungerford there were no individuals who could rival the wealth of the rural inhabitants, the wealthiest assessments were of £80 and £50 respectively. The wealth of the Newbury clothier John Winchcombe II was remarkable. He was assessed on £630 in goods, whereas the other wealthy individuals of the town were Robert Sewey (another clothier) assessed at 200 marks (£133 6s. 8d.), and two other men had goods worth £130 and £120. The wealthy inhabitants are easily visible in various documents and, as has been argued for Gloucestershire, were less likely to be overlooked by the assessors.[94] This was not necessarily the case for the rest of the population.

Table 4 *The percentage of men of western Berkshire in different categories of wealth, as indicated by assessment on movable goods in 1522*

Region	<£1	£1–<2	Sub total	£2–<5	£5–<10	£10–<20	Sub total	£20–<50	£50 +	Total no. of individuals
Downs	15.94	24.56	40.5	32	12.8	10.57	55.37	3.36	0.85	1637
Kennet	20.2	25.2	45.4	35.2	9.6	6.3	51.1	2.1	1.4	560
White Horse	2.5	31.4	33.9	46.1	11.3	4.3	61.7	3.2	1.3	914

Notes:

Downs region now includes the Mixed Parishes.

Data for Hungerford, Newbury and Wantage are found in chapter 3.

Source: TNA, E315/464.

The percentage of those with assessments of over £20 in Table 4 accords with the pattern of wealth described above, that is, the wealthy in western Berkshire

---

[91] That is, those assessed on income of £40 and over, and who were liable for payments to Wolsey's Anticipation Subsidy. The Anticipation for Berkshire appears to have been a copy of the Military Survey as the assessments were identical. TNA, Anticipation E179/73/132, Military Survey E315/464.

[92] There were 24 individuals in the Vale of the White Horse, 32 in the area of the Berkshire Downs (including ten from the mixed region) and 23 in the Kennet region.

[93] The presence in northern Berkshire of wealthy wool merchants and members of the Staple of Calais is examined in more detail in chapter 5.

[94] Hoyle, *The Military Survey of Gloucestershire*, xxvii.

were fairly evenly distributed across the region. This was not the case in the category of the majority of the population or 'middling group' of those with goods valued at between £2 and £20, where the contrasts between the Vale and the Kennet and Downs were marked. This is an important social group who were predominantly small-scale agriculturalists of half a virgate of land or more and who are discussed in greater detail in chapter 5. They were the key players in the local economy. It was the agricultural activities of these men in the Vale that underpinned the prosperous farming of the region described earlier in this chapter.

We turn now in an attempt to identify the poorer sections of society.[95] The Military Survey of 1522 included large numbers of low assessments and the numbers of those with goods assessed at less than £2 are significant.[96] There were regional differences in their distribution, with the Kennet having a greater percentage of its male population in this category than the other regions. The additional forms of employment available for those living in the Kennet area, described earlier in this chapter, may partially account for the lower assessments on moveable goods in this region. Sub-regional differences are also found in the statistical measure of inequality performed on the 1522 data with the Kennet region having the greatest inequality.[97]

A constant feature of rural England has been the requirement that large agricultural units will necessitate the employment of labour over and above that provided by the family.[98] The types of labour employed would vary between the size and type of agricultural holding, and would change over time. The opportunities for employment in agriculture therefore were never static, nor were the demands for labour. In the period around 1300, when population was exerting pressure on landholdings and many held less than half a virgate of land, probably half the population would have to augment the produce of their land to feed their families, and wage earning could provide a potential source of income, although opportunities for employment

---

[95] For the comparison with 1381 see above, p. 39.

[96] The differences in the recording of valuations below £1 were probably the result of individual commissioners, and their numbers were largely rectified in the assessments of £1–<2. The category of under £2 was chosen to overcome this discrepancy in recording, and because it should enable comparisons with those assessed on wage labour in the Lay Subsidies.

[97] The method of assessment accounts for the different size of coefficients compared with 1381. The wealth bands chosen were: less than £1, £1–<£2, £2–<£5, £5–<£10, £10–<£50 and £50 and over. Gini coefficients for 1522: Berkshire Downs 0.714; Kennet Valley 0.721; Mixed 0.616; Vale of White Horse 0.666.

[98] According to Campbell units of 30 hectares (approximately 12 acres) or more would require additional labour. B. M. S. Campbell, 'England: Land and People', in S. H. Rigby (ed.), *A Companion to Britain in the Later Middle Ages* (Oxford, 2003), 18.

were limited.[99] In the changed demographic conditions of the late fourteenth century the proportion of people who obtained most of their living from wage work probably exceeded a third over the whole country but with wide regional variations.[100] The optimal conditions for wage labourers by the middle of the fifteenth century has led to the characterisation of the period as 'the golden age of the English husbandman, the artisan, and the labourer'.[101] Nevertheless, charitable bequests made in some of the wills of the time should alert us to the presence of the poor in local society.[102] Their presence in local society may have been increasing during the sixteenth century. This has significant implications for other areas of change, such as age of marriage and fertility in the case of servants in husbandry.[103] Additionally, as wage labourers they provided the supplementary work force required to cultivate the large farms,

---

[99] R. H. Britnell, 'Specialization of Work in England, 1100–1300', EcHRev, 54 (2001), 1–16.

[100] C. Dyer, Standards of Living in the Later Middle Ages (Cambridge, 1989), 213–14. Estimated for the poll tax years 1377–81, and rising to two-thirds in parts of eastern England. For additional references to works on servants and labourers see below, n. 103.

[101] J. E. Thorold Rogers, A History of Agriculture and Prices in England, 1259–1793, vol. IV (Oxford, 1866–1902), 23.

[102] See below, chapter 5, p. 218. For literary references to the poor of the fourteenth century see William Langland's Piers Plowman, discussed in G. Shepherd, 'Poverty in Piers Plowman', in T. H. Aston, P. Coss, C. Dyer and J. Thirsk (eds), Social Relations and Ideas (Cambridge, 1983), 169–89.

[103] Service in husbandry has been viewed as a form of life-cycle employment that involved unmarried adolescents and young adults of both sexes. Pioneering work in identifying the proportion of servants within the early modern population was undertaken by P. Laslett, Family Life and Illicit Love in Earlier Generations (Cambridge, 1977). The innovative work of Kussmaul expanded our understanding of servants in husbandry: A. Kussmaul, Servants in Husbandry in Early Modern England (Cambridge, 1981), and was extended in her General View of the Rural Economy of England, 1538–1840 (Cambridge, 1990). Work on Essex provided additional data on the topic L. Poos, A Rural Society After the Black Death (Cambridge, 1991), 181–228. The association between life-cycle service, fertility and demographic change is made by R. M. Smith, 'Hypotheses sur la Nuptualite en Angleterre aux XIII–XIV Siecles', Annales Economies Societes Civilisations 38 (1983), 107–36, and P. J. P. Goldberg, Women, Work, and Life Cycle in a Medieval Economy: Women in York and Yorkshire, c.1300–1520 (Oxford, 1992), and the evidence is reviewed in M. Bailey, 'Demographic Decline in Late Medieval England: Some Thoughts on Recent Research', EcHRev, 49 (1996), 1–19. For conditions of employment and wage rates, in addition to those already cited, see S. Penn, and C. Dyer, 'Wages and Earnings in Late Medieval England: Evidence from the Enforcement of the Labour Laws', EcHRev, 43 (1990), 356–76; C. M. Newman, 'Work and Wages at Durham Priory, 1494–1519', Continuity and Change, 16 (2001), 357–78; D. Youngs, 'Servants and Labourers on a Late Medieval Demesne: The Case of Newton, Cheshire, 1498–1520', AgHRev, 47 (1999), 145–60; A. Everitt, 'Farm Labourers', in Thirsk, Agrarian History IV, 396–465.

and change in the conditions of wage labour comprise one of the features of the transition to a capitalistic system.[104]

Those dependent wholly or partially on income from wages formed a diverse social group described in the Sumptuary Legislation of 1463 as 'Servant of Husbandry', 'Common Labourer', 'Servant' and 'Artificer'.[105] In western Berkshire servants and labourers were often grouped together, as in 1522. There is evidence to suggest that there may have been the same proportion of male servants in the population in 1381 as in 1522.[106] The category of under £2 was defined as a method of distinguishing those who might have been employed as wage labourers in 1522. Their numbers were particularly marked in the Kennet region, and there were noticeably fewer living in the Vale. An investigation into the distribution of those paying the Lay Subsidy on income from wages largely substantiates this finding.

The Lay Subsidies of 1524 and 1525 are a known source for the study of the proportion of wage labour in the population.[107] Poor survival of the nominal returns prevents a detailed study of western Berkshire, but where they do survive they do confirm the distribution identified in 1522.[108] Sheail has argued that the £1 *per annum* value represented a minimum qualification for inclusion within the 1523 tax threshold and not necessarily the total income of the man.[109] It was a type of poll tax levied on all those above the age of fifteen and, unlike the clauses relating to moveable goods and landed incomes, the phrase 'for every pounde' was missing. Thus a man could earn more than £1 in wage income in a year and pay 4d. in tax provided that he did not possess goods and lands which would place him within the higher thresholds. The following investigation is therefore an analysis of the proportion within the taxable community of those assessed on wages rather than the sums that they earned. In western

---

[104] A recent overview and study of the subject with specific references to *Capital* is found in J. Whittle, *The Development of Agrarian Capitalism* (Oxford, 2000), 8–9, 225–7, 253–6.

[105] *Statutes of the Realm from Original Records and Authentic Manuscripts*, 11 vols (Record Commission, 1810–28), vol. II, 401. D. Woodward, 'The Background to the Statute of Artificers: The Genesis of Labour Policy, 1558–63', *EcHRev*, 33 (1980), 32–44. Idem, *Men at Work: Labourers and Building Craftsmen in the Towns of Northern England, 1450–1750* (Cambridge, 1995) 41, 55–6, 184–91.

[106] Where they were recorded in 1381 male servants, as a percentage of the male population, comprised 10.63 per cent, and in 1522 10.5 per cent of all resident men.

[107] For example J. C. K. Cornwall, *Wealth and Society in Early Sixteenth Century England* (London, 1988), 200–10. More recently in Whittle, *Development of Agrarian Capitalism*, 227–34.

[108] The Vale of the White Horse had particularly poor coverage.

[109] J. Sheail, 'The Regional Distribution of Wealth in England as Indicated in the 1524/25 Lay Subsidy Returns', Ph.D. thesis, London (1968), 34.

Berkshire in 1524 assessments on wages accounted for 43.1 per cent,[110] and in 1525 40.6 per cent,[111] of all men. In 1522 certain commissioners created a separate category for recording labourers and servants. In this group of sixteen parishes, which lay in the southern half of the county, labourers and servants comprised 44.98 per cent of resident men. In the Lay Subsidy of 1524, in these same parishes, those assessed on wage income comprised 44.4 per cent of all male assessments.[112] These figures can be compared with other areas of England where Sheail calculated, employing four hundreds from Norfolk, that 35.7 per cent in 1524 and 34.7 per cent were assessed on wage income.[113] Dyer has argued that those assessed on wages and those assessed on goods worth less than 40s. together constitute a reasonable approximation to the group of labourers in the localities in question.[114] He calculated that the average percentage of wage earners was 36 per cent, and ranged from 32 per cent in Gloucestershire to 41 per cent in Rutland.[115] If this procedure is adopted for the figures for Essex obtained from Poos then wage labour accounted for 43.4 per cent of taxpayers assessed in 1524.[116] These must remain minimum figures as there may have been other wage earners who were too poor to have been assessed for taxation, or whose wages comprised the smaller proportion of their total income from other sources. The Berkshire figures are shown to have been very similar to those from Essex. They confirm the findings from 1522 that there were many more wage labourers as a proportion of the population in the Kennet region than the Vale of the White Horse.[117] We can conclude that, although marred by inconsistent coverage of the region, there were marked sub-regional differences in the presence of wage labour. The observation that there had possibly been no change in the proportion of wage labour in the population between 1381 and 1522 should be re-iterated.

To conclude this investigation into shifts in the relative distribution of population and assessed wealth as revealed from a study of fiscal records it is appropriate to comment on the differences in the nature of change between the regions of western Berkshire. Notwithstanding the inherent difficulties in the fiscal data various patterns have emerged of sub-regional change in rural

---

[110] Those assessed on goods comprised 56.5 per cent and land 0.4 per cent. TNA, E179/73/121.

[111] Goods 58.9 per cent and land 0.6 per cent. TNA, E179/73/124–6.

[112] Note these figures are for men only, as female labour was inconsistently recorded.

[113] Sheail, 'The Regional Distribution of Wealth in England', 38.

[114] Dyer, *Standards of Living*, 214.

[115] *Ibid.*

[116] Poos, *Rural Society*, 29.

[117] The distribution for the Vale may be affected by the poor coverage of this area by the documents. Numbers of those assessed on wages as a percentage of total: Downs 39; Kennet region 49; Mixed 31, Vale of White Horse 18. TNA, E/179/73/121, 124, 125, 126.

western Berkshire between the fourteenth and sixteenth centuries. The taxable population in the Kennet area had grown in proportion to the other areas of the region. The Vale of the White Horse was the pre-eminent sub-region in terms of its taxable wealth until the middle of the sixteenth century. People living in the Downs region consistently paid large sums in taxation, although this was a relatively dispersed population, and there were areas that were experiencing economic difficulties in the 1340s. This decline was also noticeable in parts of the Kennet region. The region of Mixed Parishes was characterised by the experience of fluctuations in the relative distribution of assessed wealth. The presence of wealthy individuals had been most marked in the Downs in the fourteenth century and absent from the towns of western Berkshire. In the sixteenth century the wealthy rural inhabitants were fairly uniformly distributed across the regions and there were now very wealthy clothiers in the town of Newbury. By the sixteenth century there was a greater proportion of wage labour in the Kennet region than elsewhere. It was, however, the rising fortunes of the town of Newbury that had brought the most significant change to the distribution of assessed wealth in western Berkshire from that of the fourteenth century.

The landowners of western Berkshire and changes in the social distribution of land

Land, its ownership, forms of tenure, and the ways in which it was administered provide the foundations for any rural study. The impact that landlords had on the pace of change in a locality will be a recurring theme of subsequent chapters. Naturally different types of lords ran their estates with different objectives, particularly in the demands they made of their tenants. For example, it has been argued that the crown had numerous estates and manors and was a relatively undemanding landlord.[118] In comparison, the large ecclesiastical landowners were often very conservative as landlords and strove to retain the integrity of their estates and often imposed heavy, and sometimes old-fashioned, burdens on their tenants.[119] Minor lay landowners, especially the gentry, had a more direct interest in their lands and tenants and often pursued a more personal and individualistic approach to the management of their much

---

[118] R. W. Hoyle (ed.), *The Estates of the English Crown, 1558–1640* (Cambridge, 1992). M. Bailey, *The English Manor c.1200–c.1500* (Manchester, 2002), 8.

[119] C. Dyer, *Lords and Peasants in a Changing Society* (Cambridge, 1980). B. Harvey, *Westminster Abbey and its Estates in the Middle Ages* (Oxford, 1977). P. Schofield, 'Extranei and the Market for Customary Land on a Westminster Abbey Manor in the Fifteenth Century', *AgHRev*, 49 (2001), 1–16.

smaller estates.[120] Nevertheless, that does not necessarily mean that lords of large estates did not attempt to maximise their returns.[121] The landowners of Berkshire are considered now in fairly general terms to establish a context for this study.

The crown maintained a strong presence in Berkshire, particularly in the eastern end of the county and centred on their residence at Windsor Castle. There was, however, an absence of any strong indigenous noble influence in Berkshire. Even the chief baronial holder of the medieval period, Henry de Ferrers and his successor the Earl of Lancaster, who were important landowners for two and a half centuries, had their chief interests away from Berkshire.[122] Until the Dissolution the major landowners, in addition to the crown, were the two great Benedictine abbeys of Abingdon and Reading, closely followed by Beaulieu Abbey who held the whole hundred of Faringdon.[123] The management style of a major landowner might well have an effect on the economy of an area.[124] Both abbeys were important sources of employment for the Berkshire gentry as stewards or lawyers, for example Sir Thomas Fettiplace, a member of a successful local gentry family, who was steward to the abbot Abingdon in 1522. The impact, therefore, that the Dissolution had on the pattern of tenure was considerable and will be discussed in detail below.

The gentry were one of the social groups credited with taking advantage of the opportunities for obtaining lands following the Dissolution, and they have played a prominent role as energetic and innovative new landowners in some of the arguments for the transition to the early modern period.[125] The rise of the gentry, it was argued, brought a shift of emphasis in the ways in which income from land was to be maximised, and farming pursued for a profit.[126]

---

[120] Such as those in N. Saul, *Knights and Esquires: The Gloucestershire Gentry in the Fourteenth Century* (Oxford, 1981).

[121] D. Stone, *Decision-Making in Medieval Agriculture* (Oxford, 2005), who argues that they were often proactive in pursuing income-generating strategies.

[122] P. J. Jefferies, 'A Consideration of Some Aspects of Landholding in Medieval Berkshire', Ph.D. thesis, Reading (1972), 20.

[123] Jefferies, 'Some Aspects of Landholding', 19.

[124] This point was made by Hilton, referring to Stenton's analysis of the estates of Abingdon Abbey: R. H. Hilton, *The Economic Development of Some Leicestershire Estates in the Fourteenth and Fifteenth Centuries* (Oxford, 1947), 5.

[125] The works of R. H. Tawney have been particularly influential in this area. R. H. Tawney, 'The Rise of the Gentry, 1558–1640', *EcHRev*, 11 (1941), 1–38.

[126] This was Tawney's point and numerous studies of the gentry have subsequently been undertaken that reveal the wide diversity of experience of this social group: for example, C. Carpenter, *Locality and Polity. A Study of Warwickshire Landed Society, 1401–1499* (Cambridge, 1992); N. Saul, *Knights and Esquires: The Gloucestershire Gentry in the Fourteenth Century* (Oxford, 1981); and *Scenes from Provincial Life: Knightly Families in Sussex, 1280–1400* (Oxford, 1986).

Nevertheless, direct evidence for a distinctive style of estate management remains inconclusive. The origins of this social group may date back to the thirteenth century and by 1400 to be 'gentil' was still to be noble, but by 1436 they were becoming more clearly defined in legal cases and the language of statutes,[127] and characteristically they possessed a minimum income from land of £10.[128] William Harrison set out the qualifications for becoming a gentleman in his *Description of England* in the sixteenth century:

> Whosoever studieth the laws of the realm, whoso abideth in the university giving his mind to his book, or professeth physic and the liberal sciences, or, beside his service in the room of a captain in the wars or good counsel given at home, whereby his commonwealth is benefited, can live without manual labor, and thereto is able and will bear the port, charge and countenance of a gentleman ...[129]

The increasing popularity of the status of gentleman is clearly visible in the Visitations of the sixteenth century, when families flocked to have their pedigrees recorded.[130] Nevertheless, the title of gentleman was not universally adopted by those who qualified in the early sixteenth century; for example, there was inconsistent use of the designation recorded in the Military Survey for Berkshire.[131]

As the most numerous social group of landowner in Berkshire it is worth considering the gentry in more detail. The gentry families of Berkshire, in common with elsewhere in the country, were subject to fluctuations in both their fortunes and in the survival of male heirs, and there was a considerable

---

[127] For example the Statute of Additions defined greater distinctions among those claiming gentility. M. Keen, *English Society in the Later Middle Ages, 1348–1500* (Penguin, 1990), 11. More recent work on the origins of the gentry include P. Coss, *The Origins of the English Gentry* (Cambridge, 2003). M. Keen, *Origins of the English Gentleman: Heraldry, Chivalry and Gentility in Medieval England, c.1300–1500* (Stroud, 2002).

[128] Gray loosely grouped them in 1436 in the category between the baronage and the yeomanry which rather exaggerated their numbers. H. L. Gray, 'Incomes from Land in England in 1436', *English Historical Journal*, 49 (1934), 607–39. T. B. Pugh, 'The Magnates, Knights and Gentry', in S. B. Chrimes *et al.* (eds), *Fifteenth-century England, 1399–1509* (Stroud, 1995), 96–7. K. B. McFarlane, *The Nobility in Later Medieval England* (Oxford, 1973), 122–3, 275. S. J. Payling, *Political Society in Lancastrian England* (Oxford, 1991), 2, 11–13. See also Carpenter's sophisticated classification in *Locality and Polity*, chapter 3. Income of £10 was certainly the standard required by the College of Arms to bear a coat of arms, that is, to become armigerous. Pugh, 'Magnates, Knights and Gentry', 97.

[129] Reprinted from the 1587 edition in G. Edelen (ed.), *The Description of England by William Harrison* (New York, 1968), 113–14.

[130] Those for Berkshire are published in W. H. Rylands (ed.), *The Four Visitations of Berkshire* (Harleian Society, 56 1907).

[131] Among the landowners four were styled knight, nine esquire and nineteen gentleman.

turnover of families within this group in the fifteenth century that continued in the sixteenth century.[132] The Puseys were a success story.[133] They were already landowners before the Conquest and, although their fortunes fluctuated in the meantime, they were in a position by the Dissolution to profit from the changes in the availability of land. The Abberbury's were a case of a family who appeared among the Berkshire landowners at the end of the thirteenth century, then increased their landholdings by piecemeal acquisitions, and finally dissipated them, also in a piecemeal fashion, in the fifteenth century.[134] One of the main beneficiaries were the aristocratic Dukes of Suffolk. They were major landowners in the fifteenth century but were themselves the casualties of political allegiances in the sixteenth century. Several gentry families declined for lack of male heirs in the fifteenth century; for example the de la Beche family based at Aldworth, the Danvers of Winterbourn and the Chelreys. The process of decline among some landowning families continued over the next century especially the Norreys of Wytham, the Parrys of Hamstead Marshall, the Essexes of Lambourn and the Untons of Wadley. On the other hand, the Fettiplace family were particularly prolific at this time and continued to expand the different branches of the family, their landholdings, and influence into the sixteenth century and later.[135]

These gentry families, together with those local men who were of the knightly class, formed the political and administrative community of the county and wielded considerable influence locally. It was from their numbers that various appointments were made as royal servants, commissioners, collectors of customs and taxes, and other offices. Almost all of the county's representatives to Parliament had some experience of local administration in the early fifteenth century as sheriff or escheator, or appeared on royal commissions in Berkshire at various times.[136] This situation changed, however, after 1558, when the influence of London was stronger in the selection of Berkshire's Members

---

[132] Of the 12 families studied by Jefferies who held land in 1300 only four remained after 1500; the Puseys, Coudrays, Kingstons and Fettiplace. Jefferies, 'Some Aspects of Landholding', 390. From a seventeenth-century perspective of the 38 families that constituted the country gentry group in Berkshire in 1640 only 8 (21 per cent) were settled as rural landowners before 1500; another 16 (42 per cent) entered between 1500 and 1600; and the remaining 14 (37 per cent) had arrived after 1600. C. G. Durston, 'London and the Provinces: the Association between the Capital and the Berkshire County Gentry of the Early Seventeenth Century', *Southern History*, 3 (1981), 42.

[133] For details see Jefferies 'Some Aspects of Landholding'.

[134] S. Walker, 'Sir Richard Abberbury (c.1330–99) and his Kinsmen: The Rise and Fall of a Gentry Family' *Nottingham Medieval Studies* 34 (1990), 113–40.

[135] The Fettiplace family are discussed in more detail in chapter 5.

[136] J. S. Roskell et al. (eds), *The History of Parliament: The House of Commons, 1386–1421*, vol. 1 (Stroud, 1992), 264.

of Parliament, although many still held lands in the county.[137] One example from the fifteenth century was John Arches of East Hendred, who was also lord of the manor of West Hanney. He acted as escheator, tax collector, aulnager, justice of the peace, and on several commissions for Berkshire, while also fulfilling his role as bailiff of the liberty in Oxfordshire and Berkshire for the Bishop of Winchester, and also of his manor of Witney.[138] In the early sixteenth century Sir William Essex of Lambourn had served as sheriff and on several commissions on various occasions, including that of 1535.[139] These men formed the local 'political' society, and their loyalties and allegiances bound them into networks with land landowners and members of the aristocracy. For example, in 1522 Sir Thomas Fettiplace was steward to the Abbot of Abingdon, John Cheyney to the Duke of Suffolk, and Sir William Essex acted as steward for different lords on various manors. The effects of London on the county community declined in influence from east to west. Conversely, the capital's influence increased over the course of this study, and in the sixteenth century a period living in London formed an important detour in the path to land acquisition in Berkshire.[140]

The place of residence of local gentry families was concentrated in the north of the region, particularly in the Vale of the White Horse, with only John Norreys of Yattendon and John Cheyney of West Woodhay living in the Kennet region in 1522. One of the effects of the changes of the sixteenth century was to increase the number of gentry families resident in Berkshire, although they were still predominantly found in the north of the county. This was certainly the case among the freeholders for the country listed in 1561 who were styled knight, esquire or gentleman.[141] They were characterised by having the majority of their landed estates in the county, close kin and friendship networks; indeed, there was much inter-marriage within this social group, and, as has already been shown, they held many of the county administrative offices.[142] By 1640 they remained most deeply rooted in the Vale region.[143]

[137] P. W. Hasler (ed.), *The History of Parliament: The House of Commons, 1558–1603*, vol. 1 (London, 1981), 113–17.

[138] Roskell, *History of Parliament*, 264, 47–8.

[139] S. T. Bindoff (ed.), *The History of Parliament: The House of Commons, 1509–1558*, vol. 2 (London, 1982), 106–7.

[140] Durston, 'London and the Provinces', 44–5.

[141] BL, MS Lansdowne 5, number 9, folio 29. From the study area: Wantage and Ganfield hundreds 10; Farringdon hundred 3; Shrivenahm hundred 12; Faircross and Kintbury hundreds 7.

[142] Their social and family networks are examined in greater detail in chapter 5.

[143] Durston, 'London and the Provinces', distribution map on page 38.

Table 5 *Income from land in Berkshire in 1412*

Category	Number	Total Income	Percentage
Lay Barons	9	£319 6s. 8d.	17.8
More than £100	—		
£40-£100	5	£353 6s. 8d.	19.7
£20–£39	28	£623 14s. 8d.	34.8
£10–£19	12	£140 6s. 8d.	7.8
Less than £10	30	£146 8s. 0d.	8.2
Clerical (incomplete)	6	£117 2s. 0d.	9.9
Colleges	2	£30	1.7

Notes:
Clerical category is incomplete due to omission of Abbot of Reading's lands.
Sources: The data are for the whole county of Berkshire. *Inquisitions and Assessments relating to Feudal Aids*, vol. VI (Record Commission, 1920), 399–404. There are, however, problems as the lands of the Abbot of Reading were omitted.

It is important to establish what proportion of the lands of Berkshire the different types of landowners controlled and also to identify any change over time. Indeed, stability was the dominant attribute as there was little significant alteration in the social structure of landowners between 1412 and 1522, change came later in the sixteenth century with the transfer of lands after 1540. The first date is 1412 when the assessments on income from land provide an excellent insight into the social distribution of landholding for the whole county, although they omit additional properties held by individuals beyond the county borders.[144] The tax threshold was set at lands or rents with an annual value of £20.[145] The data in Table 5 suggest that most of the land in Berkshire was held by small lay landowners whose annual income from their estates was less than £40. The predominant social group of landowners were the lesser knights and gentry; this was also the case in 1522.

The largest proportion of income from land was held by men and institutions who were not resident on their manors.[146] The laity was a category that comprised all ranks of society below the aristocracy and formed the largest

[144] There was no suitable source for the country in the fourteenth century and the categories were chosen to be comparable with the results from the rest of the country in Payling, *Political Society in Lancastrian England*, 5, 11–13. See also J. M. W. Bean. 'Landlords', in Miller, *Agrarian History* III, 528–36.
[145] See Appendix 1, p. 253.
[146] Cornwall has criticised the valuations of land in the Berkshire Military Survey for being inconsistent between the different hundreds, particularly the high valuation of Wantage compared with its neighbouring hundreds. The results may reflect, in part, the returns of the different commissioners Cornwall, *Wealth and Society in Early Sixteenth Century England*, 124–5.

Table 6 *Income from land in western Berkshire in 1522*

Category	Number of persons	Number of properties	Income from land of absent landowner	Income from land of resident landowner	Assessment on goods	Total income from land	% of all land	Total
King	1	13	£223 11s. 4d.			£223 11s. 4d.	5	£223 11s. 4d.
Aristocracy	9	32	£294 6s. 0d.			£294 6s. 0d.	6	£294 6s. 0d.
Church	28	46	£242 14s. 3d.	£5 9s. 8d.	£1 6s. 8d.	£248 3s. 11d.	5	£249 10s. 7d.
Monastic	32	113	£1,276 1s. 3d.			£1,276 1s. 3d.	27	£1,276 1s. 3d.
Corporate bodies	12	25	£170 13s. 8d.	£2		£172 13s. 8d.	4	£172 13s. 8d.
Laity	537	483	£1,902 9s. 0d.	£579 8s. 8d.	£3,004 17s. 6d.	£2,481 17s. 8d.	53	£5,486 15s. 2d.
Totals	619	712	£4,109 15s. 6d.	£586 18s. 4d.	£3,006 4s. 2d.	£4,696 13s. 10d.	100	£7,702 18s. 0d.

Source: TNA, E315/464. Note, it does not cover the eastern area of the county.

group of landowners, with the highest total income from land. It is, of necessity due to the documentation that does not define status, a very broad category and one that omits important social distinctions. The assessed income of monastic landowners was the second largest group. The wealthiest individual landowner was the Abbot of Abingdon, with a total of £411 13s. 10d. that included manors, rectories, free lands and pensions which were predominantly situated in the Vale and Downland areas.[147] He was followed by the king, with income from lands of £223 11s. 4d. The other categories of landowners held only small proportions of the total lands of the region. There had been little change in the social distribution of land between the two dates. Nevertheless, this was not the case over the course of the sixteenth century when lay landowners increased their dominance as local landowners.

When we examine the data in more detail we find that many of the local landowners of 1522 held portfolios of lands from different manors.[148] The number of small parcels of land indicated by their low valuations is noteworthy, 44.26 per cent held land with an annual income of less than £1.[149] This figure is rather lower than in Babergh hundred in Suffolk where this group represented 54 per cent, and in South Erpingham in Norfolk where they comprised 56 per cent of landowners. Income from land did not represent their total wealth. The assessment of land by resident landowners was £586 18s. 4d. whilst their total assessment on goods was £3,006 4s. 2d., and thus land only accounted for 16.5 per cent of their total assessment. Of those resident landowners in the group with lands valued at less than £1 this source of income only represented 3.1 per cent of their total assessment (£41 5s. 5d. in resident land and £1,281 15s. 6d. in goods). There were regional differences; in particular, the Vale of the White Horse had many more persons assessed on land than the other regions.[150] There may have been more owner-occupiers living in the Vale than the Kennet, in which case, this extends the different characteristic features of the society in the Vale.

Change to the structure of landowning in western Berkshire occurred later in the sixteenth century, and in particular, with the transfer of lands as a

---

[147] For a detailed examination of the landholdings of Abingdon Abbey see C. J. Bond, 'The Reconstruction of the Medieval Landscape; The Estates of Abingdon Abbey', *Landscape History* 1 (1979), 59–75. Also the introduction to G. Lambrick and C. F. Slade (eds), *The Cartularies of Abingdon Abbey* II (Oxford Historical Society, New Series, 33, 1990–92), xx–lxviii.

[148] Among the 619 landowners 207 were resident, and of these 38 held additional lands elsewhere in the county.

[149] That is, of the 619 landowners 274 had lands valued at under £1.

[150] Again, this could be a product of different commissioners, or it might reflect, albeit only partially, differences in the types of society. Total number of assessments on land: Downs 217; Kennet 175; Mixed 168; Vale 357.

result of the Dissolution of the Monasteries from 1536.[151] In 1522 monastic landlords held 27 per cent of the total income from land shown in Table 6. At the Dissolution, therefore, we can reasonably presume that over a quarter of the lands of western Berkshire changed hands. These were lands that had previously been held, often for centuries, by the same landlord. The longevity and stability of many of these estates were shattered. It would have had a significant impact on the administration of these lands and the conditions for the tenants living there, if not immediately, then certainly within a generation.[152] In 1522 the three largest monastic landowners in western Berkshire were the Abbot of Abingdon described above, the Abbot of Beaulieu with a total assessment of £151 10s. 11d., and the Prioress of Amesbury with a total of £131 15s. 1d.[153] These were all major landlords in western Berkshire who did not survive the sixteenth century.

We can examine in some detail the fate of the 45 manors in western Berkshire that had been held by monastic houses for the speed of transfer and type of beneficiaries. In general, lands changed hands rapidly in the 1540s and the chief beneficiaries were those with London connections and associated with the king and Thomas Cromwell, and other members of the nobility, gentry, and merchants.

The majority of initial transfers were of grants by the king, only four being direct sales. In another four cases the current tenant or lessee obtained the manor and would have provided some measure of continuity for the tenants.[154] The king retained Boxford and East Hendred, and also the manor of Greenham, whose subsequent history was complicated by the revival by Queen Mary of the order of Hospitallers and the restoration of their lands at Greenham.[155] The remaining manors changed hands frequently, particularly in the 1540s.[156] The

---

[151] Although, as will be shown, Wolsey had earlier dissolved the priories of Poughley and St Frideswide's in 1524 to endow his college at Oxford.

[152] This point will be developed in chapters 4 and 5.

[153] Other monastic landowners in 1522 with total holdings in western Berkshire of over £10 were: Abbot of Westminster £77 4s. 1d.; Prior of St John of Jerusalem £51 5s. 11d.; Prior Poughley £47 6s. 8d.; Prior Wallingford £40 5s. 6d.; Abbot Glastonbury £40; Abbot Cirencester £31 17s. 5d.; Prior St Swithens £30; Abbot of Battle £27 13s. 4d.; Prior Shene £26; Prior St Frideswides £24 19s. 0d.; Prioress of Nuneaton £20; Prioress Goring £15; Abbot Titchfield £10.

[154] The Pusey family, mentioned earlier, had held the manor of Pusey of the Abbot of Abingdon since 1086 and took it at the Dissolution. William Pleydell held Shrivenham, Alexander Unton had Shellingford and Thomas Morris continued at Great Coxwell.

[155] VCH Berkshire, III, 319–20.

[156] There were 10 that changed hands twice between the Dissolution and 1560, 9 that changed hands 3 times, 8 changed 6 times, 7 changed 4 times, and 3 changed 5 times. 4 continued in the same hands and the king retained 2. Donnington is omitted due to the fragmentation of its lands.

priories of Poughley and St Frideswide's had been dissolved by Wolsey in 1524 and were granted as part of the foundation of his college at Oxford.[157] Fifteen manors went to Berkshire men and 13 manors were granted to royal servants and members of the aristocracy. Thomas Seymour was a notable beneficiary and his attainder meant further change when his manors reverted to the crown and were subsequently re-granted by the king. The Newbury clothier, John Winchcombe II, bought East Lockinge, West Ginge, Farnborough in the study area, and various additional manors of Reading Abbey, especially Thatcham and Bucklebury. It was probably profits obtained from the sale of wool that enabled members of the Yate family to purchase their lands and manors.[158] In the Kennet region two local men, Richard Bridges of Shefford and John Knight of Newbury, bought lands together which they subsequently divided between themselves.[159] Transfers did not all go uncontested. John Cheney of West Woodhay had unsuccessfully petitioned for Longworth; and the king's physician did not retain Welford as it had previously been granted to Sir Thomas Parry. These changes in the distribution of land at the Dissolution largely conform with the patterns identified elsewhere in the country.[160] Moreover, the transfer of lands was not necessarily viewed as irreversible, as can be seen in the example of Henry Horneclif of Newbury who, when writing his will in 1558, was worried in bequeathing his lands that they would revert to the Church by act of Parliament.[161]

Local men such as William Essex of Lambourn, Richard Brydges of West Shefford, and John Cheney of West Woodhay had acted as commissioners in 1535 undertaking the assessment of the potential wealth of the Church in Berkshire. They were therefore well informed of the local landholdings and wealth of the monasteries. Nevertheless, the majority of the properties of the large houses of Abingdon and Reading initially went to Thomas Cromwell and his colleagues from London. Cheney wrote asking for lands, but was not initially successful. Eventually, in 1542, Cheney obtained the lands of neighbouring Kintbury that had previously belonged to Amesbury. The influence of London and the royal court was much stronger in obtaining lands than that of local men.

---

[157] Those of Poughley priory eventually went to the Dean and Chapter of Westminster Abbey.

[158] John and James Yate were Staplers in the early sixteenth century. See chapter 5.

[159] They do not appear to have been buying land for others or acting as agents as they subsequently only divided the lands between themselves.

[160] J. Youings, 'The Church', in C. Clay (ed.), *Rural Society: Landowners, Peasants and Labourers, 1500–1750* (Cambridge, 1990), 103–20. Also J. Youings, *The Dissolution of the Monasteries* (London, 1971), 117–31. J. Youings, 'The Terms of the Disposal of the Devon Monastic Lands, 1536–58', *EHR*, 69 (1954), 18–38. H. J. Habakkuk, 'The Market for Monastic Property, 1539–1603', *EcHRev*, 10 (1958), 362–80.

[161] BRO, D/A1/76/22.

Contemporaries of the time, men such as Henry Brinklow whose family lived at Kintbury in western Berkshire, wrote condemning the rapacious actions of the new owners of monastic property, particularly in the increasing of the cost of land to the tenant.[162]

Consyder yow, what a wickednes is comonly vsed thorow the realme vnponysshed, in the inordinate inhansyng of rentys, and takyng of vnresonable fynys, and euery day worse than other; and euyn of them specially to whom the kyng hath geuen and sold the landys of those impys of Antichrist, Abbays and nonryes ...[163]

These allegations require testing. One method is to compare the assessments of 1522 with those of the first ministers' accounts; this can be undertaken for 29 of the Berkshire manors, and the result is a general increase in valuation.[164] Changes to the value of the lands of Amesbury can be charted for a longer period and reveal a significant rise in the totals between the documentary sources.[165] It is unfortunate that the *Valor Ecclesiaticus* exists only in summary form for Berkshire and this exercise cannot be undertaken for other lands.[166] The assessments of rectories, pensions and portions remained unchanged. The evidence is therefore ambiguous and reveals a variety of experience, but one that was certainly not on the scale implied by the authors of the polemical texts. The economic effects of these changes in landholding in western Berkshire may have been muted, but were no less dramatic for having removed a major landowner from the scene after centuries of continuity. Subsequently there was little stability in the landowning class of Berkshire. By 1640 only five of the thirty-eight county families of Berkshire of the time had either initially

---

[162] This family is discussed in more detail in chapter 5. Brinklow's comments are the subject of detailed examination in M. Yates, 'Between Fact and Fiction: Henry Brinklow's *Complaynt* Against Rapacious Landlords', *AgHRev*, 54 (2006), 24–44.

[163] J. M. Cowper (ed.), *Henry Brinklow's Complaynt of Roderyck Mors* (EETS, extra series xxii, 1874), first published 1542, pp. 9–10.

[164] William Dugdale, *Monasticon Anglicanum*, 8 vols (London, 1849) with additional material from TNA, E315/464, SC6/HENVIII/3986, 2402, 3739. An average increase of 40 per cent was calculated, but this hides a wide range of percentage increases from 464 to –87, with a median value of 15 per cent increase. These confirm Cornwall's findings of inconsistency in the valuations of land in Berkshire. For example, the manors (not total landholding) of the Abbot of Abingdon rose from £405 3s. 2d. in 1522 to £424 11s. 3d. in 1538–39; those of the Abbot of Beaulieu fell from £118 7s. 2d. in 1522 to £102 1s. 2d.; additionally, the valuation of Farringdon fell from £66 to £46 19s. 7d. Additional detail in Yates, 'Between Fact and Fiction', 36–7.

[165] In 1522 £131 15s. 0d.; in 1535 £151 0s. 7d. as the valuation in the *Valor Ecclesiasticus Temp. Henr' VIII*, vol. 2 (Record Commission, 1814), 95; in 1546 £173 14s. 6d. in the ministers' accounts in Dugdale, *Monasticon Anglicanum*, vol. 2, 341–3.

[166] A. Savine, *English Monasteries on the Eve of the Dissolution* (Oxford, 1909), 23–4.

established or considerably enlarged their Berkshire estates with monastic land.[167]

The social status of the landowners and pattern of landholding in western Berkshire had remained stable into the sixteenth century. Change had come that was driven by the exogenous factor of the transfer of lands at the Dissolution of the Monasteries. Many of the beneficiaries from this event had strong links with London. During the sixteenth century the gentry as a social group expanded their numbers resident in the region, infiltrated society in the south of the county, although they remained concentrated in their residences in the north of the county. As members of the 'political' society of the region their influence would have been wide-ranging. The effects that resident members of the gentry had upon local society is a theme that will be expanded in chapters four and five.

Conclusion

We have demonstrated in this chapter that within the relatively small area of western Berkshire there were distinctive landscapes and local economies. There was a significant shift in the distribution of the population and in the economy between the fourteenth and sixteenth centuries, and the experience of change varied between the three main regions. Overall there had been little alteration in the size of the population between 1381 and 1522; if anything the population may have fallen, although this cannot be confirmed because of the shortcomings of the sources. Yet closer examination revealed areas of growth and decline that suggest a redistribution of population within the region, with migration as an important factor. It has been possible to demonstrate an increase in mortality in the late 1540s and 1550s, and crisis mortality in the town of Newbury. Migration into the town must have played a significant role in maintaining its demographic and economic vitality. In the Vale of the White Horse economic buoyancy was a consistent and continuing feature; there were wealthy individuals resident in the area in the fourteenth and sixteenth centuries, and low amounts of wage labour recorded in the sixteenth century. By comparison, in the Downs there were a number of wealthy individuals living in the region in the fourteenth century, and there had been a period of economic decline identifiable before the Black Death. There were fewer wealthy inhabitants in the Kennet region until the sixteenth century when the most notable were resident in the town of Newbury; nevertheless there was also an increase in the number of wealthy farmers in this rural region. The population also included a large number of person assessed on income from wages, a feature explained by the opportunities for diversity of economic activity. The

[167] Durston, 'London and the Provinces', 43.

Dissolution of the Monasteries had brought about a significant change among the local landowners with the loss of longstanding monastic landlords, a feature particularly of the 1540s, and one of the effects was to increase further the gentry's influence as landowners in the locality. The fortunes of the towns of western Berkshire varied. Wantage had been a thriving market town in the late fourteenth century and was in decline by the early sixteenth century. The fortunes of Newbury were its mirror image as the town was growing rapidly by 1522 and contained a number of wealthy individuals. For convenience the urban data were isolated from the analyses of this chapter. In fact there was a symbiotic relationship between town and countryside, and the following chapter will examine this dynamic in detail and consider the impact of urban–rural relationships upon the nature of change in the area between the fourteenth and sixteenth centuries.

CHAPTER 3

Town and country relations: Newbury and its hinterland

Introduction

Urban–rural relationships are an important dynamic in any study of past societies and economies. It is readily accepted among historians that towns can be defined simply as a relatively dense and permanent concentration of residents engaged in a multiplicity of activities, a substantial proportion of which were non-agrarian.[1] This definition, however useful, isolates the town and omits the relationship with its immediate surrounding countryside, with other towns, and its place within a market network. Towns fulfilled essential social and economic functions that inextricably bound them into a series of both local and wider relationships. Geographers and archaeologists have developed theoretical approaches to their analyses of towns. In particular, they model towns in terms of central place theory, spheres of influence, urban hierarchies and marketing systems. These conceptual frameworks are not without problems, especially as they have a tendency to become static and mechanical models, but they do perform a useful function in rationalising our analysis of the function of towns and the nature of urban–rural relationships and are summarised here to proved a context for the study of a specific town.[2]

Towns can be conceived within a hierarchy based on size, economic function and social complexity. Central place theory is employed by geographers as a method for defining and quantifying towns, and then ranking them by their function. Every town possesses a distinctive role in that, to some degree, it acts

[1] R. Holt and G. Rosser (eds), *The Medieval Town. A Reader in English Urban History, 1200–1540* (London, 1990), 4. The authors employ the definition as part of their introduction to a complex examination of towns.

[2] The following is a summary of H. Carter, *The Study of Urban Geography* (London, 1995), chapters 4–6. H. Carter, *An Introduction to Urban Historical Geography* (London, 1983), 85–94. P. Clark (ed.), *Small Towns in Early Modern Europe* (Cambridge, 1995), 1–21. C. Renfrew, *Approaches to Social Archaeology* (Edinburgh, 1984), 135–53.

as a focus for the surrounding countryside and operates as a central place for collecting and distributing local produce; at the same time providing the goods and services that the countryside requires. Its centrality is measured by the number of goods and services that it offers when it acts as an administrative, social and economic centre. Towns can then be ranked by function in addition to size, particularly of the population. The notion of spheres of influence rests on the assumption that people will travel to acquire goods and services.[3] The distance travelled will lengthen in relation to the perceived value of the goods. The transaction costs incurred, particularly from transport, form part of the price of the luxury. Similarly, patterns of consumption can have a hierarchical structure, ranging from luxury goods to everyday foodstuffs.[4] Astill ranked towns not just by their immediate hinterlands, but included the country's external relationship with the continent and the strength of international trade.[5] Towns can be ranked hierarchically within a marketing network that extended from beyond London, the major ports, regional centres, to larger and then smaller market towns, and the network continued within villages, fairs, inns and other informal trading places.[6] The zones proposed by von Thünen for provisioning and supplying cities, and the impact that these had on the pattern of agriculture within the concentric circles, provide another and allied conceptual model for viewing a specific urban–rural relationship.[7] This model has proved a useful framework within which to analyse London's influence, and western Berkshire lay within the area of the 'Feeding the City' project at the Centre for Metropolitan History.[8] It is important to note that these spheres of influence and urban hierarchies were not fixed but were altered by consumer

---

[3] C. Dyer, 'Medieval Towns and the Countryside in Late Medieval England', *Canadian Journal of History*, 31 (1996), 17–35, employs the theoretical model in a detailed examination of marketing relationships between towns and the countryside.

[4] C. Dyer, *Everyday Life In Medieval England* (London, 1994), 257–81.

[5] G. Astill, 'Towns and Town Hierarchies in Saxon England', *Oxford Journal of Archaeology* 10 (1991), 95–116, particularly 99.

[6] Astill, 'Towns and Town Hierarchies'. C. Dyer, 'The Consumer and the Market in the Later Middle Ages', and 'The Hidden Trade of the Middle Ages: Evidence from the West Midlands', in his *Everyday Life in Medieval England* (London, 1994), 283–303, 258. R. H. Britnell, 'Urban Demand in the English Economy, 1300–1600', in J. A. Galloway (ed.), *Trade, Urban Hinterlands and Market Integration c.1300–1600* (London, 2000), 1–21.

[7] B. M. S. Campbell, J. A. Galloway, D. Keene and M. Murphy, *A Medieval Capital and its Grain Supply: Agrarian Production and Distribution in the London Region, c.1300* (Historical Geography Research Series, 30, 1993), 5–7.

[8] The model has also been applied to Cambridge and its hinterland, with grain coming from an area within a 10-mile radius of the town, livestock from further away, while fuel came from a more specialised area of production than the model predicted. J. S. Lee, 'Feeding the Colleges: Cambridge's Food and Fuel Supplies, 1450–1560', *EcHRev*, 56 (2003), 243–64 and especially 261–2.

demand, the development of urban specialities, and to meet changing social requirements, such as those of the guilds and fraternities of the later middle ages.

Towns can also be ranked by the size of their populations. They contained about 20 per cent of the English population in the late fourteenth and early sixteenth centuries.[9] London as the capital and commercial centre in 1540 was the dominant and most populous city in England, and on a par with others in western Europe.[10] It was followed in the hierarchy by the regional centres of Norwich, Bristol, Newcastle-upon-Tyne, York, Exeter, Coventry, Salisbury, Canterbury, and Colchester.[11] Recent research has emphasised the collective importance of England's small towns, those with a population of less than 2,000, within the urban system.[12] It has been estimated that at some point between 1270 and 1540 that there may have been around 600 small towns in England. In 1300 small towns may have contained about half of the urban population of England, and a tenth of that of the whole country.[13] Together they provided urban resources for the vast majority of the rural population who would have lived within easy reach of two or three small towns.

Urban–rural relationships are therefore an important dynamic element in any explanation of the rate of change, and yet theoretical concepts of urban hierarchies and spheres of influence have received little empirical testing, particularly for the medieval period, as only a few studies have sought to investigate the interaction between an individual town and its surrounding countryside.[14] Moreover, there has been a tendency in the past to concentrate on the better-documented sites, and as a result there are few studies of middling-sized towns, or of those at the forefront of the expansion of the cloth industry at the turn

---

[9] C. Dyer, 'How Urbanized was Medieval England?', in J. M. Duvosquel and E. Thoen (eds), *Peasants and Townsmen in Medieval Europe. Studia in Honorem Adriaan Verhulst* (Gent, 1995), 169–83, especially 177.

[10] C. M. Barron, 'London, 1300–1540', 397; and D. Keene, 'The South-East of England', *CUHB*, 545, 558–9.

[11] A. Dyer, 'Appendix: Ranking Lists of English Medieval Towns', in *CUHB*, 761.

[12] Particularly the work of Christopher Dyer.

[13] C. Dyer, 'Small Towns, 1270–1540', in *CUHB*, 506–10.

[14] Important exceptions for the medieval period include R. H. Britnell, *Growth and Decline in Colchester, 1300–1525* (Cambridge, 1986), especially chapters 10 and 17. M. Kowaleski, *Local Markets and Regional Trade in Medieval Exeter* (Cambridge, 1995), especially chapter 7. For the later period see C. M. Newman, *Late Medieval Northallerton: A Small Market Town and its Hinterland, c.1470–1540* (Stamford, 1999). J. Goodacre, *The Transformation of a Peasant Economy* (Aldershot, 1994). J. Galloway, 'Town and Country in England, 1300–1570', in S. R. Epstein (ed.), *Town and Country in Europe, 1300–1800* (Cambridge, 2001), 106–31. J. Lee, *Cambridge and its Economic Region, 1450–1560* (Hatfield, 2005). Lee, 'Feeding the Colleges: Cambridge's Food and Fuel Supplies', 243–64.

of the sixteenth century.[15] Newbury and its hinterland therefore provide an ideal site for answering important questions about the nature of change in this period. The absence of a local archive should not be a deterrent when undertaking an investigation such as this one that is question-based rather than document-driven. There are many centrally generated sources that can be employed, such as tax lists, cases of debt recorded in the Court of Common Pleas, customs accounts of various types, and all can be utilised to augment whatever local material survives: manorial, ecclesiastical and archaeological. By employing a variety of sources it is possible to create a holistic picture of the urban–rural relationship.

This chapter begins by placing Newbury within its urban and marketing context, then considers the town in some detail, followed by an examination of its cloth industry, before a general study of the economy and society of the town is undertaken with an emphasis on exchange and production as points of interaction with the hinterland. Finally a more specific study of the urban–rural relationship is achieved through an examination of investment and debt. The result is a picture of a local market town with a small hinterland, but due to its specialist cloth manufacture it was also a player on the national and international scene having strong links with London, Southampton and Antwerp.

The towns and marketing structure of western Berkshire

Newbury formed one element in the county's urban system and developments in the town cannot be viewed in isolation but have to be placed within the context of the urban hierarchy. Much of Berkshire's urban framework had been created by the later tenth century.[16] The principal Saxon settlement was Wallingford, founded by Alfred, and remained pre-eminent until at least the thirteenth century. Other early medieval urban centres included Abingdon, Reading, Wantage, Cookham, Lambourn and possibly Faringdon and Old Windsor; whilst others such as Thatcham and Aldermaston had urban plots (*hagae*) by Domesday. Newbury appears to have been in the process of being

---

[15] Works on middling-sized towns include M. Bonney, *Lordship and the Urban Community: Durham and its Overlords, 1250–1540* (Cambridge, 1990). D. Shaw, *The Creation of a Community: The City of Wells in the Middle Ages* (Oxford, 1993). On small cloth towns see D. Dymond and A. Betterton, *Lavenham: 700 Years of Textile Making* (Woodbridge, 1982). A little later but still relevant J. L. Bolton and M. M. Maslen (eds), *Calendar of the Court Books of the Borough of Witney, 1538–1610* (Oxfordshire Record Society, 54, 1985).

[16] I am grateful to Grenville Astill for his advice when thinking about Berkshire's towns, and this paragraph draws heavily on G. Astill, 'Medieval Towns', in J. Dils (ed.), *An Historical Atlas of Berkshire* (Reading, 1998), 22–3, and G. Astill, *Historic Towns in Berkshire: An Archaeological Appraisal* (Reading, 1978).

founded when captured by the Domesday survey.[17] In certain cases, such as Aldermaston, Lambourn and Thatcham, there were no further references until the thirteenth century and one cannot be certain about the level of continuity of urban status. In line with national trends, the twelfth and thirteenth centuries witnessed a number of royal and seigniorial urban foundations in Berkshire, including New Windsor by the 1130s (royal), Hungerford by the 1170s (aristocratic), and Wokingham by the early thirteenth century (episcopal). Maidenhead was rather different as it developed as a new bridging point on the Thames in the late thirteenth century.

The distribution of Berkshire's medieval towns was uneven and was concentrated on the main river valleys, especially the Thames and Kennet. Perhaps there was too much competition in these areas as some of the urban casualties of the later medieval period, such as Wallingford, Wargrave, Cookham, and Old Windsor, were on the Thames, and Aldermaston and Thatcham were in the Kennet valley.[18] Otherwise the urban framework appears to have been remarkably stable during the period of this study.[19] The population of western Berkshire was more dispersed away from the river valleys (as shown in chapter 2) where there were correspondingly fewer towns. The Berkshire Downs were served by Lambourn and Newbury situated at either end of the Lambourn valley, and by Wantage. The latter was the only town at the foot of the scarp and together with Faringdon and Abingdon fulfilled the urban requirement of the area of the Vale. The rural areas of eastern Berkshire were served by Wokingham and to a lesser extent New Windsor and Maidenhead. Wokingham was not sited on a major route and relied on serving an agricultural region that extended into north-east Hampshire and west Surrey.

The changing fortunes of the rural areas of western Berkshire between the fourteenth and sixteenth centuries were described in chapter 2 and the diversity of experience was explained, in part, by the effects of Newbury's expansion. We turn now to place Newbury within its local urban hierarchy by examining shifts in the relative distribution of population and assessed wealth between the towns of the region, beginning with the situation in the

---

[17] There is no direct evidence for the formation of the town of Newbury, the first record of its existence is in a grant of c.1079. It is not mentioned in Domesday Book but may have been part of the lost manor of Ulvritone. In 1066 Ulvritone was valued at £9; by 1086 it was worth £24, and 51 *hagae* or urban plots were mentioned. The increase in value and the number of houses suggests that the 'new town' came into existence during the second half of the eleventh century. *VCH Berkshire*, IV, 134–5. Astill *Historic Towns in Berkshire*, 50.

[18] A point made by Astill in 'Medieval Towns', 22.

[19] Dyer makes this observation in relation to the Midlands for the period from c.1300 to the sixteenth century. C. Dyer, 'Trade, Urban Hinterlands and Market Integration, 1300–1600: A Summing Up', in J. A. Galloway (ed.), *Trade, Urban Hinterlands and Market Integration c,1300–1600* (London, 2000), 105.

Table 7 *Comparison of the number of taxpayers and sums paid by the towns of western Berkshire, 1327–1522*

	1327				1381				1522			
	Taxpayers	% of taxpayers	Tax paid	% of tax paid	Taxpayers	% of taxpayers	Tax paid	% of tax paid	Resident men	% of resident men	Assessment on goods	% of assessment on goods
Newbury	79	31.85	£23 2s. 7¾d.	44.86	289	28.73	£14 9s. 0d.	28.73	250	37.76	£2,431 7s. 4d.	51.43
Wantage	59	23.79	£6 8s. 2d.	12.43	219	21.77	£10 19s. 0d.	21.77	108	16.31	£666 2s. 8d.	14.09
Hungerford	38	15.32	£6 13s. 10¼d.	12.98	123	12.23	£6 3s. 0d.	12.23	114	17.22	£579. 12s. 4d.	12.26
Faringdon	43	17.34	£7 2s. 9½.d	13.84	195	19.38	£9 15s. 0d.	19.38	86	12.99	£555 1s. 4d.	11.74
Lambourn	29	11.69	£8 3s. 7¾d.	15.87	180	17.89	£9 0s. 0d.	17.89	104	15.71	£495 7s. 4d.	10.48
Total	248	100	£51 11s. 1¼d.	99.98	1006	100	£50 6s. 0d.	100	662	100	£4,727 11s. 0d.	100
Reading	135		£13 15s. 6d.		583		£29 3s. 0d.				no data for Reading in 1522	

Note: data from the towns have been extracted from their rural parishes.
Source: TNA, E179/73/6; E179/73/43, 46, 48, 50, 55; E315/464.

fourteenth century. The data in Table 7 illustrate how Newbury was the largest town in the study area but positioned well below Reading, the principal town of that time, in the size of its population and the degree of its assessed wealth, and Newbury can be classified as a middling-size town. The ancient town of Wantage, although smaller in size than Newbury, was the only town in the study area that was taxed in 1334 at the rate of one tenth. In 1327 Newbury had a number of individuals who paid very large sums of tax, unlike Reading, and this accounts for the size of its total in comparison with the number of taxpayers. Newbury may have experienced some form of urban decline for much of the second half of the fourteenth century.[20] It was significantly smaller than Reading, which in 1381 had 583 persons assessed to pay a total tax of £29 3. od. compared with Newbury's 289 taxpayers who paid £14 9. od. Abingdon in the fourteenth century was the other important town, but there are no surviving returns for 1381 or 1522 and so it does not appear in the table.[21] Abingdon served as the regional centre for the Vale and was sited at important river and road crossings.[22] A cloth-producing town itself, it was also the centre of the rural cloth industry in the fourteenth century.[23] Leland still remarked in 1542 that it 'stondith by clothing'.[24] Wantage, although an ancient urban centre that served both the Downland and Vale regions, is classifiable as a small town by the late medieval period. The other small towns of the region, Faringdon, Hungerford and Lambourn, together with Wantage, appear as bustling urban centres in 1381. The surname evidence suggests a wide variety of occupations including the service trades of brewers, bakers, tailors, shoemakers, and those employed in the building and carrying trades. The small towns were all operating as market centres, having chapmen, while Wantage also had a merchant. There was some speciality as Hungerford had dyers, Faringdon woolmen and shearmen and also a goldsmith, there were

---

[20] It was reported in 1342 in the returns of the Inquisitions of the Ninth that there were no merchants trading in the town. *Inquisitiones Nonarum* (London, 1807), 7. Large sums were awarded as exemptions in 1352–53 TNA, E179/73/32; and Table 7 demonstrates its poor performance in 1381 compared with 1327.

[21] Wallingford had declined in importance by the fourteenth century and continued to do so, particularly after the new bridge over the Thames was built at Abingdon in 1416. *VCH Berkshire*, IV, 435.

[22] For example, Richard Cely had stopped at Abingdon on his way from London to Northleach to wait for his wool packer who was busy in Southampton packing wool for the king. A. Hanham (ed.), *The Cely Letters, 1472–1488* (EETS, Original Series, 273, 1975), 133–4.

[23] H. L. Gray, 'The Production and Exportation of English Woollens in the Fourteenth Century' *EHR*, 39 (1924), 13–35, especially 31.

[24] L. T. Smith (ed.), *Leland's Itinerary in England and Wales* (London, 1964), vol. I, 122. C. Jackson, 'Clothmaking and the Economy in Sixteenth-century Abingdon', *Oxoniensia*, 67 (2002), 59–78.

shepherds at Lambourn, and Wantage was remarkable for the number of servants who were recorded.[25]

By the early sixteenth century Berkshire's urban hierarchy had shifted, largely due to the rise in fortunes of Reading and Newbury and the relative decline of Abingdon. Newbury's place in the urban hierarchy was ranked 29 out of the 50 largest provincial towns of England in 1524–25 and classified as a town with a growing population of 2,691.[26] The principal town of Reading (population 3,452) was ranked 17, while Abingdon (population 819) was too small by the sixteenth century to qualify for inclusion in the list. The small towns of western Berkshire; Wantage, Faringdon, Hungerford (population 741) and Lambourn (population 397), continued to function as local centres.[27] Hungerford may have been expanding as part of the general trend in the Kennet valley at this time. Wantage, like its hinterland, declined in the proportion of its wealth and population in comparison with Newbury.

Towns formed an integral element within the marketing framework that extended throughout the country. Markets are also described in terms of a hierarchy based on the sphere of influence and range and type of goods that each provided. The proliferation of markets, as with towns described above, was an aspect of the expansion of the twelfth and thirteenth centuries, and markets also experienced some contraction or rationalisation in the later middle ages.[28] The marketing system that operated in western Berkshire in the fifteenth and sixteenth centuries accords with the general theories. London was the premier market in terms of the provision of luxuries and a major port. Cases of debt brought in the Court of Common Pleas reveal the widespread involvement of London's merchants in western Berkshire.[29] In c.1400 those laid in London

---

[25] Wantage had a total of 219 persons, of whom 61 were servants and 94 heads of household. Both men and women were employers of servants, and two servants were married suggesting a more permanent form of employment than that of life-cycle service.

[26] A. Dyer, *Decline and Growth in English Towns, 1400–1640* (Basingstoke, 1991), 66–7, 72.

[27] No 1524–25 figures for Wantage or Faringdon survive. Population figures were derived from J. Sheail, *The Regional Distribution of Wealth in England as Indicated in the 1524–25 Lay Subsidy Returns* (List and Index Society Special Series, vol. 28, 1998), 12–20, and Dyer's multiplier of 6.5 to convert taxpayers into population estimates was employed. Additional comparative examples of small towns in the urban hierarchy can be found in C. Dyer and J. Laughton, 'Small Towns in the East and West Midlands in the Later Middle Ages: A Comparison', *Midland History*, 24 (1999), 24–52.

[28] R. H. Britnell, 'The Proliferation of Markets in England, 1200–1349' *EcHRev*, 34 (1981), 209–21, and 'Urban Demand in the English Economy, 1300–1600', in Galloway (ed.), *Trade, Urban Hinterlands and Market Integration*, 1–21.

[29] Cases of debt laid in Berkshire that involved Londoners in the Michaelmas terms: 2 in 1439, 3 in 1450, 1 in 1459, 1 in 1469, 5 in 1478, 0 in 1489, 0 in 1500, 2 in 1510, 1 in 1520. TNA, CP40/715, 759, 795, 833, 864, 910, 954, 993, 1030.

came from the Kennet valley or northern part of the Vale; although Berkshire as a whole produced the smallest number of cases of debt laid by plaintiffs from London in 1424 and 1570.[30] As noted earlier, the study area formed the western boundary of the 'Feeding the City' project and the Vale continued to supply London with grain in the sixteenth century. Southampton was the other port that had strong links with western Berkshire. The city's brokage books recorded the numbers of carts carrying goods, especially wine, to centres in the Kennet valley and Vale; and returned with exports, such as cloth and hides, that belonged to the merchants of its city, or to Berkshire men. Reading fulfilled several of the county's administrative functions, but not necessarily as an important market centre for western Berkshire.[31] Although sited outside the county, Henley on Thames appears to have acted as an entrepot for produce from the Vale going to London.[32]

The towns of western Berkshire were all market centres. The markets of Abingdon, Wantage and Faringdon served the Vale of the White Horse. The area of the Berkshire Downs was covered by Wantage and Lambourn and, additionally, the village market of East Ilsley that had a grain market and also a specialised sheep market.[33] The receipts from the market tolls of Faringdon provided a useful source of income for Beaulieu Abbey, whilst Woolstone was supplied with hurdles purchased at Lambourn.[34] Leland was disparaging in the remarks he made about the markets of Lambourn and Faringdon, which suggests that they may have been rather small and localised in their importance by the early sixteenth century.[35] Newbury and Hungerford were the main market centres for the Kennet region. Newbury had an important grain market in the fourteenth and sixteenth centuries and was also a centre

[30] D. Keene, 'Changes in London's Economic Hinterland as Indicated by Debt Cases in the Court of Common Pleas', in Galloway (ed.), Trade, Urban Hinterlands and Market Integration, 60, 63–4.
[31] See discussion of the archaeological evidence below.
[32] B. M. S. Campbell et al., A Medieval Capital and its Grain Supply (Historical Geography Research Series, 30, 1993), 158–9, 168–9, 178. R. B. Peberdy, 'Navigation on the River Thames between London and Oxford in the Later Middle Ages: A Reconsideration', Oxoniensia, 61 (1996), 311–40, especially 323, 328–30.
[33] The existence of the market at East Ilsley is established by its dispute with Wallingford over trade. VCH Berkshire, IV, 25. Thirsk, Agrarian History IV, 590.
[34] S. F. Hockey (ed.), The Account Book of Beaulieu Abbey (Camden Society, Fourth Series, 16, 1975), 84–7. TNA., SC6/758/10.
[35] 'Sum caulle this toune Cheping-Farington; but there is other none or very smaul market now at it.' Volume 1 page 125. 'to Chepinge Lanburne a poore Friday market' Volume 5 page 79. L. T. Smith (ed.), Leland's Itinerary in England and Wales (London, 1964).

for wool, yarn and cloth.[36] There is very little evidence for activity of the village markets in western Berkshire after the initial grant of the market charter, with the exception of East Ilsley, described above.[37] In addition, and as will be discussed more fully below, East Hendred was a centre for the rural cloth industry and reputed to have had a cloth fair, perhaps as a local response to a period of specialised production.[38]

The town of Newbury

Newbury's position within the urban and marketing hierarchy has been established. The town will now be examined in some detail as it serves as a suitable site for investigating the economic and social functions of a middle-sized town, and a town that was expanding by the end of the fifteenth century largely due to the importance of its cloth industry. The production of cloth has been described more generally as the dynamic sector of the economy in the fifteenth century and may be seen as the motor for subsequent economic expansion in the late 1470s, particularly through its exports.[39] Newbury provides a useful opportunity for examining the expansion of the cloth industry in detail and the antecedents to the high levels of production that are identifiable by the early sixteenth century. The famous entrepreneurial clothier John Smallwood also Winchcombe, otherwise known as 'Jack of Newbury', has traditionally been portrayed as playing a pivotal role in explaining the rise in the town's fortunes. The town's cloth industry, however, was based on earlier foundations. To understand these developments we need a context, and we will begin by describing Newbury's urban framework in terms of its physical layout and administrative structure.

Newbury is located in a strategic position for capturing passing road and river traffic. The town lies in the south-west corner of the county at an

---

[36] Miller, *Agrarian History* III, 349–50, Thirsk, *Agrarian History* IV, 495, 591. Newbury's market functions are dealt with in detail below.

[37] Grants of markets in western Berkshire: Balking in 1217, Catmore 1306, East Garston 1238, East Hendred 1415, East Ilsley 1232, Faringdon 1218, Hinton Waldrist 1217, Hungerford pre-1246, Kingston Lisle mid-13th century, Kintbury 1267, Lambourn no date, Newbury pre-1228, Shrivenham 1257, Speen 1218, Stanford in the Vale 1230, Wantage pre-1224, West Woodhay 1317, Yattendon 1258. J. Sims, 'Markets of Medieval Berkshire', in Dils (ed.), *An Historical Atlas of Berkshire*, 24–5. Astill *Historic Towns in Berkshire*, 8.

[38] *VCH Berkshire*, IV, 294. Gray, 'Production and Exportation of English Woollens', TNA E101/343/24.

[39] D. C. Coleman, *The Economy of England, 1450–1750* (Oxford, 1977), 49–55. J. H. Munro, 'The 'New Institutional Economics' and the Changing Fortunes of Fairs in Medieval and Early Modern Europe: the Textile Trades, Warfare and Transaction Costs', *Vierteljahr-schrift fur Sozial- und Wirtschaftsgeschichte* 88 (2001), 1–47.

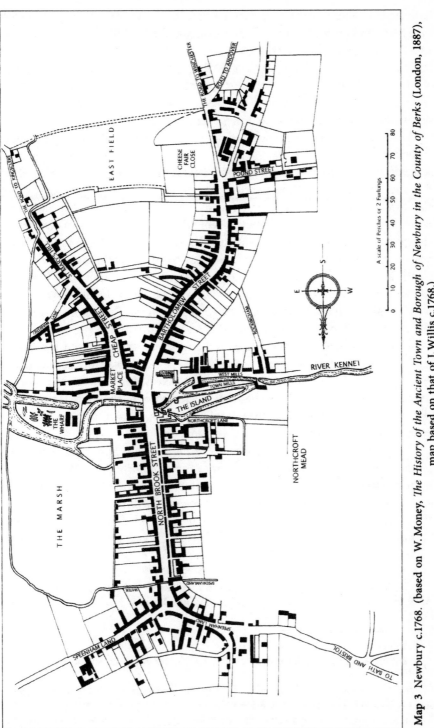

Map 3 Newbury c.1768. (based on W. Money, *The History of the Ancient Town and Borough of Newbury in the County of Berks* (London, 1887), map based on that of J. Willis c.1768.)

important crossing of the river Kennet, and to the west of the junction with the river Lambourn. The road from Oxford and the Midlands to Winchester and Southampton runs north–south crossing the river Kennet in the town centre, and the road from London to Bath passes east–west and just north of the town through the township of Speenhamland. Until 1835 the town was coterminous with the parish of St Nicholas' and contained upwards of one thousand acres.[40] The medieval town was centred on the parish church and market place that lie to the south of the river crossing, and the original plots around Cheap street and Bartholomew street appear to have been regularly laid out at that time.[41] The three main streets of the town form an inverted Y shape. To the south of the river lie the two main thoroughfares; East street also known as Cheap street which leads from the market place, and West street also known as Bartholomew street which runs south from the bridge and past the parish church and then St Bartholomew's Hospital. The latter formed the southern limit of the medieval town.[42] Northbrook street runs northwards from the river crossing and towards Speenhamland.[43] Over the course of this study the town expanded physically both to the north of the river along Northbrook street, and to the south along Bartholomew street.[44] The town was surrounded by open fields and pasture: it had two arable fields – east and west field – to the south, and pasture on the Marsh to the north-east and also in the Northcroft which lay to the north-west of the town. The town was encircled by the parishes of Speen to the north, Enborne to the west, Greenham to the east, and the chapelry of Sandleford to the south. Investment in the lands of the town and these parishes will be shown to have formed a dynamic element of the urban–rural relationship.

The manorial history of the town was rather tortuous and divided after the death of William the Marshall in 1274 into three minor manors.[45] By 1400 the lands of Hastings and part of those of Zouch were granted to a certain John Roger. The king held another third and those of Mortimer passed to the Duke of York. The latter was held by Richard, Duke of York from 1425 to 1460 and thus during the period of his challenge for the throne, after which it came to

[40] A. E. Cockburn, *The Corporations of England and Wales, Collected and Abridged from the Reports of the Commissioners for Inquiring into Municipal Corporations* (London, 1835).

[41] Astill, *Historic Towns*, 49–57.

[42] *Ibid.*, 50–1.

[43] Northbrook street may have been laid out as a secondary extension to the town. Astill, *Historic Towns*, 50.

[44] Seen, for example, in the payments for new tenements in the accounts of 1457–58 and 1493–94. TNA, SC6/750/5, SC6/HENVII/1226.

[45] The full history of the manorial descent before 1596 is found in *VCH Berkshire*, IV, 134–40.

the crown. In 1461 Edward IV bestowed manor, lordship and borough on his mother, Cecily Duchess of York, and from that point until the grant of the second charter of incorporation in 1627, the town was held by members of the royal family.[46] Newbury's status as a town or borough is confused. Within the Assize roll of 1224-25 it was listed on separate occasions as both *burgus* and *villa*.[47] Burgesses were first mentioned in 1189;[48] Newbury was cited as a borough in the Hundred Roll;[49] and the town sent two members to the Parliament of 1275, and representatives attended the King's Council in 1337, but this level of representation did not continue.[50] It was not listed among the boroughs in the Feudal Aid of 1316 and was taxed at a fifteenth in 1334.[51] In 1596 the town received its first charter of incorporation and government was placed in the hands of thirty-one burgesses from whose ranks the mayor and six aldermen were to be elected.[52]

The method of administration of the town while the manor was divided remains unclear. It would appear to have been managed as a unit and the profits, such as from the tolls of the market and courts, were divided into three parts between the holders of the manors.[53] What follows on the town's government prior to incorporation has had to be reconstructed from various references.[54] The town, in theory, was ruled by its lord whose steward held the twice-yearly court leet at which the bailiffs and reeves were appointed. It

---

[46] Money, *History*, 169-73. *VCH Berkshire*, IV, 136. Walter Money and the *VCH* are the two main secondary works for the history of the town.

[47] TNA, JUST 1/36.

[48] *VCH Berkshire*, IV, 136. Reference in the 1189 Pipe Roll when the burgesses owed £6 18s. '*de dono*'.

[49] *Rotuli Hundredorum*, vol. I (Record Commission, 1812), 18.

[50] *VCH Berkshire*, IV, 137.

[51] *Feudal Aids*, vol. I (Record Commission, 1899), 47. R. Glasscock (ed.), *The Lay Subsidy of 1334* (London, 1975), 6-14.

[52] Newbury, *The Borough Charter of 1596* (Newbury District Museum, 1996).

[53] The chief manor was that of Mortimer which was subsequently held by the duke of York and then by the king. *VCH Berkshire*, IV, 135-6. The account of 1445-46 was rendered by the named reeve 'of the town' and also the bailiff, TNA SC6/750/5. The accounts record receipts of the third part of the tolls of the market and profits of the courts, TNA, SC6/750/3, 4, 5. By the account of 1493-94 it would appear that the total profits of the courts were being received in their entirety, TNA, SC6/HENVII/1226.

[54] The absence of a town archive means that all details are derived from a variety of disparate sources. Newbury was fairly typical of the government of small towns generally. Dyer, 'Small Towns, 1270-1540', 526-32. There are a series of estreats for Northbrook street for 1464 WCM, 14646. There is only one extant court roll, and one set of jury presentments, TNA, SC2/154/49 court roll for 1527; and SHC, LM/317/3 presentments for 1549. Although both are from the sixteenth century, it is presumed that the nature of town government had not changed radically since the fifteenth century, especially after 1461.

was probably the reeve who held the more frequent port moot, held 18 times in the year 1449–50, 17 in 1457–58 and eight times in 1493–94.[55] There were bailiffs from the reign of John if not before.[56] The bailiffs and reeves were responsible to the lord for such matters as collecting rents and submitted their accounts each year. These reveal their involvement in the everyday running of the town, such as collecting various fines and market tolls, as well as dealing with infringements of property.[57] The twelve jurors of the court were all substantial townsmen. The annual appointment of the town's four constables and four bailiffs were divided equally between the lord's steward and the court. These were influential men and were also viewed as witnesses to the various charters concerning the transfer of land in the town. Gentry involvement in the running of the town is found in the position of the two port reeves, one appointed by the steward and the other by the court.[58] These were members of local families such as Thomas Essex and John Norreys in 1549, and not necessarily inhabitants of the town.[59] Other appointments made in the court included the gatewardens, haywards, wardens of the bakers and butchers. Newbury was divided into six tithings based on the three main streets of the town and their east and west sides. Each tithing was represented by elected tithing men who were smaller traders and less wealthy individuals than the jurors. Presentments in the court for various commercial offences, such as infringements of the assize, were made through the unit of the tithings.

The regulatory role of town government can be identified in the proceedings of the court leet and cases of presentment. Trade in the town was controlled in a variety of ways. In the market place, forestalling was limited; profits were maintained by fining outsiders who used the market such as the regraters Richard Hed of Winterborne and William Cokkeshed of Speen in 1527; and the storage of goods in the town for sale after the market had ended was prohibited. Standardisation of weights and measures was maintained, and the price of bread and ale was regulated, as were the number of ale houses (they were too many in 1549). Quality controls were exacted on butchers and fishmongers to secure the sale of fresh meat and fish; on the candlemakers to ensure the candles were of full weight; and on the tanners to maintain the quality of the leather that was subsequently used by the shoemakers. The rate of toll exacted by the millers to grind corn was regulated. The urban environment was maintained

---

[55] The numbers of these courts are recorded in the ministers' accounts: TNA, SC6/1115/1, SC6/750/5, SC6/Hen VII/1226.

[56] VCH Berkshire, IV, 139.

[57] TNA, SC6/1115/1, SC6/750/5, SC6/Hen VII/1226.

[58] For the significance of the gentry in towns see R. Horrox, 'The Urban Gentry in the Fifteenth Century', in J. A. F. Thomson (ed.), Towns and Townspeople in the Fifteenth Century (Stroud, 1988), 22–44.

[59] SHC, LM/317/3.

through the maintenance of the roads and ditches, the clearing of gutters and the removal of rubbish, and attempts were made to remove buildings that encroached into the roads and overhanging pentices. Agricultural issues were dealt with, such as the allocation of pasture and the grazing of animals on the stubble, the ringing of pigs, and the maintenance of the gates, presumably those leading to the open fields. The pasture of the Marsh was protected from damage done by iron-bound carts crossing it. The court was also concerned with maintaining law and order in the town and passed on appropriate cases to the higher courts.[60]

Cloth manufacture in Newbury

In the more theoretical explanations concerning the nature of social and economic change the roots of the capitalist system were said to be found in the specific conditions of the fifteenth and sixteenth centuries. The study of Newbury will provide evidence for capital investment in fixed assets and the employment of wage labour on a large scale by the early sixteenth century, but it will also show the transitory nature of this enterprise. A warning is given against placing too much emphasis on these early incidences of capitalistic production. Additionally, it will be argued that the continued buoyancy of Newbury's industrial sector during the fifteenth century explains, in part, its position as one of those towns that were classified as expanding by the early sixteenth century. Evaluating the impact of the town as a force of acceleration in the rate of change will be examined in the section on urban–rural relations. It is essential, therefore, to begin by describing the manufacture of cloth in Newbury.

Newbury's expansion as a centre of cloth production was based on earlier foundations. Archaeological excavations revealed items associated with cloth production in the contexts of the twelfth and thirteenth centuries.[61] The first mention of a fulling mill operating in the town was in 1204 and is indicative of cloth production.[62] The town's merchants were exporting wool from Southampton and Portsmouth without licence in 1275 during the war with Flanders.[63] There were dyers in the town in 1327.[64] In the aulnage account of 1341–42 there were thirteen Newbury men paying tax on a total of 63¼ cloths.[65]

---

[60] Cases of violence and disorder in the town were found in the records of the royal courts of Kings Bench and Common Pleas. See chapter 5.
[61] A. G. Vince, S. J. Lobb, J. C. Richards, L. Mepham *Excavations in Newbury, Berkshire, 1979–1990* (Salisbury, 1997), 156.
[62] *VCH Berkshire*, IV, 136.
[63] *Rotuli Hundredorum*, 18.
[64] TNA, E179/73/6, from surname evidence.
[65] TNA, E101/343/23.

In the same document there were only nine men from Abingdon who paid aulnage on 33½ cloths. Over fifty years later the manufacture of cloth had apparently shifted to the north of the region associated with Abingdon, with very little production in Newbury.[66] The fortunes of Abingdon appear to have been the inverse experience of those of Newbury.

In addition to manufacture in the towns there was also a rural cloth industry in western Berkshire in the fourteenth century. Production was centred on Abingdon and the rural parishes of Steventon and Hendred.[67] Much of the evidence comes from aulnage accounts, whose reliability has been questioned.[68] There are, indeed, very real problems with the account of 1394–95 as C. R. J. Currie has pointed out, but he concluded that there must have been significant production of cloth in the north of the county, even if other villages besides those mentioned were involved.[69] Furthermore, there is corroborative evidence of cloth production in the region. For example a Clothmongers cross at Stanford in the Vale was recorded as a geographical point in 1334.[70] Traditionally East Hendred is regarded as a centre of cloth production and may have had a cloth fair.[71] There were certainly a large number of cloths, 483 for East Hendred alone, recorded in the aulnage accounts of 1395.[72] There were also a group of wealthy individuals assessed in East Hendred in 1381 who employed several servants; their link with the manufacture of cloth cannot be established, but the concentration of several wealthy individuals at that time is noteworthy.[73] A John Hatter of Hendred 'clothman' also 'kerseyman',

[66] Aulnage account of 1394–95. TNA, E101/343/24. Newbury had a total of 53 cloths compared with 385.5 for Abingdon. See below for additional aulnage figures from this document and for cloth production in the rural areas.

[67] Aulnage account of 1394–95. TNA, E101/343/24. In addition to Newbury and Abingdon, the other places were: Aldermaston 105.5 cloths, Benham 128.5, Boxford 108, Faringdon 4, East Garston 6, East Hendred 483, West Hendred 137.5, Ilsley 5, Maidenhead 30, Reading 45, Steventon 575.5, Wallingford 13, Wantage 185.5, Welford 192, Windsor 39 cloths.

[68] E. Carus-Wilson, *Medieval Merchant Venturers* (London, 1954), 279–91 was pessimistic. A. R. Bridbury, *Economic Growth* (London, 1975), 33–5 and again in his *Medieval English Clothmaking* (London, 1982), 47–61 was more optimistic.

[69] C. R. J. Currie 'Smaller Domestic Architecture and Society in North Berkshire c.1300–c.1650 with Special Reference to Steventon' D.Phil. thesis, Oxford (1976), Appendix 3.

[70] BRO, D/EB p/T57.

[71] *VCH Berkshire*, IV, 294.

[72] It was probably significant that the lord of the manor of Arches in East Hendred, John Arches, was Aulnager for Berkshire at the time. J. S. Roskell (ed.), *The History of Parliament: The House of Commons, 1386–1421*, vol. 1 (London, 1992), 47–8.

[73] For example Thomas More paid a poll tax of 6s. 8d. and had six servants; William Kete paid 5s. 0d., John Fynamour 5s. 0d., Thomas Kene 4s. 4d., Richard Hose 4s. 0d.; these were all exceptional sums. A similar pattern of wealth was also found at West Hendred. TNA, E179/73/46.

along with William Hatter citizen and mercer of London, were owed £20 by a man from Wallingford.[74] In the church of East Hendred there is a memorial brass of 1479 to William Whitwey, *pannarius et lanarius*, and another brass to two brothers, Henry and Roger (d. 1439) Eldysley, who were merchants of the town and one figure has two merchants marks.[75] From her study of the deeds of the Pusey family P. Jefferies argued for a fairly widespread area of rural cloth manufacture in the medieval period.[76] It is certainly not possible to say when rural production declined, or indeed, why manufacture became concentrated in Newbury and Reading. Cloth continued to be manufactured at Abingdon into the sixteenth century, although the scale of operation became dwarfed by that of production at Newbury and Reading.[77] Indeed, there is evidence that individuals were considering re-invigorating the cloth industry at Abingdon in 1538.[78] Manufacture in this north Berkshire town may also have had a similar impact on its hinterland as that of Newbury. From the evidence of the aulnage accounts there may have been some decline in the proportion of cloth produced in Newbury at the end of the fourteenth century.

The situation changed in the fifteenth century and when there is evidence again it reveals Newbury merchants[79] producing between 15 per cent and 22 per cent of the cloths of the two counties as shown in Table 8.[80] Thereafter the percentage share of cloths produced by these merchants fell. Kerseys were the main type of cloth manufactured in Newbury and were a smaller and lighter fabric than a broadcloth; three kerseys were usually assessed at the customs as the equivalent of a broadcloth.[81] English kerseys were doing fairly well abroad at this time, particularly in comparison with traditional broadcloths, and were to play a major role as exports later in the century.[82] The changing

---

[74] *CPR* 1452–61, p. 320.

[75] *VCH Berkshire*, IV, 301.

[76] P. J. Jefferies, 'A Consideration of Some Aspects of Landholding in Medieval Berkshire', Ph.D. thesis, Reading (1972), 380. BRO, D/EB p/T.

[77] Jackson, 'Clothmaking and the Economy in Sixteenth-century Abingdon', 59–78.

[78] *L&PHenry VIII* 13 (i), 113, 154. A Burford clothmaker called Tucker wanted to lease the fulling mills of the dissolved Abbey of Abingdon and provide employment; whilst Thomas Cade was offering to provide employment in carding and spinning in the town.

[79] Consistently: John Bedford, John and Robert Croke, Thomas Love; less frequently Robert Bedford and Robert Devenys.

[80] The aulnage accounts for the fifteenth century did not differentiate the type of cloth produced or list specific locations of production, but grouped together the merchants for the counties of Oxfordshire and Berkshire. The names of Newbury's merchants were known from other sources.

[81] Carus-Wilson, *Medieval Merchant Venturers*, 263.

[82] J. Munro, 'Industrial Protectionism in Medieval Flanders: Urban or National?', in H. A. Miskimin (ed.), *The Medieval City* (New Haven, 1977), 229–67, especially 240, tables 13.3 and 13.5. J. Munro, 'Industrial Transformations in the North-West European Textile

Table 8 *Cloths paying aulnage in the counties of Berkshire and Oxfordshire during the fifteenth century*

Date of account	1468–69	1468–69	1469–70	1470–71	1471 half	1471–74	1471–72	1472–73	1473–74	1474–76	1476–82
Total number of cloths, Berkshire and Oxfordshire	1498	1493	1492	799.5	908	106	1503	1504	1173	2348	1653
Total number of cloths, Newbury	297	224	223	181	197	18	238	238	258	190	113
Percentage of cloths from Newbury	19.8	15.0	14.9	22.6	21.6	16.9	15.8	15.8	21.9	8.0	6.8
Cloth merchants in Berkshire and Oxfordshire	31	31	31	29	29	24	29	29	30	40	38
Cloth merchants in Newbury	6	6	6	5	5	4	5	5	5	4	4

Notes:

Newbury is never specified in the documents, but the merchants are known from other contexts.

The accounts of 1469–70 closely follow those of 1468–69, and there is a similar affinity between those of 1471–72 and 1472–73.

Sources: TNA, E101/346/23, E101/343/26, E101/347/8–11.

demands of the European market were an important dynamic in the Newbury story. Cloth was exported via Southampton. Merchants from Newbury were paying brokage as they exported kerseys from the city in the first half of the fifteenth century. In the accounts of 1439 and 1443 both John Doget and John Underwood entered Southampton with kerseys.[83] In 1443 John Doget exported 70 pieces of kerseys and an unspecified number of others. Kerseys were not mentioned again in a Newbury-Southampton context until those of John Winchcombe and John Helyer in 1527.[84] In the fifteenth century several men had occupational designations that were related to the production of kerseys.[85] The aulnage accounts of the fifteenth century may not have specified the type of cloth exported, but it would appear that Newbury had an established history of kersey production before the arrival of John Winchcombe. It should be noted that the cloths exported may not have been produced exclusively in the town itself as some may have been manufactured in the surrounding area. We can be confident, however, that Newbury merchants were trading in significant numbers of cloths before 1474.

The data for the imports of woad into the town imply that some of the cloth was dyed, and a dye house was operating in the town in the 1460s when Robert Dyer of Newbury was in dispute over its terms of ownership and repairs.[86] In 1477 a Richard Dyer was importing quantities of woad into the town. There was an increase in the amount of woad going to the town between 1466 and 1478. Other dyes imported from Southampton to Newbury included alum and madder. Thus the cloths exported from Newbury may have been dyed and finished, unlike those from many other areas of the country. The numbers of fullers and dyers identified in the various documents supports this assumption.[87] In Berkshire in the sixteenth century much of the wool was dyed

---

Trades, c.1290–c.1340: Economic Progress or Economic Crisis?', in B. M. S. Campbell (ed.), *Before the Black Death* (Manchester, 1991), 110–48, especially 134.

[83] B. D. M. Bunyard (ed.), *The Brokage Book of Southampton, 1439–40* (Southampton Records Series, 40, 1941), 46–7, 51, 52, 55, 118. O. Coleman (ed.), *The Brokage Book of Southampton, 1443–44* (Southampton Records Series, 4, 1960), 190, 209, 231, 262, 279.

[84] K. F. Stevens (ed.), *The Brokage Books of Southampton for 1477–78 and 1527–28* (Southampton Records Series 28, 1985).

[85] 1441 William Archer kersey weaver, 1449 Roger Chillond kerseymaker, 1452 John Chippes chapman also kerseyman, 1460 John Haddam kerseyman. Note, this was not a sixteenth-century designation.

[86] TNA, C1/28/530, date unspecified but probably between 1460 and 1465.

[87] The process of dyeing may have declined at the end of the century when the imports of woad into the town from Southampton fell. Further evidence is found in the inventory of Nicholas Frere also Weaver in 1495 whose kerseys were white. TNA, PROB2/95. An alternative explanation for the decline in imports of woad could be the result of a shift in the market for dyestuffs, perhaps importing through London. Dyeing was certainly taking place again in 1535 when the imports of woad increased as shown in Table 9.

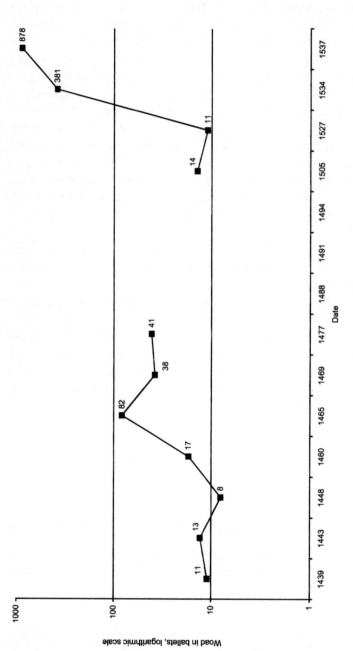

Figure 4 Woad imports to Newbury through Southampton.

Note logarithmic scale. Bunyard, *The Brokage Book of Southampton from 1439–40*; Coleman, *The Brokage Book of Southampton, 1443–44* vols I and II; E. A. Lewis (ed.), *The Southampton Port and Brokage Books, 1448–49* (Southampton Records Series 36, 1993); Stevens, *The Brokage Books of Southampton for 1477–78 and 1527–28*; Southampton City Archives, SC5/5/12 Brokage Book for 1460–61; SC5/5/19 for 1469–70; SC5/5/28 for 1491–92; SC5/5/31 for 1494–95; SC5/5/32 for 1505; SC5/5/34 for 1534–35; SC5/5/35 for 1537–38. Note: these figures are via Southampton only and do not include the woad purchased via London, especially from Thomas Gresham. See below.

before becoming cloth and this may also have been the stage in the production of cloth in the fifteenth century.[88] Dyeing in the wool in order to maintain an even colour was particularly useful in areas of hard water. Woad, moreover, was a pigment and not a dye and had to be chemically reduced to its soluble form before dyeing could take place.[89] Woad often served as a base before other dyes were added, and cloths could be woven from woad-dyed wools and then re-dyed in the piece with other dyes to produce various colours.[90]

The men associated with the cloth industry in the fifteenth century – especially clothmakers, fullers, and weavers – were generally wealthy men with widespread trading contacts, both in the hinterland and beyond. The Bennets were a family of prosperous fullers, and there were three generations operating in Newbury in the fifteenth century. John Bennet leased the fulling and tanning mills of the town in 1436, was a bailiff, and was active as a witness to various charters relating to lands in the town. In 1445 he was pursuing Conrad Ros, a German merchant, in the Guildhall of London over a debt of £36.[91] Nicholas Frere also Weaver was styled 'clothemaker' and when he died in 1495 his inventory included 200 pounds of yarn, and in the warehouse four packs and 24 pieces of white kerseys, and in the shop various looms, more yarn and kerseys. His inventory included debts owed to him by men in Southampton, Winchester, Reading, Newbury, and the seamen on board the ship *New June*.[92] One of the Southampton debts was due from William Ambrose, probably an Italian merchant there.[93] John Chippes and John Haddam were both kerseymen in the mid-century. The latter owed £12 to a London draper, the former owed £100 to William Deaunvers esquire.[94] The weaver Vincent Walery was owed £8 each from men from Witney, Deddington and Standlake in Oxfordshire in 1439.[95] These were not isolated examples. The documentary sources may be skewing the data towards the wealthy inhabitants of the town, but they are revealing a vibrant cloth industry in the fifteenth century associated with widespread trading contacts.

Within the town, Newbury's merchants, clothiers and fullers operated within a complex network of social and commercial relationships. These can

---

[88] C. Jackson, 'The Berkshire Woollen Industry 1500–1650', Ph.D. thesis, Reading (1993), 51.

[89] The whole process is described in detail in J. Edmonds, *The History of Woad and the Medieval Woad Vat* (Chalfont St Giles, 1998), especially 2–5, 7, 25.

[90] J. H. Munro, *Textiles, Towns and Trade* (Aldershot, 1994), I, 23, V, 54–6.

[91] Corporation of London Record Office, Guildhall, MC1/3/44.

[92] TNA, PROB2/95, PROB11/10/29.

[93] Ambrose were a Florentine family based in Southampton; the most famous was Christopher Ambrose. A. A. Ruddock, *Italian Merchants and Shipping in Southampton, 1270–1600* (Southampton, 1951), 183–5. Stevens, *Brokage Books*, xv, xvi.

[94] CPR 1441–46, 116 Haddam, CPR 1446–52, 489 Chippes.

[95] TNA, CP40/715, r. clviii.

be reconstructed across the sources and are particularly evident when they witnessed each other's wills.[96] John Flaget is a good example of a man who was exporting cloth through Southampton and importing wool in 1505. He was the supervisor of the wills of Richard Bedford, Nicholas Frere also Weaver, Thomas Collins and others. His own will was witnessed by John Winchcombe I in 1510. Henry Bennet, one of the family of fullers, supervised the will of Thomas Leech and his own supervisors in 1485 were John Elys, Henry Okeham and Richard Goddard. His son Roger inherited the lease of the fulling mill and was in turn a witness to the will of John Winchcombe I, left a bequest to John Winchcombe II, and his overseers included John Bennet, Robert Carter and Richard Snell. Furthermore, these relationships brought in men from outside the town such as Maurice Smart of Shaw. Networks were also created further down the social scale such as Thomas Long who was a 66s. householder in 1522, bailiff in 1527, executer to a weaver's will and witness to Richard Warrand's will who was a cloth maker.

The manufacturing context in which these men operated in the fifteenth and sixteenth centuries can be created by briefly describing the various stages of production.[97] The chief raw material was wool and Berkshire was a wool-growing county producing a short-staple, good-quality wool suitable for the manufacture of broadcloths and ranked in price below Cotswold wool in the fifteenth century.[98] It had a market both at home and abroad and Berkshire was one of those counties included in the act of 1489 whose wool was to be

[96] To reconstruct the various social and commercial relationships all nominal references from the different documentary sources were entered into a relational database. This is now deposited with the ESRC Data Archive 'Town and Countryside in West Berkshire, c.1400–1600 (Study Number 4339)'.

[97] Jackson, 'Berkshire Woollen Industry' is an exhaustive study of the subject for Berkshire. For neighbouring Wiltshire see E. Carus-Wilson, 'The Woollen Industry before 1550', in E. Crittall (ed.), *A History of the County of Wiltshire*, vol. 4 (Oxford, 1959), 115–47. G. D. Ramsay, *The Wiltshire Woollen Industry in the Sixteenth and Seventeenth Centuries* (London, 1965). J. Hare, 'The Wiltshire Risings of 1450: Political and Economic Discontent in Mid-Fifteenth Century England' *Southern History*, 4 (1982), 13–31. J. G. Jenkins (ed.), *The Wool and Textile Industry in Great Britain* (London, 1972). E. Lipson, *The History of the Woollen and Worsted Industries* (London, 1921), 46–9, 128–42. For the emphasis on wool E. Power, 'The Wool Trade in the Fifteenth Century', in E. Power and M. M. Postan (eds), *Studies in English Trade in the Fifteenth Century* (London, 1933). T. H. Lloyd, *The English Wool Trade in the Middle Ages* (Cambridge, 1977). P. J. Bowden, *The Wool Trade in Tudor and Stuart England* (London, 1971).

[98] Bowden, *Wool Trade*, 34. Power noticed a rise in the price of Berkshire wool from rank 7 to 3 in the fifteenth century, Power, 'Wool Trade', 49. Berkshire wool was approximately 2 marks per sack cheaper than Cotswold. A. Hanham, *The Celys and their World* (Cambridge, 1985), 146.

reserved for English clothiers.[99] By the early sixteenth century merchants of the Calais staple were living and operating out of the Vale and growing wool on the Downs; indeed, in 1533 Mr John Yate was regarded as a 'stapler of reputation'.[100] Newbury clothiers purchased the wool in a variety of ways.[101] John Winchcombe II was able to deal directly with the wool growers.[102] Wool could also be purchased from wool broggers or merchants; for example in 1551 William Twyne, a Newbury clothier, had bought 130 tods of wool from a London grocer.[103] Newbury clothiers were among those who in 1577 complained to the Privy Council against the activities of wool middlemen.[104] Once the wool had been purchased it was sorted, the dirt and impurities removed or washed out, and then it was ready for dyeing.[105] Quantities of wool, both white and dyed, were present among the goods of the deceased. For example, in 1552 John Sawndersone (draper) had 140 lbs of blue wool and yarn, a tod of russet wool, 9 tods of coarse wool and 60 lbs of coarse wool total value of £11 among his possessions.[106] The wool was then carded in preparation for being spun into yarn. Cards were imported from Southampton, and both cards and spinning wheels were among the inventoried goods of the deceased of the town.[107] These were never of great monetary value; for example in 1573 John Jones had a spinning wheel and a pair of cards valued at one shilling.[108] The spun yarn was valuable and stocks of yarn were appraised in the inventories.[109]

[99] R. H. Tawney and E. Power (eds), *Tudor Economic Documents* II (London, 1924), 5–6.

[100] *L&P Henry VIII*, Addenda, vol. 1 1509–47, 320–1. TNA, SP1/238, 265. John Yate lived at Charney in the parish of Longworth before buying the manor of Lyford in Hanney and moving there. See Chapter 5 for a more detailed discussion of wool merchants and this family in particular.

[101] The following are representative of the disparate nature of the references before the systematic entries in the seventeenth-century Newbury Clothiers' Book, BRO, D/EPT/uncat.

[102] In 1550 he offered Mistress Elmes 25s a tod, cash down, for her wool. B. Winchester, *Tudor Family Portrait* (London, 1955), 176.

[103] TNA, REQ2/17/16.

[104] Bowden, *Wool Trade*, 137.

[105] The sheep were usually washed and their coats dried before shearing. Bowden, *Wool Trade*, 22–3.

[106] BRO, D/A1/132/183.

[107] In 1537 Mr Bory imported over 14 dozen cards into Newbury. Southampton City Archives, SC5/5/35.

[108] BRO, D/A1/199/25.

[109] For example, in 1495 Nicholas Frere also Weaver had 200 pounds of yarn valued at 6 marks in a chamber and another 40 pounds in the shop appraised at 13s. 4d. TNA, PROB2/95.

The yarn was then woven into cloth. Kerseys were produced on shorter looms than traditional broadcloths and could be operated by one man.[110] Looms were assessed on average at five shillings in the first half of the sixteenth century. They were sufficiently valued by the testators to be bequeathed separately and in some instances the various parts of the loom were itemised, such as the gears, warping bars, harness and quilling wheels (for the wound yarn).

Once the cloth was woven it was burled to remove stray particles and then fulled. The process of fulling matted the fibres together by pounding the cloth in a detergent solution such as fullers earth. Newbury had at least two fulling mills in the town itself in the fifteenth century[111] and the townsmen also leased fulling mills in the hinterland.[112] The fullers who leased these mills were wealthy individuals, such as the members of the Bennet family already described. Once fulled, the wet cloths were then stretched to dry outside on tenters. John Winchcombe I had a close of land allocated for this purpose.[113] The final process was the raising of the nap (also known as rowing) and then cropping it as closely as possible with shears. This was a highly skilled process using large pairs of blades attached to wooden handles.[114] Finally the cloth was pressed and packed ready for the market.

Cloth production in Newbury has been made famous by Thomas Deloney's poem and biography of the legendary 'Jack of Newbury', first registered in 1596–97 during a difficult time for the cloth industry.[115] This poem has been influential in previous accounts of Newbury's cloth industry and it is worth placing it in context before employing it as evidence. In the introduction to his edition Mann argued that, from internal evidence of names and places, Thomas Deloney knew Newbury and its traditions, customs and myths.[116] Deloney was a yeoman weaver of silk of the London Weavers' Company (but not a master) before becoming a balladeer-novelist and polemicist.[117] In his poems he blended ideology and polemic about his craft and current political and social concerns, and placed them in a fictional, nostalgic and idealised

---

[110] Jackson, 'Berkshire Woollen Industry', 58.

[111] West Mills and Town Mills; but there was a complex relationship between the mills, and there were probably others. Certainly by 1544 the king granted to John Knight three fulling mills, Upper, Middle and Nether while he was also holding the mills belonging to St George's Windsor at the time.

[112] A point that will be expanded later in urban–rural relations.

[113] TNA, PROB11/19/27, he bequeathed 'all the Rakkys and teynters as ther now stonde within a close called the culverhouse'.

[114] The shears and handles were valued items. Their assessments in the inventories varied for example: 1546 6 pairs 30s., 1566 5 pairs 26s. 8d., 1571 7 pairs 40s.

[115] F. O. Mann (ed.), *The Works of Thomas Deloney* (Oxford, 1912), xii.

[116] Mann, *Works*, xi.

[117] R. A. Ladd, 'Thomas Deloney and the London Weavers' Company', *Sixteenth Century Journal*, 32 (2001), 981–1001.

past. Events of Henry VIII's reign were expressed in Elizabethan terms such as concerns about poverty, the power of guilds, government involvement in manufacture and women's employment.[118] This was the context for describing Jack's employment of the labour of poor people in his 'factory', his organisation of manufacture, petitions and lobbying government, his marriage to his first wife, and becoming master of his craft, a position that Deloney did not achieve. Deloney was an advocate for his craft and he entered the discourse of the time with his poems, including *The pleasant historie of John Winchcomb*, in an attempt to bring about reform.[119]

Turning to the evidence, the poem appears to conflate the first two John Winchcombes into one person. John Smallwood also Winchcombe (John Winchcombe I) died in Newbury in 1519, left a will in which his son was the main beneficiary,[120] and a memorial brass in the parish church of St Nicholas whose rebuilding he had largely financed, but remains a very shadowy figure. The assessment of his son three years later in 1522 (£632 6s. 8d.) must be, in part, a reflection of his father's fortune and the joint wealth that they had amassed by that date. John Winchcombe II (d. 1557) is better known and much of the evidence of cloth production is related to him. Winchcome II's wealth was exceptional in 1522 (the highest in western Berkshire) and also in his inventory totalling £1,223 4s. 9d.[121] There are many similarities between John Winchcombe II and William Stumpe of Malmsbury. John Leland's description of Stumpe's organisation of cloth manufacture in the old abbey buildings is reminiscent of Deloney's poem that describes Winchcombe's large and centralised method of cloth production.[122]

> Within one roome being large and long,
> There stood two hundred Loomes full strong:
> Two hundred men the truth is so,
> Wrought in these Loomes all in a row.
> By every one a pretty boy,

[118] *Ibid.*

[119] Ladd, 'Thomas Deloney and the London Weaver's Company', 981–3, 986–99. D. Rollison. 'Discourse and Class Struggle: The Politics of Industry in Early Modern England', *Social History*, 26 (2001), 166–89, especially 189 where he argues that there is no evidence that cloth manufacture was ever centralised as Deloney portrayed Jack bringing it together. He does not, however, engage with verifying the person or the evidence for manufacture in Newbury at the time.

[120] TNA, PROB11/19/27.

[121] TNA, PROB2/345. For a detailed study of Winchcombe and his manufacturing and trading activities see D. Peacock, 'The Winchcombe Family and the Woollen Industry in Sixteenth-century Newbury', Ph.D. thesis, Reading (2003).

[122] *Leland's Itinerary*, I, p. 132. G. D. Ramsay, *The Wiltshire Woollen Industry* (London, 1965), 31–41.

Sate making quils with mickle joy;
And in another place hard by,
An hundred women merrily,
Were carding hard with joyfull cheere,
Who singing sate with voices cleere.
And in a chamber close beside,
Two hundred maidens did abide,
In petticoates of Stammell red,
And milke-white kerchers on their head:
Their smocke-sleeves like to winter snow,
That on the Westerne mountaines flow,
And each sleeve with a silken band,
Was featly tied at the hand.
These pretty maids did never lin,
But in that place all day did spin:
And spinning so with voices meet,
Like Nightingals they sung full sweet.
Then to another roome came they,
Where children were in poore aray:
And every one sate picking wool,
The finest from the course to cull:
The number was seven score and ten,
The children of poore silly men:
And these their labours to requite,
Had every one a penny at night,
Beside their meat and drinke all day,
Which was to them a wondrous stay.
Within another place likewise,
Full fifty proper men he spies,
And these were Shearemen every one,
Whose skill and cunning there was showne:
And hard by them there did remaine,
Full fourscore Rowers taking paine.
A dye house likewise had he then,
Wherin he kept full forty men:
And likewise in his fulling Mill,
Full twenty persons kept he still.[123]

---

[123] Thomas Deloney, *The pleasant historie of John Winchcomb in his yonguer* [sic] *ye Jack of Newbery, the famous and worthy clothier of England* STC (2nd edn)/6560 (London, 1626).

Even allowing for a great deal of literary embellishment the poem does provide a picture of large-scale production. Moreover, the evidence from other sources tends to confirm the scale of manufacture. The great increase in the woad imports of 1537 shown in Figure 4 was principally due to his personal total of 676 ballets in that year. A decade later he was purchasing large quantities of woad from Thomas Gresham in London, for example 300 ballets in December 1549.[124] He was trading with Southampton on such a large scale that he was able to arrange a special, and reduced, rate of custom with the mayor in 1538. This was both on the rate of woad imported, and for the packs of kerseys exported, provided he kept exporting his kerseys from Southampton.[125] In the copybook of letters for the Antwerp commission house, Pieter van der Molen and Brothers of 1538 to 1544, it states that the quality of Winchcombe's kerseys was setting the standard for production of that type of cloth in Antwerp. The demand for his kerseys was obviously greater than supply, as an agreement was made in 1540 requiring merchants to buy double the number of other, inferior kerseys, for each Winchcombe.[126] In 1539 Cromwell had ordered 1,000 pieces of kerseys but John Winchcombe wrote to him and explained that time was short and he was hoping to have 500 pieces ready by Easter.[127] In 1544 Winchcombe's kerseys were said to 'make great heaps of money' in Antwerp.[128] He was successful, along with other unnamed clothiers, in securing the suspension of the Act of 1536 regulating the manufacture of woollen cloth.[129] The continuing scale of Winchcombe's production is best illustrated in the number of cloths bought and shipped by the London mercer, Thomas Gresham.[130] For example during the month of December 1546 Gresham bought a total of 600 kerseys from John Winchcombe.[131] The picture drawn from these various sources is one of large-scale production by a successful entrepreneurial manufacturer.

[124] Mercers' Company Archive, Thomas Gresham's Day Book, number 5250. For an analysis of Thomas Gresham's trading activities see P. H. Ramsey, 'The Merchant Adventurers in the First Half of the Sixteenth Century', D.Phil. thesis, Oxford (1958), and Peacock, 'The Winchcombe Family'.

[125] Merson, *Third Book of Remembrance*, 61-2.

[126] F. Edler, 'Winchcombe Kerseys in Antwerp', *EcHRev*, First Series 7 (1936), 60.

[127] *L&P Henry VIII*, vol. 14, 151.

[128] *L&P Henry VIII*, vol. 19, 723.

[129] H. Nicolas (ed.), *Proceedings and Ordinances of the Privy Council of England Volume VII, 1540-1542* (Record Commission, 1837), 156.

[130] Itemised in Mercers' Company Archive, Thomas Gresham's Day Book and analysed in the doctoral theses of Ramsay and Peacock above.

[131] Mercers' Company Archive, Thomas Gresham's Day Book, numbers 1056, 1062, 1078, 1084-5, 1092, 1097-8, 1100, 1101, 1109. Peacock calculated that between November 1546 and November 1549 Gresham shipped out 3,775 of Winchcombe cloths. Peacock, 'The Winchcombe Family', 19.

But Winchcombe did not have a monopoly of the production of kerseys in the town. Indeed, he was not listed among the clothiers 'which make fyne karses' in the country in the middle of the sixteenth century when Newbury was the only place mentioned in Berkshire.[132] There were five men: Thomas Dolman, Brian Chamberlain, Philip Kystell, Humphrey Holmes and William Blandy. Thomas Gresham was purchasing kerseys from John Winchcombe, Thomas Dolman and William Benet of Newbury in 1549.[133] Thomas Dolman was the second generation of clothiers as his father William was said to have been in the employ of John Winchcombe I;[134] he was certainly a beneficiary of Winchcombe's will where he received 40s. 'besides all thinges of his covenurnts'.[135] William died in 1531.[136] His son, Thomas (d. 1575) may also have manufactured cloth in a centralised or 'factory' system, again producing coloured kerseys.[137] Peacock calculated that between March 1548 and July 1550 Thomas Dolman produced 4,005 kerseys for Thomas Gresham.[138] In 1544 he bought the manor of Shaw and initiated the building of a prestigious house there (still standing) that was finished by his son, also Thomas, in 1581.[139] The withdrawal of the Dolmans to Shaw, and from their involvement in the manufacture of cloth, caused resentment in the town, illustrated in the rhyme:

> Lord have mercy on us miserable sinners!
> Thomas Dolman has built a new house, and has turned away all his
>   spinners![140]

The Winchcombes and Dolmans were probably unusual in their centralised method of manufacture.[141] Other clothiers in the town may have employed an

---

[132] TNA, E101/347/17. The reasons for the compilation of this document remain uncertain, as does Winchcombe's omission.

[133] In 1549 of the 5,672 kerseys that Gresham bought no less than 1,400 were supplied by John Winchcombe, 1,550 by Thomas Dolman and 549 by William Benet. Ramsey, 'The Merchant Adventurers', 184.

[134] VCH Berkshire, IV, 138. For detailed studies of the Dolmans see Jackson, 'Berkshire Woollen Industry, and Peacock, 'Winchcombe Family'.

[135] TNA, PROB11/19/27.

[136] BRO, D/A1/1 r. 172.

[137] Jackson, 'Berkshire Woollen Industry', 100.

[138] Peacock, 'The Winchcombe Family', 23.

[139] The Dolman family will be mentioned again in relation to the manor of Shaw in chapters 4 and 5. They are an important example of a family whose fortune had been made from cloth and subsequently invested in land. The house is pictured on the front cover.

[140] VCH Berkshire, IV, 141.

[141] A. R. Bridbury, Medieval English Clothmaking (London, 1982), 11. Stumpe is the other well-known example, Ramsay, Wiltshire Woollen Industry, 32–3.

integrated workshop system of production.[142] By the early seventeenth century the evidence for that form of production is very detailed.[143] The various stages in the manufacture of cloth were given to outworkers and overseen by the clothier. Newbury clothiers in 1629 leased spinning houses in Wantage, Ham and Longparish, weavers were paid for the cloths woven, and fullers for the cloths that they had 'milled', the final finishing may have been undertaken in the clothiers' workshops as there were very few disbursements for this process. It would appear that the centralised form of fixed-capital manufacture of cloth was a short-lived enterprise and was related to certain individuals.

Can we gauge the extent of integration and level of involvement by the rural population in the manufacture of cloth? We have already shown that Berkshire wool was used in the production of cloth. There were strong links between John Winchcombe II and John Yate of Buckland, one of the family of Staplers, although wool was never directly referred to.[144] Large amounts of wool and flocks of sheep were recorded in the probate inventories of neighbouring Shaw and Kintbury.[145] The putting-out system of manufacture should have involved the rural hinterland but references are too disparate to calculate the extent of integration.[146] The evidence is stronger for involvement in the finishing of cloth in the surrounding region. Both the rivers Kennet and Lambourn supported fulling mills.[147] Townsmen were among the lessees of these rural mills. Indeed, John Bullford of Newbury built a fulling mill at Shaw in the 1440s on free land belonging to Ingram atte Moore.[148] In the sixteenth century John Winchcombe II had the lease of the mills at Bagnor and Thomas Dolman of those at Colthrop. Cloth was also manufactured in the town of Hungerford where there was a fulling mill at Dun mill.[149] It was men from Hungerford

---

[142] Jackson, 'Berkshire Woollen Industry', 102.

[143] Newbury Clothier's Book, BRO, D/EPT/uncat. Now published as C. Jackson (ed.), *Newbury Kendrick Workhouse Records, 1627–1641* (Berkshire Record Society, 8, 2004).

[144] John Yate was one of the executers of Winchcombe's will in 1557. TNA, PROB11/40/26.

[145] For example at Kintbury in 1558 John Brinklow had 495 sheep of various sorts and 35 tods of wool; in 1577 John Elgar had 370 sheep and 16 tods of wool; at Shaw Thomas Hatt had 267 sheep and lambs and 10 tods of wool. Chapter 5 contains a more detailed examination of wool growing in Berkshire where it will be shown that more was produced in the Downs at Ashbury.

[146] John Norcott at Shaw had a narrow loom among his possessions, there were no weavers at Kintbury, and only isolated references to spinning wheels and cards.

[147] M. Yates, 'Watermills in the Local Economy of a Late Medieval Manor in Berkshire', in T. Thornton (ed.), *Social Attitudes and Political Structures in the Fifteenth Century* (Stroud, 2000), 184–201. C. Jackson, 'The Berkshire Woollen Industry c.1500–c.1650', in J. Dils (ed.), *An Historical Atlas of Berkshire* (Reading, 1998), 52–3.

[148] Yates, 'Mills', 195.

[149] Nicholas Passion from Hungerford were fined at Blackwell Hall for defective cloths. TNA, E159/350, 330, 332.

who leased the fulling mill at neighbouring Kintbury, such as John Dyne in the middle of the fifteenth century. There were cloth finishers at both Shaw and Kintbury in the sixteenth century.[150] In sum, it would appear that the manufacture of cloth was centred on the town and occasionally drew in the services of the rural hinterland, particularly for the finishing of the cloth, and certainly for the purchase of wool.

The final outcome of production was the marketing of the cloth. It has not been possible to establish what proportion of the cloth produced was for the home market, and how much for export. Newbury's merchants were exporting kerseys from Southampton in the fifteenth century. In *A Speciall Direction for Divers Trades* of c.1575–85 Newbury kerseys had a market in the Levant, in France at Rouen, Morlaix in Brittany and Saint Malo, Andalucía in Spain, Tripoli in Syria.[151] We have shown that Winchcombe's kerseys had a market in Antwerp and that he was trading directly out of Southampton. Peacock has shown that he was trading in large numbers of cloths with Thomas Gresham, as was Thomas Dolman.[152] Other clothiers may have been using Blackwell Hall in London. It is worth noting that Newbury men did not appear in the lists of clothiers fined for producing defective cloths at Blackwell Hall during Elizabeth's reign.[153] These memoranda rolls are not an infallible source for identifying centres of cloth production in the later sixteenth century.[154] The networks of relationships of the fifteenth-century merchants and clothiers of the town have revealed strong contacts with London and imply trade with the capital in addition to that with Southampton. Nevertheless, there must also have been a local market for the cloth and enough trade to sustain the town's cloth and wool market.[155] Certainly lengths of cloth were among the goods of the deceased in the rural areas.[156]

---

[150] There may have been others in the neighbouring parishes, but these have not been systematically studied. At Shaw 18 probate inventories survive before 1600 and of their subjects one was a weaver and two were cloth finishers. At Kintbury from 83 inventories before 1600 three related to cloth finishing: a shearman, a tucker, and one identified from his goods. Their diversified economic activities are discussed in more detail in the section in chapter 5 'The middling or modal group'.

[151] Tawney and Power, *Tudor Economic Documents* III, 201–2, 208.

[152] Peacock, 'Winchcombe Family'.

[153] TNA, E159/350 mm. 329–32, 7 Eliz I Hilary term. Nor found in E159/354 part 1, or E159/358, E159/359 part 1.

[154] G. D. Ramsay, 'The Distribution of the Cloth Industry in 1561–62', *EHR*, 57 (1942), 361–9 was rather optimistic in his appraisal.

[155] See section on marketing below.

[156] For example John Brinklow of Kintbury had 36 yards of russet and 4 yards of broad russet in 1558. BRO, D/A1/39/129, and John Woodward had an unspecified number of yards of kerseys. BRO, D/A1/132/198. The trading activities of the Brinklow family are discussed in detail in chapter 5.

The widespread market for the cloth produced in the town, and the fact that Winchcombe's kerseys were setting the standard at Antwerp, imply that the town had a reputation for manufacturing high-quality cloth. How standards were maintained and the methods by which the industry was regulated in the town prior to incorporation remain obscure. It is said that a guild or fraternity of weavers was founded in the reign of Henry VIII and incorporated in 1601 under the title of 'the Fellowship of the Weavers at Newbury'.[157] The only evidence for the existence of a merchant guild is that mentioned in the manor court roll of 1527 when no one came to that court to pay a fine for licence to enter the merchant guild, and presumably to trade.[158] The local evidence for regulation may be rather vague but the sixteenth century witnessed concerted government attempts to regulate the industry through legislation, proclamations and grants of letters patent in an attempt at standardisation of production to maintain quality, particularly of the cloths for export.[159] Responsibility for the regulation of the industry lay with the craft guilds and local justices of the peace, among whose numbers were the Winchcombe and Dolman families.[160] One has to assume in the light of the lack of documentary evidence that the high quality of manufacture was maintained on an informal, individual, and *ad hoc* basis regulated by the clothiers and their employees and founded on the personal reputation of the individual clothier.[161] The elaborate Ordinances of 1597 removed all vestiges of informality and regulated the town's industry through five companies comprising all the trades in the borough. The government of each company was in the hands of a master and two wardens appointed by the mayor, and no person could practise a craft or set up a shop without belonging to a company.[162]

The death of John Winchcombe II in 1557,[163] the eventual loss of the Antwerp market by 1563, the withdrawal of other clothiers such as Thomas Dolman

---

[157] VCH Berkshire, I, 390.

[158] TNA, SC2/154/49.

[159] Ramsay, *Wiltshire Woollen Industry*, 50–64. Jackson, 'Berkshire Woollen Industry', 79–87.

[160] Jackson, 'Berkshire Woollen Industry', 87.

[161] Possibly a continuation of the successful operation of a system of informal regulation that had been in operation in the medieval period. See also C. Dyer, 'Taxation and Communities in Late Medieval England', in R. Britnell and J. Hatcher (eds), *Progress and Problems in Medieval England* (Cambridge, 1996), 168–90, especially 188–90 on local arrangements for the collection of tax and poor relief.

[162] VCH Berkshire, IV, 140–1. Newbury, *The Book of Ordinances of 1599* (Newbury District Museum, 1996).

[163] His eldest son John Winchcombe III had already left Newbury by the time of his father's death and was embarked on a political career. S. T. Bindoff (ed.), *The History of Parliament: The House of Commons, 1509–1558* (London, 1982) vol. III, 632. The second son, Henry, was involved in manufacture but on a smaller scale than his father's from

to their rural manors, mark the end of the period when Newbury was one of the country's leading cloth-producing towns. Thereafter the new clothiers who emerged did not share the same level of entrepreneurial skill, wealth or international standing as their predecessors. Just as spectacular fortunes could be made in the industry – such as those of the Winchcombes and Dolmans – they could also be lost and the clothier Brian Chamberlain was a Newbury example being bankrupt in 1571 with debts of £6,000.[164] The evidence suggests that the centralised form of production did not continue and that by the early seventeenth century the putting-out system was being operated by the Newbury clothiers. Cloth was still being manufactured in the town, but the heyday of the industry was over. The transitory nature of the centralised form of fixed capital industrial production employing large numbers of wage labourers that has been described in this chapter as operating in Newbury in the first half of the sixteenth century must be noted. Those historians seeking the origins of capitalism in this period should not be beguiled by the apparent presence of these conditions as they were linked to the activities of specific men and did not outlast their individual entrepreneurial activities.

Trade

It would be wrong to describe Newbury's economy purely in terms of its cloth industry, and to ignore its other economic functions – particularly trade – and their relationship with the hinterland. The model of reciprocity is a familiar one: medieval rural cultivators took their surplus products to the local market in the town to sell and had the opportunity to purchase manufactured goods, while at the same time, townspeople were not self-sufficient in foodstuffs, fuel and raw materials and relied on the hinterland for their supply. We have already described Newbury's place in the region's marketing hierarchy as a local centre serving the area to the south of the Downs. Hungerford, eight miles away, was its nearest marketing rival. Newbury had a weekly market and several annual fairs. The first reference to a fair was that of St Bartholomew, granted to the hospital in 1215.[165] The right to the tolls from the market and fairs were granted with the manor, and in proportion to the size of the grant of the manor. For example, in 1465 a third part of the tolls of the weekly market held every Thursday, along with the two annual fairs held at the feast of Corpus Christi and on the eve of the Nativity of St John, were granted to Thomas Herbert the elder along with rents of lands and tenements, and a third of the court

the evidence of his inventory, and certainly his total wealth recorded there. BRO, D/A1/132/183, inventory total £254 8s. 1d.

[164] BL, Lansdowne MSS. 13, no. 13.

[165] VCH Berkshire, IV, 136, Money, History, 130.

profits.[166] The tolls and court profits in the middle of the fifteenth century were itemised in the manorial accounts as representing a third part of the total collected, usually fixed at 5s. as the third part of the 15s. taken as market toll and 3s. 4d. as a third of the court profits.[167] In 1554 a grant was made of the lease of the stallage, picage, tolls and other profits of the fairs and markets to four townsmen, one presumes representing the inhabitants of the town. This was confirmed, in general terms, in the charter granted in 1596, when four annual fairs were specified.[168] At the end of the fifteenth century the market had extended along the western part of Cheap street towards the New lane end.[169] Many of the stalls and shambles of the market were fairly permanent structures with new buildings erected over the course of the fifteenth century. There is a sense obtained from the documents that traders grouped themselves together and that the market was divided into specialist areas for merchants, butchers, tanners and shoemakers.[170]

There is evidence that Newbury had an important grain market in the fourteenth and sixteenth centuries. The Abbot of Bec's reeve on the manor of Coombe in Hampshire travelled to the markets at Andover and Newbury to sell grain seventeen times in the summer of 1307.[171] And the bailiff of Ogbourne St Andrew in Wiltshire had occasion to eschew the market at Marlborough (four miles away) for that at Newbury (twenty miles away) to sell grain, presumably because he could obtain a better price.[172] In the sixteenth century Newbury had one of the specialist grain markets, and men from Hungerford sold their corn there.[173] Newbury also had a wool and cloth market.[174] At the moothall in the fifteenth century toll was taken for weighing the cloth and wool of non-residents of the town.[175] In the seventeenth century the rate was 1d. per tod of wool levied for weighing if it was sold to an inhabitant of the borough, and 2d. per tod to an outsider.[176]

Trade in the town was not confined to the market place. The accounts reveal the construction of various pentices to tenements such as that constructed by

---

[166] CPR 1461–67, 424.

[167] TNA, SC6/750/3, 4

[168] Money, History, 190. TNA, SP12/35 m.98. Newbury. The Borough Charter of 1596, 3, 23–4.

[169] TNA, SC6/Hen VII/1226.

[170] TNA, SC6/Hen VII/1226 and in the rental of SC11/47 Henry VI where Richard Boucher paid rent for a stall at 'boucheres schamell', in Chepestreet.

[171] Miller, Agrarian History III, 349–50.

[172] M. Morgan, The English Lands of the Abbey of Bec (Oxford, 1968), 49.

[173] Thirsk, Agrarian History IV, 495, 500, 589.

[174] Thirsk, Agrarian History IV, 591.

[175] TNA, SC6/1115/1, SC6/750/5, SC6/Hen VII/1226.

[176] Bowden, Wool Trade, 95.

Henry Wormstall in Northbrook street.[177] Also, rentals referred to various 'shops' albeit workshops. Shops on the bridge were catching the passing trade from those using the town as a thoroughfare. For example, Thomas Kenetbury and John Goldsmith both had shops on the bridge in the fifteenth century.[178] In 1390 a grant of pontage had been made to the bailiffs and good men of Newbury.[179] On those occasions when occupational designations were given those associated with trade included mercer, merchant, huckster, chapman, and some more specialist entries such as jeweller and goldsmith. Details of the contents of the shops are found in the sixteenth-century probate inventories. A particularly detailed example is that of William Saunders, a mercer in 1541, who had a wide variety of goods including ribbons, cord, pack thread, knives, spoons, inkhorns, combs, and lengths of velvet, silk, damask, worsted, fustian, holland, lockram, canvas, as well as ready made shirts, jerkins, aprons, and many more items.[180] The more specialised stock of Edward Hormer, hardwareman, in 1580 included a large range of different sorts and sizes of knives, along with locks, bells, compasses, arrow heads and fork heads.[181]

Newbury also functioned as a service provider for the area. As a thoroughfare town it had inns, such as 'The Hart' on Northbrook street, and the usual large numbers of hostellers and beer and ale sellers.[182] There were also the brewers and bakers, butchers and fishmongers who dealt in foodstuffs. They were ammerced according to their tithings along with the candle makers.[183] In 1549 the jurors attempted to limit the number of alehouses in each tithing as there had been much 'dyshorder by certeyne lewde persons resorting to sum of the seyd ale howses'.[184] Tailors, glovers, cappers, and shoemakers could provide ready made clothes. The smiths and saddlers catered for the horses.

The town also acted as a re-distribution centre for the area. This is especially identifiable in those goods imported into the town from Southampton. It is uncertain whether all the imported woad, shown in Table 9 and discussed earlier, was processed within the town or went elsewhere. Table 9 also shows the amount of wine that went to Newbury from Southampton. This was a fairly constant supply, with a small decline at the turn of the century that was part

---

[177] TNA, SC6/1115/1.

[178] TNA, SC11/47, rental Henry VI.

[179] CPR 1388–92, 307.

[180] BRO, D/A1/114/90. Total inventory appraised at £38 16s. 9d.

[181] BRO, D/A1/76/189.

[182] There were other inns whose names were not recorded. 'The Hart' belonged to St George's Windsor, and was also referred to in the Winchester College documents.

[183] TNA, SC2/154/49 for 1527, also mentioned in 1464 ammercements for Winchester College, WCM, 14646.

[184] SHC, LM/317/3.

Table 9 *Imports of woad and wine to Newbury through Southampton*

	Woad in ballets	Wine in pipes	Number of carts going to Newbury
1439–40	11	14	18
1443–44	13	21 (27)	35
1445–46	—	27	—
1448–49	9	21	31
1460–61	17	11	21
1465–66	88 (82)*	18 (16)	23
1469–70	55 (38)	20	19
1477–78	41	22	41
1488–89	0	33 (29.5)	18
1491–92	0	3	11
1494–95	0	6	4
1505 (half)	7	7	10
1527–28	11	39	79
1534–35	381	29	100
1537–38	878	23	113

* My figures, in parenthesis, are given where they differ from O. Coleman (ed.), *The Brokage Book of Southampton, 1443–44*, vol. II (Southampton Records Series, 1961), 322–7.

Sources: Bunyard, *The Brokage Book of Southampton from 1439–40*; Coleman, *The Brokage Book of Southampton 1443–44*, vols I and II; E. A. Lewis (ed.), *The Southampton Port and Brokage Books, 1448–49* (Southampton Records Series 36, 1993); Stevens, *The Brokage Books of Southampton for 1477–78 and 1527–28*; Southampton City Archives, SC5/5/12 Brokage Book for 1460–61; SC5/5/19 for 1469–70; SC5/5/28 for 1491–92; SC5/5/31 for 1494–95; SC5/5/32 for 1505; SC5/5/34 for 1534–35; SC5/5/35 for 1537–38.

See also Appendix II: comparative data for imports of woad and wine through Southampton from 1439–10 to 1491–92.

of a much wider shift in trade.[185] The quantities were small compared with other places such, as Salisbury and Winchester, shown in Appendix II. This may reflect the ease of access to other markets from Newbury such as London itself. The type of wine was rarely specified in the brokage books, but there were references to malmsey and wine of Gascony going to Newbury. The main merchants were usually Southampton burgesses, but others were Newbury men such as John Bedford and John Croke in 1448, and William Goldsmith and John Colyns in 1477. Merchants who were said to be from Newbury may in fact have lived in the hinterland. For example, Maurice Smart was a wealthy tanner in Shaw, but was said to come from Newbury when he was importing

[185] A. B. W. Chapman (ed.), *The Black Book of Southampton* (Southampton Records Series, 8, 1912), xxvi.

wine in 1527; two barrels of malmsey, and one barrel and one ton of wine (unspecified).

Fish was another commodity taken to Newbury in large amounts. This was particularly a winter trade, and there was no dramatic increase during the period of Lent. The majority of fish were herring, both red and white, and there were also carts carrying hake, mulwell, ling, salmon, Newlond fish, salt fish and wet fish. The amounts taken could be large and implies supply for a market that was larger than the town. For example, 900 Newlond fish and four barrels of herring were carried to Newbury on 10 March 1527 in five carts belonging to Robert Devenes, a prominent merchant and burgess of Southampton. In 1477 large numbers of eels were imported; 300 congers were carried on 23 July 1477, and another 100 congers on 8 August 1477.

To deduce the size of a town's sphere of market influence it is necessary to go beyond the institutional framework and look at the number and variety of commodities traded, and to consider any specialist products, and the impact of choice exerted by consumers.[186] We are becoming increasingly aware of trade that was being conducted in an informal manner away from the formal marketing structures.[187] The variety of goods taken to Newbury suggests a wide market area. For example, in 1443 there were 39 carts going to Newbury which took, apart from woad and wine, small quantities of sayme (grease), herrings, fruit, alum, wax, hides, teasels, canvas, oxhides, battery, oil, salt, woolfells and even a feather bed.[188] Luxurious goods were imported to Newbury, especially Mediterranean fruits such as raisins and others specified simply as pieces of fruit. In 1477 six bags of almonds were imported. In 1537 two barrels of peaches were on the same cart that carried raisins. Although it has been noted elsewhere that there was an increase in the number and variety of luxury items over time, it has not been possible to identify this happening in Newbury as luxurious items seem to have been imported throughout the period studied.[189]

The sphere of contacts of the merchants of Newbury ranged beyond the confines of the town and the immediate hinterland, particularly as many were trading with Southampton and London. These merchants were based at Newbury, were integrated into the society of the town, but have to be viewed

---

[186] C. Dyer, 'Market Towns and the Countryside in Late Medieval England', *Canadian Journal of History*, 31 (1996), 17–35, and 'The Hidden Trade of the Middle Ages: Evidence from the West Midlands of England', *Journal of Historical Geography*, 18 (1992), 141–57.

[187] The details of John Winchcombe II's trading activities described above is a good example. Christopher Dyer is the leading author on this subject; see the references above.

[188] Coleman, *Brokage Book*, xxxiii.

[189] Chapman, *Black Book*, xxiii.

in a wider context of trading activity.[190] John Deneman of Newbury was owed money from various woolmen in London and Marlborough in 1404, was also owed £45 by Richard Clerk citizen and grocer of London, had lands in Newbury, witnessed charters there and was the collector of the tenth and fifteenth between 1401 and 1407. John Doget traded through Southampton where he exported kerseys and wool, and imported woad and wine. He also traded with Salisbury and Andover. He was a freeholder in Newbury, witnessed various land charters, was constable and bailiff and collector of the tenth and fifteenth in 1453. John Dering of Newbury was also the owner of lands in Southampton when he died in 1403. John Bedford was active in the town as a patron of the hospital, setting up Wormstall's chantry, and was also a bailiff and constable. He paid brokage in Southampton, paid aulnage on cloths, and was in receipt of goods from a citizen and mercer of London. John Croke senior had very similar experiences to those of John Bedford. John Winchcombe II traded in Southampton, London and Antwerp and had debts owed to him in his inventory from men across much of southern England. Although the scale of Winchcombe's operation was exceptional, he came from a tradition of successful Newbury merchants.

Archaeological evidence is an important source for the study of trade. A field-walking survey of the area between Newbury and Reading produced pottery sequences corresponding more closely with those of Newbury than Reading, even from those areas at the eastern end of the survey area.[191] The conclusion reached was that Newbury drew on an area that covered the west of the county, whilst Reading was a more commercial centre with a catchment area to the east.[192] Pottery sequences from a production site either in, or just outside, Abingdon reveal its influence in northern Berkshire that extended down to Newbury.[193] The distribution may have been related to the relationship between Abingdon Abbey and its estates and granges.[194] Excavations within the town of Newbury produced a sequence for the late thirteenth to mid-fourteenth centuries and first half of the fifteenth century that was concentrated on the Kennet valley and included north-west Wiltshire, Oxfordshire and northern Hampshire, but was almost absent from Reading. The pottery was mainly for domestic use. The source of this type of pottery remains unknown, but

[190] The following details are drawn from a wide range of sources entered into a relational database so that the connections could be made; they are now deposited with the ESRC Data Archive, see above.
[191] S. J. Lobb and P. G. Rose, *Archaeological Survey of the Lower Kennet Valley, Berkshire* (Salisbury, 1996), 97. Vince *et al.*, *Excavations in Newbury*, 158.
[192] *Ibid.*
[193] M. Mellor *et al.*, 'A Synthesis of Middle and Late Saxon, Medieval and Post-Medieval Pottery in the Oxford Region', *Oxoniensia*, 59 (1994), 17–217, especially 78–9.
[194] *Ibid.*

was probably from the northern border of Savernake Forest in the parish of Mildenhall. In the fifteenth and sixteenth centuries Newbury was supplied by the Surrey ware industry based on the Hampshire–Surrey border. This shift in supply from a centre near Savernake to Surrey wares was part of a wider movement also identified in Reading and Windsor.[195] There was very little non-local pottery found in the Newbury excavations, only three sherds of imported wares.[196] Excavations did not reveal the trade with Southampton recorded in the brokage books.

Although Newbury's function as an administrative centre was not directly associated with trade, it does reveal another area of interaction between town and countryside. Newbury's sphere of influence covered south-west Berkshire. This was the area of the Newbury deanery and the archdeacon of Berkshire held his court in the town. Probate was granted at these sessions and rural dwellers would have had occasion to visit the town when a relative died.[197] The churchwardens of the rural parishes also attended these courts.[198] Moreover, royal jurisdiction was also administered from the town, for example at the court of quarter sessions which sat at Newbury at Easter.[199] These drew people from a wide area and the mayor of Reading and other officials from that town attended the sessions held at Newbury in 1421.[200] We know from other sources that the meetings of this court would have required the presence of representatives of the rural areas.[201] These occasions presented additional fora for urban–rural contacts.

Other economic pursuits

The various industrial activities of the town drew upon raw materials from the region and provide another area in which to explore the points of contact

---

[195] Vince *et al.*, *Excavations in Newbury*, 157.

[196] They were one of medieval Saintonge ware and two from Tudor contexts, one from Spain and another from the Rhineland. Vince *et al.*, *Excavations in Newbury*, 157–8. This is consistent with the limited distribution of late medieval pottery in Southampton. D. Brown, *Pottery in Medieval Southampton, c.1066–1510* (CBA, 2002).

[197] BRO, D/A1 original wills were inscribed with the date and place of the grant of probate; for example Kintbury's wills were proved at Newbury.

[198] For example, 25 November 1516, Brightwalton's churchwardens were paid 4d. for their expenses made at Newbury. BRO, D/P24/5/1.

[199] Although the records of the court at Newbury do not survive before 1703. *Guide to the Berkshire Record Office* (Berkshire County Council, 1952), 1.

[200] C. Slade (ed.), *Reading Gild Accounts, 1357–1516* (Berkshire Record Society, 6 and 7, 2002), vol. 6, 51; and there were other occasions when they visited the town and their expenses were recorded, vol. 6, 123, vol. 7, 186.

[201] A. L. Brown, *The Governance of Late Medieval England, 1272–1461* (London, 1989), 123–6.

between town and countryside. The town's grain mills would have processed more than just the grain grown in its arable fields. There were two mill complexes to the west of the bridge and south of the river Kennet – Town Mills and West Mills – and there may also have been another to the east of the bridge. The complex physical relationship of these mills is illustrated in Henry Bennet's will of 1485 where he bequeathed his fulling mill and also the corn mill that he had 'of the Dean of Windsor which is next door'.[202] Malt was manufactured in the town and some exported from Southampton. London may also have provided a useful market for this product; the 'value added' element and reduction in transactions costs making malt a more attractive commodity to transport over longer distances than unprocessed grain.[203] Tanning relied on skins from the surrounding area and was an important activity in this region more generally. There were tanning mills at Shaw, Speenhamland and Kintbury, in addition to those in Newbury. The rural tanners were wealthy individuals, many from families with several generations of tanners.[204] The market for their products was widespread, and Newbury's merchants exported skins from Southampton; for example, John Croke exported 25 hides from Southampton in 1448.[205] Allied to tanning were the parchment makers of Shaw and Newbury.[206]

Tiles were manufactured in Newbury. Paving tiles were bought by Winchester College from Newbury to pave the library of the college in c.1412. The tiler also came from Newbury to lay the floor.[207] Excavations in the town centre unearthed tiles that were similar to these, although the production site was not identified.[208] The accounts of the manor of Shaw recorded purchases of roof tiles from Newbury for the repair of the mills and manor.[209] In addition to the tilers, other members of the building trades were represented in occupational designations, such as carpenters, plasterers, painters and stainers. The carpenters also appear to have travelled widely, as individuals from Newbury were among those employed by various Oxford colleges on their building

---

[202] TNA, PROB11/7/15.

[203] J. Galloway, 'London's Grain Supply' *Franco-British Studies*, 20 (1995), 23–34.

[204] For example the Walrond family at Kintbury in the fifteenth century, the Barkesdales at Speen in the fifteenth and sixteenth centuries, and Maurice Smart and his descendants at Shaw in the sixteenth century.

[205] Lewis, *Southampton Port and Brokage Books, 1448–49.*

[206] In 1495 Shaw supplied Winchester College with parchment. WCM, 22158. I am grateful to Winifred Harwood for this reference. In 1439 John Townsend parchment maker of Newbury owed the Abbot of Abingdon 40s., TNA, CP40/715.

[207] E. C. Norton, 'The Medieval Paving Tiles of Winchester College', *Proceedings of the Hampshire Field Club and Archaeology Society* 31 (1974), 23–41.

[208] Vince et al., *Excavations in Newbury,* 157.

[209] In 1404–05 there were 6,000 tiles taken in 12 carts to tile the mill; in 1406–07 a further 1,000 tiles were taken to the mill in two carts; in 1416–17 the granary was roofed with 3,000 tiles from Newbury. BRO, D/ENm M12, 13, 22.

projects.[210] Large-scale building activity in Newbury itself would have required raw materials and also provided employment. Several public-spirited, and wealthy, individuals left bequests to finance building projects. The parish church was almost completely rebuilt at the beginning of the sixteenth century.[211] The other major building project was the construction of the guild hall, funded by a bequest in the will of Henry Bennet in 1485.[212] Less altruistic was the construction of a new fulling mill in the town financed by William Bennet in 1454.[213] On a smaller scale, but important for their cumulative impact, new tenements were built by various landowners as the town expanded, particularly in the early sixteenth century.

Agricultural activity in the urban context also involved the rural parishes. Townsmen and women leased acres in the two arable fields of the town, and, additionally, in the neighbouring parishes of Enborne and Greenham. Newbury's large farms were located to the south of its parish. John Stylman amassed several properties belonging to the College of St George Windsor, and incorporating lands in Enborne, to create Bartholomew's farm in the early sixteenth century.[214] The wills of the inhabitants of Newbury included bequests of their lands in Enborne and Greenham, in addition to their holdings in Newbury.[215] Agricultural activity was regulated by the court leet, especially the maintenance of the commons. For example in 1549 Henry Winchcombe was ordered to refrain from bringing his iron-bound carts carrying wool across the Marsh and damaging it.[216] By the sixteenth century there had been some piecemeal enclosure of the lands of the parish. Farming was never a dominant economic activity in the fifteenth century, and from the sixteenth-century probate evidence there was very little evidence of agricultural activity, even as a by-employment, in Newbury.[217]

Nevertheless, taking into consideration the diversity of economic activity described above, an examination of the occupational designations of Newbury's testators reveals the dominance of the cloth industry in the life of the town.

---

[210] E. A. Gee, 'Oxford Carpenters, 1370–1530', *Oxoniensia*, 17–18 (1952–53), 112–84.

[211] It is the best example of a 'cloth' church in the area. Although John Winchcombe I left the substantial sum of £40 towards its reconstruction there were many other bequests for the rebuilding of the church made in the wills of the fifteenth and early sixteenth centuries.

[212] TNA, PROB11/7/15.

[213] TNA, SC6/750/5, account for 1457–58 records date of construction.

[214] St George's Chapel Windsor, XV.54.88, m 2.

[215] For example, John Winchcombe II bequeathed both his farm at Greenham and Bartholomew's farm in his will. TNA, PROB11/40/26.

[216] SHC, LM/317/3.

[217] In 53 of the 104 inventories some livestock was appraised, such as a pig, horse, cow or poultry. Although the town had its own arable fields there were only 26 inventories that contained any form of crop, even a load of hay

Table 10 *Occupations of the testators of wills in Newbury, 1403–1580*

Cloth	Service	Shopkeeper	Clothing	Agricultural	Building	Widows*	Priests	Unknown	Total
fuller (27)	butcher (2)	mercer (4)	tailor (3)	yeoman (4)	carpenter (1)				
weaver (22)	brewer (4)	draper (4)	glover (3)	husbandman (2)	joiner (1)				
cloth maker (6)	barber (2)	haberdasher (4)	shoemaker (3)		painter and stainer (1)				
clothier (4)	innkeeper (2)	hardwareman (1)	capper (1)						
dyer (3)	chandler (2)		bocher (1)						
cloth finisher (3)	smith (2)		cordwainer (1)						
shereman (2)	fishmonger (1)								
	miller (1)								
	cook (1)								
67	17	13	12	6	3	14	4	71	207

* Includes only those specified as such.

Some 207 wills survive for the period 1403–1580, and they increase in number over time, skewing the data towards the sixteenth century: 1403–50 – 2; 1451–1500 – 10; 1501–50 – 68; 1551–80 – 127.

There are of course weaknesses with the occupational data as we rely on the titles given either by the testator or the appraisers. These may not reflect accurately the full occupational activity of the individual. We know that both John Winchcombe II and his son Henry were styled 'gentlemen', both had large farming concerns, and their industrial activity was barely mentioned.[218] Nevertheless, the probate data does confirm the dominance of employment opportunities in the various processes of cloth production. From a more general study of all occupational designations some chronological change was identified, particularly those styled 'clothier' who appeared after 1485, in contrast 'kerseymaker' was a fifteenth-century designation. Furthermore, there were more individuals identified as weavers and fullers in the sixteenth than in the fifteenth century.[219]

The economic fortunes of the town

Changes in the economic fortunes of the town over time have been alluded to and are now collated and presented in a systematic manner. The debate among historians on urban decline is based on opposing examples of towns that were either growing or in decline, and no consensus has been reached.[220] Furthermore the fluctuations in the economy of the fifteenth century, particularly the mid-century recession, have received very little empirical testing. The data presented here make a useful contribution to these topics of broader historical interest. The evidence for Newbury suggests that it probably benefited from an expansion of its textile industry in the 1430s. Cloth exports from Southampton were particularly high in the years 1439–43.[221] By this period Newbury merchants had built up strong long-distance patterns of credit. They were prosecuting for debt in the Court of Common Pleas in 1439 and in the Mayor's Court in London in 1441. Imports of woad through Southampton may have risen into the mid-1440s. There are some ambiguities about the following period from the mid-1440s to the early 1460s. Judging from the data in Table 9, woad imports through Southampton perhaps suffered a temporary contraction in 1448–49 and then increased during the 1460s and 1470s, though the force of this evidence is problematic given that we do not have annual figures and that Southampton was not the only source of supply. Imports of wine through Southampton may also have declined between 1445–46 and 1460–61. However, even the middle

[218] See below.
[219] Those identified in the fifteenth century were all wealthy individuals who left wills proved in the PCC and so this conclusion may be a product of documentary survival.
[220] See above, chapter 1. Dobson summarises the current state of research concerning the fortunes of towns as characterised by a variety of experience. B. Dobson, 'General Survey 1300–1540', in *CUHB*, 273–90, especially 274–7.
[221] See above, p. 85, on the export of kerseys by John Doget and John Underwood.

years of the century may have been less problematic for Newbury than for some larger and better established cloth towns. An extra four new market stalls were erected in 1449, and another five in 1457, although these may simply have replaced five other stalls from which the rent could not be collected.[222] In 1454 a new fulling mill was constructed, and this suggests that the cloth industry was attracting investment at a time when other clothmaking centres were experiencing hard times. There seems little doubt that following the mid-fifteenth-century recession the economy of Newbury performed exceptionally well. Between 1468 and 1474 Newbury merchants accounted for about 18 per cent of all merchants paying aulnage in Berkshire and Oxfordshire, and for the same proportion of total cloths sold.[223] Imports of woad through Southampton were particularly high in 1465–66, 1469–70 and 1477–81, and imports of wine recovered to a new high level in 1488–89.[224] In the last decade of the century Newbury's imports through Southampton dropped away, probably because of closer trade links with London, so we have no evidence from this period of woad or wine imports particular to Newbury. However, there is little reason to doubt that the town continued to benefit from increasing cloth exports. In 1493 six new market stalls were constructed.[225] In 1495 a new guildhall was built, even though in 1495 and 1496 the College of St George was paying as much for repairs to its properties as it was receiving in rents.[226] The 1490s are now thought to have witnessed a period of high mortality and, if this were the case in Newbury, would help to explain these events.[227] Any difficulties were quickly resolved and by 1506 the College of St George was constructing new tenements in the town,[228] obtained additional properties, and in 1517 they were able to raise their rents.[229] Nevertheless, at the same time some rents remained remarkably unchanged.[230]

---

[222] TNA, SC6/1115/1, 750/5.

[223] See Table 8.

[224] See Table 9.

[225] TNA, SC6/Hen VII/1226.

[226] St George's Chapel Windsor, XV.48.60–1. Part of a more general problem see A. K. B. Evans, 'The Years of Arrears: Financial Problems of the College of St George in the Fifteenth Century', in C. Richmond and E. Scarff (eds), *St George's Chapel, Windsor in the Late Middle Ages* (Windsor, 2001), 93–105.

[227] Paper delivered by J. Hatcher at the 38th International Congress on Medieval Studies, University of Western Michigan, Kalamazoo, 2003. See also the sharp fall in life expectancy of the monks of Canterbury and Westminster in B. Harvey, *Living and Dying in England, 1100–1540. The Monastic Experience* (Oxford, 1993), 127–9.

[228] St George's Chapel Windsor, XV.54.83.

[229] St George's Chapel Windsor, XV.49.13.

[230] For example a tenement in Northbrook street east side owed an annual rent of 42s. in 1527, and 43s. 4d. in 1564 and 1585. In Bartholomew street the rents on a Culverhouse and barn remained unchanged at 6s. and 5s. between 1518 and 1540.

Table 11 *Rents due to the College of St George, Windsor*

Date	Place	Total rent
1453	Newbury only	£7 14s. 0d.
1487	Newbury and Greenham	£17 16s. 6d.
1517	Newbury only	£22 15s. 0d.
1520	Newbury only	£27 4s. 11d.
1569 and 1573	Newbury only	£33 5s. 8d.

Sources: St George's Chapel Windsor, XV.29.46, XV.54.92, XV.53.5.

Winchester College also raised the rents on their properties in Newbury in the 1530s.[231] The evidence for Newbury during the first half of the sixteenth century is consistently that of growth, as seen particularly in the production of cloth, and by 1547 the town had expanded physically along Northbrook street and to the south on the west side of West street. A comparison of two rentals of 1436 and 1547 reveal these extensions to the town, the amalgamation of several properties into the hands of fewer tenants, and an increase in rent.[232] A noticeable feature was the increase in the number of entries which referred to composite holdings of 'the lands and tenements of ...', and these usually had significantly higher rents.

Newbury's fortunes may have fluctuated, but from the middle of the fifteenth century, when elsewhere in the country there were signs of depression, there is evidence of growth in the economic activity of the town. This may not have brought universal prosperity, as Newbury was one of those towns that experienced unrest in 1450 and 1460.[233] Nevertheless, expansion in the sixteenth century can be identified in the size of its population,[234] its manufacturing output, its trading networks, and in the physical growth of the town. Concurrently in the surrounding countryside growth was also experienced. We turn now to consider how these changes affected the inhabitants of the town.

---

[231] WCM, Bursars receipts 22158–22212.

[232] TNA, SC11/62, and LR2/187 fols 112–16. These are not directly comparable as that of 1436 relates to the manor of John Roger which was one of the three manors included in the rental of 1547 held by the king. Nevertheless, a number of properties were identifiable in both documents from which to chart change and draw these conclusions.

[233] Social unrest is discussed in more detail in chapter 5. See also J. Hare, 'The Wiltshire Risings of 1450: Political and Economic Discontent in Mid-Fifteenth Century England' *Southern History*, 4 (1982), 13–31.

[234] Demonstrated in chapter 2.

Urban society

It has been possible to demonstrate the diversity of occupations typical of other urban centres and, in addition, to show the dominance of those involved in the cloth industry in Newbury. In the early sixteenth century the manufacture of cloth was largely in the hands of the capitalist clothiers, especially the first two Winchcombes and the Dolmans. They were reputed to have invested fixed capital in a centralised form of manufacture and employed large numbers of wage labourers. To investigate the effects that this had on the urban society we need to examine any changes in the distribution of wealth and number of those dependent on wage labour within the town; and also to identify the wealthy and prominent members of that urban society and their role in the running of the town.

Table 12 *Distribution of sums of tax paid in 1381*

Town*	Less than 12d.		12d.		More than 12d.		5s. or more	Total number of individuals
Newbury	8.1%	6	82.4%	61	9.5%	7	0	74
Hungerford	36.5%	42	30.5%	35	33%	38	0	115
Wantage	31.5%	69	57%	125	11.5%	25	0	219

Note: This table only includes the data from the nominal returns that are legible, and it is presumed that they are representative of the whole return.

* Lambourn and Faringdon have been omitted.

Sources: For documentary references see Table 7.

Wealth, as reflected in the different amounts of tax paid, was fairly evenly distributed in the taxpaying society of Newbury in 1381. The majority of the urban taxpayers were paying the shilling poll tax and there were less than 10 per cent who were either poor, or wealthy. This is in comparison with Hungerford and Wantage where approximately a third of the taxpayers might have been poor and paid less than a shilling. The large sums paid in tax by the rural inhabitants of western Berkshire, as described in chapter 2, were not to be found in the towns.

Table 13 *Men in different categories of wealth, as indicated by assessment on movable goods in 1522*

Town	Less than £2		£2–£5		£5–£10		£10–£50		£50–£100		£100–£150		£630		Total no.
	%	no.	%	no.	%	no.	%	no.	%	no.	%	no.	%	no.	
Newbury	49	120	26	62	9	24	11	26	3	7	1	3	0.4	1	243
Hungerford	56	63	19	21	8	9	15	17	2	2	0		0		112
Wantage	51.9	56	23.1	25	12	13	9.3	10	3.7	4	0		0		108

Source: TNA, E315/464.

By 1522 there were a number of very wealthy men in the town of Newbury. The largest sum, that of John Winchcombe II, was unique in western Berkshire; the next in wealth, with £400 on goods, was the merchant of the Staple, Thomas Snodenham of Stamford in the Vale,. The three other wealthy individuals of the town, Robert Sewey, Edward Sharpe and Thomas Flaget, had significantly smaller assessments than Winchcombe: 200 marks, £130 and £120 respectively. Together with Winchcombe these four men controlled 42 per cent of the assessed taxable wealth of the town.[235] The category 'less than £2' was created to consider the proportion of the population who might have been assessed on wages in the Lay Subsidy.[236] There is, however, a very real possibility that the total number of assessments recorded for Newbury in 1522 may have emphasised the householders, and that those with less than £2 who were not householders are under-represented. The total number of those assessed in 1522 is certainly smaller than the 414 taxpayers Sheail calculated for 1524 for Newbury.[237]

Wealth as recorded in probate inventories confirms this unequal distribution. The 104 probate inventories that survive for Newbury between 1495 and 1580 range in value from £1 15s. 8d. to £1,223 4s. 9d., and the majority (82) were appraised at less than £50.[238] The two wealthiest inventories were the Winchcombes, John II and his son Henry, who styled themselves as 'gentleman', and although their wealth was founded on the cloth industry, their inventories do not reflect this.[239] The industrial side of their lives had, presumably, already

[235] That is, £1,013 6s. 8d. from a total of £2,431 7s. 4d.
[236] The nominal returns for the Lay Subsidy for Newbury have sections that are illegible and it is difficult to make an accurate calculation of those assessed on wages. TNA, E179/73/124, and see footnote 240 below.
[237] J. Sheail. *The Regional Distribution of Wealth in England as Indicated in the 1524–25 Lay Subsidy Returns* (List and Index Society, Special Series, 29, 1998), 13.
[238] Four were proved in the PCC, the remaining wills in the archdeacon's court.
[239] Neither did John Winchcombe II's *IPM*, TNA, C142/111/10, E150/822/6. Their inventory totals were £1,223 and £254 respectively. TNA, PROB2/345; BRO, D/A1/132/183.

been bequeathed before they died, apart from the lease of the dye house. The next group of four wealthy inventories, with totals of between £100 and £175, belonged, in ascending order of wealth, to men who were referred to as parson, haberdasher, clothmaker and clothier. John Winchcombe II's wealth may have been extraordinary in the western Berkshire context, but the assessments made on the other wealthy urban dwellers were also of a greater order of magnitude than had been the case in the fourteenth century. Nevertheless, these sources are not including the poorer sections of society.

Did the success of the clothiers result in an increase in the number of those dependent on wage labour? It would be useful to calculate the proportion of those who were wage labourers. In Table 13 49 per cent of those recorded in the Military Survey had assessments of less than £2 and may have been liable to have paid the Lay Subsidy on their income from wages. The Subsidy of 1524, although partially illegible, indicates that perhaps two-thirds were assessed on wages.[240] Deloney's poem implied that Winchcombe employed a workforce of over one thousand individuals and included women and children.[241] This sum seems unlikely in the context of the fiscal data and may relate to Deloney's desire to portray Jack as providing employment for the poor in the period before statutory poor relief.[242] Nevertheless, we gain an impression from John Winchcombe II's will that his workforce was large; in addition to the 83 named individuals who received bequests, he left £13 7s. 10d. to poor people who were named in a separate bill.[243] It would appear that the poorer inhabitants of the town were not liable for taxation, and we cannot determine their numbers. This is an important omission when attempting to quantify the distribution of wealth of the inhabitants of the town and the number of wage earners.[244]

Another category of employee were those classed as aliens or foreigners. There were aliens listed as living in Newbury in the fifteenth and sixteenth centuries. Their influence is said to have been linked to developments in the cloth industry of the town, but this has been impossible to prove.[245] In the alien subsidy of 1439-40 there were 46 aliens listed in Newbury and of these only one, an Irishman, was given a specific country of origin.[246] The majority, 25,

[240] TNA, E179/73/124. It was possible to count 411 entries, and of those that were legible: three were assessed on lands, 77 on goods, and 128 on wages

[241] Mann, *Thomas Deloney*, 20–1. 200 weavers, 200 boys, 100 carders, 200 spinners, 150 children, 50 shearmen, 80 rowers, 40 employed in dye house, 20 at the fulling mill, a butcher, a brewer, a baker, 5 cooks, 6 scullery boys.

[242] Ladd, 'Thomas Deloney and the London Weaver's Company'.

[243] TNA, PROB11/40/26, the accompanying bill does not survive.

[244] Particularly in the light of the rate of increase of the population calculated in chapter 2.

[245] *VCH Berkshire*, IV, 138.

[246] TNA, E179/73/91. S. Thrupp, 'Aliens In and Around London in the Fifteenth Century', in A. E. J. Hollaender and W. Kellaway (eds), *Studies in London History* (London, 1969),

were servants linked to merchants and clothiers of the town, perhaps reflecting their widespread trading interests. Otherwise there were two tailors, a butcher, a fuller and a labourer. In the subsidy of 1484 there were 12 aliens listed for Newbury and no place of origin was given.[247] Again the majority, eight, were servants and there were two shoemakers and a goldsmith. More detail is given in the 1522 Military Survey, where 10 aliens were listed and places of origin were recorded as: two from Brittany, two Normans, two Scots, a Frenchman, one born in 'Holond under the emperor' and another born 'under the obeysaunce of the Emperor'. The links with the cloth industry cannot be established, for the servants of the town's clothiers could have held a variety of occupations. It is worth noting, however, that migrants were attracted to prosperous areas, and there was obviously something about Newbury that drew them to the town during the fifteenth and sixteenth centuries.

The majority of English towns were ruled by some form of restrictive oligarchy, and this was also the case at Newbury in both the fifteenth and sixteenth centuries.[248] The increase in the wealth of certain individuals, described above, did not radically alter the situation. From at least the fourteenth century a small group of wealthy men can be identified whose names reappear on a number of significant occasions. At times they were expressly described as acting on behalf of the 'commonality' of the town, particularly over the appointment of the warden of St Bartholomew's hospital. In 1391 Roger Russell was instituted priest to the chapel of St Bartholomew's hospital and the patrons were 'the commonalty of Newbury'.[249] In 1466 the warden was presented to the bishop by John Croke senior and John Bedford senior, and in 1540 by Richard Bridges and John Winchcombe when they were styled 'patron' of the hospital.[250] These were wealthy men of the town and seem to have been acting on behalf of the urban community. The hospital had been founded by c.1200 and was staffed by a warden and brothers and sisters who cared for the sick. By 1267 they were given the right of burial and had a chapel.[251] The hospital survived the Reformation but in an altered form, due in part to the activities and influence of these wealthy individuals, and was converted during the second half of the sixteenth century into provision for the

---

251–72 for the background to these taxes.

[247] TNA, E179/73/109.

[248] Although this is a contentious issue see S. Reynolds, 'Medieval Urban History, and the History of Political Thought', *Urban History Yearbook* (1982), 14–23. S. R. Rigby, 'Urban "Oligarchy" in Late Medieval England', in J. A. F. Thomson (ed.), *Towns and Townspeople in the Fifteenth Century* (Stroud, 1988), 62–86.

[249] T. C. B. Timmins (ed.), *The Register of John Waltham Bishop of Salisbury, 1388–1395* (The Canterbury and York Society, 80, 1994), number 587.

[250] TNA, E315/121.

[251] *VCH Berkshire*, IV, 151.

poor and almshouses, whilst some of the lands were used for the foundation of the school discussed below.[252] This group of wealthy individuals were also active as the witnesses and feoffees to the various charters recording land transfers in the town. For example in 1454 a 'snapshot' can be made of the town's notables, especially merchants, when they were granted lands that were later given to Winchester College. These included Robert Shotesbrook knight, John Roger esquire, Richard Aubrey, William Lamborn, William Smith, John Croke senior, Stephen Wyard, Henry Wormstall, Robert Brokehampton, John Doget, John Bedford and Thomas Robyns.[253] The foundation of Wormstall's chantry in 1469 was another occasion that involved the prominent men of the town. John Wormstall left his lands and tenements in Newbury to endow a chantry and instructed various men to implement his will.[254] These included the prominent merchants of the town, John Bedford, John Croke senior, John Haddam and Thomas Love, and also Thomas Roger who held the nearby manor of Benham Valence. A parallel incident in the middle of the sixteenth century was the setting up of the school with an endowment of some of the lands of the hospital of St Bartholomew.[255] The list of participants was headed by John Winchcombe the elder, and then his two sons Thomas and Henry, followed by the clothier Thomas Dolman, and then John Goldwire, Walter Collins, John Green, William Blandy, Robert Arnold, John Lychepole, Henry Horncliff, John Millet, Thomas Kerry and William Bennet. All were prominent freeholders in the town and many were clothiers rather than the predominantly merchant group of the fifteenth century.

There was some change over time in the social standing of the officers of the town. The bailiffs and constables, who have already been mentioned with reference to the town's government, were often wealthy merchants in the fifteenth century such as John Chippes (he was also described as kerseyman), Robert Croke and John Bedford. But they also comprised non-mercantile men such as Richard Devenyssh who was styled 'yeoman'. Constables remained men of standing in the sixteenth century; for example, in 1549 they included Henry Winchcombe, Thomas Dolman, Walter Collins, and William Bennet.[256] However, there appears to have been a change in the social standing of the bailiffs at the turn of the sixteenth century when the really wealthy men of the town, such as John Winchcombe and Richard Bridges, did not hold this office. By the 1520s the town's bailiffs came from the group who were assessed

[252] TNA, C1/1276/75.
[253] WCM, 14641.
[254] TNA, PROB11/5/27.
[255] TNA, C1/1276/75.
[256] SHC, LM/317/3.

in 1522 as 40s. to 60s. householders, such as Nicholas Skinner, John Freeman and John Adderley.

As a social group the gentry were never prominent members of Newbury's urban elite in the period of this study. They do not appear to have lived in the town itself, but rather on their rural manors, and held freehold land in the town.[257] They included men such as Richard Adderbury of Donnington, John Norris of Yattendon and John Cheyney of West Woodhay. Newbury was said to have been one of the centres for Buckingham's rebellion in 1483 as the commission of array stated that the town was their headquarters; the men listed, however, were from the surrounding area.[258] The Cheyneys were in trouble again at the end of the century when they entered the town with a large group of armed retainers and threatened the peace of the inhabitants.[259] As mentioned before, the gentry were involved in the town as port reeves, such as Thomas Essex esquire and Sir John Norreys. Otherwise they seem remarkably silent in the records. Newbury did not send representatives to Parliament at this time; nevertheless, there were two men living in the town in the middle of the sixteenth century who were members. Henry Brydges represented Ludgershall in 1529, and possibly also in 1523 and 1536. He held lands in the town, and witnessed several wills there, for example that of John Elys in 1503.[260] The other was John Winchcombe II who was MP for Great Bedwyn in 1545 and Cricklade in 1547.[261]

Historical sources are always biased in their emphasis on recording the wealthy members of society, and this has certainly been the case with Newbury. The wealth and influence of these men appears to have remained consistently greater than the rest of the town's population over the fifteenth and sixteenth centuries. Whether they formed a restrictive oligarchy cannot be established. The influence of the wealthy members of the 'commonality' of the town became institutionalised and formalised with the granting of the town's charter of incorporation in 1596, government now lay in the hands of the thirty-one burgesses from whose members the mayor and six aldermen were to be elected.[262]

[257] John Winchcome II was a notable exception. In his will he mentioned his house in Newbury where he lived. TNA, PROB11/40/26.

[258] *Rotuli Parliamentorum* VI, 245–6. See chapter 5.

[259] TNA, REQ2/16/25. *Cal. Close Rolls* Henry VII, vol. 1, 329.

[260] TNA, PROB11/13/26.

[261] Bindoff (ed.), *The Commons, 1509–1558*, Brydges, vol. I, 531–3; Winchcombe, vol. III, 632–3.

[262] Newbury. *The Borough Charter of 1596* (Newbury District Museum, 1996).

Urban–rural relationships: investment and debt

The investigation of urban–rural relationships is expanded now through an examination of investment and debt.[263] Investment in land can be employed as a means of looking at both sides of the relationship. We begin by identifying the geographical location of those individuals who were investing in the lands of the town. Among the freeholders of Newbury who were listed in 1522 only 40 per cent were residents of the town.[264] There were six freeholders who came from beyond the area of western Berkshire. Three were Londoners, and the other three were heads of institutions: the warden and scholars of Winchester College, the Dean of St George's Chapel in Windsor Castle and the Prioress of the Abbey of Wherwell in Hampshire. Also enumerated in the Military Survey were 24 individuals who lived in the countryside and who had assessments on lands in the town; these came from Hungerford (3), Speenhamland (5), Greenham (4), Woodspeen (3), Enborne (3), Donnington (2), Shaw (2), and then one each from Hidden, Churchspeen, Welford, Shalbourn, West Woodhay, West Ilsley and East Ilsley. These places are characterised by their proximity to the town; indeed, Speehamland was almost a suburb of Newbury. They comprised a group of wealthy rural inhabitants who were investing in freehold tenancies in the town. For example, John Hore was the farmer of the demesne lands at Shaw, a man individually assessed at £40 in 1522 and a freeholder in Newbury with lands assessed at 16s.[265] This was not a new phenomenon, or a feature of this particular documentary source, as men from Shaw had invested in urban properties in the past. For example, in 1431 John Bedford and William Hull were leasing additional tenements in Newbury.[266] And John Tanner and Katherine Adderbury, both from Donnington, held tenements in Newbury in 1436.[267]

In sharp comparison, there were very few townsmen who invested in the freehold lands of the surrounding area as listed in the Military Survey. There were only ten individuals assessed on goods in the town who were also assessed as freeholders elsewhere and one presumes owned property that lay outside

---

[263] Urban–rural links between Newbury and its hinterland in matters of political and religious dissent are dealt with in chapter 5.

[264] TNA, E315/464: 73 freeholders, of whom 29 were also assessed on goods and thus considered to have been resident in the town. There were 14 names where it was impossible to trace a place of residence.

[265] My conclusion is that land was assessed on its yearly value, that is, its rental value and not sale value. For details of John Hore as farmer of the demesne at Shaw see chapter 5, p. 203.

[266] WCM, 14618.

[267] TNA, SC11/62.

Newbury.[268] Again the distribution of properties was concentrated in the surrounding area: Speenhamland 5, Enborne 3, Shaw 2, Greenham 2, and then one each in Churchspeen, Benham Valence, East Challow and Hungerford. This is startling evidence given the great wealth of the inhabitants of the town. Nevertheless, it does conform with the changing pattern of investment identified in Colchester. When the economy of that town was expanding its inhabitants were not interested in the countryside; and conversely, when expansion slowed down in the fifteenth and sixteenth centuries the townsmen invested in rural properties and were less interested in trade and industry.[269] The majority of John Winchcombe II's wealth in 1522 lay in the assessment of his goods that probably included industrial items related to his enterprise as a clothier.[270] Robert Sewey's was the second assessment in rank order – £133 16s. 8d. – and thus in a different league of wealth. He was also a clothier of the town, and he did invest in lands outside the town, in Enborne and Shaw. Indeed at Shaw he was the lessee of the mills there.[271] Income from rents in the town attracted outside investment, particularly from the surrounding countryside, whereas townsmen were less inclined to buy property in the countryside. This pattern was to change in the massive re-distribution of land later in the century, when wealthy townsmen, such as the clothier families of Winchcombe and Dolman, bought lands and manors in the countryside to which they eventually moved.

Bequests of land made in the wills of the inhabitants of Newbury before 1550 confirm a similar pattern of investment to that of the Military Survey. The emphasis was on lands in Greenham, Speenhamland, Enborne, and Hamstead Marshall.[272] The only exceptions were the lands in Southampton owned by Newbury men in the fifteenth century, John Dering in 1403 and John Wormstall in 1469, perhaps a reflection of the strong trade links with that town. The location of the county boundary just south of Newbury may account, in part, for the lack of references to places in north Hampshire.[273]

---

[268] From a total of 206 householders.

[269] Britnell, *Growth and Decline in Colchester*, 260–1.

[270] He was assessed on 46s. 8d. in lands in the town and £630 in goods. He had no assessment on lands beyond the town.

[271] WCM, 22992.

[272] Speen and Speenhamland 7; Enborne 4; Greenham 2; Hamstead Marshall 2; Hungerford 1; Newtown in Hampshire 1; Southampton 2.

[273] It formed one of Phythian-Adams' 'boundaries of cultural provinces'. C. Phythian-Adams, 'Frontier Valleys', in J. Thirsk (ed.), *The English Rural Landscape* (Oxford, 2000), 236–62, especially 239. The distribution may have been affected by the method of compilation of the Military Survey, but not the probate material.

Nevertheless, townsmen did engage in an active association with the rural hinterland. They maintained social and religious ties, as can be seen in the bequests in their wills to churches and religious institutions in the surrounding countryside, and there were important social networks that can be observed in the ways in which they witnessed each other's wills. Bequests made to religious institutions can be employed as an indication of some form of contact made with that place during the testator's lifetime. The distribution does widen, although it remains centred on those places within Newbury's immediate hinterland.[274] The probate evidence has revealed more of the towns-people's contacts with the hinterland, but given the size of the sample of 207 wills, it is not a very dynamic picture. The evidence for rural dwellers' involvement by investing in the lands of the town does appear to have been the dominant side of that particular relationship.

Patterns of debt have been employed by historians to examine a town's sphere of influence.[275] Debts can also provide indirect evidence for networks of trade, and both credit availability and the perceived credit worthiness of individuals. In this study an examination of the pattern of debts is made both for the town of Newbury, and also for five rural locations, for evidence of trading activity and the spheres of contact of an economic nature of the inhabitants of both town and countryside. The evidence for Newbury is unusual because there were very few debts owed to or from people in the hinterland, the majority of cases of debt lay within the town itself. The absence of a local archive for the town prohibits a study of the distribution of small debts, particularly those of less than 40s., and may provide a partial explanation for the distribution.

Table 14 provides the evidence from all documentary sources, both debts owed and owing to Newbury people. The greatest number were due within the town, followed by London. Windsor had eleven cases, all owed to the College of St George and due upon bond, often taken out at the same time as the lease of a property from the College. There were more debts that involved Southampton than Reading people, perhaps a reflection of greater trade links with the former. This is of interest as Reading was the county's principal town and point of entry to the Thames from Newbury, whether by road or the river Kennet. Those due in Dorset probably had a kinship link with members of the Bedford family living there. Otherwise there were single cases in Newbury's hinterland (apart from Speen), and scattered throughout the south of England. It is also worth noting the paucity of debts in the region

---

[274] Bequests to churches and institutions beyond Newbury: Thatcham (2), and then single entries for Shaw, Speen, Greenham, Bucklebury, Padworth, Hungerford, Lockinge, Kingsclere, Lynckenholt, Southampton, New College and Merton College Oxford. The vicars of: Chievely (4 times), Sandleford, Compton, West Shefford, Letcombe Basset.
[275] Dyer, 'Small Towns', 519–20.

Table 14 *The origins of litigants in pleas of debt involving Newbury people as creditors and debtors, from all documentary sources, 1403–1570*

Newbury	91	Shaw	1	men from Essex	1
London	22	Lambourn	1	Laverton	1
Windsor	11	Buttermere	1	Sodbury	1
Southampton	6	Clewer	1	Standlake	1
Reading	5	Garford	1	Stomhouse	1
Oxfordshire	4	Wantage	1	Kinstanly	1
Speen	3	Andover	1	Uxton	1
Abingdon	2	Salisbury	1	Hadcot	1
Dorset	2	Winchester	1	German merchant	1
Sussex	2	Marlborough	1	seaman on the *New*	
Speenhamland	1	Wells in Somerset	1	*June*	1
Enborne	1	Buckingham	1		

The main sources were: probate records – 103 cases, debts laid in the Court of Common Pleas –49 (CP40), Chancery – 11 (C1), Patent and Close Rolls – 8, and one from the Mayor's Court of the Guildhall in London (Corporation of London Record Office, MC1/3/44). Their chronological distribution was: 1400–1450 – 25; 1451–1500 – 32; 1501–1550 – 38; 1551–1570 – 77.

to the west of the town. 'Foreign' debts included those cases already mentioned of John Bennet's action in 1441 against Conrad Ros the German merchant in the court of the Guildhall in London,[276] and also the debt owed to Nicholas Frere also Weaver in 1495 from Richard Osteler aboard the *New June*.[277] The debts recorded in the probate inventories should have included the smaller sized debts that involved the hinterland and did not.[278] Newbury's widespread trading contacts are clearly demonstrated in the evidence from the cases of debt recorded in the Court of Common Pleas.[279] There was some variation chronologically; notably a fall in the number of cases between 1470 and 1500, and a rise in 1510 and then further in 1520. The data are, of course, skewed towards debts of more than 40s. – the threshold for consideration by the

[276] Corporation of London Record Office, MC1/3/44.
[277] TNA, PROB11/10/29.
[278] In Table 14 those cases of debt only recorded in probate inventories included: Within Berkshire: Speen, Greenham (2), Ham, Lamborne, Woolstone, Isbury, Reading. Outside Berkshire: London (5), Southampton (3), Winchester, Essex (diverse men, unspecified number), Laverton, Uxton, Standlake, Sodbury, Stomhouse, Kingston Lacey, Sussex (unspecified number), aboard the 'New June'.
[279] The sample is derived from the Michaelmas term: 1439, 1450, 1459, 1469, 1478, 1489, 1500, 1510, 1520. TNA, CP40/715, 759, 795, 833, 864, 910, 954, 993, 1030. There were 49 cases relating to men from Newbury.

royal courts – but the distribution has revealed the importance of commercial contacts with London.[280]

The analysis of debt has revealed a number of points of interest: first the paucity of local cases involving the hinterland; second the importance of the London connection; and, third, the stronger links with Southampton than with Reading. The pattern of debts did not emphasise Newbury's integration with its rural hinterland, but rather revealed wide-ranging contacts covering much of south-eastern England and some 'foreign' elements.[281] We saw earlier how men from Newbury were manufacturing cloth for export, and how foreign merchants were trading directly with townsmen. The Winchcombes may have been the most outstanding examples, but they remained an integral element within the broader context of manufacture and export within the town.

We turn now to examine the pattern of debt in the countryside itself so that both sides of the urban–rural relationship are considered. There was never a sufficient number of cases of debt derived from national records to make a satisfactory analysis of any single rural community and so the emphasis here is on those debts recorded in the probate wills and inventories. The data relate to places employed in the detailed analyses of chapters 4 and 5.[282]

Shaw is situated in the Kennet region and in Newbury's immediate hinterland. There were remarkably few debts recorded in the probate documents, only to men in Wallingford, Newbury, Donnington and Frilsham. However, there were a significant number of bequests made in wills to Newbury men; and townsmen were often used as witnesses to these wills. Maurice Smart, a wealthy tanner from Shaw, was closely involved with prominent men from Newbury; Walter Collins was his executor and John and Thomas Winchcombe were appointed as overseers of his will. There was obviously a close relationship between the inhabitants of this rural manor and the town. By contrast, the debts in the probate records of Kintbury, also situated in the Kennet region, were numerous and widespread and ranged over an area of southern England from Oxford to Chichester.[283] Local society in Kintbury included a number of wealthy individuals who cultivated large areas of arable land and also kept

---

[280] Where places were specified: Newbury inhabitants 3; Londoners 3; single cases locally at Speen, Benham, Wantage and Garfield; Reading 2; Abingdon 2; Oxfordshire 4; Chichester 1.

[281] The types of documentary source employed and lack of a local archive may be affecting these conclusions.

[282] In addition to sums of money the debts were predominantly amounts owed for grain, wool and cloth.

[283] Avington, Bampton (Oxon), Bishopstone (unknown), Bristol, Chichester, Chipping Ilsley, Dunyll (unknown), Enborne, Falley, Froxfield, Hungerford, Inkpen, Newbury, Oxford, Pearnerd (unknown), Peasemore, Reading, Salisbury, Up Lambourn, Whitchurch (Hampshire), Winchester, Woolly (unknown), Wyst (unknown).

considerable flocks of sheep. Some families, such as the Brinklows discussed in chapter 5, had very wide-ranging familial and commercial contacts.

The northern area of the study region was served by the towns and marketing facilities of Wantage and Abingdon, and the smaller urban centre of Lambourn. As we saw earlier, the characteristic feature of these towns was their mirror-imaging of the fortunes of Newbury; they were thriving centres in the fourteenth century but were losing their pre-eminence by the early sixteenth century.[284] Ashbury is situated on the northern slopes of the Berkshire Downs and was a very successful area for the farming of sheep by both lords and peasants. Debts here were concentrated in the area of northern Berkshire, with only a few beyond the county border.[285] At West Hanney, in the Vale of the White Horse, debts covered a fairly wide geographical area and there was a concentration on the local towns of Wantage, Abingdon and also on East Hendred.[286] West Hanney had a buoyant local economy based on mixed farming and the probate records were those of prosperous agriculturalists. The economic interests of this group were concentrated in both the local towns and other rural areas, and there were also more widespread links with London and Hampshire. Those debts from Buckland, also in the Vale, and where there was more emphasis on pastoral – especially sheep – than arable husbandry, were concentrated in northern Berkshire and southern Oxfordshire, and one in Gloucestershire.[287] Links with the latter appear to have been relatively strong as serfs were reported as living there in the fifteenth-century manor court rolls.[288] In the early sixteenth century the wool grown at Buckland formed part of the trade from the Cotswolds.[289]

What type of individual was responsible for these debts? Those with wide-ranging contacts, both as creditors and debtors, were tenants who farmed on a substantial scale. Men such as William Slatter of Buckland who, when he died in 1495, had over 110 acres largely sown with barley, various types of cattle, and 300 sheep and 100 lambs. He claimed to be owed money by men from Coleshill, Wantage and Abingdon, and he owed money to William Battenian of Gloucestershire.[290] Robert Clark also Wace of Templeton in Kintbury was a

---

[284] Above and chapter 2.

[285] Ashbury, Ardington, Beedon, Coxwell 2, Faringdon 3, Longcott 2, Lydyngton (unknown, possibly Rutland), Marlborough (Wilts), Uffington, Woolstone, Wroughton (Wilts), Weke (unknown), Winterbourne, Chayste churgo (unknown).

[286] Wantage 6; Abingdon 4; Hendred 4; London 3; single cases at Chaddleworth, Charlton, Harwell, Kingsclere (Hants.), Steventon, Sutton.

[287] Abingdon, Beedon, Coleshill, Wantage, Broughton (Hants), Morton (Glos), Donsurth (unknown), Hyeworth (Wilts), Gloucester.

[288] See chapter 5.

[289] A point that is expanded in chapter 5 in an analysis of the trading and agricultural activities of the merchants of the Staple of Calais in northern Berkshire.

[290] TNA, PROB2/455.

similar figure, although on a rather larger scale, and claimed debts in his will of 1529 due locally from men at Kintbury, Inkpen, Hungerford and Newbury, as well as from further away from Oxford (2), Reading, Bristol, Winchester, Salisbury, and Wyst.[291] The distributions were derived more typically from individuals with just one or two small debts, people such as Elizabeth Beslye of Ashbury, whose debts included £1 owed to her for wool.[292] Additionally, there were many others where the place of residence of the other party in the debt was not specified and so do not appear in the distributions. Nevertheless, they represent a broader level of commercial activity that was occurring in these communities but cannot be located geographically.

Apart from Shaw, which was heavily influenced by its proximity to Newbury, the pattern of debt in the villages of western Berkshire reveals their integration into a network of market activity. These people did not live in isolated rural communities, nor were their activities limited to the towns in the immediate vicinity, but rather, they were integrated into a variety of trading relationships that covered a large area of southern England. Furthermore, the analysis of patterns of investment demonstrates the introverted nature of urban interests during periods of rapid expansion, in contrast to their widespread trading activities. By comparison, the rural inhabitants were willing and able to invest in the properties of the expanding town. This investigation of urban–rural relationships has shown how the theoretical models of hierarchies of trading networks are flawed by their inability to incorporate the variety of experience identified in detailed studies. Marketing structures remained fluid and much of the activity was related to individuals rather than institutions.[293]

Conclusion

The economy of Newbury has been shown to have been buoyant for much of the fifteenth century, with marked expansion by the end of the century that was clearly demonstrable by the early sixteenth century. The manufacture of cloth was the dominant form of economic activity and the acceleration in production was based on earlier foundations. Nevertheless, the enterprising entrepreneur played a pivotal role in explaining the rapid increase in production in the town. The great success of the town's cloth industry accounted for the rise in its position in the country's urban hierarchy. The merchants and clothiers of the town traded with London and Southampton and the market for its cloth had an international dimension. The town was integrated into the economy of the area of south-western Berkshire through interaction in the arenas of marketing,

---

[291] BRO, D/A1/1 fols 100–101.
[292] BRO, D/A1/39/110.
[293] Britnell, 'Urban Demand', 1–21.

manufacture and investment where the rise in the town's fortunes were felt. The rural inhabitants of the area exploited the situation by taking advantage of Newbury's expansion and investing in urban properties. Furthermore, their spheres of economic activity ranged beyond the confines of the local market centres. We must move away from an emphasis on institutions to identify the complexity of the situation derived from the activities of enterprising individuals. The exploits of the rural entrepreneurs were as much a feature of the fourteenth to sixteenth centuries as their urban and industrial counterparts. Town and country dwellers reacted in different, but equally innovative, ways to the conditions of the late fifteenth and early sixteenth centuries. We should note the cumulative impact of the rural inhabitants in particular, who in the past have been considered as rather unusual, but in fact were present in many of the larger villages of England and who were not constrained by their locality but had much wider horizons.[294] Forces for change can be found in both town and countryside and in the interaction between the two as this chapter has shown. We turn now to the role of landowners in shaping the pace of change.

[294] A point that will be expanded in chapter 5.

CHAPTER 4

Estate Management and Profitability

Introduction

It is stating the obvious that landlords did not form a homogenous social group and the problem to be addressed in this chapter is the extent to which the different administrative regimes of the various lords affected the pace of change in the locality and the profitability of their estates.[1]

Land formed the basis of any agrarian economy and therefore who owned the land and how it was administered would have had wide-ranging social consequences. The style of administration adopted would be influenced by various factors including the size of the estate,[2] region in which it was situated,[3]

---

[1] For a general introduction to the subject see J. M. W. Bean, 'Landlords', in Miller, *Agrarian History* III, 526–46, 568–86. E. Miller and J. Hatcher, *Medieval England. Rural Society and Economic Change, 1086–1348* (London, 1978), 179–204.

[2] See note 1 above, and important studies of individual estates by Harvey and Dyer. B. Harvey, *Westminster Abbey and Its Estates in the Middle Ages* (Oxford, 1977). C. Dyer, *Lords and Peasants in a Changing Society: The Estates of the Bishopric of Worcester, 680–1540* (Cambridge, 1980). Other studies of estates include E. Levett, 'The Black Death on the Estates of the See of Winchester', in P. Vinogradoff (ed.), *Studies in Social and Legal History* (Oxford, 1916). R. H. Hilton, *The Economic Development of Some Leicestershire Estates in the Fourteenth and Fifteenth Centuries* (Oxford, 1947). E. Miller, *The Abbey and Bishopric of Ely: The Social History of an Ecclesiastical Estate from the Tenth Century to the Early Fourteenth Century* (Cambridge, 1951). J. A. Raftis, *The Estates of Ramsey Abbey* (Toronto, 1957). F. R. H. DuBoulay, *The Lordship of Canterbury: An Essay on Medieval Society* (London, 1966). E. King, *Peterborough Abbey, 1086–1310: A Study in the Land Market* (Cambridge, 1973). T. A. R. Evans, and R. J. Faith, 'College Estates and University Finances, 1350–1500', in J. I. Catto and T. A. R. Evans (eds), *The History of the University of Oxford*, vol. 2 (Oxford, 1992).

[3] For regional differences see below, p. 128. An overview of landlords that considers the differences between areas of 'strong' and 'weak' lordship can be found in P. Schofield, *Peasant and Community in Medieval England, 1200–1500* (Basingstoke, 2003), 44–5, 47–51. For an in-depth comparison of region and landholding between Norfolk and Berkshire see J. Whittle and M. Yates, '*Pays Réel* or *Pays Légal*'? Contrasting Patterns of Land Tenure and Social Structure in Eastern Norfolk and Western Berkshire, 1450–1600', *AgHRev*, 48

the underlying economic conditions of the time,[4] and the personal inclinations of the individual lord. In addition to these factors income from an estate would be affected by the relationships between lord and tenant.[5] Furthermore, the fifteenth century has been characterised as a difficult time for landlords, especially in maintaining the income from their properties, although the reasons for this observation are disputed.[6] Indeed, these difficulties may have a longer history, dating from at least the early fourteenth century.[7] Therefore the interaction between the different factors should be considered when exploring the reasons for change in a locality. Previous studies have correctly stressed the large variations in the practices of different lords, but have not examined with the same degree of emphasis the effects that this diversity had on the tenant population, a theme that will be addressed in this and the next chapter. We will begin with an examination of the manor as a unit of estate administration and the criteria for the selection of the Berkshire case studies; and then compare the different manors for details of administration, revenue, enclosure, and finally

(2000), 1–26. An example from a wood pasture region is A. Watkins, 'Landowners and Estates in the Forest of Arden in the Fifteenth Century', *AgHRev*, 45 (1997), 18–33, in which he provides useful references to other studies of seigniorial income.

[4] See above, chapter 1. For an example of a lord responding to the economic conditions of the mid-fifteenth century see R. H. Britnell, 'The Pastons and their Norfolk', *AgHRev*, 36 (1988), 132–44.

[5] Dyer identified the advantages for the peasantry in C. Dyer, 'A Redistribution of Incomes in Fifteenth-century England?', *Past and Present*, 39 (1968), 11–33. In response to Dyer see B. J. Harris, 'Landlords and Tenants in England in the Later Middle Ages: The Buckingham Estates', *Past and Present*, 43 (1969), 146–50.

[6] Postan was pessimistic in his assessment of the ability of large landowners to improve their incomes, although he was more optimistic about lesser landlords. M. M. Postan, 'Medieval Agrarian Society in its Prime: England', in M. M. Postan (ed.), *The Cambridge Economic History of Europe* (Cambridge, 1966), 595–6. Lander adopted a more optimistic approach and argued that conditions varied across England and that some lords could be proactive in the management of their estates in order to maintain their income. J. R. Lander, *Conflict and Stability in Fifteenth-century England* (London, 1977), 26–33. McFarlane, however, observed that the income of the nobility could be maintained through the acquisition of additional properties. K. B. McFarlane, *The Nobility of Later Medieval England* (Oxford, 1973), 186, 212, 213–27 esp. 223. For a detailed examination of conditions in Warwickshire in the fifteenth century see C. Carpenter, *Locality and Polity: A Study of Warwickshire Landed Society, 1401–1499* (Cambridge, 1992), 153–95. The income of the lesser landowners of fourteenth-century Gloucestershire are examined by N. Saul, *Knights and Esquires: The Gloucestershire Gentry in the Fourteenth Century* (Oxford, 1981), chapter 6. The situation in the Welsh marches was studied by Pollard, who was pessimistic in his assessment of the Talbot's ability to increase their income and raise large sums of ready cash. A. J. Pollard, 'Estate Management in the Later Middle Ages: The Talbots and Whitchurch, 1383–1525', *EcHRev*, 25 (1972), 553–66.

[7] B. M. S. Campbell, 'The Agrarian Problem in the Early Fourteenth Century', *Past and Present*, 188 (2005), 3–70, especially 69.

make a brief assessment of profitability as net income. The result is a pattern of contrasting administrative regimes, especially noticeable when the gentry were compared with the crown and institutional landlords. Moreover, they had repercussions for the tenants of marked differences for them in the cost of land and opportunities for economic expansion. Nevertheless, a new landlord did not bring about an immediate transformation as the underlying institutions of custom and tenure continued to exert a modifying influence on their ability to impose change.

The manor as a unit of estate administration and lordship[8]

The large and often dispersed lands of the estate of a lord were usually divided into a number of manors whose functions were twofold: they acted as the individual administrative units of the landed estate, and also provided a private court where the lord exercised his rights of jurisdiction over his tenants.[9] During the fifteenth century possession of the right to hold a court defined a property as a manor and became its technical legal meaning.[10] This court was known as the court baron; its rights of jurisdiction were limited to the local concerns of the lord and his tenants, its law was that of the custom of the manor, and within this context it regulated the tenure of customary land. Additional rights of jurisdiction to hold a court leet or view of frankpledge might be granted as a minor royal franchise. This court's origins were founded on a system of mutual sureties, the frankpledge system, while its function remained that of the maintenance of local law and order with the right to try minor breaches of the king's peace. Other functions of the court leet included the imposition of quality controls on trading standards, especially of the brewers, bakers and butchers, and responsibility for the maintenance of the king's highways. The tenants of the manor made use of the lord's court for dealing with personal disputes, debt, and the administration of common resources, such as the open fields and pasture, which were regulated through the passing of agricultural bye-laws enforced in the court.[11] During the period of study the level of activity and influence of the manor court changed as its function for regulating the local community and settlement of personal altercations declined in the face of rising inflation in the sixteenth century, increasing use of the royal courts, and the growing importance of the parish

---

[8] This section draws upon P. D. A. Harvey, *A Medieval Oxfordshire Village: Cuxham, 1240 to 1400* (Oxford, 1965); *idem, Manorial Records* (London, revised edn, 1999), M. Bailey, *The English Manor, c.1200–c.1500* (Manchester, 2002).

[9] Harvey, *Manorial Records*, 2, 45–7.

[10] *Ibid.*, 2.

[11] The regulation of local society by its members is discussed in detail in chapter 5.

as an administrative unit;[12] nevertheless it continued to act as an important court of record for the transfer of land. The court, therefore, was the forum in which the lord exercised, in a very public and practical sense, his authority over his tenants. Furthermore, as has already been mentioned, the manor was also an area of land and a unit of administration, either on its own or within a large estate, and as such it was concerned with the functional aspects of land and revenue that are the concerns of this chapter.

There were significant variations in the manors of medieval England, especially between the different regions of the country, in their size, social composition, and the level of enforcement of seigniorial authority. For example, in much of East Anglia manors were made up of relatively small areas of land, sometimes several within one parish; they often belonged to the lesser nobility and gentry and comprised a predominantly free peasantry. On this type of manor seigniorial restrictions were few and the regions in question are often referred to as 'lightly manorialised' or even 'non-manorial'.[13] Berkshire, by contrast, belonged to that area of central and southern England that has been described as 'heavily manorialised', where manors were large and often formed just one small part of an estate, especially those belonging to the crown and great ecclesiastical houses.[14] In regions such as this seigniorial demands and restrictions could be heavy, there were proportionately fewer free peasants, and manors could be coterminous with their parishes.

Except for small estates, manors were rarely administered directly by their lords. Rather, the various aspects of management were delegated and undertaken by their own officials or servants, or by members of the local community, and the choice depended on the nature of the activity. Thus the actual running of the manor, particularly those belonging to large estates, was delegated to the lord's steward, who was usually an outsider. He oversaw the administration of the estate and came and held the manor court as the lord's representative. The steward was the point of contact between lord and tenant.

[12] The 40 shilling threshold for access to the royal courts became less of an obstacle in the economic conditions of the sixteenth century.

[13] A recent summary of the differences between the manors of England can be found in Bailey, *English Manor*, 2–18. Kosminsky employed the Hundred Rolls of 1279 and classified manors by their size. E. A. Kosminsky, *Studies in the Agrarian History of England in the Thirteenth Century* (Oxford, 1956), 96. Detailed studies of contrasting areas include Whittle and Yates, '*Pays Réel* or *Pays Légal*'?', 1–26; J. Whittle, 'Individualism and the Family-Land Bond. A Reassessment of Land Transfer Patterns Among the English Peasantry, c.1270–1580', *Past and Present*, 160 (1998), 25–63; Z. Razi, 'The Myth of the Immutable English Family', *Past and Present*, 140 (1993), 3–44. It was Postan who employed the term 'non-manorial', in M. M. Postan, *The Medieval Economy and Society* (London, 1972), 97.

[14] *VCH Berkshire*, II, 180 where it is suggested that the manorial system in Berkshire provides an excellent example of the manor in its typical form.

The day-to-day administration of the manor was left to resident members of the local community and the tasks were divided between a number of local officials drawn from the tenant population, and whose function and title varied between the manors.[15] The local officials, most commonly known as the reeve, and less frequently as bailiff, were required to answer for the everyday management of the manor, upkeep of the tenancies and their occupancy, any part of the demesne that remained in direct control of the lord, and submit a written annual account.

The selection of manors

Thus there were marked variations in the social composition of landlords, size of landed estates, structure of manors, and level of seigniorial influence. Even within the relatively small area of western Berkshire the impact that these differences had on conditions in the locality could be significant. The optimal method for investigating this level of diversity and assessing its effects is to undertake a series of detailed case studies for the region and compare the results. Thus the manors of different types of landlord – aristocratic, gentry, monastic, and collegiate – are examined from across the regions within western Berkshire. Detailed studies can identify the specific nature of both continuity and change. Furthermore, they make a significant contribution to topics of broader historical interest, such as the impact that the transfer of lands at the Dissolution of the Monasteries had on local society, the role played by the gentry in these changes and in shaping local society. Moreover, they enable us to identify the effects that the different management strategies of the various landlords had on conditions in the locality.

Methodological difficulties can be encountered when undertaking this type of regional investigation, particularly due to the imperfect survival of the documentation. As will shortly become evident, the manorial archives of these different lords are fragmented, but with careful scrutiny, and an awareness of their limitations, they can provide important evidence.[16] It is from these detailed studies that the data are drawn that provide the evidence for this chapter and chapter 5.

The selected manors therefore had to reflect the three regions within western Berkshire as well as the different social backgrounds of the lords. The manors lying in the Vale of the White Horse were situated in the parishes of West Hanney and Buckland. Both parishes contained several manors. The lands of

[15] For the duties of the reeve and other manorial officials see Harvey, *Cuxham*, 63–74, Bailey, *The English Manor*, 98–100.
[16] For a discussion of the methodology employed to overcome the difficulties with the documentation and their chronological coverage see Appendix III.

West Hanney were divided between the manors of Priors Court, Seymours Court, Andrews Court and the Rectory.[17] Detailed studies were made of the first two manors. Priors Court was a manor held by New College Oxford from 1441 following the earlier closure of the alien priory of Newton Longville. Seymours Court was held by a local gentry family from East Hendred and could descend in the female line when there were no male heirs. Ralph Arches held the manor in 1412 and after his death it descended in the female line until c.1455 when Isabel Stowe married John Eyston, also of East Hendred, and the manor remained with the Eyston family for the rest of this study.[18] The large parish of Buckland contained five manors and several minor estates.[19] The two manors of Dukes and St Johns were studied in the greatest detail, Dukes being the largest and principal manor and cited unless specificied otherwise. The parish also included the manor of the Rectory, and the manors of the hamlets of Barcote and Carswell were added to the main manor for administrative purposes. Dukes manor was named after the Dukes of Suffolk, who held the manor between 1434 and 1513, prior to which it had been held by the gentry family of Bessels, and after 1544 by various members of the Yate family who were already resident on the manor.[20] St Johns was named after its medieval lords, the Order of Knights Hospitaller, who held the manor until the Dissolution when it was also purchased by John Yate.

Situated in the Kennet valley are the parishes of Shaw and Kintbury. The manor of Shaw was coterminous with its medieval parish[21] and was held by Winchester College from 1404 until 1543 when it passed to the king,[22] and then

[17] The relative size of the different manors can be calculated by dividing the total acreage of the parish of 1,383 acres from *VCH Berkshire*, II, 242, by the number of yardlands for each manor and the Rectory. The number of yardlands were recorded in 1599 in the resolution of a dispute over pasture rights between the three manors, NCA, 1360; they were Priors Court 18 yardlands, Seymours Court 11.25, Andrews Court 17, and the Rectory 4 yardlands.

[18] To avoid confusion the lords are always called Eyston for the rest of this study. For full details of the manorial descent see *VCH Berkshire*, IV, 286, 298.

[19] A parish of 4,505 acres. *VCH Berkshire*, IV, 453.

[20] Members of the Bessels family were lords of the manor until 1428 when Thomas Chaucer held the manor. He died in 1434 when it passed to his daughter and heir Alice, wife of the Duke of Suffolk. Edmund duke of Suffolk was executed in 1513 and Henry VIII granted the manor to Charles Brandon who was created Duke of Suffolk, but in 1535 exchanged it with the king again until it was bought by John Yate in 1544 for £1,408 14s. 7d. *VCH Berkshire*, IV, 454–5.

[21] Shaw was approximately 1,000 acres in size and would be classified as of medium size by Kosminsky in *Studies in Agrarian History*, 96. Note in Map 2, Shaw is joined with its neighbouring parish of Donnington to form Shaw cum Donnington.

[22] Very little work has been done on the crown's estates, see the collection of essays R. W. Hoyle (ed.), *The Estates of the English Crown, 1558–1640* (Cambridge, 1992).

in 1554 it was bought by Thomas Dolman, a wealthy clothier from Newbury.[23] Kintbury was a large parish which contained six manors of varying sizes by the fifteenth century.[24] Kintbury Eaton was named after its lady the Prioress of Nuneaton who held the manor until the Dissolution when it passed to the king who granted it to Edward Earl of Hertford in 1542. He sold the manor in 1544 to Richard Bridges of Shefford.[25] Kintbury Amesbury was held by the Prioress of Amesbury until the Dissolution when it passed to the king, and in 1542 was exchanged with another manor belonging to John Cheyney of neighbouring West Woodhay.[26]

The manors in the Downs were studied in less detail due to the more fragmentary nature of their archives.[27] Ashbury was held by the abbot of Glastonbury Abbey until the Dissolution, when it passed to the king who granted it in 1543 to Sir William Essex of Lambourn.[28] Woolstone was once a chapelry in the parish of Uffington.[29] The manor belonged to the prior of St Swithun's, Winchester who held it until the Dissolution.[30] It was then granted to Sir Thomas Seymour and at his attainder in 1549 was returned to the crown and passed to a succession of different men over the rest of the sixteenth century.[31]

Manors were not necessarily discrete blocks of land; for example, at West Hanney the strips of arable land belonging to the various manors were interspersed in the common fields of the parish.[32] As discussed in chapter 2, the lands of the Berkshire manors were held predominantly in standard units

---

[23] *VCH Berkshire*, IV, 89. Winchester College was not granted a view of frankpledge until 1461 and prior to that time it only held the court baron.

[24] Kintbury covered an area of approximately 7,800 acres which were divided between the two principal manors belonging to the nuns of Amesbury and Nuneaton, and the smaller manors or estates of Templeton, Titcombe, Inglewood, Balsdon, Anville's, and Denford. For a description of the manors of this parish see *VCH Berkshire*, IV, 206–14.

[25] *VCH Berkshire*, IV, 208.

[26] *VCH Berkshire*, IV, 207.

[27] In the early sections of chapter 2 Ashbury and Woolstone were initially classified as 'Mixed parishes' but this category was found to have very few distinguishing characteristics and, as the majority of the lands of the parishes were situated on the Downs, and their local economies were dominated by sheep husbandry, they were subsequently classed as parishes of the Berkshire Downs. See chapter 2, pp. 46–7.

[28] *VCH Berkshire*, IV, 505–6. Asbury covered an area of 5,609 acres.

[29] *VCH Berkshire*, IV, 544, 545, 549–51. As a parish it now contains 2,012 acres. It was one of the Anglo-Saxon estates studied by Hooke, see D. Hooke, 'Anglo-Saxon Estates in the Vale of the White Horse', *Oxoniensia*, 52 (1987), 129–43.

[30] It was also studied in detail by Ross Faith see R. Faith, 'Berkshire: Fourteenth and Fifteenth Centuries', in P. D. A. Harvey (ed.), *The Peasant Land Market in Medieval England* (Oxford, 1984).

[31] *VCH Berkshire*, IV, 545.

[32] See description in chapter 2, footnote 13, p. 26.

of yardlands or virgates. These were units of assessment and contained varying numbers of acres of arable land with pasture allocated in proportion to the arable, often described in terms of the number of animals that could be grazed, and rents were levied on a property as a unit rather than by the number of acres that it contained.

Thus a variety of manors of different sizes, held by lords from a range of social and institutional backgrounds, many of which changed hands, and situated within the three regions of western Berkshire, are employed to provide the detailed evidence on which much of this study is based.

Administration

Different landlords had correspondingly different objectives in the management of their manors and estates. It is worth emphasising that the concerns of an aristocratic lord such as the Duke and Duchess of Suffolk towards their manor in Buckland would be different from those of John Yate, a man who aspired to the rank of gentleman and lived on the manor in the sixteenth century. Again, an institutional body such as New College Oxford would not administer its manor at West Hanney in the same way that the Eyston family managed its lands nearby. At Buckland during periods of political upheaval there was some increase in violence on the manor, although the underlying administrative structures remained unchanged. The fortunes of lords changed, such as the fall from favour of Charles Brandon, and this might entail a new lord of the manor. On a larger scale, the transfer of lands at the Dissolution of the Monasteries brought a new group of personnel to the manor. Yet it will become apparent that the immediate impact that the changes brought by the Dissolution were remarkably muted and often took several decades before the effects were visible.

The stewards administering the manors were of varied social status and geographical origins depending on the size and type of estate; many were enumerated in the returns of the Military Survey.[33] The social standing of officials could change over time. For example, the principal steward of the priory of Nuneaton in 1448 was John Stokes, and in 1468 Edward Langford, and they each held the courts at Kintbury Eaton; in contrast, at the beginning of the fourteenth century the Kintbury manors were managed and courts held by lesser officials of the priory, either bailiffs or lay brothers.[34] Yet all authority

---

[33] Examples of the stewards included Sir Thomas Fettiplace, who was steward on all the manors of the abbot of Abingdon; in comparison there were several different men who acted as stewards on the crown manors, and at Woolstone Master Froste of Hampshire acted for the Prior of St Swithun's Winchester. TNA, E315/464.

[34] BL, Add Roll 49235 court of 13 June 1448; Add Roll 49238 court of 17 November 1468. B. Kerr, *Religious Life for Women, c.1100–c.1350* (Oxford, 1999), 184.

was not necessarily delegated as the warden and fellows of New College and Winchester College inspected their manors on their twice-yearly progresses as set out in the procedures of their founder's statute.[35] In direct contrast, members of the Eyston and Yate family held the manor court themselves, although it was often a junior representative of the family. This more personal approach will be seen to have had an effect on the tenant population.

The responsibilities and duties of the local officials also varied between the manors. Reeves often acted as the local collectors of rent, as was the case at Kintbury. In comparison at Shaw, where the demesne lands were leased with the customary rents, all responsibilities were handed over to the farmer of the demesne who collected the various rents and subsequently paid a fixed sum to the lord. The various duties of the reeve could be very onerous, and remuneration was often by the remission of their year's rent, or exemption from payment of pannage for their pigs. For example, at Kintbury both Laurence Corf in 1455 and John Nalder in 1456 were excused payment of pannage on account of being reeve.[36] There were occasions when it may be inferred that their duties became very onerous. For example, in the middle of the fifteenth century, a period when it was difficult to find tenants to fill all the properties of a manor, the reeve at Buckland was responsible for the loss of income on eight properties lying in the lord's hands.[37] An individual who had been elected to the office could pay for permission for another tenant to take his place as reeve. Or alternatively be fined for non-compliance in holding the office as was the case with William Hayward of Kintbury in 1438 who was fined £1 for not acting as reeve or finding a substitute.[38] Stockmen rendered accounts for the sheep when the manorial flocks of sheep and pasture were retained in the direct control of the lord, such as by the Prior of Edington Priory.[39] Other local manorial officials were concerned with additional aspects of the agricultural life of the community; for example, the hayward's duties were to guard the corn in the field and present to the court those who trespassed or damaged it.[40] At Buckland in the early fifteenth century the hayward submitted an account with the farmer of the sums he had

---

[35] William of Wykeham founded both colleges and the 36th statute set out the method and procedure of the visitations for inspection and audit. T. E. Kirkby, *Annals of Winchester College* 511–13 quoted in L. C. Latham, 'A Berkshire Manor at the Close of the Middle Ages', *Transactions of the Newbury District Field Club*, 6 (1931), 74. A valor of 1476 for New College demonstrates that the strict level of supervision was continuing on their estates. Evans and Faith, 'College Estates', 670.

[36] BL, Add Roll 49237 court 10 November 1455; 49237 court 9 November 1456.

[37] SBT, DR5/1968, 1962, courts of 18 May and 1 December 1441.

[38] BL, Add Roll 49229 court 3 July 1438.

[39] Faith, 'Berkshire', 171.

[40] Harvey, *Manorial Records*, 46.

raised, the totals being recorded in the court rolls.[41] The gate warden, whose functions were less clear, sometimes aided them. The wood warden, such as Laurence Corf in 1442, was an official at Kintbury who had responsibility for the maintenance of the large areas of woodland on this manor and also the upkeep of the boundaries and fences of the woods.[42] There was a warden of swans at Buckland in the early fifteenth century when they were reared for the lord's table.[43] There were also opportunities for these individuals to profit from their office-holding, chances for advancement and to implement change, and by the sixteenth century the manorial office holders were usually large and wealthy farmers. Yet, as we will see when examining the profitability of the manors, the lords had formal and often stringent methods of account and audit in which the local official had to report to the lord for all sums owing once every transaction had been allowed for. Many reeves or farmers in the fifteenth century went into arrears in their accounts. These were assiduously carried forward to the next year as the income generating function of the manor was of great interest to the lord.[44]

Revenue

We turn now to examine the various sources of revenue available to the lords from the manors. Each manor provided the lord with different types of revenue. These included income taken directly from the tenants for the lands mainly in the form of rents, including those for the demesnes which were now predominantly on lease, plus the occasional payments of fines and heriots;[45] from exploitation of the natural resources on the manor such as woodland, mills and fisheries; and income derived from the jurisdictional aspects of the manor, especially the profits of the manor court taken in fines and ammercements. These will each be considered in some detail as their method of exploitation varied between the different lords.

Income from the lands of the manor[46]
The lands of the manor can be divided into two main categories; those of the lord – the demesne, and those of the tenants either as free land or land held

[41] For example in 1406 the sums were 10s. 1d. and 2s. 8d. as recorded in the two courts. SBT, DR5/1943.
[42] BL, Add Roll 49233, court 10 November 1442.
[43] SBT, DR5/1942, 1945, 1946, 1950, 1952.
[44] Below pp. 166, 168 for a discussion of arrears in the accounts.
[45] An entry fine was paid at the beginning of a customary tenancy and a heriot on the death of the tenant. See below, p. 144.
[46] This general description of change in tenure and estate for the medieval period employs: Bailey, *The Medieval Manor*, 5–18, 21–41. Schofield, *Peasant and Community,*

by local manorial custom.[47] The amount of income derived from these lands was influenced by the events of the past, the terms of tenure, the duration – or estate – of the tenancy, and the legal framework of the common law.[48] Changes to the conditions of tenure related to the demesne and customary lands by the fifteenth century, as opposed to free lands, as on many free lands the rents and conditions had been fixed at an earlier date and remained very largely as token payments. The lands of the demesne had been managed directly by the lord and were gradually leased to individuals until by 1450 the majority were held on lease for a specified number of years and for an economic rent set by the lord of the manor at the beginning of the tenancy.[49] In comparison villein land, or customary land as it became known, was held at the will of the lord and according to the custom of the individual manor.[50] From the fourteenth century tenants could obtain a copy of their terms of tenure as specified in

Part 1. Harvey, P. D. A. *The Peasant Land Market in Medieval England* (Oxford, 1984), Introduction. Harvey, *Westminster Abbey and Its Estates*. B. M. S. Campbell, *English Seigniorial Agriculture, 1250–1450* (Cambridge, 2000). An excellent introduction to the subject that covers both the medieval and early modern developments is M. Overton, *Agricultural Revolution in England* (Cambridge, 1996), 30–5, 147–86, 191–2. For the sixteenth century see R. C. Allen, *Enclosure and the Yeoman* (Oxford, 1992), Appendix 1. R. W. Hoyle, 'An Ancient and Laudable Custom: The Definition and Development of Tenant Right in North-Western England in the Sixteenth Century', *Past and Present*, 116 (1987), 24–55. Idem, 'Tenure and the Land Market in Early Modern England: Or a Late Contribution to the Brenner Debate', *EcHRev*, 43 (1990), 1–20. Thirsk, *Agrarian History IV*, Chapter 5. A. L. Erickson, *Women and Property in Early Modern England* (London, 1993), 23–31, 61–78, 163–5. Compare Tawney's pessimistic view of the conditions of tenure for customary tenants with those of Kerridge: R. H. Tawney, *The Agrarian Problem in the Sixteenth Century* (London, 1912); E. Kerridge, *Agrarian Problems in the Sixteenth Century and After* (London, 1969).

[47] In those areas covered by the Hundred Rolls of 1279 the proportion of arable acres held as demesne was 32 per cent, villein 40 per cent, free 28 per cent. Kosminsky, *Studies in the Agrarian History of England*, 92. More recently Campbell and Kanzaka have argued that there were nearly as many free as unfree holdings. Campbell, 'Agrarian problem', 9, 27. J. Kanzaka, 'Villein Rents in Thirteenth-century England: An Analysis of the Hundred Rolls of 1279–1280', *EcHRev*, 55 (2002), 593–618, Table 2. Seigniorial income in the early fourteenth century was derived as: income from demesne lands 30 per cent of total revenue; rents of tenanted lands 37 per cent; banalities and other prerogatives 13 per cent; and tithes 20 per cent. Campbell, 'Agrarian problem', 19.

[48] Overton, *Agricultural Revolution*, 30–4. Kanzaka, 'Villein Rents', 617, where he argues for the importance of local custom in constraining lords' ability to raise customary rents in the early fourteenth century.

[49] Campbell, *English Seigniorial Agriculture*, 58–60, 431–3, 436.

[50] The term 'villein land' is employed here to refer to land which was unfree in the legal sense that disputes were settled in the lord's court and not those of the king; and the tenant might be subject to the arbitrary demands of the lord for services or other dues in return for the land. Schofield, *Peasant and Community*, 12–17. R. M. Smith, 'Some Thoughts on 'Hereditary' and 'Proprietary' Rights in Land Under Customary Law in

the court roll and over the next century the term 'copyhold' was applied with reference to customary tenure.[51] Conditions of tenure varied considerably but in all cases the custom of the manor afforded some level of protection to the tenant against the arbitrary demands of the lord.[52] By the end of the fifteenth century the royal court of Chancery was willing to assist in disputes over customary tenure and recognise the custom of the manor.[53] The rent from customary land was usually a cash payment which included the monetary value of labour and renders in kind that had been commuted at some point, usually in the fourteenth century. The estate in these customary lands differed between regions and manors and ranged from the term of a single life, number of lives – usually the tenant, his wife and a child, or was heritable, and again this varied between regions as to whether the land went to the eldest child, the youngest, or was divided between the heirs.[54] In Berkshire the estate by which customary lands were held was usually for a specified number of lives.[55] In the specific conditions usually associated with the fifteenth century of low demand for land there were references to informal agreements or tenancies 'at will' whereby land was usually held at an economic rent, for a short period of time, without long-term commitments by either party, or the protection of the custom of the manor or common law.[56]

Changes in the conditions of tenure in England in the fifteenth and sixteenth centuries lie at the heart of Robert Brenner's thesis. According to Brenner English lords took advantage of the demographic decline of the fourteenth and fifteenth centuries to convert empty customary tenancies to leasehold tenure, and in the sixteenth century had the ability to charge arbitrary rents and entry fines, respond to inflation, and evict tenants at the end of a tenancy rather than allow a reversion or renewal.[57] The result was the creation of large capitalist farms through the displacement of smaller tenants. He assumed that landlords had the foresight to see that it would be economically advantageous

Thirteenth- and Early Fourteenth-century England', *Law and History Review*, 1 (1983), 95–128. Kanzaka, 'Villein Rents', 593–618.

[51] J. H. Baker, *An Introduction to English Legal History*, 3rd edn (London, 1990), 347–50. Harvey, *Peasant Land Market*, 328–30.

[52] Miller, *Agrarian History* III, chapter 7.

[53] Baker, *Introduction to English Legal History*, 349–50.

[54] Primogeniture where land descended to the eldest son; ultimogeniture in which the youngest son inherited; partible was divided between all sons or all daughters and found in parts of the north, Kent and the East Anglia. C. Howell, 'Peasant Inheritance Customs in the Midlands, 1280–1700', in J. Goody, J. Thirsk and E. P. Thompson (eds), *Family and Inheritance* (Cambridge, 1976), 112–55.

[55] See below p. 142. Regional differences were marked, see Whittle and Yates, 'Pays Réel or Pays Légal?'.

[56] See below, p. 179.

[57] Aston and Philpin, *The Brenner Debate*, 46–50.

to convert customary tenancies into leasehold, an assumption that Richard Hoyle refutes.[58] Rather, Hoyle argues, it was fortuitous on the part of landlords that during the sixteenth century changes in property rights occurred that were disadvantageous for the tenant. The legal changes came about by accident in a context of rising agricultural prosperity and demand for land that allowed lords to pressurise their tenants into paying higher rents and entry fines to the detriment of the tenants of smaller holdings.[59]

We turn now to examine the evidence for Berkshire and the detailed contribution that it makes to these more theoretical discussions. By 1400 manorial land was divided into demesne, customary or free and the proportions varied between the manors with customary land forming the largest sector. Each type of land will now be considered in detail to investigate the various management strategies of the different lords.

Demesne land

Changes to the management of the demesne lands of the manors in Berkshire largely conform to the general pattern that has been described by others.[60] That is, they had previously been retained by the lord and worked by the labour of a combination of the hired *famuli*, labour services of the customary tenants, and some additional waged labour; subsequently many services became commuted for a cash payment in the fourteenth century and sometimes earlier. The process of leasing some of the lands of the demesne accelerated under the conditions of the second half of the fourteenth century as direct farming became increasingly onerous, and the cost of labour increased. There was great diversity in the ways in which the lands of the demesne were leased. In general, the majority of demesne lands in western Berkshire were being leased by 1450 and many had been leased by 1400.[61] Even a conservative lord such as William of Wykeham, bishop of Winchester and founder of New College, gradually leased his properties. New College itself slowly leased its manors during the first half of the fifteenth century until only one remained in hand in 1440.[62] The leasing of the demesne lands was not always a continuous process as lords sometimes changed their minds, and lands might revert to the lord in unusual circumstances, particularly if they were having difficulties in finding suitable tenants. An example of this happening occurred at Woolstone in 1458 when

[58] Hoyle, 'Tenure and the Land Market', 11.
[59] Ibid., 10–11.
[60] In particular see Campbell, *English Seigniorial Agriculture*.
[61] L. C. Latham, 'A Berkshire Manor at the Close of the Middle Ages', *Transactions of the Newbury District Field Club*, 6 (1931), 3, 150–65; *VCH Berkshire*, II, 191–3; Faith, 'Berkshire', 108–10, 165–8, especially page 109 for detailed examples that show that many were leased between 1422 and 1486.
[62] Evans and Faith, 'College Estates', 673.

Richard Combe, the farmer of the demesne, absconded with all the demesne stock – that is, 87 sheep, 5 cows, 4 oxen, 10 quarters of wheat, 13 of barley, 7 of beans and various utensils – and the Prior then took the demesne back in hand for a few years.[63] The ways in which the demesnes were leased also varied. At Shaw by 1405 the lease of the demesne also included the rents of the customary tenants. At the same date in Buckland and Kintbury the commutation of labour services had become a fixed annual payment of £8 8s. 8d. and £3 10s. od. respectively.[64] The payments continued in the accounts at Kintbury until 1428 when customary rents were revised and these sums were incorporated, although some services such as carting continued to be demanded.[65] A lord might lease the arable lands of the manor whilst retaining the pasture, particularly if he retained flocks of sheep and other animals as was the case on several of the manors on the Downs. The lease of the demesne stock might occur at a considerable interval after that of the arable land. For example at Coleshill the lord only gradually leased the pasture on the manor, while at Woolstone the farmer of the demesne was still leasing 201 sheep from the prior of St Swithins Winchester in 1537.[66] The length of the leases of the demesnes varied between different lords on the manors studies and ranged from between 8 and 32 years.[67]

Table 15 Data for annual income from manors

Manor and Date	Lease of demesne	Customary rent	Free and customary rents	Court profits	Lease of mills	Notes
Vale White Horse						
Priors, West Hanney						
1443	£6 6s. 8d.	£6 14s. 2d.	£9 8s. 11d.	£1 2s. 8d.		
1490	£6 0s. 0d.	£6 14s. 4d.[a]	£9 9s. 0d.	£0 2s. 4d.		[a] mean per virgate 13s. 4d.
1518	£6 0s. 0d.		£9 9s. 0d.	£0 12s. 6d.		
1541	£6 13s. 8d.		£9 10s. 0d.	£0 2s. 0d.		
1595	£6 13s. 8d.	£6 10s. 4d.[b]	£9 13s. 3d.	£1 18s. 0d.		[b] mean per virgate 11s. 4d.

[63] TNA, SC6/758/12.

[64] See Chapter 5 for a detailed discussion of the process by which labour services were commuted in western Berkshire.

[65] BL, Add Roll 49272–49273.

[66] For Coleshill see Faith 'Berkshire', 171; for Woolstone TNA, SC6/HENVIII/104.

[67] At West Hanney New College leased their demesne for terms of 10–20 years, and in comparison the Eyston's leased theirs for 8–10 years. At Shaw the duration of the leases of Winchester College varied between 10 and 32 years. The nuns of Nuneaton leased their demesne at Kintbury for 21 years.

Manor and Date	Lease of demesne	Customary rent	Free and customary rents	Court profits	Lease of mills	Notes
Seymours, West Hanney						
1492		£6 16s. 2d.c				c mean per virgate 14s. 6½d.
c.1600		£5 14s. 6d.d				d mean per virgate 14s. 3d.
Buckland						
1405	£10 13s. 4d.		£40 19s. 7d.	£4 16s. 2d.		
1535	£13 3s. 10d.		£35 1s. 1d.	£1 12s. 7d.		
Kennet Region						
Shawe						e Farmer has rents & court profits
1406	£12 10s. 0d.			£2 2s. 7d.	£3 13s. 4d.	
1449	£10 0s. 0d. [£4 19s. 2d.]			£2 6s. 9½d.	£2 5s. 0d.	
1498	£12 12s. 4d.			£0 2s. 0d.	£5 6s. 8d.	
1528	£13 2s. 4d.			£0 4s. 10d.	£6 13s. 4d.	
1547	£13 2s. 4d. [£7 9s. 10d.]			£0 18s. 0d.	£6 13s. 4d.	
1570					£8 0s. 0d.	
Kintbury Eaton						
1406		£13 1s. 1d.		£1 14s. 2d.		
1421	£6 0s. 0d.	£13 1s. 1d.		£1 1s. 10d.	£1 13s. 4d.	
1450	£5 6s. 8d.	£14 14s. 5d.		£0 18s. 11d.	£3 6s. 8d.	
1539	£5 6s. 8d.	£11 15s. 11d.		£0 15s. 8d.	£4 0s. 0d.	
Kintbury Amesbury						
1535	£15 10s. 2½d.		£20 14s. 3d.	£1 6s. 8d.		
1540	£16 13s. 4d.		£21 2s. 11d.	£8 7s. 0d.		
Berkshire Downs						
1413		£10 13s. 11d.f		£3 9s. 1d.		f direct farming
1457	£11 10s. 0dg	£18 14s. 6d.		£2 16s. 6d.		g 320 sheep & 30 rams
1477	£14 0s. 0d.h	£19 19s. 5d.		£1 6s. 5d.		h 200 sheep
1537	£14 0s. 0d.i	£18 12s. 5d.		£1 3s. 1d.		i 201 sheep

Note: There were more fluctuations than appear in the table; these are just the main trends.

Sources: Priors West Hanney NCA, 7191, 4075, 1777, 1735, 1977. Seymours West Hanney BRO, D/EX1/M7, D/EX1/M5,6. Buckland SBT, DR5/1941, TNA, SC6/HENVIII/6900. Shaw TNA, SC2/154/53, LR2/187, BRO, D/ENm M13, 52, 55, D/ENm1 T2. Kintbury Eaton BL, Add Roll 49266, 49268, 49236, TNA, SC6/HENVIII/3739. Kintbury Amesbury *Valor Ecclesiasticus*, vol. 2 (Record Commission, 1814), 242, TNA, SC6/HENVIII/3986. Woolstone TNA, SC6/758/2, 11, 24, SC6/HENVIII/104.

The conditions implied in the leases also varied in certain respects, and some were more responsive to changes in the underlying economic conditions than others. All required payments of annual rents, and many included strict conditions for the maintenance and upkeep of the property during the term of the lease; the enforcement of which can be an indication of a strong demand for land.[68] The level of rent varied over time on the various demesnes as shown in Table 15 with some evidence for decline in the middle of the fifteenth century on the manors in the Kennet valley, whereas it was later in 1490 at West Hanney. Similarly, the date for the recovery of rental value also varied between the various manors.[69] Additional expenses could be incurred, as at Kintbury where the farmer also had to provide 'bred and ale and a motton and hors meyte' for the officers of the priory when they came to hold the court there in the sixteenth century.[70] Other aspects of the lease could be beneficial to the lessee, such as his right to have the use of timber from the manor for major repairs, and the accounts at Shaw reveal that this was a worthwhile perquisite.[71] The success of the different lords in adjusting the level of rent and conditions of the lease in response to a changing economic environment, and ensuring a reasonable return of income for the effort expended on administration, will be assessed below when considering net income.

Free lands

The treatment of income from the free lands of the manor varied widely and the origins of these differences may be found long before the fifteenth century.[72] The creation of the free lands often lay in the great period of tenurial change of the eleventh and twelfth centuries.[73] The actual extent of free land remains a great unknown factor due to inconsistency in its recording in manorial documents, and may have been large. The distribution of free tenures had marked regional variations with a greater incidence in the east of England.[74]

---

[68] For the significance of repairs see below, p. 161.
[69] This was not unique to western Berkshire as Blanchard demonstrated variations in the moment when rents on arable lands rose in I. Blanchard, 'Population Change, Enclosure, and the Early Tudor Economy', *EcHRev*, 23 (1970), 433–5, and on pastoral lands in Derbyshire in *The Duchy of Lancaster's Estates in Derbyshire, 1485–1540* (Derbyshire Archaeological Society Record Series, 3, 1971), 3–16.
[70] BL, Add Ch 47444 which is a new lease of 1531 made with the farmer of the demesne, Bartholomew Paroke.
[71] For example in 1439, BRO, D/ENm M31.
[72] For general discussions see Campbell, 'Agrarian Problem', 3–70, and Kanzaka, 'Villein Rents', 593–618.
[73] For additional examples of different forms of free tenure and the services owed in Berkshire generally see *VCH Berkshire*, II, 168–9, 202–3.
[74] Kosminsky, *Studies in the Agrarian History of England*, 92–4, 204–6. R. H. Hilton, *The Decline of Serfdom in Medieval England* (London, 1970), 18–19.

The size of freeholdings and conditions of tenure also varied enormously, with many free tenants holding very small plots of land. Common to all was the concept of a fixed rent; the value of the land was reflected in the price paid when it was sold and does not appear in the manorial records.[75] The transfer itself, however, was recorded in the court roll and illustrates the concept of tenure in the manorial system; that land was held of the lord however nominally. Free tenants of elevated social standing held by military service. Several in Berkshire held by the less significant feudal tenure of serjeanty.[76] For example, services included the keeping of a hawk for the manor of Titcombe in Kintbury parish, or at Buckland in 1469 the payment of two shillings instead of having to appear with a sparrow hawk at the lord's mealtimes.[77] Additionally, the amount of free land could be increased through the process of assart, that is, clearing land and bringing it into cultivation, that had occurred before 1400. The proportions of free land varied between the different manors of this case study,[78] was always the smallest component of the total land of the manor, and frequently was held in small parcels of land.[79] The social composition of the tenants of free land also varied and included members of the aristocracy such as the Duke of Lancaster who owned land at Kintbury, neighbouring manorial lords such as the Yate family of Lyford who held additional free lands in West Hanney, and customary tenants such as the Fox family at Shaw who held just a few acres of free land. The level of rent and other dues also varied on the free lands of western Berkshire and frequently involved token payments such as a red rose, pound of pepper or cumin, or just 2d. On some free properties a payment was due at the end of the tenure, known as a relief, and this also varied widely in size of payment both between manors and even on properties within a manor.[80] Most tenants of free holdings were obliged to perform suit of court.

Customary lands

As we have observed already, customary land may have formed the largest component of the manor and conditions by which this land was held varied

---

[75] Harvey, *Westminster Abbey and its Estates*, 107ff.

[76] E. G. Kimball, *Serjeanty Tenure in Medieval England* (New Haven, 1936).

[77] See *VCH Berkshire*, IV, 209 for Titcombe; and SBT, DR5/1993 court of 14 October 1467 for Buckland example.

[78] It was impossible to establish the total acreage of free land as it was often just recorded as 'free lands' and the size was not specified.

[79] As illustrated by the large numbers of small sums for land recorded in the Military Survey, see chapter 2, table 6.

[80] For example in the court of 22 October 1523 at Priors Court, West Hanney the payments of relief ranged from 2d., 4s., and a horse valued at 10s. NCA, 4061.

considerably.[81] The estate by which tenants held their lands in western Berkshire usually comprised three lives: in many, cases, though not all, the named tenant, his wife (so long as she did not remarry when her continuation in the tenancy would require special permission), and a named child. All transactions in the manor court specified that the tenant held 'according to the custom of the manor' which usually meant that they owed suit of court, and at Buckland and Kintbury it also included serving as reeve and rent collector. Various permutations existed within this type of customary tenure. For example at Priors Court in West Hanney after naming the tenants the clause stated 'Habendum et tenendum sibi et suis ad voluntatem domini secundum consuetudinem manerii'; which on this manor meant the named tenant and his wife during her widowhood, but not if she remarried. At Seymours Court there was a slight shift in the terms of tenure as between 1433 and 1445 tenure was for one life as 'terminum vite sue', and after 1470 for the three lives of the tenant his wife and son, and daughters on occasion. The potential existed for tenants to renew their tenures and extend their tenancies and these had chronological significance as will be discussed later. It became increasingly common, particularly over the course of the sixteenth century, for tenants to refer to their copy of the court roll where the original land transfer was recorded. Nevertheless, there were wide variations in the practice. Copy of court roll was mentioned specifically at Kintbury from 1415 onwards, and tenants produced their copies in the court and quoted from them. By contrast, this did not happen at Buckland until 1535, Shaw 1546, Seymours West Hanney 1528; and at Priors West Hanney there was only a vague reference in 1599. The Survey of Shaw in 1547 illustrates the interchangeable use of nomenclature where, under the heading of 'Rents of the Customary Tenants', each 'holds by copy given' on a specific date.[82]

Some labour services were still being demanded by individual lords in the fifteenth century as part of the payment for the customary lands of their tenants. This form of manorial revenue varied in its incidence, the level of demands between the different lords in the study area, and ranged from New College who did not demand any labour services from their tenants at Priors West Hanney, to Glastonbury Abbey who in 1520 were still demanding that many of their customary tenants wash and shear the lord's sheep every year.[83] At Kintbury a detailed custumal of the fifteenth century recorded a variety of labour services that were still owed in principle. For example, Alexander of Holt in Kintbury who held a virgate of land from the prioress of Nuneaton

---

[81] For a detailed comparison of the customary tenures of Norfolk and Berkshire see Whittle and Yates, 'Pays Réel or Pays Légal?'.
[82] TNA, LR2/187 fol. 102.
[83] BL, Harley MS. 3961.

was, along with other virgaters and half virgaters, to provide services that included the mowing of an acre and half of meadow and to raise a haycock, to plough an acre at the feast of St John the Baptist, to reap half an acre of corn and bind a sheaf, and in autumn to carry a cartload of the prioress's corn wheresoever she wished, and another cartload within the manor of Kintbury.[84] The gradual erosion of the old system occurred at different rates on the manors belonging to the various lords. It was more general in Berkshire, however, for many of these tasks to have been commuted for a money rent over the course of the fourteenth century.[85] The demands made on those who were personally unfree, as opposed to holding villein or customary land, will be examined in chapter 5.

In general, the cost of customary land to the tenant was a combination of rent, entry fine and heriot. Rents were charged on a property as a unit rather than by acreage and usually included a tenement and a fraction, or number, of virgates or yardlands. Customary rent had largely been established at a time before 1400 and changed only occasionally, for example when holdings were amalgamated it might be increased, or more commonly, rents were reduced as an inducement to take the property in the fifteenth century. This is demonstrated in the sums recorded in Table 15 above. The level of rent could vary between manors even within the same parish, and this was the case at West Hanney where the lands of Seymours at the end of the fifteenth century were more expensive than those at Priors.[86] The sum of rent demanded for customary land might change, as demonstrated in the case of Seymours. The rental of 1492 was compiled at a time when the cost of pasture and its allocation were matters of dispute between the lord and his tenants. The tenants appear to have been attempting to obtain a reduction in rent in lieu of the rights of pasture they had lost. The accompanying court roll records the process of clarification. In 1492 there were several smaller parcels of land belonging to Seymours in addition to those of the standard virgate holdings. During the process of rationalisation these became incorporated into the standard holdings and their individual rents were subsequently lost. As a result by the end of the

---

[84] BL, Add Mss 36905 fols 215ff. This document is said to be a custumal of the fifteenth century, but the names of the tenants suggest that it may have been a fifteenth-century copy of an earlier document; nevertheless it is interesting that it was thought worthwhile to make a copy. There is no evidence for the enforcement or performance of these services.

[85] L. C. Latham, 'The Decay of the Manorial System During the First Half of the Fifteenth Century with Special Reference to Manorial Jurisdiction and the Decline of Villeinage, as Exemplified in the Records of Twenty-Six Manors in the Counties of Berkshire, Hampshire and Wiltshire', MA thesis, London (1928). Faith, 'Berkshire', 108–10.

[86] The larger manor of Priors had a total rent of £6 14s. 4d., whereas the total rent for a smaller area of customary land at Seymours was £6 16s. 2d. There are rentals for 1490 and 1492 respectively Priors Court, NCA, 4075; Seymours Court, BRO, D/EX1/M7.

sixteenth century the total customary rent at Seymours was approximately £5 14s. 6d., a fall of nearly £1.[87] Change in the level of rent when it did occur had been a matter of negotiation between the lords and their tenants.

Entry fines varied more frequently over time, between the different lords, and reveal marked variations in the cost of land to the tenant. Entry fines were the initial payment made by the tenant to the lord on taking up the tenancy, usually as a large one-off cash payment. The level at which they were set was determined by the lord and his freedom in this course of action could be modified by the custom of the manor. Entry fines can reflect the underlying economic conditions of the period and the different policies of the various lords towards the income-generating aspects of their manors. Nevertheless, methodological difficulties are encountered when analysing their data due to the wide variations in the level of fines on different properties, even within the individual manors. Some general observations, however, can be made before we study the evidence in more detail. There was consistency in the treatment of entry fines on the manors of Priors West Hanney and Kintbury Eaton in comparison with the variations in the level of fines at Seymours West Hanney, Shaw, and Duke's manor Buckland.[88] Where change can be observed it reveals that entry fines tended to be relatively high before 1430, they subsequently declined in amount in the Vale but only slightly in the Kennet, recovery varied in amount and chronology during the second half of the fifteenth century, and there was some evidence for a significant increase in entry fines after 1560, which in some instances could be very sharp indeed.

There were occasions in the early fifteenth century at Shaw and Buckland when entry fines were paid as large sums of money. This occurred more consistently at Shaw between 1405 and 1412, when payments were made of 5 shillings for those properties with a half virgate of land, or 6s. 8d. for a messuage and two half virgates of land. At Buckland the majority of entry fines before 1525 were paid as capons, or their monetary equivalent. There were two exceptional occasions in 1406 when £2 was paid for two separate holdings of a messuage and approximately three virgates of land. There were other, and infrequent, occasions when the sums of 3s. 4d. and 6s. 8d. were paid for smaller properties of a virgate or less.[89] Payments of a mark, or fraction

---

[87] No rental exists at this date and data were derived from the individual properties when they were transferred in the court rolls of 1567–1607.

[88] These are the main manors where there are data on entry fines that cover the period of this study. At Buckland on St John's manor the level of entry fines varied widely between the different properties; for example, in 1509 sums of 3s. 4d., 2s., 1s. 8d., or 2 capons were levied as entry fines.

[89] Between 1406 and 1462 from a total of 92 transfers these sums were demanded in 1408, 1419, 1421, 1440, 1451, and 1456. There were 16 occasions when the payment of

of a mark, became proportionately more numerous at Buckland after 1462.[90] In the case studies generally, there was a more widespread decline in the level of entry fines in the middle of the fifteenth century, or even the complete waiver of the fine on occasion, particularly if repairs were to be made to the property by the tenant. This occurred at Buckland along with the payments of entry fines that we have observed.[91] Payments were also made in capons at Seymours Court in West Hanney between 1438 and at least 1445, perhaps even 1470 due to a break in the archive. At Shaw some reduction in the payment of entry fines can be observed by 1434, for example for the property Pudmannes 5s. had been paid in 1405 but 2s. in 1434, and for Colburyes in 1406 10s. paid as entry fine but 3s. 4d. in 1434.

There was evidence for a rise in the sums paid as entry fines after these dates. Seen at Seymours from 1471 to the equivalent of a year's rent, usually 10s. for a property that contained a virgate of land.[92] At Shaw there was a gradual rise in the fines for the rest of the century for example from 6s. for the composite holding of Pudmannes, Rolfs and Smartysland in 1434, to 10s. in 1442, and further increases in 1486 and 1490. At Buckland we have already observed a small increase in the proportion of cash payments that occurred between 1462 and 1525 that were set against the background of the majority of payments as capons. Alongside this pattern of fluctuations and change must be placed the consistent pattern of levying entry fines on the manors of Priors Court West Hanney and Kintbury Eaton. On the first manor payments were made at the rate of approximately one year's rent, while at Kintbury they remained steady at fractions of a mark.[93]

There were sharp increases in the level of fines towards the end of the sixteenth century, although charting the precise chronology is hampered by gaps in the archive. The sums of money paid could be very large indeed; for example at Buckland £40 was paid in 1588 as entry fine for a messuage and two virgates of land, and 40 marks for a messuage and one virgate of land. At Seymours Court from 1559 the sum of £10 was paid consistently as entry fine

an entry fine was pardoned; otherwise if payments were made it was as a capon or its monetary equivalent.

[90] Between 1462 and 1525 from a total of 61 land transfers 19 were demanded as a mark or fraction, the remaining entry fines were paid as capons or their monetary equivalent except for 7 occasions when the tenants were excused payment of an entry fine.

[91] See chapter 5 for the informal nature of some tenancies at Buckland between 1470 and 1520.

[92] BRO, D/EX1M2/1 in court of 10 December 1471 entry fines were demanded as £1 for a property containing 2 messuages and 2 virgates of land, 10s. for a messuage, croft and a virgate of land, 10s. for a messuage and a virgate of land.

[93] A mark for a messuage and virgate of land and half a mark for a messuage and 'cotsetle' or cotland. At Kintbury Amesbury entry fines were levied, in general, at 13s. 4d. for a messuage and virgate of land.

and continued at this rate, regardless of size of the property or level of rent, for the rest of the century. At Shaw a more general increase continued throughout the sixteenth century typically for example on Dikars, a standard holding of a messuage and half virgate of land, in 1480 3s. 4d. was paid, in 1538 11s. 4d., and in 1605 £2. Entry fines on cottages were proportionately greater; for example, 13s. 4d. was paid for two cottages in 1539 and £4 13s. 4d. in 1605. Properties with additional and valued assets could incur very high entry fines, such as the £12 5s. 4d. paid for a holding that included a coppice of wood.[94] The rise in entry fines that has been described must be seen in conjunction with the unchanged level of customary rent during a period of inflation. During the second half of the sixteenth century, and for a variety of reasons, the majority of the manors in this study belonged to small lay landowners. Priors West Hanney belonged to an institutional lord, New College, which was the only manor studied where there had been no marked rise in the level of entry fine by the end of the sixteenth century. Thus the cost of land at West Hanney by 1600 varied considerably between the two different lords. Chapter 5 will consider how the tenants on the two manors reacted to these differences.

The final customary payment was that of the heriot, usually paid on the death of the tenant as the first life. A heriot was traditionally stipulated as being the best beast belonging to the tenant, but it might also comprise the equivalent amount of grain; on occasion an anvil for the forge at Seymours was levied. At Kintbury the level of heriot was set by custom and usually amounted to 1s. 8d. for a cottage and 5s. for a virgate of land. Gradually heriots became converted into money payments during the course of this study and the manorial accounts record that they were received as such into the exchequer of the lord.

The management of the lands of the manor and the revenue derived from these estates have been shown to have differed markedly. The contrasts between the two lords at Hanney were significant. In particular, the gentry lord was more reactive to the underlying economic conditions of the period than the institutional lord whose management remained largely unchanged. On those occasions when the crown was temporarily landlord there was little noticeable dislocation. The monastic estates that were studied passed initially to the king at the Dissolution but the conditions of the tenants changed very little before 1542 when they left the crown estate.[95] This was also the case at Shaw immediately following the exchange with Winchester College. In this instance when the documentary series survives again at the beginning of the seventeenth century there is evidence from the levels of entry fines, that significant change had

---

[94] BRO, D/EN m1, Court of 1605 a messuage, the coppice, a close and parcel of land.
[95] Apart from the lease of Kintbury Amesbury that had increased between 1535 and 1540.

been undertaken by the lord in the second half of the sixteenth century. At Buckland on the manor of St Johns following the suppression of the Order of Hospitallers in 1540 the manor passed to the king who granted it to John Yate, the lord of Duke's manor, in 1545. A new rental was made at the time that recorded no change in the level of rent. The court rolls of 1547 also reveal no alteration in the level of financial exactions on the manor. By the 1580s, following the gap in the archive, a marked change had taken place, particularly in the rate of entry fine which had risen sharply and was in line with those of Duke's manor. It would appear that the underlying institutions of tenure were strong and did not react to the change in seigniorial administration during the first decades after the transfer.

Income from the natural resources of the manor

Additional sources of seigniorial revenue were available from the exploitation of the natural resources of the manors, especially the rivers and woodland, which the lord often claimed as a manorial monopoly. The ways in which these sources of income were managed also varied between the different lords, as did the opportunities available to tenants to make a profit, and both are considered now.

Western Berkshire was well supplied with rivers, including the Thames forming its northern boundary, the Kennet and Enborne in the south, and the various tributaries of these rivers.[96] The rights to these rivers were jealously guarded, including the natural resources such as fishing, and also for industrial purposes. Mills provided an important source of manorial revenue for the lord both in terms of rental income and also the requirement that the tenants should grind their grain at the manorial mill. We can also note that mills were not solely confined to those driven by water power; for example, at Buckland in 1405, in addition to the two water mills there were also two horse mills.[97] A study of seigniorial attitudes towards income from water mills can demonstrate a variety of responses and management strategies. At Shaw, a manor with good documentation, the evidence allows us to identify a balancing act between revenue from rents and the cost of repairs which is presented here as an example of one lord's response to the changing economic conditions of the period.[98] The mills at Shaw included, at various times, one for grinding corn,

[96] For a more detailed analysis of the rivers and numbers of mills that they supported in Berkshire, and Shaw in particular, see M. Yates, 'Watermills in the Local Economy of a Late Medieval Manor in Berkshire', in T. Thornton (ed.), *Social Attitudes and Political Structures in the Fifteenth Century* (Stroud, 2000), 189–91.
[97] SBT, DR5/1941.
[98] See Yates 'Watermills' for a more detailed discussion of this mill complex. Also Chapter 5, pp. 203–6, where the millers are described.

another for milling malt, for grinding bark for tanning, and a fulling mill.[99] The rents from the mills could represent a significant proportion of the total income from a manor. At Shaw this ranged from a third in 1406 to a half by the sixteenth century.[100] Rents varied over the course of the fifteenth century as did seigniorial attitudes towards the cost of repairs. In 1406 the annual rent of the corn mill was £3 13s. 4d. and in 1410 the rent was increased by 6s. 8d. with the addition of the tanning mill. This sum may reflect the lord's uncertainty as to how profitable this venture would be, and in the end must have been a realistic amount given the combined rents of later years. The mill was rebuilt in 1415 at a cost of £29 0s. 3d. and the annual rent in the next year was increased to £5. Twelve years later the level of rent returned to £4 but in 1439 it was reduced to £2 4s. 0d. and remained at this level until 1451. The reduction in rent at Shaw occurred at the end of ten years when Winchester College had not received the full income expected, and was perhaps a realistic action on the part of this landlord.[101] Changes in the level of rent may have been offset by a different policy towards the payment for repairs. Although not specified as a change in the conditions of the lease, the fall in rent did coincide with an absence of repairs recorded in the manorial accounts. This suggests that these became the responsibility of the lessee in return for a reduction in rent, a situation that was made more explicitly between 1488 and 1498.[102] Detailed analysis of the total sums for the period 1478 to 1488 revealed that out of a potential rent of £55 16s. 8d. in total over this ten-year period only £36 13s. 1d. was received in Winchester and, when the £15 15s. 8d. spent by the College on repairs to the mills was deducted, the net receipt in that accounting year was £20 17s. 5d. This sum can be compared with the following period of ten years of reduced rent when the lease specified that repairs were the responsibility of the lessee. The rent was paid in full amounting to £26 13s. 4d. and thus an increase in net receipt at Winchester. In a period of economic recession this lord chose to pass the charge of repairs down the hierarchy of responsibility to the lessee. The reduction in rent and transfer of maintenance costs were a rational response that resulted in an increase in the profitability of the mills, reduced financial outlay and investment, and a higher proportion of anticipated

---

[99] This variety in the types of mill was not unusual. J. Langdon, *Mills in the Medieval Economy* (Oxford, 2004). R. Holt, *The Mills of Medieval England* (Oxford, 1988). On the manor of Kintbury Eaton in addition to the corn mill, there was a fulling mill and, at the beginning of the fifteenth century, also a tanning mill.

[100] On other manors, such as Kintbury Eaton, the documentation is less comprehensive and the mill complex was much smaller. Here income from the mill represented 13 per cent of total income from the manor in 1433 and 14 per cent in 1539.

[101] See Figure 8 later in this chapter recording the receipts from the mills at Shaw.

[102] This analysis is based on a comparison of the ministers' accounts and College receipts. BRO, D/ENm1 M12–M55, and WCM, 22100–22200.

income received. Any study of changes in the level of rent if taken in isolation will not necessarily reveal the underlying and sometimes positive effects on seigniorial income. The reduction of rent in 1439 may have made the lease of the mills an attractive proposition for entrepreneurial activity. John Bullford of Newbury had taken the lease of the mills in 1436 and expanded his activity by building his own fulling mill on the free land at Shaw belonging to Ingram atte Moore, and with no reference to Winchester College. His widow Isabella was prepared to face the College's disapproval and renewed the lease in 1447 when she paid £40 for entry but only one shilling extra in rent for water rights to the fulling mill.[103] An adverse period for a local lord, who was unable to collect all income and had to reduce rents was, however, conducive to entrepreneurial activity. A period of economic uncertainty did not preclude expansion by an individual operating within the specific conditions of his locality.

Turning to the history of Shaw mills in the sixteenth century we find many similarities even though there was a change of manorial lord in 1554. In 1498 the rents on the mills were increased to £5. 6s. 8d. *per annum* and now Winchester College were paying for the repairs. The mill was rebuilt in 1528 at a cost of £18 0s. 10d. and the rent was subsequently increased to £6 13s. 4d. *per annum*, where it remained until 1570 when it was increased to £8 *per annum*. In the interim period the manor had changed hands and in 1554 it was sold to Thomas Dolman who had previously been a successful clothier in Newbury. The lease of the mills themselves attracted men from Newbury including the clothier Robert Sewey in 1503,[104] and in 1570 Thomas Dolman leased the mills to a Newbury clothworker, Henry Lynch.[105] Nevertheless in the 1530s and 1540s it was leased to a local miller Thomas Morne and subsequent members of his family. The change of lord of the manor does not appear to have radically altered the management of the mill complex, unlike the alterations to the cost of customary land that were discussed earlier.

The rivers Thames and Kennet were excellent sources of fish. Rights to fishing at Buckland provided the lords with an additional and lucrative element within their income from customary tenures; for example, in 1405 these were attached to five properties.[106] Tenants were prepared to pay higher rents and entry fines for properties that included fishing rights, even at times when the demand for other lands on the manor was reduced. For example, in 1481 John Stone paid 13s. 4d. as entry fine and an annual rent of 15s. for a messuage with adjoining

---

[103] WCM, 22992 'Liber Albus' fol. 121.
[104] WCM, 22992 fol. 164. Sewey leased the mills from Michaelmas 1503 to Michaelmas 1528. J. H. Harvey, 'A Map of Shaw, Berkshire, England, of ca.1528–29' *Huntia*, 3 (1979), 154.
[105] Lease of 1570 BRO, D/EN m1 T2.
[106] SBT, DR5/1941.

croft and an acre of arable land and fishing rights on the river Thames.[107] This can be compared with the one shilling entry fine and 9s. 6d. annual rent paid by Richard Freman for a messuage and virgate of land in the previous year.[108] Fishing on the river Kennet also provided important manorial income and was regulated in the manor court at Kintbury Eaton where tenants had to purchase licences to fish and, additionally, attempts were made to maintain the stocks of fish and not to over-fish the river. This gave rise to numerous cases, and subsequently fines, against tenants who had been caught employing various types of nets and 'engines' to fish with, or who had blocked the millpond with traps used for catching eels. For example in 1449 John Plecy and John Walcote took trout and other fish from the separate water of the manor without licence to such as extent that they were served a writ.[109] It also led to disputes with men from neighbouring Hungerford who fished in the water of the manor.[110] Trout were a valuable fish in the river Kennet in the late medieval period as they continue to be today. The river Thames at Buckland was used for the last element of direct farming at Buckland, the raising of swans.[111]

The wood that grew on the manors remained the property of the lord and this woodland provided another important source of revenue. This was particularly the case in areas of wood-pasture such as in the Kennet valley. The methods of management varied between the lords but common to all lay the assumption that the trees growing on the manor were a valuable resource and capital asset belonging to the lord. In addition, access to woodland was an essential element of the tenants' livelihoods as it provided fuel, building materials, and grazing for pigs. Thus the management of wood and its exploitation were concerns for both lords and tenants. The woodland on the manor could be leased by the lord, or retained in hand and managed directly, and this further emphasises its importance. Conditions at Shaw support this assertion as the woods were retained by Winchester College and not leased with the manor, unlike the rents of the tenants. It can be illustrated in the lease of the manor in 1542 when the manor with its lands and rents were transferred to John Bekensall, but all wood and coppice growing upon any part of the premises were specifically excepted from his lease.[112] The lord, however, did agree at Shaw and elsewhere, to provide all the large timbers for repairs on the manor and to the mill. At Buckland, after timber had been taken for repairs, it was the tenants'

---

[107] SBT, DR5/2006.
[108] SBT, DR5/2005.
[109] BL, Add Roll 49235, court of 10 November 1449.
[110] BL, Add Roll 49222, court of 21 November 1420.
[111] SBT, DR5/1942, 1945, 1946, 1950, 1952.
[112] WCM, 22993.

responsibility to replant and maintain the replacement tree.[113] A reflection of the perceived value of woodland can be seen in the many detailed surveys of woodland that were made by the crown's officials in the sixteenth century. Its importance is further illustrated in the exchange of the manor of Shaw with Henry VIII in 1543 when the woodland was itemised, but not the manors, mills, arable lands or other parts of the manor.[114]

It is therefore logical that the tenants' access to woodland was closely regulated, usually by the granting of licences to fell wood, and fines were levied in cases of infringements against the rules, thus providing additional sources of seigniorial revenue. Manorial officials were employed to look after the woodland on the lords' behalf for example at Kintbury a woodward was appointed specifically to look after Foxlease wood. The various areas of woodland at Kintbury were surrounded by hedges to protect them and delimitate their boundaries. On all manors, whether in woodland areas or not, tenants were fined for felling wood unlawfully, and in severe cases they could be pursued through the royal courts. For example at Shaw in 1426 William atte Burgh of Speenhamland felled and removed 4,000 saplings of thorn, hazel and beech, a case that continued in the manor courts and then royal courts until 1433.[115]

Moreover, the sale of the large timber on the manor produced an important source of seigniorial revenue. Winchester College may have been selling their capital asset of wood at Shaw in order to maintain a reasonable level of income as a response to the economic conditions of the fifteenth century.[116] A study of receipts from the manor in the bursars' accounts reveal a tendency whereby sales of wood often followed periods of reduced income, as in 1459, 1475–77, and 1509.[117] This may be a coincidence and only reflect normal woodland management, although the distribution appears too regular for this to be a chance occurrence.[118] The sales of wood did not follow a change of warden as had occurred on the Bishop of Winchester's estate when new bishops used the sale of timber to help pay for their heavy initial expenses.[119] When wood was sold it appeared in the bursars' accounts but not when it was used in the

[113] This was set out in a bye law of c.1590 that dealt with both manors of Dukes and St Johns. SBT, DR5/2097, 15v.

[114] WCM, 22993.

[115] TNA, SC2/154/53; royal court extract of an earlier case of 1405, WCM, 11471A.

[116] Pollard also found that this policy was adopted by the Talbots of Whitchurch in the fifteenth century. A. J. Pollard, 'Estate Management in the later Middle Ages', EcHRev, 25 (1972), 533–66.

[117] Based on receipts in the bursars' accounts.

[118] Yates thesis, Figure 6.3 All Receipts, p. 229.

[119] D. Farmer, 'Woodland and Pasture Sales on the Winchester manors in the Thirteenth Century', in R. H. Britnell and B. M. S. Campbell (eds), A Commercialising Economy (Manchester, 1995), 111–14 and 129.

buildings or repairs to the manor or mill. On these occasions it was an internal accounting procedure. It is reasonable to conclude that the sale of wood may have been one of the strategies employed by Winchester College to maintain their income at periods when profitability was reduced. The study of seigniorial revenue, however, should not blind us to the activities of the tenants on the manor who also exploited this resource in a commercial manner, for example as charcoal burners and coopers.[120]

Finally, before leaving this section on revenue from the natural resources of the manor we must mention other associated sources. For example, warrens and dovecotes were found on many of the manors in western Berkshire during these two centuries.[121] They provided an important source of protein and sales for the lord. We cannot quantify the proportion of income from this source due to the nature of the documentation, but their importance can be gauged by the number of occasions when tenants were prosecuted for stealing from the lord. Furthermore, tenants dug clay and chalk on the manor of Shaw for making bricks and daubing and the lord attempted, largely unsuccessfully, to profit from these exploits.[122] Indeed, lords were rather conservative in comparison with their tenants in exploiting the natural resources of the manor for commercial purposes such as fishing and making bricks.

The natural resources of the manor were actively managed and preserved as sources of income by all the lords of this study. The detailed examination of the manor of Shaw has revealed how this institutional lord, who had delegated other forms of revenue collection such as the rents of the manor, was actively engaged in maximising income, particularly during periods of more general contraction in the economy. The study of the mills at Shaw revealed a complex balancing of income from rent with the costs of repairs to maintain a dependable source of revenue.

Income from jurisdiction

As we have seen, the manor court was a forum for the expression of seigniorial authority and it was also a source of profit. Was there a decline in the relevance of the manor court to rural society?[123] There was certainly a reduction in the number of cases and profits from the manor court.[124] Yet this was not

---

[120] See chapter 5, p. 217.

[121] For the significance of the warren in the medieval economy see M. Bailey, 'The Rabbit and the Medieval East Anglian Economy', *AgHRev*, 36 (1988), 1–20.

[122] See below, chapter 5, p. 217.

[123] See chapter 1, p. 17.

[124] The activities of the manor court are discussed in some detail with special reference to Norfolk in J. Whittle, *The Development of Agrarian Capitalism* (Oxford, 2000), 47–65. For income from the manor courts of the bishop of Worcester see Dyer *Lords and Peasants in a Changing Society*, 174–5.

entirely straightforward or necessarily true, as there appears to have been a shift in the types of cases heard in the court; for example, fewer inter-personal pleadings were brought in comparison with the scrupulous recording of land transactions in the later sixteenth century. In western Berkshire there were certainly signs of decline in the use of the manor court for inter-personal cases, in the number of cases against the assize of bread and ale, in the incidence of tenants obtaining licences or paying fines for the pannage of their pigs, and in the sums of money taken as fines and amercements.[125] The tithing penny had become a fixed sum of money, usually two shillings, on the Berkshire manors at some point before 1400. Moreover, there was a decrease in the number of cases relating to the activities and jurisdiction of the court leet, such as the maintenance of law and order. This trend might be explained as a result of the 40 shilling threshold of access to the royal courts becoming less of a barrier in a period of inflation. There were also fewer cases concerned with the maintenance of the king's highways. Furthermore, these trends were affected by the underlying decline in the actual number of times that the courts were held each year.[126] Nevertheless, it was income from the transfers of land that account for the continued buoyancy of court profits within manorial receipts shown in Table 15. Those lords who developed a policy for charging high levels of entry fines, described above, would have a correspondingly high level of income shown as court profits.[127] Increasingly the manor court was used for the passing and enforcing of agricultural bye-laws, as at Buckland in 1593.[128] Failure to repair properties continued to attract large sums of money in fines as we will see, especially given the reduction in the total number of properties due to engrossment. Rather than decline in the relevance of the manor court we would argue for a shift in its response to the changing demands of the period.

Enclosure, engrossing, subtenants and repairs

The lords of western Berkshire had different attitudes towards the enclosure and engrossing of lands, taking of subtenants and enforcement of repairs which reflect their disparate styles of administration and could, arguably, affect net income received from their estates. Historians are generally agreed that enclosure was an act that resulted in the removal of common rights from a piece of land, usually associated with the erection of a fence or hedge that

---

[125] Although the latter trend would have been exacerbated by the inflation of the sixteenth century.
[126] See table 24, 'Cases in the manor courts'.
[127] For example the Kintbury Amesbury figure in Table 15.
[128] SBT, DR5/2097, and see chapter 5.

created a clear boundary and thus separated the land from the others of the village, and brought it under private control.[129] The effects of enclosure form a recurring element in the older economic histories of this period and also in the transition debates, especially the ability to enclose, and the effects of enclosure that are seen as important features in the development of agrarian capitalism.[130] When enclosure is considered in association with the more general features of the fifteenth century, especially the rise in the numbers of large farms, we can observe that structural change had occurred to the layout of fields and in the delineation of the rural landscape.

One of the consequences of enclosure was to withdraw vital assets from the local community. Common land was available to all on the manor and supplied additional resources to those of a smallholding, particularly providing access to areas of pasture. In addition, common rights often included important access to additional grazing for animals, even if only on the stubble in the arable fields after the harvest had been taken. Common rights might also include the important asset of gathering underwood for fuel. Taken together the resources of access to common land and common rights on a manor were valuable amenities and formed an important element in making a smallholding viable. The extent and value of common rights varied over the country and between manors.[131] Once enclosure had taken place it was extremely difficult to reverse. It was the perceived widespread acts of enclosure, especially in the Midlands, associated with the eviction of tenants, which elucidated the greatest condemnation from commentators of the sixteenth century who viewed enclosure as one of the causes of their current problems, particularly poverty and vagrancy.[132] They considered that the key players in the drama were rapacious landlords, and especially those who were members of the gentry. Separating the reality from contemporary comments remains difficult;[133] for

[129] The definition employed here is based on J. Thirsk 'Enclosing and Engrossing', in Thirsk, *Agrarian History*, IV, 200–1. There is a vast literature on the subject usefully annotated in the bibliography in Overton, *Agricultural Revolution*, 218–19. A recent reassessment of the importance of enclosure can be found in R. C. Allen, 'Progress and Poverty in Early Modern Europe', *EcHRev*, 56 (2003), 403–43. For a comprehensive study of enclosure in Berkshire see J. R. Wordie (ed.), *Enclosure in Berkshire, 1485–1885* (Berkshire Record Society, 5, 2000).

[130] See chapter 1 p. 15.

[131] The value of common resources is very difficult to quantify and this has led to controversy over the effects of enclosure. J. M. Neeson, *Commoners: Common Right, Enclosure and Social Change in England, 1700–1820* (Cambridge, 1993). L. Shaw-Taylor, 'Labourers, Cows, Common Rights and Parliamentary Enclosure: The Evidence of Contemporary Comment, c.1760–1810' *Past and Present*, 171 (2001), 95–126.

[132] Thirsk, 'Enclosure and Engrossing', 213–39.

[133] M. Yates, 'Between Fact and Fiction: Henry Brinklow's *Complaynt* Against Rapacious Landlords', *AgHRev*, 54 (2006), 24–44.

example, assessing Thomas More's often quoted description of sheep eating men, the reports of Wolsey's commission of inquiry into enclosures and village desertions, and the associated concerns of government over depopulation, landless men, vagrancy and poverty that were all strong in their condemnation of enclosure.[134] Nevertheless, as we will see, the actual amount of land that was enclosed had a regional dimension and was much smaller in some areas than the contemporary comments would suggest.

The detailed evidence for enclosure suggests a more complex process than the rather simplistic descriptions of sixteenth-century commentators. In Berkshire, particularly in areas of wood-pasture such as the Kennet valley, as elsewhere, enclosures had been occurring, albeit in a piecemeal fashion, before 1400.[135] Many had occurred within a more general context of a shift in emphasis towards pastoral husbandry as less labour-intensive than arable in a period of low population, while greater *per capita* incomes and raised standards of living brought changes in diet and dress and increased demand for the products of both sheep and cattle for the home and export markets. Furthermore, there was greater variety in the social status of those participating in enclosures than just the lords and gentry of the theorists and commentators. Tenants were rationalising their holdings, enclosing, engrossing and creating larger farms, and many turned to pastoral farming. Moreover, in many areas there was a contraction of settlement from village or hamlet to perhaps one large farm.[136] Nevertheless, if desertion of a village occurred it was usually the final act at the end of a long period of decline and only rarely the result of enclosure.[137]

Thus enclosure was neither uniform nor monolithic, and in the context of this chapter we are particularly interested in how the different lords' attitudes towards enclosure and engrossing permitted greater opportunities for tenants to rationalise their holdings, that in turn, affected the nature of change in an area. Nevertheless, these concerns have to be explored within the overarching context of the different landscapes and so we begin with a general examination of the incidence of enclosure in Berkshire, the amounts of land involved, and change over time.

---

[134] The evidence is reviewed and considered in Thirsk, *Agrarian History* IV, 214–18 and 239. For more specific detail on Berkshire see I. S. Leadam, *The Domesday of Inclosures* (London, 1897).

[135] For a useful chronology of enclosures see Overton, *Agricultural Revolution*, 147–53.

[136] Examples from the study area include Carswell in Buckland and Holt and Templeton in Kintbury.

[137] C. Dyer, *Everyday Life in Medieval England* (London, 1994), chapters 2 and 3.

In Berkshire as a whole 23.9 per cent of the land had been enclosed by 1600.[138] The most open parishes lay in the north of the county in the Vale of White Horse and situated close to the Midland Plain with which there were many shared characteristics. The Downs were also very open and contained extensive areas of common grazing. The parishes of the south of the county roughly from Kintbury and Inkpen, through Shaw and Bucklebury, to Pangbourne and Reading, and then Swallowfield, comprised the most highly enclosed part of the county in 1600, with on average 38.5 per cent of their lands enclosed. In the east of Berkshire there were still significant areas of open land in 1600, much of it wasteland, common grazing and common woodland, although some open field arable remained. Three small parishes were entirely enclosed by 1600, Eaton Hastings, Hatford and Tubney.[139] Wordie calculated that by 1485 18 per cent of the county was enclosed and a further 6 per cent was enclosed before 1599.[140] The most intensive period for enclosure in Berkshire occurred much later, in the nineteenth century, and was achieved mainly through Parliamentary procedures.[141] The chronology of enclosure in Berkshire was delayed in comparison with other areas of England.

The rate of enclosure in the detailed case studies supports these general conclusions, confirms the regional dimension to enclosure, and provides additional insights into the process. By 1400 both Kintbury and Shaw in the Kennet region had areas of enclosed land held in individual closes. The full extent of enclosure was often hidden within the landholding structure of the virgate. At Shaw the details of these holdings can be observed in the Survey of 1547 when,[142] for example, the customary holding of William Chalke was described as a messuage and half virgate of land[143] and was made up of four and a half acres of arable land dispersed in the common fields, four piddles of one acre each, two closes of a half acre each, one close of two acres of pasture, and twelve acres of arable held in three closes. This can be compared with the holding of John Howchyns that was also described as a messuage and half virgate of land but in his case comprised 12 acres of arable land dispersed between the three common fields of the manor and a close containing 5 acres of pasture. By 1547 large areas of the manor of Shaw, between 50 per cent and 60 per cent, had been enclosed and was typical of this area of the Kennet more generally.

---

[138] The evidence for this paragraph is largely drawn from Wordie, *Enclosure in Berkshire*, Introduction, and here specifically at xxvi.

[139] *Ibid.*, xxvi–xxvii.

[140] *Ibid.*, xxx.

[141] *Ibid.*, xxx.

[142] TNA, LR2/187.

[143] As had also been the case in 1450 when this half virgate consisted of 18 acres of land.

The process of small-scale enclosures at Kintbury continued quite briskly in the first half of the fifteenth century when tenants were prosecuted in the manor court. For example, in 1414 John Hynton made an enclosure next to his existing close that he had to account for in the manor court.[144] In 1517 Wolsey's commissioners had encountered the activities of John Houne who was reported for converting one ploughland to pasture for animals in 1506 and evicting four people. He was a wealthy tenant farmer of Kintbury Eaton, assessed at £30 in goods in 1524, and active in the parish. Was he culpable? In the context of a parish where piecemeal enclosures were an established feature of its landscape this is very difficult to establish.[145] Kintbury was moreover, a parish with a number of shrunken settlements by this time, most noticeably those of Holt and Templeton.[146]

The Berkshire Downs were predominantly used as common grazing. Nevertheless, the detailed studies revealed that these were divided, managed and regulated in diverse ways. There were large areas of common grazing at Woolstone on the Downs, but this was not unlimited as the number of animals was regulated according to the size of the arable holding.[147] By 1547, in addition to the lands of the common fields, there were a few small scattered closes and some enclosure of the demesne lands.[148] Ashbury contained an area known as 'Aysshen parke' that was wooded and separated from the other lands of the manor.[149] The rest of the manor was open with arable in the two fields, and there was common grazing for sheep on the Downs, and for cattle in the meadows below. There were very few closes on this manor and when they did occur, in case of that, for example, belonging to Thomas Horton, they were restricted and only allowed to be separate until 1 August.

The amount of enclosure varied between the case studies of the Vale. West Hanney was open; there were very few closes, the arable of the common fields was shared between the manors and Rectory of the parish, and rights of pasture were allocated in relation to the amount of arable. By contrast, in Buckland there were areas of enclosure in addition to the common lands in the large open fields of the parish, but this land amounted to only a small fraction of the

---

[144] BL, Add Roll 49220, court of 12 November 1414.
[145] Wordie calculated that by 1600 as much as 40 per cent of the lands of this parish were enclosed. Wordie, *Enclosure in Berkshire*, 97.
[146] M. W. Beresford and J. G. Hurst, 'Introduction to a First List of Deserted Medieval Village Sites in Berkshire', *Berkshire Archaeological Journal*, 60 (1962), 97. They were also investigated by the DMVRG, whose files are deposited at the National Monuments Record Centre, Swindon, who were, however, unable to identify the specific locations of the medieval settlements.
[147] TNA, LR2/187/166–169.
[148] *Ibid.*
[149] BL, Harley MS. 3961, Terrier of Glastonbury Abbey.

whole parish.[150] The commissioners of 1517 also received reports of enclosure and evictions at Buckland.[151] Four of the five men who were accused can be identified and they came from a variety of different social backgrounds. The two wealthy men were Thomas Costard who was from a family of free tenants and did not live on the manor; and Edmund Whitehill, gentleman, who was a wealthy householder and large tenant farmer of the lands of the Rectory. In comparison William Wyx and John Baker were smaller tenants of the rank of husbandman and came from families resident on the manor from at least the previous generation. There were no distinguishing characteristics common to these men except their reported enclosing activities. Beresford and Hurst included Barcote, Carswell, and Newton as deserted sites in their list.[152] Indeed, the case of violent assault at Carswell in 1465 that resulted in land lying uncultivated and the loss of 200 sheep, may have been part of the process of its desertion.[153] If enclosure was a factor in the desertion of these hamlets it was only one part of a more complex process.

The amount of enclosure in western Berkshire was influenced by region; nevertheless, within the general trends there was some degree of diversity due to local conditions; especially a lord who was willing to allow enclosure to take place, and enterprising individuals who were prepared to undertake the expense and effort of enclosure. Local circumstances or vendettas might also partially account for the reporting of certain individuals to Wolsey's commissioners at a time when others were overlooked.

An additional and associated feature in the context of the rise of the large farm was the incidence of engrossment of holdings, that is, the amalgamation of several pieces of land into one holding. This course of action might occur when tenants wanted to rationalise their dispersed lands; or, as more land became increasingly available, to join properties together and create a large farm. One of the consequences of the creation of large multiple holdings would be the requirement for labour beyond that of the family to work the farm, or even the subletting of tenancies. Landlords' attitudes towards engrossing varied as some allowed it to take place, and at the same time, others wanted to ensure the continued integrity of the landholdings of the manor

The engrossing of holdings was not a new phenomenon in 1400 as at both Kintbury and Buckland there were tenants with large multiple holdings by this date. For example at Buckland in 1405 John Sewall was holding a total of three messuages, three virgates of land, one carucate of land and fishing rights on

---

[150] Wordie estimated that no more than 15 per cent of the parish was enclosed by 1600. Wordie, *Enclosure in Berkshire*, 32.
[151] Leadam, *Domesday of Inclosures*, vol. I 129, 141–3; vol. II 518–19, 532–5.
[152] Beresford and Hurst, 'Introduction to a First List', 97.
[153] TNA, C1/27/421. For further details see chapter 5.

the Thames. A method of establishing the amount of engrossing of holdings that had taken place on a manor, and by inference the landlords' attitudes towards this type of activity, is to calculate change in the number of direct tenants holding the customary lands of the manor. The case studies provide evidence for a general decline in the number of direct tenants.[154] West Hanney is a good example of how the policies of different lords affected change. On the New College manor of Priors there had been a decline in the number of direct tenants and fall in customary rent per acre as was shown in Table 15. We have seen that on the manor of Seymours, where the number of tenants had only fallen by one, there had been a rationalisation of the allocation of pasture in the early sixteenth century. Before rationalisation the majority of landholdings had been held as standard virgates but there were several additional parcels of land of a few acres, tofts and closes. These became incorporated into the standard holdings and their rents lost. This occurred in the context of a period of high mortality in the parish, especially in 1511. Moreover, large composite holdings were not a consistent feature of Seymours. Occasionally an individual such as Francis Coggen did acquire several properties during his lifetime, but these did not survive intact after his death. This landlord was able to impose his wishes in maintaining the integrity of holdings on his manor which had a direct impact on his tenants' abilities to bring about change.

Attitudes towards the taking of sub-tenants on customary land also varied between the different lords. On many manors in England, such as those of St Albans, licences were required if a subtenant was to be taken for two years or more, and these were recorded in the manor court.[155] One presumes, therefore, that the short-term subtenancies went unrecorded. It is generally accepted that the identification of subtenants is notoriously difficult to quantify.[156] Nevertheless they comprised an important sector of local society and are worth investigating. At Shaw tenants were required to obtain a licence to take subtenants and in 1484 John Carver was commended in the proceedings of the manor court for doing this, perhaps in an attempt to encourage other tenants to do the same. Winchester College was particularly interested in the revenue-generating aspects of subtenancy. For example, Richard Person held a close of land, which was probably a chalk pit, within which he leased individual

---

[154] Buckland in 1405 there were 52 tenants and 8 properties were in the lord's hands compared with 35 tenants in 1547. Priors West Hanney there were 9 tenants in 1490 and in 1605 there were 5 tenants and an additional 2 on newly erected cottages. Seymours West Hanney there were 8 tenants in 1492 and 7 c.1600. At Kintbury there were 19 tenants in 1448 and 13 in 1522. At Shaw in 1450 there were 9 tenants and 2 properties were in the lord's hands and in 1547 there were 8 tenants. At Coleshill in 1394 there were 44 tenants, in 1424 18 tenants, and in 1520 23 tenants. Faith 'Berkshire', 152–4.

[155] M. M. Postan, *Essays on Medieval Agriculture* (Cambridge, 1973), 140–3.

[156] C. J. Harrison, 'Elizabethan Village Surveys: A Comment', *AgHRev*, 27 (1979), 82–9.

acres to men from Newbury who would pay him larger sums as rent than that paid to the lord. In total, 5 acres were transferred and 2s. 2d. paid to the College and 13s. 4d. to Richard Person. The College's interest in the matter is revealed in the records of the detailed sums of money made annually in the ministers' accounts, along with the length of each lease to the subtenants. This example also illustrates the potential economic benefits to the tenant of subletting a property, and additionally, it reveals how heavily a subtenant might be charged for a holding. The current level of economic rent was being paid by the subtenant and not necessarily by the primary tenant.

It is worth attempting to identify the prevalence of subtenancy in local society, albeit in a qualitative manner. Most of the landlords in the studies of western Berkshire allowed subtenants on their manors, but some were more overt in granting permission than others. At Shaw the conditions of the leases of both the manor and mills had specified that subtenants were forbidden and yet there were millers fined for taking excessive toll in the manor courts who were not mentioned in the accounts or leases and must have been subtenants.[157] Additional indirect evidence reveals the presence of subtenants on the customary lands of the manor. For example in the nominal returns of the 1522 Military Survey for Shaw there were 34 individuals listed of whom 19 did not hold land directly from the manor. Six of these were junior members of families; the other 13 or 38 per cent may therefore have been subtenants.[158] This was also the case in 1547 when the manorial survey listed the demesne farmer, miller and eight customary tenants, and the court rolls of 1543–46 listed nine jurors who were neither in the survey nor recorded acquiring land, and were therefore likely to have been subtenants. We cannot establish what their relationship was with the manorial lord, or how this action had been countenanced. The lands of the free tenants, however, appear to have been exempt from the restrictions on subtenancy as the construction of the fulling mill on the land of Ingram ate Moore illustrated. By contrast, on the neighbouring manor of Speenhamland subtenancies were allowed by the Despensers as they were recorded openly in the rentals of the fourteenth and fifteenth centuries.[159] At Kintbury licences were granted throughout the period to allow individuals to take subtenants on their properties and these increased in number after 1480.

The differences between the two manorial lords at West Hanney can also be observed in their treatment of subtenancy. There were subtenants at Priors but

---

[157] Between 1406 and 1500 5 millers from a total of 28 individual millers were identified in this manner.

[158] A similar situation was found at Ashbury where four customary tenants were not listed as resident in the Military Survey whilst there were 17 persons assessed who were not direct landholding tenants.

[159] Faith, 'Berkshire', 143–5.

they were not, however, found on the manor of Seymours until licences were granted from 1576.[160] A comparison of the Military Survey with the manorial records revealed that, from a total of 34 individuals there were eleven in the Survey who did not appear in the manorial records. They could either have been tenants of the third manor of Andrews, or else they were subtenants. The courts surrounding the rentals of 1490 and 1492 revealed the names of jurors who were not associated with a landholding. At Priors between 1489 and 1491 there were 14 men who were jurors and neither appeared in the rental, nor were observed taking land, in comparison at Seymours between 1491 and 1494 there were only two such men. It would appear that these men may have been subtenants and that their incidence was more common at Priors than Seymours, further emphasising the different management styles of the two lords.

The incidence of repairs to tenements can be employed as a measure of a lord's interest in the maintenance and integrity of the properties on the manor. In an era of low demand for land there with greater opportunities for the engrossing of holdings; in many cases there would have been buildings that were superfluous to the needs of the larger holding, and these could be left to decay. A lord who wished to maintain the integrity of the holdings on the manor, and his income from the properties, would attempt to ensure that the buildings were kept in good repair. The routine maintenance and repairs to customary holdings were the responsibility of the tenant, and lords objected to non-compliance.[161] Repairs to tenements were enforced through all the manor courts of this study, with increasing levels of fines for repeated non-compliance, and eventual eviction as the final sanction. For example, at Buckland John Wyke was first asked to repair his tenement in 1476 but did not; on each subsequent occasion that he was ordered to make repairs the penalty for non-compliance was doubled, rising from 3s. 4d. to £2, after which forfeiture was threatened in 1480 and 1481, and eventually he was evicted from the property in 1482. Moreover, the differences between the incidence and chronology of these events on the manors were significant as revealed in Figure 5. In particular at West Hanney the contrast between the activities of the two lords was marked. There was significantly more activity at Seymours than at Priors. Demands for repairs ceased after 1532 at Priors and 1572 at Seymours, and one might conclude that tenants were then cooperating with their lord after the choice of available tenancies had declined. At Buckland there was a general fall in activity in the sixteenth century, but repairs continued to be enforced

---

[160] Licences to take subtenants were granted three times between 1576 and 1594 at Seymours, but at Priors this occurred only once in 1599.
[161] Large timbers for repairs were provided by the lord.

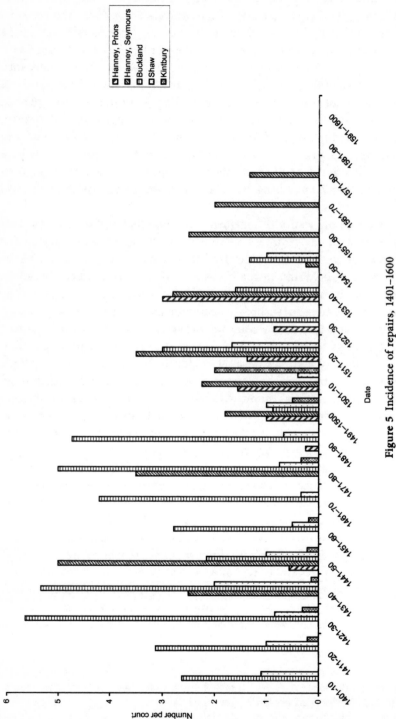

Figure 5 Incidence of repairs, 1401–1600

Source: Buckland SBT, DR5/1939–2048. Priors, Hanney NCA, 4060–4062. Seymours, Hanney BRO, D/EX1 M1–6 and Hendred House. Kintbury BL, Add Roll 49210–49284. Shaw TNA, SC2/154/52–54, 18.

with forfeiture as the final outcome in 1481, 1482 and 1537.[162] At Kintbury the incidence of cases of buildings requiring repairs actually increased in the sixteenth century, although the overall number of cases was much smaller.

To sum up this section, we have seen how the lords of the different manors varied in their attitudes towards enclosure, engrossment, subtenants, and the repair of tenements. The amount of enclosure varied between the regions and was already an established feature of the landscape by the early fifteenth century, particularly in the Kennet valley. The subsequent rate of engrossment and enclosure was affected by the lords' attitudes towards the integrity of their holdings. This is most clearly demonstrated in the comparison of the two manors at West Hanney. On the manor of Seymours the gentry lord pursued a conservative policy and attempted to maintain the integrity of holdings, suppressed engrossing, and actively enforced repairs to properties, a situation that was not happening to the same extent on the New College manor. The effects of this strategy can be seen in the tenants' reactions to these policies.[163] In particular, there was a greater take up of the properties on the New College manor that had important consequences for seigniorial income and profitability, and also the social distribution of land.

Finally, an additional feature that might affect the workings of the manor would be in those cases where the lord possessed distinctive and attractive exemptions that could be conveyed to his tenants. This was the situation pertaining to the tenants at Buckland holding lands on St John's manor that belonged to the Order of Hospitallers. This Order was entitled to certain privileges and exemptions from taxation as granted by the king and they may have been able to pass some of these benefits on to their tenants whose properties had to be identified.[164] The surviving court rolls of this manor are not as numerous as those of Duke's manor, but they do suggest that the problem of vacant tenements as cases in the court, particularly in the middle of the fifteenth century, was never a concern on this manor. Rents and entry fines were set at a similar level to those of Duke's manor. An action that was novel was the insistence by the manorial officials that tenants paint crosses on the gable ends of their tenements. General orders to this effect were made in the first court of a new reign, such as occurred at the start of Henry VI's reign and again in 1509 at the beginning of Henry VIII's reign.[165] After each general order tenants were fined for non-compliance in painting their crosses. This

---

[162] Numbers at Buckland may be a reflection of the larger number of tenements on this manor. The chronological trend, however, would not be affected by the size of manor.

[163] See chapter 5.

[164] Examples of grants and privileges in *Calendar of Charter Rolls. vol. 1, 1226–1257*, 5, 9. J. Delaville le Roulx (ed.), *Cartulaire Générad de l'Ordre des Hospitaliers de S. Jean de Jerusalem, vol. 2* (Paris, 1897), 358.

[165] SBT, DR5/1957, DR5/2017.

was a feature that has been described for town properties, such as occurred in Rochester.[166] It would appear from the evidence of Buckland that it was also the case in rural settlements, and one that continued into the sixteenth century. The marking of properties with crosses identified them as belonging to the Order and the tenants may have benefited from the privileges granted to the Hospitallers, especially exemption from various exactions.[167] If this were the case then these tenancies would have been very attractive to the inhabitants of Buckland, and might help to explain why there were no problems with empty tenements on this manor in the mid-fifteenth century.

Net income

We have demonstrated a range of different ways in which the various lords administered their manors which affected conditions for their tenants and the pace of change in a locality. We turn now to examine the rationality of these actions through a brief assessment of net income on certain manors. We have described in general terms the difficulties encountered by landowners of maintaining levels of income in the fifteenth century and the variety of experience between the different social groups.[168] Detailed studies reveal the effects of external influences on profitability at this time. For example although the Talbots were vigorous in the administration of their Whitchurch estate they could not overcome the effects of a downturn in the economy, whereas the effect of the cloth industry in Wiltshire was to strengthen the rural economy and maintain demand for land and rental income in those areas associated with production.[169] In the Berkshire manors maintaining net income was a balancing act between expenditure of effort and returns of income in the context of more general economic change. We have already observed the strategies adopted by Winchester College in the administration of their mill complex at Shaw to provide a predictable level of income in a period of economic uncertainty. Moreover, their management of the capital asset of woodland was viewed as an additional source of income that could be exploited in times of hardship. We have seen how New College pursued a

[166] C. Perkins, 'The Knights Templar in the British Isles', *EHR*, 25 (1910) 209–30, especially 218.
[167] For the effects of these privileges for the tenants of Templar properties and the similarities see Perkins, 'The Knights Templar in the British Isles', 209–30.
[168] Above, p. 126.
[169] Pollard, 'Estate Management in the Later Middle Ages', 553–66. J. N. Hare, 'The Lords and their Tenants: Conflict and Stability in Fifteenth-century Wiltshire', in B. Stapleton (ed.), *Conflict and Community in Southern England* (Stroud, 1992), and his 'Growth and Recession in the Fifteenth-century Economy: the Wiltshire Textile Industry and the Countryside', *EcHRev*, 52 (1999), 1–26.

fairly consistent strategy in the level of demands for income from the lands of their estates, particularly in comparison with the other lords.[170] They also allowed engrossing of holdings, taking of subtenants, and were less assiduous in insisting on the maintenance of properties. In chapter 5 we will observe how they suffered less from empty tenements than their neighbours on Seymours manor. It is worth considering now whether their actions were economically sound, given that we are examining a period of fluctuations in the economy, especially the slump in the middle of the fifteenth century and the inflation of the second half of the sixteenth century. One method of examining net income on a manor is through a study of the various annual accounts.

The aim of the account was to establish the state of affairs between the local official and his lord, and both parties had a personal interest in the record.[171] Assessing the net income of the manor was not the main purpose for the compilation of the document, although some lords did make these calculations.[172] The New College archive allows us to examine income on the manor of Priors West Hanney over two centuries and consider the validity of their style of administration on the manor. Two types of account are suitable for our purposes: those compiled at the centre being the College receipts and accounts that provide data for the lord's side of the relationship; and the local ministers' and bailiffs' accounts that represent the manorial officials' perspective. It is acknowledged that reading fifteenth-century accounts, whose style is formulaic, is an exercise in distinguishing between theory and reality, but parts of the account are suitable for analysis.[173] In particular the *Liberaciones denariorum* entries represent the amount of cash that the farmer and rent collector were able to collect and pay to New College in any year. It would appear that New College bursars' accounts recorded, rather than theoretical income, real sums even if they were not strictly net.[174] It is a reasonable assumption that the sums of the *Liberaciones denariorum* entries really were paid in cash to the College, even during periods when coin may have been in short supply. Although New College had agricultural property

---

[170] Above p. 143.

[171] Harvey, *Manorial Records*, 28. Also see his description of the compilation of the accounts for Cuxham, Harvey, *A Medieval Oxfordshire Village*, 10–11.

[172] Harvey, *Manorial Records*, 28–9. D. Stone, 'The Productivity of Hired and Customary Labour', *EcHRev*, 50 (1997), 640–56.

[173] Harvey references above. Dyer, *Lords and Peasants in a Changing Society*, 162 for the warning on reliability. A general introduction to medieval accounting procedures is found in N. Denholm Young, *Seigniorial Administration in England* (Oxford, 1937), chapter iv. For checks on the reeve see J. S. Drew, 'Manorial Accounts of St. Swithun's Priory, Winchester', *EHR*, 62 (1947), 20–41. For the treatment of arrears see R. R. Davies, 'Baronial Accounts, Incomes, and Arrears in the Later Middle Ages', *EcHRev*, 21 (1968), 211–29. Dyer, 'A Redistribution of Incomes in Fifteenth-century England?', 11–33.

[174] Evans and Faith, 'College Estates', 691.

within easy transportation distance, as did Merton College, it does not appear to have relied on the estates to supply the College with food but obtained provisions from the local market.[175] Payments in kind from nearby estates were sold at Oxford market, and the cash raised was then paid to New College.[176] New College was receiving its revenues from the manors as cash payments. There was a strong statistical correlation between the *Liberaciones denariorum* entries in the ministers' and bailiffs' accounts and the amount received by New College.[177]

Figure 6 charts the differences between the sums expected and the amounts actually received. A reasoned expectation of income is that which was 'Owed', calculated as the sum of the rents of the manor (there were no entries for 'decayed' rents, nor evidence of peasant resistance to paying rents) plus the court profits which included episodic items such as entry fines, heriots and the confiscated goods of felons. 'Received' income is that which should have been paid to the College and is the total *Liberacio denariorum* entries plus any items that had been allowed against the account, such as fees and building repairs. We will assume, therefore, that the sums 'Owed' and 'Received' should, in theory, be the same and that on those occasions where they differ they reflect changes in the local economy. The graph demonstrates that revenue at West Hanney was more variable in the fifteenth than sixteenth centuries. There were prolonged periods when New College did not receive its anticipated income, particularly between the accounts of 1460 and 1464, and also 1449 and 1452, and 1470 and 1472. This is evidence to support those who argue for a period of economic downturn in the middle of the century. Change occurred after 1495 when years of arrears were followed by years of additional payments, such as 1526–27. There appears to have been an economic turning point in 1495 when income from the manor changed from being an unreliable source to one of economic stability and dependable receipts.

Others have discussed the question of the treatment of arrears within manorial income, particularly in the fifteenth century.[178] Arrears were certainly a problem for New College in the fifteenth century and the Valor of its manors in 1476 shows that the most important factor in the shortfall in income was the failure of the lessee to pay their rent in full.[179] Although the carrying forward of previous arrears may have been a formal accounting procedure,

---

[175] *Ibid.*, 661.

[176] I would like to thank Dr Ros Faith for this insight into the management of New College estates, and, additionally, for all her helpful comments and advice on the Berkshire material.

[177] Spearman's rank order correlation coefficient was 0.926 and significant at the 0.05 level with 60 degrees of freedom.

[178] See above, footnote 173.

[179] Evans and Faith 'College Estates', 689.

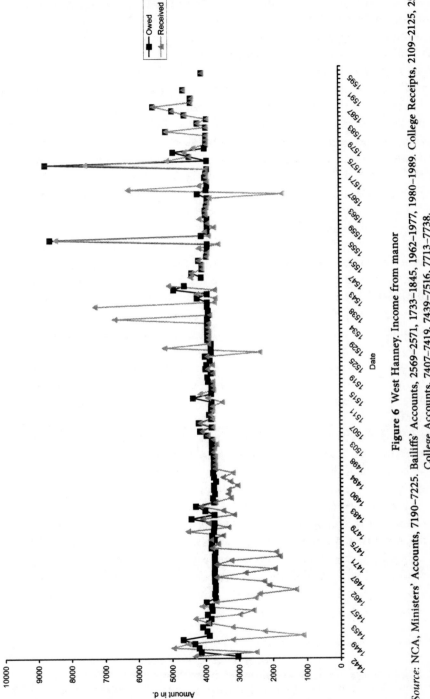

Figure 6 West Hanney. Income from manor

Source: NCA, Ministers' Accounts, 7190–7225. Bailiffs' Accounts, 2569–2571, 1733–1845, 1962–1977, 1980–1989. College Receipts, 2109–2125, 2578. College Accounts, 7407–7419, 7439–7516, 7713–7738.

New College was assiduous in following up and collecting its debts.[180] The continuation of a person's arrears could be recorded for several years without any hope of payment; for example, those of the rent collector William Benbur' continued for eighteen years. In the account of 1479 the arrears of a group of six individuals were brought together as desperate debts, and they continued to be recorded in the accounts in this manner. There was no evidence of any unwillingness on the part of the tenants to pay their rents such as occurred on the Worcester estates,[181] although there were occasions in the 1460s when two separate tenements were in the lord's hands and their *defectus* rent amounted to 11s. 4d. The terms of the lease of the demesne specified that, should the farmer amass any arrears, then the College would distrain his goods as payment, or he would be evicted. The accounts reveal that the farmers did pay off their arrears, and this could occur over several years. For example, William Gye had been the farmer of the demesne from 1443 until 1452 and continued to pay off his arrears in small sums until the account of 1465 when the rest were excused due to the benevolence of the warden and the poverty of William Gye. The rent of the demesne had been reduced after his tenancy, perhaps in recognition of the economic conditions of the time.[182] Another farmer, Henry Hopkins, had died by 1463 and it was his executors who made the subsequent payments towards the arrears until they were finally paid in full. New College may have been unable to collect its total income from this manor but it persevered in the pursuit of the payment of arrears. We can conclude that New College's management strategies were flexible given the difficulties they experienced in receiving income in the middle of the fifteenth century. As we will see in chapter 5 they did not experience as many empty tenements and difficulties in finding tenants as their neighbours. Perhaps a more permissive attitude to engrossing, maintenance and taking subtenants in association with a consistent level of rent was a sensible response when the population was low. It may not have been worth the extra effort to negotiate an increase in rents in a period of fluctuating trends in the economy generally.

Other manors in western Berkshire which have been studied do not have the same chronological coverage of documentation as those belonging to New College, but they do show some marked variations, particularly in the absence of a significant downturn in receipts in the middle of the fifteenth century. The chronological pattern of change was rather different on Winchester College's

---

[180] West Hanney was in line with other New College manors where debts could go back over 50 years. Evans and Faith, 'College Estates', 690

[181] Dyer, *Lords and Peasants in a Changing Society*, 180–2.

[182] New College had reduced the rent on other manors in the fifteenth century. Evans and Faith, 'College Estates', 681.

manor of Shaw just outside Newbury.[183] Receipts from the manor of Shaw in Figure 7 reveal a more dependable source of income throughout the period 1401–1528. There were, however, more fluctuations in the sums received from the mills shown in Figure 8, and the period 1439–59 was a lean time when even a reduction in rent did not ensure full payment by the lessees. After this date receipts from the mills became a more dependable source of income. A similar analysis of the accounts for the manor of the prioress of Nuneaton at Kintbury, also in the Kennet valley, Figure 9, although for a shorter period, 1406–50, reveal a fairly reliable receipt of the income generated from the manor, apart from the short period between 1428 and 1433.[184] Profitability on St Swithun's manor of Woolstone situated in the Downs, Figure 10, is more difficult to discern due to the fragmentation of the archive, especially the gap between 1437 and 1457, and in 1463 after the farmer had absconded with the demesne stock. Nevertheless, the general impression is one of a fairly dependable level of manorial receipts for period from 1414 to 1477, with perhaps some decline in total income after 1463.

To sum up, we have seen how different landlords adopted a variety of administrative strategies in the management of their estates, and had correspondingly different attitudes towards net income. This affected the conditions under which tenants held their lands and pursued their own economic activities. Furthermore, the underlying conditions in the regional economies had an additional impact on the income from the manors studied. In particular, the more general economic problems of the mid-fifteenth century were not felt as acutely in the Kennet valley or Downs as in the Vale. The management of estates and profitability provide only one element in determining the pace of economic change in a locality and must be taken in conjunction with other factors.

Conclusion

It has been possible to identify several contrasting aspects of the administrative regimes of the different lords in the study area. It has been shown that there were variations in the amount of active involvement in the running of the manors and that the gentry families who were resident in the locality pursued a personal and direct approach to management. In contrast, New College and Winchester College relied on the regular pattern of visits as opportunities to

---

[183] The peaks in Figure 7 are the result of major repairs to mill and construction of new sheepfold in 1415, and the re-roofing of the grange in 1459 which were recorded in the ministers' accounts.

[184] Figures 9 and 10 for Kintbury and Woolstone are only based on a study of the ministers' accounts.

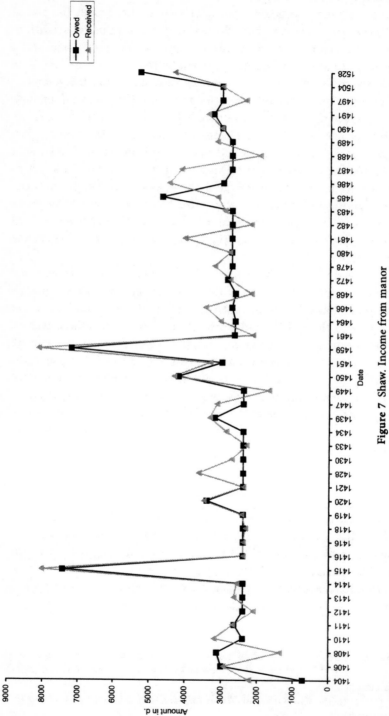

Figure 7 Shaw. Income from manor

Sources for both graphs for Shaw WCM, Bursars' Accounts, 22100–22200. Ministers' Accounts, BRO, D/ENmM12–55 and Newbury Museum for 1461–62 and 1466–67. Previously published in M. Yates, 'Change and continuities in rural society from the later middle ages to the sixteenth century: the contribution of west Berkshire', *EcHRev* 52 (1999), figures 4 and 5; reprinted by the kind permission of the publishers.

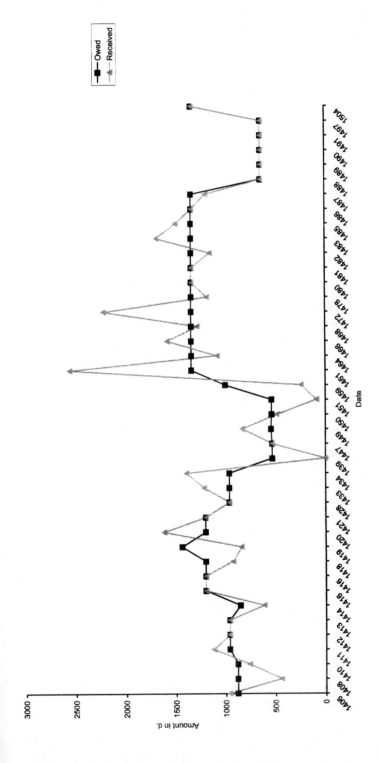

Figure 8 Shaw. Income from mills

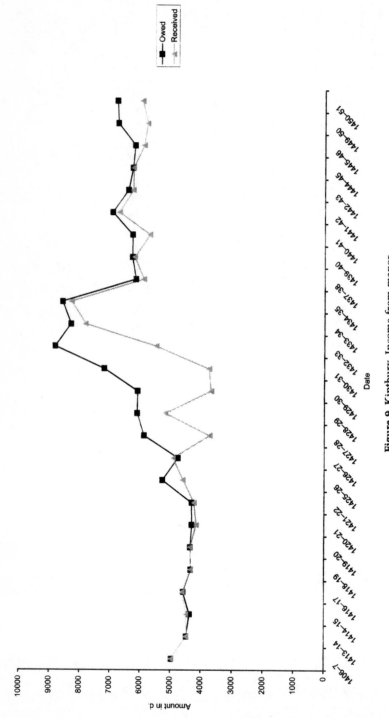

Figure 9 Kintbury. Income from manor

Sources: Ministers' accounts BL, Add Roll 49266–49284, 49236.

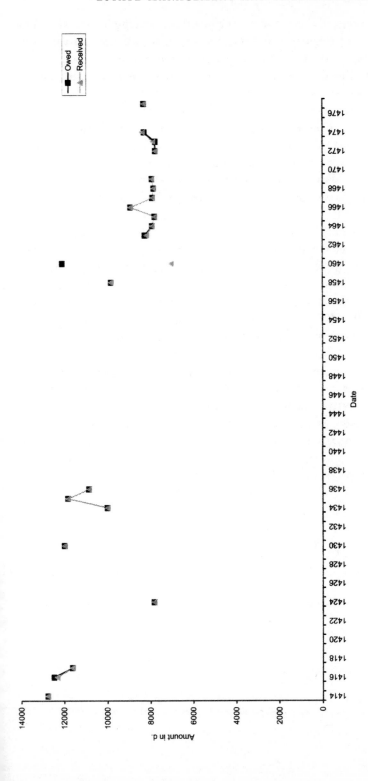

Figure 10 Woolstone. Income from manor
Sources: Ministers' accounts TNA, SC6/758/2–12, 14–25.

oversee the workings of their manors. Income from the manors was always an important aspect of seigniorial revenue and one that came from a variety of sources, including land, the natural resources of the manor and the profits of the manor court. The methods by which income was managed varied between the lords. The cost of land to the tenant also differed between the manors, even when they lay in the same parish and common fields. In addition to the management of income, lords pursued different policies in the treatment of engrossment, enclosure, and the maintenance of tenements. These had a direct impact on the pace of change in a locality as on those occasions where engrossing was not allowed and buildings had to be kept in good repair, there were consequently fewer opportunities for tenants to take advantage of the more general conditions of the period. Nevertheless we have also seen how the less proactive policies of New College and Winchester College did not necessarily result in a decline in revenue. Net income was maintained through the interaction of various forces including the management strategies adopted by the lord, and was partly shaped by the underlying economic conditions of the period and regional differences. It has been possible to show the various ways in which the different administrative practices of the manorial lords influenced the nature and pace of change in a locality. Nevertheless, a new landlord could not instigate change in the cost of land immediately; the underlying institutions of custom and tenure appear to have had a modifying influence. In the next chapter we will examine the tenants' reactions to these different administrative strategies of the lords by considering the ways in which tenancies were taken, and the numbers of holdings that lay vacant and in the lords' hands with a corresponding reduction in seigniorial income. The focus therefore shifts now to the tenants' perspective, and we examine the role of the individual in determining the nature of change.

CHAPTER 5

Tenant Society

Introduction

The main objective of this chapter is to examine the social and economic events of the fifteenth and sixteenth centuries from the tenants' view-point. Tenant society in western Berkshire was the dynamic element in the process of change. These were the people who took up the tenancies, paid the rents and entry fines, worked the land, and traded across most of southern England, and as far away as Calais and Antwerp in some instances. They also operated within the more general, and often restrictive, economic conditions of the period. Nevertheless, we will argue that they remained the proactive force in shaping the nature of change in a locality.

We noted previously how a number of generalisations have been made about changes in society between the fifteenth and sixteenth centuries that require examining in the light of detailed case studies now and present the evidence from western Berkshire. We need to establish whether, in the words of J. E. Thorold Rogers, 'The fifteenth century, and the early years of the sixteenth, were the golden age of the English husbandman, the artisan, and the labourer'.[1] To what extent were tenants free to innovate and can we observe the activities of entrepreneurs? Furthermore, did conditions deteriorate for the small farmer over the sixteenth century? Was access to land reduced, and can we discern a rise in wage labour? By 1600 were there fundamental differences in society from what had gone before?

Tenant society is studied here in some detail as the final contributing factor in determining the pace of change in western Berkshire. This will be achieved by examining the role of tenants in the management of customary landholdings, and the results of their actions will be observed in the changing distribution of land and wealth. We cannot fully appreciate these changes without understanding the diverse nature of rural society both within individual

[1] J. E. Thorold Rogers, *A History of Agriculture and Prices in England, 1259–1793*, vol. IV (Oxford, 1866–1902), 23.

villages and between the regions, and each of the constituent social groups will be examined in some detail for evidence of both continuity and change. Finally, there were inherent tensions within these communities, especially at times of rapid social change, and we end with an examination of the regulation of local society.

Changes to customary landholdings in western Berkshire.

As we have seen, the mid-fifteenth century has traditionally been portrayed as a time of low population, empty tenements, decline in income from rents, and an increase in the availability of land for the tenants. In contrast, the second half of the sixteenth century was a period of rising population, inflation, a proliferation in the number of large farms associated with a growing demand for small affordable landholdings, and an increasing reliance on income from wages. We saw in chapter 4 how the various lords in western Berkshire reacted differently to the changing conditions of the period. Were the different policies of the lords reflected in the occupancy of their tenements? In other words, did tenants exercise their freedom of choice and take the relatively unencumbered and less expensive properties in preference to those of a more restrictive lord? Did the changes to conditions of tenure result in the impoverishment of certain sectors of society by the end of the sixteenth century? These questions have implications for the pace of change in a locality, and the opportunities for tenants to profit from their landholdings. We will see how tenants responded to both the changing conditions of the time, and to their own individual needs. This is particularly discernible in the analysis of customary landholdings.

Customary landholdings formed a major category of the lands of the manor that were available to tenants and are therefore ideal for this type of investigation.[2] In western Berkshire customary land was usually held in standardised units of a yardland or virgate that were usually transferred in their entirety. They could be amalgamated with other lands to make a larger holding, but were rarely broken up into smaller units. As we saw in the last chapter the number of direct customary tenants fell, with a corresponding increase in the size of farms, although this was not a universal feature as the lords of Seymours in Hanney strove to retain the integrity of their landholdings. There was little evidence for a market in small parcels of land consisting of a few acres as occurred in eastern England, or of any adjustment to the size of the holding during the lifetime of the tenant.[3] It may have been happening on

[2] See chapter 4, p. 135.
[3] See the detailed discussion of the land market below, p. 181. For a comparison between the two regions of the different types of tenure and land markets see J. Whittle and M. Yates "*Pays Réel* or *Pays Légal*"? The Contrasting Patterns of Land Tenure and Social

an informal basis for short periods of time and was therefore not recorded in the manor court. One would presume that it would have been necessary for a widow with a large holding to make some sort of provision, albeit to employ additional labour to work her holding. We are left with the impression that accommodating this type of necessity was occurring outside the formal proceeding of the manor court. One can safely assume, however, that if there had been long-term implications for seigniorial income, then records of these transactions would have appeared in the manorial documentation.

Table 16 *Summary data relating to land transfers, 1401–1600*
(Full data in Appendix IV, Table 23)

Place	Total number of courts	Total number of land transfers	One way	Transfer to family	Transfer no relationship specified	Reversions
Priors, Hanney	54	68	32	20	16	1
Seymours, Hanney	48	80	56	11	13	2
Buckland	146	277	191	48	38	8
Shaw	71	111	50	22	38	0
Kintbury	150	116	50	44	22	14

Note: Explanations for the significance of the different types of transfer are found in the text.
Sources: Buckland SBT, DR5/1939–2048. Priors, Hanney NCA, 4060–4062. Seymours, Hanney BRO, D/EX1 M1–6 and Hendred House. Kintbury BL, Add Roll 49210–49284. Shaw TNA, SC2/154/52–54, 18.

We will now examine the rate of take-up and turnover of properties to discern the tenants' reactions to the policies of the different landlords described in chapter 4. The actual rate of transfer of properties did vary between the manors; for example, at Priors in Hanney on average every 17.67 years, Seymours in Hanney every 15.23 years, and at Shaw every 10 years. Meanwhile, Faith identified a more rapid transfer of properties on the manors that she studied in Berkshire.[4] The numbers of transfers of land in the manor courts may not have been very great, but there are discernible chronological trends that can be observed in the full data presented in Appendix IV. At Seymours the total number of transfers increased in the second half of the sixteenth century and coincided with the payments of large entry fines for the lands. At Hanney

Structure in Eastern Norfolk and Western Berkshire, 1450–1600', *AgHRev*, 48 (2000), 1–26.
[4] For example, a villein holding could change hands five times in as many years. R. Faith 'Berkshire: Fourteenth and Fifteenth Centuries', in P. D. A. Harvey (ed.), *The Peasant Land Market in Medieval England* (Oxford, 1984), 119–20.

there was an increased number of *post mortem* transfers at Seymours in 1511 and in the 1520s at Priors following a period of high mortality. At Buckland the period from 1470 to 1520 witnessed a marked decline in activity, especially in the 1510s.[5] At Shaw there was a peak in the total number of transfers in the 1430s, but a more marked fall in their numbers in the sixteenth century. The latter may be a reflection of the decline in the number of direct tenants and increased size of holdings. In comparison, there was a lower level of activity at Kintbury than elsewhere. Tenants, therefore, were reacting to the different conditions on the manors.

A marked feature of the pattern of land transfers in western Berkshire was the number of occasions when land resided in the lords' hands rather than being a direct transfer between two tenants. During this time it is assumed that the land remained unoccupied. This type of incident has important implications for seigniorial revenue and, albeit indirectly, demonstrates the changing relationship between lords and tenants. The transfer of land emphasised the superior role of the lord in the transaction as the acts of surrender and admittance to each holding were formal and public demonstrations of the lord's role as the major landowner, and he took the opportunity to levy a fine for the transaction. Those cases where the land remained in the lords' hands are classified in Table 16 as 'One way'. When combined with the records of empty tenements lying 'in the lord's hands', they reveal a pattern of low take-up of holdings. Of note is the difference between the two lords of Hanney. There was a significantly greater incidence of this type of event occurring on the gentry manor, and a decline in their numbers after 1520. One might infer that tenants were choosing the cheaper and less restrictive tenancies of the New College manor. At a time when tenants could pick and choose their landholdings and landlord these decisions had important implications for seigniorial revenue. Once there was greater pressure on holdings in the second half of the sixteenth century, options were more limited, and there was full occupancy on both manors. At Buckland there was a decline in these one-way transfers after 1470. Nevertheless, one-way transfers and land lying in the lords' hands were not a feature of the manor of St John's Buckland. At Shaw they did not occur in the sixteenth century. They were never a marked feature on the manor at Kintbury. Therefore, the effect of tenants' reaction to the policies of the various lords is observed in the occupation of tenancies.

An alternative strategy may have been adopted during periods when both lords and tenants were willing to have properties taken on an informal basis. This was probably happening on the Bishop of Winchester's estates in the

---

[5] The significance of this is discussed below when considering the informal nature of land transactions at the time.

late fourteenth century.[6] Titow described a situation whereby a property was handed over to an individual who could pay a rent, but only until another person came forward who was willing to hold it by ancient custom. The land remained cultivated, the lord received at least some income from the property, but the arrangement was not formally recognised in the manor court. At Seymours in 1435 a messuage and four acres of land were granted to Thomas Crippe *quousque melior tenens advenerit* for a rent of 4s. 6d. and no entry fine.[7] The next year the lord seized the property because the rent had not been paid. At Buckland there appears to have been a period of informality in the take-up of land between about 1470 and 1520, and especially in the 1510s.[8] The holdings were still filled as there were no recorded cases of empty tenements in the courts, and buildings were still having to be maintained. A fairly typical example of the number of informal tenancies of a property is the cottage which had been held by Thomas Brasyer and which was in the lord's hands in 1466; the next year it was given to John Porter for the year at the full rent of 4s.; and two years later John Porter was still holding it on probation. The cottage was subsequently held by William Walter until it reverted back into the lord's hands. In 1479 it was let for a year to John Floodgate and he was still holding it in 1483 with other properties. There were no official records of these transactions or any mention of the payment of an entry fine. Yet, for some unknown reason, the situation changed after 1520 when tenants once again paid entry fines and received a formal copy of the land transfer from the manor court roll. The irregular nature of tenure may have been a temporary measure to meet the needs of a particular economic and demographic situation. We should be aware, therefore, that the absence of a formal record in the court roll may mask the true state of occupancy of the tenements of the manor.

In contrast to this informality there were other occasions when tenants renewed their tenancies at the end of the three lives for which customary tenures were normally held,[9] or they arranged a reversion of the tenancy to another party. They often paid a heavy entry fine for these forms of transaction, and one presumes actively chose to do so. The payment of a large sum of money for the transaction would suggest that there was pressure on landholdings, or alternatively, that these were attractive tenancies and worth retaining. At Kintbury in the first half of the fifteenth century cases of renewals or reversions occurred as 20 per cent of all transactions, that is, 14 cases out of a total of 71 transfers. Three transfers were renewals to other members of the Wallrond family; the

[6] J. Titow, 'Lost Rents, Vacant Holdings and the Contraction of Peasant Cultivation after the Black Death', *AgHRev*, 42 (1994), 97–114.
[7] BRO, D/EX1 M1/1, court 20 April 1435.
[8] At Kintbury this type of incident occurred during the 1490s.
[9] See chapter 4, p. 142, on the conditions of customary tenure.

remaining eleven holdings passed as reversions to individuals where there was no family relationship discernible. These reversions appear to have been the result of previous peasant agreements which were subsequently formalised in the courts, and may be indirect of evidence of inter-peasant sales.[10] The current tenant would appear in court, confirm the manner in which he held the land, and agree to the transfer. The new tenant would pay the, often large, entry fine for the holding, but would not enter the property until the current tenant had died.[11] On that occasion the new tenant would come to court and confirm the previous transfer and no further monies were required from him to enter the property. At Hanney and Buckland the reversions in the second half of the sixteenth century were by the third life (usually family members) renewing or extending the tenancy for another three lives. They were prepared to pay heavily for the extension of their tenure, for example at Buckland between 1586 to 1595 £28 for a messuage with one virgate of land and an annual rent of 15s., or £40 for a messuage with two virgates of land and an annual rent of £1 3s. od., or £60 for a messuage, two virgates, fishing rights, and closes of land that rendered an annual rent of £3 10s. 3d. These were large sums of money and probably also reflected the possession of certain additional features of a property, such as the fishing rights. The ability to obtain a renewal or reversion on a property was obviously considered a valuable asset and one for which it was worth paying a large sum of money. It is also indirect evidence of pressure on landholdings, as at Kintbury in the first half of the fifteenth century, and at Buckland and Hanney at the end of the sixteenth century.

Individual tenants were able to maximise their opportunities by selecting lands from the different manors. The ability to observe the tenurial situation at Hanney enables us to identify those tenants who were building portfolios of lands for themselves from the different manors of the parish. This activity has also to be viewed in the wider context of the engrossment of holdings discussed in chapter 4. It is significant that this type of activity was usually associated with the larger tenants such as Richard Burymill. He took a customary holding from Seymours in 1438, another in 1441, and in 1445 he became the lessee of the demesne lands of the manor. In the same year he was non-resident on his two customary holdings at Priors and was perhaps letting them to subtenants. Local manorial lords also engaged in the activity of taking lands from several manors. For example Thomas Yate who held the manor of Andrews Court in Hanney in the sixteenth century was a large freehold tenant of Priors and held a smaller property at Seymours. Thus there was potential for individuals to exploit the local tenurial situation to their own advantage, and there were

[10] See pp. 181–2 for peasant land market and associated references.
[11] For example 40 shillings for a messuage and virgate of land and another 10 acres of land, although more usually the fine was levied at the rate of a mark or half mark.

a number of enterprising people who took advantage of these openings and increased the size of their landholdings. We will see below how this had important implications for changes to the social distribution of land over the fifteenth and sixteenth centuries.

The evidence presented in chapter 4 on the cost of land and the decline in the numbers of direct tenants, combined with the data in Appendix IV, Table 23, on the take-up of landholdings, reveal certain trends that have chronological significance and these need drawing together. The lords in the Vale appear to have had difficulties in finding tenants in the middle of the fifteenth century. This was particularly the case on the gentry manor of Seymours in Hanney. At Buckland there was a period of informal tenure at the end of the fifteenth and early sixteenth centuries that may have been the result of a strategy for maintaining some income from the lands.[12] The problem of empty tenements was not a major feature of the Kennet valley on the manors studied. Furthermore, individual tenants were able to take advantage of a variety of different opportunities for amassing lands. At Hanney, in particular, they appear to have preferred the lands of New College. In the changed conditions of the second half of the sixteenth century the tenements of the different lords were fully occupied, many tenants were charged large sums as entry fines for the properties, and tenants were also paying to extend their tenancies. Yet it should be noted that entry fines remained fairly constant on the manor belonging to New College. There was evidence that some engrossment of holdings and enclosure had already taken place on certain lands before 1400, and enclosure was a particular feature of the lands in the Kennet valley. On those manors where engrossment of properties had been tolerated by the lord this resulted in a decline in the number of direct customary tenants. Some individuals were building up portfolios of land from the different manors. By the end of the sixteenth century there were, in general, fewer tenants holding larger properties in western Berkshire. The total cost of customary land to the tenant had, with one exception, increased dramatically, particularly on smaller properties and cottages. This had been achieved through a combination of landlord policy and proactive tenants, and the end result was fewer tenants holding a greater proportion of land as larger properties.

Was there a land market and did money change hands? There is some discussion among historians concerning whether money or resources actually passed between individuals, and in particular, the relative significance of the economic obligations of transfers between family members, such as payments of maintenance for widows, or dowries for younger siblings; as opposed to those

---

[12] It should be remembered that empty tenements were not an item in the court rolls of the manor of St John's Buckland.

transfers which are more directly identifiable as sales.[13] There were certainly transfers of land that were not market-orientated. Nevertheless, the payment of money or resources is a distinction that is useful in any analysis of the land market. 'Market' implies the sale of property, and no evidence for Berkshire was found of sums of money passing between individual tenants with the transfer of land as was the case in Norfolk.[14] The cases of reversions of tenancies discussed above for Kintbury do suggest some form of private transaction between individuals undertaken outside the manor court. The number of transfers per court in western Berkshire was never very great, although they did have chronological significance. The role of the lord, as seen in the number of one-way transfers, was important. A land market in a purely commercial sense is not discernible from the records of the manors studied. Rather, it might be more appropriate to think in terms of the relationship between the persons transferring land, whether direct family members or others where the relationship was not specified. We need to consider the relative significance of the family and its landholding and how this changed over time.

Much ink has been expended on debating the existence and longevity of the attachment that families had to a specific landholding, often referred to as the 'family-land bond'.[15] The notion, as Faith described it, of 'keeping the name on the land ... An established holding ought to descend in the blood of the men who had held it of old,"[16] may have been fairly widespread among English peasants before the Black Death, but was broken at some point in the fourteenth or fifteenth centuries.[17] The reasons given for this perceived shift are various and include changes in demand for land as the population fell after the Black Death, migration of family members away from the manor, or, indeed, that it had never existed as medieval tenants were self-optimising

[13] Harvey, Peasant Land Market. For a full discussion of the subject and data from Norfolk see J. Whittle, The Development of Agrarian Capitalism (Oxford, 2000), 86–177. A summary of the debate can also be found in R. W. Hoyle, 'Land and Landed Relations in Craven, Yorkshire, c.1520–1600', D.Phil. thesis, Oxford (1986), 92–4.

[14] Whittle, Development of Agrarian Capitalism, 110–19.

[15] For a summary of the key aspects of family, land and inheritance see Whittle, Development of Agrarian Capitalism, 86–100.

[16] R. Faith, 'Peasant Families and Inheritance Customs in Medieval England', AgHRev, 14 (1966), 77–95.

[17] Smith summarises the various aspects of the relationship between family and land in his introduction to R. M. Smith (ed.), Land, Kinship and Life-Cycle (Cambridge, 1984). Faith and Lomas suggest that the bond was broken by the Black Death in Harvey, Peasant Land Market, 106–77, 253–327. Razi identified the erosion of the family-land bond as occurring between 1431 and 1500 in association with a corresponding fall in the survival rate of peasant families at Halesowen and fall in kin density on the manor in Z. Razi, 'The Myth of the Immutable English Family', Past and Present, 140 (1993), 28–33, 43.

individuals and market orientated in their treatment of land.[18] An additional feature of the late fourteenth and fifteenth centuries was the instability of larger landholdings. There was a tendency for large peasant landholdings which had been built up over several generations to fragment and pass out of the family, as Faith found in her study of Berkshire.[19] The situation was subsequently reversed as, under the very different demographic, economic and tenurial conditions of the sixteenth century, it has been shown that there was an increasing tendency for tenants to remain on their lands for several generations.[20] The following discussion of the evidence presented in Table 16[21] will reveal a high level of choice exerted by the tenants in their selection of land, one that was conditioned as much by the availability and cost of land, as any notion of an emotional attachment to a specific holding.

One cannot ascertain in western Berkshire whether sums of money passed between tenants on the transfer of a property either as an inter-peasant sale, or in provision for any family members who gave up a tenancy, since they were not recorded in the manor court rolls. Nevertheless, we have to acknowledge that payment may have been occurring away from the manor court. On the manors studied in detail there were noticeable differences between the numbers transferring to family compared to non-family members. In Hanney on Priors manor there was a higher incidence of family transfers (20:16) compared with Seymours manor (11:13), and perhaps a greater incidence of non-family transfers at the end of the sixteenth century at Seymours. At Buckland there were more family transfers (48:38) with a marked increase at the end of the sixteenth century. At Kintbury, where the evidence survives only for the fifteenth century, the number going to family members was double those where there was no relationship specified (44:22). In contrast, Shaw was different as there were more non-family transfers (22:38), perhaps influenced

---

[18] The latter argument was put forward in A. Macfarlane, *The Origins of English Individualism* (Oxford, 1978). This has subsequently been countered by Whittle, who compares the land markets of 'East Anglia' and the 'Midlands' and demonstrates that a tenant's relationship with a specific holding was influenced by many more and competing factors than Macfarlane suggested. J. Whittle, 'Individualism and the Family-Land Bond: A Reassessment of Land Transfer Patterns Among the English Peasantry', *Past and Present*, 160 (1998), 25–63.

[19] Faith, 'Berkshire', 167–8. C. Dyer, 'Changes in the Size of Peasant Holdings in Some West Midland Villages, 1400–1540', in R. M. Smith (ed.), *Land, Kinship and Life Cycle* (Cambridge, 1984), 283–93.

[20] Dyer, 'Changes in the Size of Peasant Holdings', 282–94. Whittle, *Development of Agrarian Capitalism*, 100–10.

[21] Family where the relationship was specified and includes widows. This strict definition omits those with the same surnames unless the relationship was given. But as customary tenure was for three lives, usually named, the family relationship was normally specified.

by proximity to Newbury.[22] It would appear that, in general, when the demand for landholdings was high families tended to retain their holdings, although this did not happen at Seymours. At Kintbury there was a lower incidence of one-way transfers and empty tenements, and one might infer that these were attractive tenancies, or alternatively, that there was pressure on landholdings for most of the fifteenth century.[23]

Aggregate data, even at the level of the individual manor, tend to flatten the variety of experience and reduce our ability to observe the ways in which individual tenants were exercising their freedom to choose when taking landholdings, and whether there was any family association with a particular property. For example at Shaw, as elsewhere, an analysis of specific families was undertaken where the particularities of change were found to have been more complex. Two cases can usefully illustrate this point. The free lands of the Fox family had been passed from father to son for three generations by 1442 when Thomas Fox took additional customary lands which he added to the family holding, and later became farmer of the demesne lands of the manor.[24] By 1461 he held approximately half of the available land of the manor. His landholdings were exceptional in size. On his death in 1485 his son did not take up these holdings, but came into court and alienated the free holding to Richard Bedford, and the customary lands went to other non-family persons, although Thomas had been named as the third life. The Fox family had held a large amount of land, some with a strong family tie but, for some unknown reason, the son and heir had not wished to take the properties. Yet this situation can be compared with that of the Person family at Shaw who remained on their holding throughout the two centuries of this study. These examples reveal the diversity of experience, even within one manor, that was the result of individuals exercising their freedom of choice.

One group who did remain consistently on the property were widows. Wives were usually recorded as the second life on the tenancy, and attended the manor court on the death of their husband to be formally recognised as the tenant of the property. The conditions under which they held the property usually stipulated that they should not remarry, but remain chaste and single.[25] Nevertheless, permission to remarry could be obtained in the manor court. For example, at Buckland in 1426 John Lynby paid 13s. 4d. for

---

[22] Discussed below, p. 189.

[23] The latter may be the more appropriate explanation given the incidence of cases of ancient demesne discussed later in this chapter.

[24] For a more detailed description of the lands of this family see M. Yates 'Continuity and Change, in Rural Society, c.1400–1600: West Hanney and Shaw (Berkshire) and Their Region', D.Phil. thesis, Oxford (1997), 248–50.

[25] This was not a universal feature away from the study area; for example, at Long Wittenham, widows could remarry. B. Todd, 'Freebench and Free Enterprise: Widows

permission to marry Alice, the widow of John Hyche, and enter her property of a messuage with half virgate of land and fishing rights.[26] During the time that a widow was the tenant of a property she had to maintain the premises, and widows were frequently fined for not making the necessary repairs to their buildings. In the sixteenth century many of their probate inventories contained farming implements, sheep and cattle that suggest their continued and active involvement in husbandry during their widowhood. For example, Annes Stanbroke of Shaw was obviously held in high regard by her husband Thomas who in his will made her sole executrix, and left instructions to her that included, 'and bestowe of our goods and cattle upon our natural children according to her good and motherly discrecione as god shall put in her myne'.[27] Annes died in 1588 and in her inventory, valued at £27, there were seven acres of winter wheat growing in the fields in addition to the rye, maslin, wheat and barley in the barn, which together suggest that she had continued to cultivate the holding during her widowhood.[28] Another example of a widow from Shaw was Isabella Bullford, who was active as a miller after her husband's death. She was the widow of John Bullford and renewed the lease of the mills in 1447, including the additional fulling mill, and actively continued to operate as a miller until 1449 when she remarried Roger Coryngdon who subsequently became the miller.[29] Widows might also act as court jurors on specific occasions, for example at Hanney in 1511, 1520, 1545 and 1587, during periods of high mortality, when their role as manorial officials was probably related to their tenure of a particular holding. Nevertheless, on those occasions when a widow did not continue to cultivate the holding she might be provided with some form of maintenance while her son entered the property during her lifetime. For example, at Seymours in Hanney, Thomas Donnesdon employed the manor court to record the agreement between himself and his mother Jane that he would provide her with food and lodging in the house, and the payment of £2 a year for the rest of her lifetime.[30] On other occasions husbands would make provision in their wills for the maintenance of their wives during their widowhood. For example John Cole of Ashbury in 1561 ordered his brother Richard 'too governe & honestly kepe my wife during her wedowhed & my children tyll theyr maryete & he to have for hys paynes the leace & right of

and their Property in Two Berkshire Villages', in J. Chartres and D. Hey (eds), *English Rural Society, 1500–1800* (Cambridge, 1990), 175–200.

[26] SBT, DR5/1961, court of 14 October 1426.

[27] BRO, D/A1/115/71, will of Thomas Stanbroke 1570.

[28] BRO, D/A1/116/6A, will and inventory of Annis Stanbrooke 1588.

[29] During the years of her widowhood between 1446 and 1449 she appeared in the ministers' accounts as the miller who paid the rents and fulfilled her obligations.

[30] BRO, D/EX1/M6, court of 10 October 1594.

my farme'.[31] Once again, we have observed individuals, in this case widows and their families, making arrangements concerning their landholdings that were unique and appropriate to their particular circumstances.

For further insights into the family's association with a particular holding we can expand this investigation and consider the mobility of the population more generally and how this changed over time. The fifteenth century has been characterised as a period of increased peasant mobility; in fact, in some villages three-quarters of families changed every 50 years.[32] The increase in population previously identified in the Kennet region in chapter 2 may have been fuelled by migration into the area and the figures for the introduction of new surnames on the manors further supports this assertion. A number of reasons lie behind this mobility, as peasants moved to towns or other rural areas at a time of increased employment opportunities and availability of landholdings. An examination of the number of new surnames on a manor has important implications for understanding migration into an area or, conversely, the underlying stability of the population. At Hanney the highest increase in the numbers of new surnames was in the period 1451 to 1500, and there was a total absence of new surnames after 1551.[33] Within the broader trends there was a more rapid turnover of population at Seymours from 1470 to 1520 and at Priors from the late 1480s to around 1515 and again in 1525. This may be explained by the coincidence with periods of high levels of mortality that have already been mentioned. The stability of the population after 1550 is of particular note. At Shaw there was an increasing tendency for families to remain on their holdings after 1450, which was a century earlier than at Hanney.[34] At Kintbury, also within the Kennet region, the influx of new surnames dwindled rapidly after 1450, apart from a peak in the 1490s.[35] People were on the move in search of employment and other tenancies to those of the family and, through a study of surnames we are able to glimpse the mobility of the population in the fifteenth century. There does appear to have been an increasing tendency for families to remain on their holdings in the sixteenth century. This was a time when property was more expensive to enter, and we have observed instances where families who could afford to, were renewing their tenancies, often with considerable financial outlay. Demand

---

[31] BRO, D/A1/51/180.

[32] C Dyer, *Making a Living in the Middle Ages* (New Haven, 2002), 354.

[33] There are methodological difficulties after 1551 due to the uneven survival of the documentation discussed in Appendix III, but the trend remains the same. Data of new surnames from both manors: 1401–50 – 43; 1451–1500 – 62; 1501–50 – 52; 1551–1600 – 0.

[34] New surnames at Shaw: 1405–50 – 43; 1451–1500 – 19; 1501–47 – 15.

[35] New surnames at Kintbury: 1410–19 – 64; 1420–29 – 44; 1430–39 – 25; 1440–49 – 21; 1450–59 – 9; 1460–69 – 12; 1470–79 – 12; 1480–89 – 2; 1490–99 – 27; 1500 – 4.

may have been outstripping supply, and, under these conditions, tenants were concerned to hold onto property and keep it in the family.[36] This study of the family's association with land has revealed the wide variety of choices that were available to tenants, how these changed over time, and the different strategies that were adopted by individuals to meet their specific needs. Whether this was an emotional or pragmatic response we cannot establish. What we have seen, however, were tenants as an essential element in the process of bringing about change in an area.

Social distribution of land and wealth

We have observed how the number of direct customary tenants declined with a corresponding increase in the size of farms, and how some tenants were proactive in taking advantage of opportunities to increase the size of their landholdings. We now need to consider the effects of these changes. In particular, were some tenants getting rich at the expense of others, and was there a polarisation of wealth in the sixteenth century? In chapter 2 we saw how the social distribution of assessed taxable wealth differed between the sub-regions of western Berkshire both in the fourteenth and sixteenth centuries. In this section we extend the investigation by examining in more detail the distribution of land and wealth. We will employ the evidence from fiscal, manorial and probate sources for three case studies from the regions of western Berkshire: West Hanney, Shaw, and Ashbury; and, to a lesser extent, it is possible to consider Buckland and Kintbury. These will create a framework for understanding social change before embarking on an examination of the different sectors of society. A detailed comparison of those recorded in the fiscal records with their manorial landholdings overcomes the partial nature of the sources and, in particular, the Military Survey exposes a social group who were not found in association with a landholding. The results reveal marked differences between the regions at the level of the individual community that strengthens our understanding of the nature of regional variations in local society. Nevertheless, the farmers of the demesnes across western Berkshire remained a constant feature of local society as they dominated the distribution of land, and were consistently wealthy individuals.

[36] For a similar pattern in Norfolk see Whittle and Yates, *"Pays Réel* or *Pays Légal"?',* 15–17.

Table 17 *The percentage of men of western Berkshire in different categories of wealth, as indicated by assessment on movable goods in 1522.*

Place	<£1	£1–<2	Subtotal	£2–<5	£5–<10	£10–<20	£20–<50	£50+	Total number of individuals
Ashbury	11.1	33.3	44.4	33.3	11.1	7.4	3.7	0	27
Buckland	15.4	26.9	42.3	34.6	17.3	1.9	3.8	0	52
Hanney	2.9	23.5	26.4	55.9	5.9	5.9	2.9	2.9	34
Kintbury	4.5	35.2	39.7	35.2	13.6	6.8	1.1	3.4	88
Shaw	20.6	25.5	47.1	29.4	8.8	2.9	5.8	5.8	34

See Chapter 2, Table 4, for comparison with their regions.
Source: TNA, E315/464.

Table 18 *Percentage of customary land held by individual tenants*

Ashbury		Priors, Hanney		Seymours, Hanney		Shaw	
1519[a]	1519[b]	1490	1605	1492	c.1600	1450[c]	1547
15.5[d]	54.7[f]	30.8	33.3	28.6	27.6	26.7	32.5
11.0	7.0	20.5	30.8	14.3	27.6	15.9	31.0
10.4	5.0	15.4	20.5	14.3	13.8	13.6	18.7
9.4[e]	4.7	10.3	10.3	14.3	13.8	12.5	10.0
7.6	4.3	10.3	5.1	14.3	13.8	11.4	7.0
7.5	3.4	5.1		7.1	3.4	10.2	0.4
7.5	3.4	5.1		7.1	0	6.8	0.2
6.4	3.4	2.5		0		1.1	0
6.1	2.9	0				1.1	
5.9	2.8					0.6	
5.4	2.7						
4.0	2.4						
3.3	1.8						
	1.5						
13	**14**	**9**	**5**	**8**	**7**	**10**	**8**

Notes:
The totals in bold type represent the total number of customary tenants.
[a] Customary tenants only.
[b] Includes the farmer of the demesne.
[c] This was the date when the pattern of landholding has stabilised, particularly after the fluidity of the 1430s.
[d] Unfree tenant.
[e] Unfree tenant.
[f] Farmer of demesne lands.

Sources: Ashbury BL, Harley MS. 3961. Priors, Hanney NCA, 4075, 4076. Seymours, Hanney BRO, D/EX1/M7, D/EX1/M5,6. Shaw TNA, SC2/154/53, LR2/187.

A comparison of the data in the two parts of Table 18 for Hanney in the Vale reveals how land was distributed more equitably on the manor of Seymours than Priors where there had been more engrossment of holdings (the result, as we have observed, of different seigniorial policies). Neither manor, however, experienced widespread polarisation of landholding, nor a high proportion of cottagers. Indeed, cottagers were noticeable by their absence in the records before 1599. There was no evidence for investment in land by outsiders on either manor. Furthermore, few people in Table 17 were assessed on goods of less than £2 and who might have been dependent in part on income from wages. The distribution of wealth was concentrated in the hands of those who had goods assessed at around £5. Thus the majority of the population had access to land and maintained a comfortable level of wealth, and one presumes, standard of living.

At Shaw in the Kennet region there was a less equitable distribution of the customary land of the manor, especially by 1547. The number of cottages had risen from two to four, and may have been associated with the larger numbers of those assessed on goods worth less than £2 who were styled 'labourers and servants'.[37] Many of these individuals did not have direct access to a landholding and one presumes that they were able to find waged employment in nearby Newbury. In addition there were more wealthy persons resident at Shaw than at Hanney, and fewer in the middle range of wealth, which was, arguably, the result of the concentration of landholdings and formation of large farms. The impact of Newbury can be observed in the additional opportunities for employment and distribution of wealth in this society.

At Ashbury in the Downs, although it was not possible to quantify change over time, the farmer of the demesne dominated the distributions in both the proportion of land and wealth that he had, and in comparison, that of the customary tenants was fairly evenly distributed, if rather lower than elsewhere. There were no very wealthy persons resident at Ashbury in 1522 and there was a high proportion of those assessed at under £2, including two customary tenants. Of particular note were the unfree tenants at Ashbury who held land and were assessed at around £1 in goods. The lack of personal freedom by this date was not an impediment to accumulating land. The pattern of distribution of wealth in this downland community was unlike both Hanney, where there was one wealthy individual but relatively few assessed at under £2, and Shaw, where there were several wealthy individuals and a high proportion of low assessments. This pattern of distribution of wealth at Ashbury changed over the sixteenth century, as is shown in the distribution of wealth in probate inventories.

---

[37] Not a category made in the enumeration of vills in the Vale region.

Table 19 *Distribution of wealth as indicated by probate inventories from five parishes*

	The percentage of testators in different categories of wealth							
Place	<£5	£5–<£20	£20–<£50	£50–<£100	£100–<£150	£150–<£200	£200+	Total number of testators
Ashbury	5.08	33.90	33.90	10.17	5.08	3.39	8.47	59
Buckland	5.88	31.37	23.53	23.53	11.76	3.92	0.00	51
Hanney	13.51	48.65	24.32	2.70	5.41	2.70	2.70	37
Kintbury	8.43	46.99	26.51	10.84	3.61	1.20	2.41	83
Shaw	11.76	17.65	23.53	29.41	11.76	5.88	0.00	17

Summary statistics of total wealth assessed in probate inventories (in pence, d.)

Place	Dates	Mean	Stan Dev	Max.	Min.	Total number of testators
Ashbury	1539–1600	15,667.15	25507.31	142,086	380	59
Buckland	1495–1600	11,873.57	11395.17	45,920	652	51
Hanney	1544–1600	8,647.58	13646.50	66,493	277	37
Kintbury	1528–1600	8,433.74	11705.78	75,816	194	83
Shaw	1550–1600	12,128.29	11001.71	37,028	558	17

Proportion of assessed wealth held as crops* and stock (in pence, d.)

Place	Total in d.	Crops in d.	Stock in d.	Crops as percentage of total wealth	Stock as percentage of total wealth
Ashbury	924,362	163,610	395,184	17.70	42.75
Buckland	605,552	150,127	224,595	24.79	37.09
Hanney	319,960½	99,220	117,091	31.01	36.60
Kintbury	700,480½	146,786	294,051	20.96	41.98
Shaw	202,761	42,144	113,148	20.79	55.80

* Crops includes those growing in the fields and stored in the barn.
Sources: All at BRO, D/A1, except TNA, PROB2/455 inventory of William Slatter of Buckland 1495.

We turn now to examine the distribution of wealth of those who left probate inventories in the sixteenth century and a rather different pattern emerges.[38] The main similarities were in the trends for Hanney and Kintbury, a trend which cuts across regional boundaries. In particular, they had the largest

[38] Due to the legal requirements for the drawing up of an inventory this source will not include the poorer members of local society. M. Spufford, 'The Limitations of the Probate Inventory in J. Chartres and D. Hey (eds), *English Rural Society, 1500–1800* (Cambridge, 1990), 139–74.

number of those in the category of inventoried wealth of between £5 and £20, and the greatest proportion of the population assessed at less than £100. In addition to this broad-based wealth there were also individuals who were particularly wealthy. At Hanney the farmer of the demesne of Priors, Richard Sury, was assessed at £277 1s. 1d. in 1586.[39] Moreover, at Kintbury, the large farmers John Brinklow and John Elgar were also assessed at over £200.[40] They were fairly typical of the large farmers of Kintbury who emerged over the course of the sixteenth century and who dominated the landholding structure of this community. They had not been a feature of local society in the fifteenth century. Although there were no exceptionally wealthy individuals at Shaw, it did have the largest percentage of those with over £100. The low numbers of inventories from Shaw is significant and could be considered indirect evidence of those in society who did not have the wealth in goods to necessitate the compilation of an inventory. Perhaps another indication of the wage-earning sector of society at Shaw due to its proximity to Newbury.

The number of wealthy individuals at Ashbury (5) on the Downs was exceptional.[41] The wealthiest man was Richard Mills, also known as Carter, a yeoman sheep farmer who was assessed at £559 8s. 0d. in 1565.[42] The importance of sheep in this local economy was reflected in the inventories as 39 included sheep and these were spread across the different sectors of this society. Additionally, many of the testators left bequests of sheep or lambs in their wills.[43] The relatively large number of wealthy individuals at Ashbury would appear to suggest that there had been a degree of polarisation of wealth in this society over the sixteenth century, and one that was based on the successful raising of sheep.[44]

The proportions of wealth held as crops and stock in Table 19 also varied between the case studies and reflects the regional differences in the local economies. The percentage held as crops at Hanney is an indication of the success of arable husbandry here, especially by the farmer of the demesne, and was typical of this part of the Vale. The cultivation of arable at Buckland in the west of the Vale was also important, although to a lesser extent than in

---

[39] BRO, D/A1/116/2.

[40] John Brinklow in 1558 assessed on £315 8s. 0d. that included large numbers of sheep. BRO, D/A1/39/129. John Elgar yeoman in 1577 was assessed on £220 0s. 3d. and in his will left several large bequests of money. BRO, D/A1/65/60.

[41] 1560 Thomas Pearce also Rede, 1565 Richard Mills also Carter yeoman, 1580 Roger Weeks gentleman, 1593 Richard Cole yeoman, 1598 Robert Harding yeoman.

[42] BRO, D/A1/96/99.

[43] Thomas Holcott gentleman left bequests totalling 753 sheep in his will of 1551. TNA, PROB11/34/25.

[44] A direct link between the change of landlord at the Dissolution of the Monasteries and this shift in the distribution of wealth in the local society cannot be made.

the east. By contrast, the low level of wealth in crops at Ashbury in the Downs was unsurprising given the nature of the terrain. Cattle were relatively more important than sheep at Buckland and Shaw. Nevertheless, the numbers of sheep included in the inventories of all five study areas was noticeable and is a reflection of the more general changes in agriculture, the increasing emphasis on pastoral husbandry and a response to the demand for wool.[45]

This examination of the social distribution of land and wealth in the five case studies of western Berkshire has supported the arguments for a regional dimension to the different societies and economies. Wealth was fairly equitably distributed among those living in the Vale and was based on the success of agriculture in the region, and, additionally at Hanney, on the effects of seigniorial policy. Sheep dominated the local economy of the Downs and there was some polarisation of wealth at Ashbury over the course of the sixteenth century. This was also the case in the Kennet region, where there was an increase in the size of landholdings and numbers of large tenants. Nevertheless, as will be shown below, the diversification of employment opportunities available in this region helped to mitigate some of the negative effects of this trend. The polarisation of wealth in the sixteenth century was not a universal feature of western Berkshire, and was identifiable most noticeably at Shaw situated in Newbury's immediate hinterland.

Tenant society

We can turn now to take a more qualitative look at the diverse nature of rural society in western Berkshire by examining the different social groups, their changing composition and distribution within the region. In doing so we continue the theme of the interaction between landscape, economy and society, whilst at the same time it is possible to glimpse those individuals who made up this society. The impact that these individuals made on the pace of change in a single locality continues to be the concern of this chapter. We will begin by examining the numerically small but influential group of landowners and merchants, and then the other taxpayers with assessments of wealth over £20; then analyse the middling taxpayers, and finally consider those taxpayers assessed at less £2 a year. It will become apparent that the key to understanding local society is to recognise the number and variety of its constituent elements.

---

[45] C. Dyer, 'Warwickshire Farming, 1349–c.1520', *Dugdale Society Occasional Papers*, 27 (1981). *Idem*, 'Sheepcotes: Evidence for Medieval Sheepfarming', *Medieval Archaeology*, 39 (1995), 136–64.

Taxpayers assessed on wealth over £20

LOCAL LANDOWNERS

The presence of local landowners and members of the gentry who were resident within the community is the first concern. In chapter 2 we saw how some historians have emphasised the role and actions of the gentry as one of the catalysts for bringing about change. They were shown to have been the largest social group of landowners in western Berkshire, and that they held relatively small estates. Their distribution was uneven, with a greater concentration in the Vale, and an increase in their numbers throughout western Berkshire in the second half of the sixteenth century. We now need to consider the effects that the presence of this group had when they were resident members of local society as opposed to their administrative policies discussed in chapter 4.

In terms of their wealth and social status they can be characterised by their dependence on land for their major source of income; in addition, they were often trained as lawyers or had strong professional contacts, especially with London. Their total wealth, however, might be less than that of the successful demesne or large farmer. Furthermore, their influence in the localities was enhanced by being officers of the crown and when they acted as local commissioners, assessors of the tax, Members of Parliament and justices of the peace. The case studies of Hanney and Buckland will illustrate some of these general points.

Both Hanney and Buckland had members of gentry families resident in the parish as manorial lords and minor landowners, and they were seen as active participants in the community and were involved in local affairs. The wealthy members of the local society of Hanney illustrate the diverse social composition of this group as they included the lords of the manor and their relatives, and also a wealthy gentleman landowner. In chapter 4 we saw the impact that a local gentry lord might have on the nature of change on his manor. It was on the manor of Seymours that the seigniorial management policy included an attempt to keep landholdings intact, prevent engrossment, and where the cost of renting land rose dramatically in the sixteenth century. These lords were members of the Eyston family of East Hendred (descended by marriage from the Arches family). It was one of their sons, William, who was farmer of the demesne lands at Hanney in the first half of the sixteenth century, and was actively involved in the life of the local society. William's wealth in terms of land and goods when he died, was valued at £113 1s. 0d. in his inventory,[46] and was neither as great as that of the previous farmer of the demesne, John Shepereve, or of other men resident on the manor. The wealthiest individual living in Hanney in 1522 was Oliver Welsborne gentleman, with goods assessed

---

[46] BRO, D/A1/65/36 inventory of 1559, will in Register B dated 1558.

at £60. He had been the king's bailiff of the manors of Abingdon, Marcham and Hanney in 1539.[47] His will of 1553 revealed that he owned lands both in Hanney and elsewhere in the county.[48] Other members of the Welsborne family were active in the area and his brother John, who was a member of the king's household and held numerous official posts, was involved in the disposal of the lands and dissolution of Abingdon Abbey.[49] Furthermore, the other lords of the manors at Hanney, especially members of the Yate and Fettiplace families, held additional lands both in the parish and within the area of the Vale, as we will see.

At Buckland there were also several different landowning and gentry families living in the parish and holding lands from the various manors. In chapter 2 we saw how members of the Fettiplace family were successful in acquiring lands in the Vale and a minor branch of the family held lands at Buckland from the fourteenth century.[50] They amassed additional lands there over the fifteenth century, and at neighbouring Pusey, and later also acquired Andrews manor in Hanney. At Buckland they were active in participating in local society, as jurors of the court of the main manor, and keeping the roads mended and ditches clear; they were also fined for allowing their pigs to roam in their neighbours' pastures, stole rabbits from the manorial warren using ferrets, and were involved in a couple of violent incidents. Although they conveyed their manor at Buckland to John Yate in 1511,[51] they remained active in local society after this date.[52] Another wealthy landholding family in the sixteenth century were the Sowthbys who lived at Newenton in Buckland and also held lands in Barcote and Carswell.[53] They were active, too, on the main manor of Dukes Buckland from which they held additional lands and were involved in various incidents on that manor. Although an essential part of the local society at Buckland, their impact on the pace of change there cannot be fully established.

The decline of the hamlets of Barcote and Carswell, however, may have been influenced by the actions of the local gentry families, although the evidence

---

[47] *L&P Henry VIII* 14 i, 593.

[48] BRO, will D/A1/10040 p. 72, inventory D/A1/132/55. His inventory was valued at £180 4s. 8d. with debts of £4 13s. 4d. owed to men in Abingdon and Wantage. Lands were in East Hanney, Cumnor, Drayton, Steventon, Sutton Courtney, Sutton Wick.

[49] S. T. Bindoff (ed.), *The History of Parliament: The House of Commons, 1509–1558*, vol. 3 (London, 1982), 575–7.

[50] P. J. Jefferies, 'A Consideration of Some Aspects of Landholding in Medieval Berkshire', Ph.D. thesis, Reading (1972), 247–8.

[51] *Ibid.*, 248.

[52] The Yate family are discussed below as their wealth had originated from trading in wool.

[53] The lands at Barcote and Carswell were held of Goring Priory and leased 7th April 1534. TNA, SC6/HENVIII/2924, 6v. Bodleian, MS ch Berks 1596.

is rather tenuous.[54] The Holcott family of Barcote had held this small estate or manor since the thirteenth century and eventually died out in the direct line in 1575.[55] They also held lands from the main manor of Dukes, and were involved in the upkeep of that manor, maintaining the roads and ditches, and also in certain violent incidents. In 1381, there had been 35 individuals who had paid tax in Barcote. By 1522, however, the settlement had dwindled to just John Holcott gentleman, Margery Holcott widow, and their servants.[56] The settlement must have been deserted at some point between these two dates, but the reasons remain unknown.[57] There was a similar situation of shrinkage at Carswell, from 30 persons in 1381 to 10 individuals in 1522. The reason for contraction here may have been the result of a violent incident and forcible eviction of tenants. This had occurred at Carswell in 1465, when the tenants appear to have had their lands spoiled, and their sheep and cattle driven away by order of Sir Robert Harecourt, and, as a consequence, were afraid to dwell in their houses.[58] If this was the case, and they did not return to their properties, it could account for the decline of this settlement.

The absence of active participation by members of the gentry at Shaw and Kintbury in the Kennet region before the middle of the sixteenth century stands in sharp contrast to what we have observed in the Vale, but, nevertheless, was typical of the Kennet area generally.[59] Local society, as a result, was very different. The situation changed from the second half of the sixteenth century. We have seen how John Winchcome II bought up many of the lands of the dissolved house of Reading Abbey. His eldest son John inherited these properties and lived at Bucklebury but was not involved in the cloth industry; rather, he was active in county administration and as a Member of Parliament.[60] Another clothier from Newbury, Thomas Dolman, bought the manor of Shaw

---

[54] See chapter 4, p. 158.

[55] VCH Berkshire, IV, 456–7.

[56] TNA, E315/464. John Holcott was assessed on £22 in lands and £20 in goods, Margery Holcott on £10 in lands and £50 in goods.

[57] J. Brooks, 'The Deserted Medieval Villages of Northern Berkshire', Ph.D. thesis, Reading (1982), 235–41.

[58] TNA, C1/27/421. '... come to Carsewell aforeseid and then and there not only your seid suppliaunter but also diverse other of your pore tenunts of the seid manoir assaunted bete wounded and grevously manassed so that your seid pore tenauntes for dred of deth and other outrageous and mischievous casueltees dare not abide in ther houses nor menure their lond but let it stand desolat as it were in land of were and over this have dryvs awey cc shepe and other diverse cately of your seid tenauntes and theyn yet kepe reteyne and dispose at ther will to the utter destruccion of your seid pore tenaunts ...'

[59] The two main families in the Kennet region were the Cheyneys of West Woodhay and Norris of Yattendon.

[60] P. W. Hasler (ed.), The History of Parliament: The House of Commons, 1558–1603, vol. 3 (London, 1981), 633.

and built a prestigious house there that was finished by his son in 1581.[61] The Dolmans were active as manorial lords and when the records of their manor survive again at the end of the century they are shown to have been actively exploiting the income-generating resources of their manor.[62] At Kintbury the lands of the dissolved religious house of Amesbury were eventually acquired by John Cheyney of neighbouring West Woodhay whose widow was living there in 1545.[63] The Cheyneys had acquired the manor of West Woodhay through marriage in the early fifteenth century,[64] and by the sixteenth century were actively involved in county affairs.[65] They are a good example of the close relationships formed by marriage within this social group. John Cheyney II was married to Jane, the daughter of Sir William Norris of Yattendon, and their son married Dorothy the daughter of John Yate of Charney.[66] They were members of the network of relationships covering western Berkshire and southern Oxfordshire discussed in chapter 2.[67]

This social group, therefore, was important in bringing about change in their communities. They were particularly effective when acting as lords of the manor, and when fulfilling their roles as royal officials. In the latter case they acted as an important link between local society and the state. Although not involved in the day-to-day running of the manors, they were integrated into the general workings of the manor such as in the maintenance of the highways and commons. Whether their absence from the Kennet region was a factor in the relative freedom of economic activity in this area cannot be established. Their legacies and endowments, moreover, could make a positive contribution to local society as in the foundation of the almshouses and schools at Lambourn and Childrey.[68]

---

[61] This house still survives as an excellent example of the architecture of the period as illustrated on this book's cover. VCH Berkshire, IV, 87, 89.

[62] See chapter 4 for their treatment of entry fines and the rents of the mills at Shaw.

[63] TNA, E179/74/181.

[64] VCH Berkshire, IV, 243.

[65] John Cheyney II was a Member of Parliament, JP for Berkshire, and held various commissions in the county: Bindoff, House of Commons, vol. 1, 633. He was also one of the commissioners of the Lay Subsidy of 1545 for the Hundreds of Kintbury Eagle and Faircross, TNA, E179/74/181.

[66] Bindoff, House of Commons, 633.

[67] This can be illustrated in the ways in which they acted as witnesses to each other's wills. For example those acting as witnesses to John Yate of Buckland in 1579 were John Eyston, John Arderne, Michell Moseley, Francis Yate, Roger Brasgirdle, John Wirdnam, Robert Fettiplace and Humphrey Fettiplace. TNA, PROB11/61/23.

[68] John Eastbury endowed an almshouse at Lambourn in 1501 and a priest to teach a free grammar school there: VCH Berkshire, IV, 252, 263–5. In 1526 William Fettiplace founded a school and almshouse at Childrey: VCH Berkshire, II, 275–6.

MERCHANTS

Merchants have been accorded a key role in the development of capitalism when acting as entrepreneurs.[69] Several were active participants in the acquisition of land at the Dissolution, and were later to abandon the style 'merchant' for 'gentleman', although in terms of their wealth were qualified to use the title before. The merchants of western Berkshire fall into two main categories: those who dealt in wool, especially the merchants of the Staple of Calais; and those who were involved in the manufacture and sale of cloth, such as clothiers and Merchant Adventurers. In 1522 they were the two wealthiest individuals in the region; that is John Winchcombe II clothier of the town of Newbury, and Thomas Snodenham of the rural parish of Stanford in the Vale, merchant of the Staple of Calais.[70]

We have already seen how wool from Berkshire formed an important element in the country's exports and was used more locally in the manufacture of cloth. Large flocks of sheep were kept by both lords and peasants.[71] An illustration of the importance attached to both the sheep and their products can be shown in the ways in which bequests of sheep were frequently made in the wills of testators, and flocks of sheep were often retained in hand after the other parts of the demesne were leased as at Coleshill and Woolstone.[72] Moreover, we have seen how at Ashbury the washing and shearing of the lord's sheep remained a labour service in the early sixteenth century.

We become aware in the early sixteenth century of the presence of a number of wealthy wool merchants resident in the Vale. Several were members of the Staple of Calais, such as Thomas Snodenham who has already been

---

[69] The main elements of this argument can be found in R. Brenner, *Merchants and Revolution: Commercial Change, Political Conflict, and London's Overseas Traders, 1550–1653* (Cambridge, 1993), Part I.

[70] John Winchcome II was assessed on land and goods of £632 6s. 8d., and Thomas Snodenham on goods of £400 0s. 0d.

[71] Peasant flocks were seen when their owners were fined in the manor court. For example at Buckland William Richards caused damage when he was moving flocks of his sheep numbering 400 and 300 in 1425 and 1426. SBT, DR5/1958, DR5/1960. And William Slatter had 300 sheep and 100 lambs itemised and assessed in his inventory. TNA, PROB2/455. At Kintbury Robert Woodrose was droving 100 of his sheep in 1479, and in 1481 Henry Gunter was droving at least 400 of his sheep from Templeton to Kintbury. BL, Add Roll 49244, 49247. A total of 676 sheep of different types were mentioned in the inventory of William Wolridge of Kintbury in 1539 BRO, D/A1/132/3. The flocks of sheep kept on the Downs were even larger; for example, Richard Mills also Carter of Ashbury had 1,393 sheep in his inventory of 1564 BRO, D/A1/96/99. Thomas Holcott bequeathed a total of 753 sheep in his will of 1551. TNA, PROB11/34/25.

[72] For Woolstone see chapter 4. At Coleshill the lord kept flocks of between 1,000 and 2,000 sheep. Faith 'Berkshire', 170–3.

mentioned,[73] and various members of the Yate family. John Yate appears to have been trading with his eldest son James from at least 1505[74] and they are discussed in greater detail below. The list of those from Berkshire who were supplying wool for export in 1530 included Sir William Essex, Mr Umpton, John Yate, Mr Leytton, Mr Hyde, William Pledwell, Sir John Abryges, Simon Yate, Thomas Goddard, John Goddard and John Stevyns.[75] This group of men shared many of the characteristics of the wool merchants of Gloucestershire and south Oxfordshire with whom they had commercial and family links.[76] Abingdon was integrated into both the local network of wool producers, and also acted as a wider trading centre located on the routes from the Cotswolds to London, and also from the Midlands to Southampton.

The Yate family of wool merchants were very successful and rose from quite obscure beginnings in the county in the fifteenth century. They are considered here in some detail to illustrate the rise of a gentry family, the characteristics of a more widespread pattern of trade, and the family connections of this social group. In the early fifteenth century there may have been several branches of the family in northern Berkshire. In 1405 John Yate of Buckland held a messuage and two virgates of land, and later another holding of a virgate. The family then disappeared from the records of Buckland until the 1490s, a time when they also appeared at Hanney. Meanwhile, in the middle of the fifteenth century Richard Yate settled at Charney Bassett and died there in 1498. He had a son John who also initially lived at Charney, and from where he traded as a member of the Calais Staple. In 1505 he was exporting wool to Calais with his eldest son James.[77] In 1507 John Yate was referred to as of Charney, 'gentilman' alias 'wolman' and merchant of the Staple of Calais. By 1533 he was referred to as a 'Stapler of reputation' and was among those exporting wool.[78] It was presumably on some of the proceeds of his trading activity that he was able to buy the manor of Lyford in Hanney to which he moved. He also bought lands on the Downs, and in his will of 1537 had farms

---

[73] Referred to as 'merchant of the Staple' in 1522, TNA, E315/464, and his will of 1541 as 'merchant of the staple at Calleys dwelling in Stanfourde in Berks', TNA, PROB11/28/34.

[74] CPR 1494–1509, 447–50, especially 448.

[75] TNA, SP1/237 fol. 4. A total of 611 sacks.

[76] For example Geoffrey Dormer of Thame was a merchant of the staple in the last quarter of the fifteenth century, M. D. Lobel (ed.), *The Victoria History of the Counties of England. Oxfordshire* VII (London, 1962), 181. Rirchard Wenman of Witney was a merchant of the staple in 1524 and assessed on £1,200, J. L. Bolton (ed.), *Calendar of the Court Books of the Borough of Witney, 1538–1610* (Oxfordshire Record Society, 54, 1985), liv.

[77] CPR 1494–1509, 448.

[78] *L&P Henry VIII*, Addenda, volume 1, 1509–47, 321.

in the parishes of Wantage and Lambourn on which he had sheep running.[79] His eldest son James was also referred to as a Stapler of Calais, and another son Bartholomew who died in 1521.[80] James moved to Buckland at a date after 1523 and died there in 1544.[81] In the same year his son John, along with his widowed mother, were able to buy the manor of Buckland, for £1,408 14s. 7d. John continued to buy lands and manors until his death in 1579 and he is commemorated in a memorial brass in the church of Buckland.[82] The Yate family were part of a wider network of family and commercial contacts. John married Mary Justice, daughter of William Justice of Reading, an important burgess of the town and first mayor after the Dissolution. John was related by marriage to several branches of the Fettiplace family, the Eystons of Hendred, the Pleydells of Farringdon, Cheyneys of West Woodhay, Hydes of Denchworth and others in the county of Berkshire.[83] There was another branch of the Yate family in Standlake, Oxfordshire. Commercial contacts are implied when John Yate acted as the executor of John Winchcome II's will in 1557. Their interests were not solely devoted to those of land and trade as Edward, his son, was a lawyer of the Middle Temple in London, and was given books in John's will. By the sixteenth century they were thus fairly typical of the gentry and merchant families of north Berkshire and south Oxfordshire.

There were also wealthy merchants who dealt in cloth and were resident in the rural areas. Furthermore it was on the proceeds of their urban manufacturing enterprise that the successful clothiers were able to buy the rural manors to which they eventually moved and joined the ranks of the landowning group. We observed in chapter 3 how, in the fourteenth century, there was a thriving rural cloth industry centred on Abingdon and its rural hinterland, including East Hendred. We also saw how the manufacture of cloth in the town of Newbury had an impact on the economy of the surrounding area. There may have been a link between the town and the Brinklow family of Kintbury, although this was never specified. There were, however, members of this family who exported cloth from London as Merchant Adventurers. They are described here in some detail as an important illustration of the network

---

[79] TNA, PROB11/28/26, will dated 1537 and proven 1541.

[80] In his will of 1521 Bartholomew was referred to as Merchant of the Staple of Calys, TNA, PROB11/20/16. The other sons were not involved in the wool trade, but became local landowners, and one was a member of the clergy. Richard was given Charney by his father, Thomas had Lyford, and Peter was a fellow of Magdalen College, Oxford and went on to become vicar of Denchworth and rector of Longworth.

[81] TNA, PROB11/30/11, will dated 1543 and proven 1544.

[82] The extent of his landholdings at the time of his death can be found in his will which mentioned lands and manors in Buckland, Stanford in the Vale, Wantage, Tullwick, Hinton, Longworth, Draycot Moor, Hatford, Charleton, Grove, Letcombe Regis, Challow, East Ginge, Sutton, West Hendred and others. TNA, PROB11/61/23.

[83] W. H. Rylands (ed.), *The Visitations of Berkshire* (Harleian Society, 56, 1907), 60.

of commercial contacts that existed in rural England.[84] Robert Brinklow was one of the large farmers of Kintbury in the early sixteenth century, farming Anville's and in the retinue of Sir Edward Darell as the keeper of his park at Balsdon in Kintbury.[85] Robert Brinklow mentioned his nine children in his will of 1543,[86] including John who remained at Kintbury and inherited the lease of the farm of Anvilles, and Henry, Hugh and Anthony who were London merchants. This family remained in close contact with each other. The sons in London were the executers and overseers of Robert's will, and in 1558 Anthony was the overseer of John's will in which two local men were asked to look after the goods 'until the time that my brother can come down'.[87] The three London brothers were all merchants engaged in the export of cloth, particularly as Merchant Adventurers who traded with Antwerp, and the three men operated as a family firm similar to the Johnson brothers; indeed, John Johnson had a trading account with Henry Brinklow.[88] After Henry's death in 1545 his brothers Hugh and Anthony continued to trade as mercers, and John's will specifically mentioned Anthony Brinklow of Antwerp.[89] Henry Brinklow is more famous as the author of *The Complaynt of Roderyck Mors* first published in 1542.[90] These brothers had travelled far from their roots in western Berkshire, but maintained close links with the family members who continued to farm at Kintbury. This pattern of behaviour has been identified elsewhere, such as the Tate family from Coventry.[91] These are important examples of the integration of familial and trading relationships that connected the rural areas with the urban centres, and London in particular, drawing the rural inhabitants into a wider commercial network.

FARMERS OF THE DEMESNE

The farmers of the demesne were an important and constant feature of local society in western Berkshire. They rose to pre-eminence in association with the leasing of the lands of the demesne. It was as lessees, or farmers as they became known, of these lands that they became a fairly universal feature of

[84] For further details of Henry Brinklow and his family and their agricultural activities see M. Yates, 'Between Fact and Fiction: Henry Brinklow's *Complaynt* Against Rapacious Landlords', *AgHRev*, 54 (2006), 24–44.

[85] TNA, E315/464 Military Survey, he was also listed in the 1524 Lay Subsidy.

[86] TNA, PROB11/29/24.

[87] BRO, D/A1/39/129.

[88] B. Winchester, *Tudor Family Portrait* (London, 1955), 45, 212.

[89] BRO, D/A1/39/129.

[90] J. M. Cowper (ed.), *Henry Brinklow's Complaynt of Roderyck Mors* (EETS, Extra Series, 22, 1874).

[91] A. Sutton, *A Merchant Family of Coventry, London and Calais: The Tates, c.1450–1515* (London, 1998).

English rural society by the middle of the fifteenth century.[92] They came from a variety of different social backgrounds but common to all was their standing as substantial and wealthy farmers, who produced a considerable marketable surplus, and were usually the regular employers of non-family labour.

The farmers of the demesne lands of western Berkshire were a constant feature of rural society both chronologically over the period of study, and spatially across the regions. The continuity of the relative wealth and social standing of this group in rural society has to be noted.[93] Their social origins were as existing tenants of large customary holdings, although not necessarily of the manor whose demesne they leased, and they were rarely newcomers to the area.[94] There was a strong family link among them, as farms were often passed from father to son. They were a constant feature of rural society, unlike the resident landowners and merchants who were found only infrequently. Throughout the period of this study the farmers of the demesne dominated the wealth and landholding of their local societies. They were consistently the largest farmers in terms of acreage, and often took additional landholdings to those of the demesne. Their farms were sufficiently large to necessitate the employment of additional labour to that of the family.[95] This can be observed in the Subsidies of the 1520s when servants, or individuals assessed on wages, were often listed after the entry of the farmer.[96] In addition to the manorial documents that recorded their landholdings, their probate inventories revealed the scale of their agrarian enterprise, and also their wealth as reflected in the furnishings of their houses. The detailed characteristics of these farmers are best illustrated by describing several individuals.

[92] F. R. H. du Boulay, 'Who Were Farming the English Demesnes at the end of the Middle Ages?' *EcHRev*, 17 (1965), 443–55. J. Hare, 'The Demesne Lessees of Fifteenth-century Wiltshire', *AgHRev*, 29 (1981), 1–15. B. Harvey, 'The Leasing of the Abbot of Westminster's Demesnes in the Later Middle Ages', *EcHRev*, 35 (1982), 17–27.

[93] New College often accepted sons of their tenants as students and education provided another important route to social advancement. T. A. R Evans and R. J. Faith 'College Estates and University Finances, 1350–1500', in J. Catto and T. A. R. Evans (eds), *The History of the University of Oxford* (Oxford, 1992), 687.

[94] This was also the modal category of farmer found in Wiltshire and on the Westminster Abbey estates. Hare, 'The Demesne Lessees of Fifteenth-century Wiltshire', 1–15. Harvey, 'The Leasing of the Abbot of Westminster's Demesnes in the Later Middle Ages', 17–27.

[95] Campbell notes that on farms of 30 hectares (12 acres approximately) or more hired labour usually exceeded that of the family. B. M. S. Campbell, 'England: Land and People', in S. H. Rigby (ed.), *A Companion to Britain in the Later Middle Ages* (Oxford, 2003), 18.

[96] Kintbury is a good example of this type of entry as the farmers of the demesne and other large farmers were followed by those assessed on wages, TNA, E179/73/125.

The farmers of the demesnes at Hanney included John Burymyll who was actually the lessee of both demesnes in 1442. In 1512 John Shepereve was the farmer of Seymours' demesne lands comprising four virgates, by which time he was already the tenant of three messuages and two and a half virgates of customary land. William Eyston has already been discussed as the son of the lord of the manor, was subsequently farmer there and he also had an additional customary holding of a messuage and virgate of land.[97] The lessees of the demesne at Priors also cultivated large areas in addition to the four virgates of demesne land and there was a strong family connection between them. William Robyns was the farmer in 1460 and was succeeded by his son, also William, in 1482. The latter took several additional customary holdings amounting to another messuage, two and half virgates of land, three tofts, and a piece of free land of unspecified size[98] and was assessed on goods of £24 in 1522. He was succeeded in 1525 in all his lands by Richard Sury, previously described as his 'heir'. In 1541 the lease was granted jointly to Richard Sury and his son, also Richard, and the elder Richard died in 1554. His son continued to cultivate these lands and when he died in 1586 his inventory was valued at £277 1s. 1d.; in his will he mentioned both the corn growing on the lands of the demesne and on the copyhold lands, and was presumably working them both himself. The remaining years of the lease were bequeathed to his sons and the copyhold lands to his wife Dorothy.[99] Her inventory of 1613 was valued at £235 13s. 4d. and included £50 of corn growing in the fields, £36 of sheep and lambs and also ten cows valued at £25.[100] She was able, presumably, to maintain an agricultural concern during her widowhood in line with the other widows discussed above.

Although a century earlier there were many similarities with the case of William Slatter who was the farmer of the demesne at Buckland in the late fifteenth century and which strengthen our argument for continuity in the characteristic features of this social group. When he died in 1495 he left an inventory assessed at over £67 6s. 0d.[101] He was growing barley (100 acres sown), wheat, pulse and had 40 quarters of malt among his possessions. He also had 300 sheep, 100 lambs, 4 cart horses, 6 oxen, 6 steers, 8 cows, 20

---

[97] That is, he farmed 44 per cent of the land of the manor. He died in 1558 and his inventory was valued at £113 1s. 0d. BRO, D/A1/65/36.

[98] Together he held approximately 40 per cent of the lands of the manor.

[99] BRO, D/A1/116/2 Will and inventory of Richard Sury 1586. The emphasis on arable cultivation at Hanney is a notable feature of this inventory.

[100] BRO, D/A1/117/100 Will and inventory of Dorothy Sury 1613 which does not appear in Table 19 as it was compiled after 1600.

[101] TNA, PROB11/10/15 will, and PROB2/455 inventory, parts of the document are illegible and the total given here is of those legible entries.

yearlings, and poultry. His wife Alice continued the enterprise and left several bequests of sheep in her will along with a cow and quantities of barley.[102]

The farmers of the demesne at Shaw in the first half of the sixteenth century were members of the Hore family. They were successful agriculturalists who also invested in the free lands in the town of Newbury. In 1522 John was assessed at £40 in goods at Shaw and 16s. on lands in Newbury. He was succeeded in his lands by his son Thomas. At Shaw they cultivated 187 acres of demesne land, or 27 per cent of the total arable of the manor. They were actively involved in the proceedings of the manor court and agricultural life of the manor. Thomas died in 1550 and his inventory was appraised at £101 10s. od. in which he had 57 acres sown with wheat, barley, rye, oats, vetches and peas, 13 horses and colts, 300 sheep and 15 small, 5 oxen, 14 cows, 6 bull oxen, 7 calves, and numerous poultry and pigs.[103] It was perhaps the success of their farming activities that enabled them to invest in the lands of the town.

At Ashbury, to an even greater extent, land and wealth in moveable goods were dominated by the farmer of the demesne, who in 1519 was Clement North also known as Hardyng.[104] He held 475 acres or 54.7 per cent of the lands of the manor,[105] was assessed on goods worth 40 marks in 1522, and when he died in 1548 his inventory was valued at £84 18s. 8d.[106] He had been educated at Winchester College where he was admitted in 1474 as the son of a college tenant at Ashbury, his father John.[107] In 1539 he rendered his account as reeve of the manor of Ashbury while also being the farmer of demesne and holding additional free and customary lands.[108] The family tie remained, and his three sons continued to farm at Ashbury throughout the sixteenth century.[109]

MILLERS

Millers are a difficult group to place within a social category as they were very varied. Nevertheless they played an essential role in the rural economy and one

---

[102] Her agricultural bequests amounted to 85 sheep, a cow, 3 quarters of barley plus four bushels of barley to each godchild (number unspecified). TNA, PROB11/11/13.

[103] BRO, D/A1/75/26.

[104] It has not been possible to trace change over time on this manor.

[105] BL, Harley MS. 3961. Free land has been omitted from the calculations as the acreages were not specified.

[106] He was a successful sheep farmer and his inventory included 303 sheep. BRO, D/A1/75/18.

[107] G. F. Lytle, 'The Social Origins of Oxford Students in the Late Middle Ages: New College, c.1380–c.1510', in J. Ijsewijn and J. Paquet (eds), *The Universities in the Late Middle Ages* (Leuven, 1978), 431.

[108] TNA, SC6/HENVIII/7406.

[109] Furthermore he made additional provision for the younger sons in the memorandum added to his will. BRO, D/A1/6 fol. 58. Robert Harding was one of those with an inventory assessed at over £200 and discussed above.

that was not directly associated with farming. They also acted as employers of labour on their industrial complexes. As a group they came from diverse social backgrounds, and had varying levels of wealth and skill. They ranged in social composition from the wealthy lessees to their employees; and from the lowly millers of the horse-powered corn mill at Buckland in the early fifteenth century, to the wealthy tanners of sixteenth-century Shaw. As we have seen, western Berkshire was amply supplied with rivers that powered a variety of different types of mill including grain, malt, fulling and tanning, in addition to those driven by wind or horse power.[110] At Shaw there was some specialisation in milling, in particular the tanning mill was often held separately from the grain and malt mills. It was demonstrated in chapter 4 that income derived from mills formed an important source of manorial revenue and one that was actively managed, particularly in balancing the costs of repairs with income from rents. We will now consider each of the different types of mill and miller for their role in the local economy and society.

Fulling mills have already been mentioned in relation to the cloth industry as a dynamic aspect of rural involvement in an otherwise town-centred industry by the sixteenth century. The lessees of the fulling mills were often townsmen, such as the Newbury clothiers John Bullford and Robert Sewey who held the mills at Shaw, and men from Hungerford were the lessees of the fulling mill at Denford in Kintbury. John Winchcombe II leased mills at Bagnor, and John Dolman at Colthrop.[111] Otherwise the lessees were local men such as Richard Davy who was the farmer of the three mills at Shaw in the 1460s,[112] and certainly it would have been local men who laboured at these mills.

The tanning, or more accurately bark mill, was the other non-agrarian mill operating in western Berkshire. Bark was crushed between the millstones to extract the tannin for curing hides, probably employing a modified version of the corn mill.[113] Tanning was an important industry, particularly in the Kennet region. It utilised the bark from this woodland region and the hides of the animals. Merchants from Newbury were exporting hides from Southampton in the fifteenth century. Allied to tanning was parchment making and Winchester

[110] Chapter 4, p. 147. For additional details of the rivers and mills of the region see M. Yates, 'Watermills in the Local Economy of a Late Medieval Manor in Berkshire', in T. Thornton (ed.), Social Attitudes and Political Structures in the Fifteenth Century (Stroud, 2000), 184–201.

[111] C. Jackson, 'The Berkshire Woollen Industry, c.1500–c.1650', in J. Dils (ed.), An Historical Atlas of Berkshire (Reading, 1998), 52–3.

[112] He submitted the annual account for the mills and paid a millers toll along with Richard Millward during these years, and until the fulling mill was damned up in 1468.

[113] R. Holt, The Mills of Medieval England (Oxford, 1988), 148–9.

College were obtaining parchment from Shaw in the late fifteenth century.[114] The lessees of the tanning mills were often different from the millers of the other mills, as was the case at Shaw and Kintbury. The wealth of these tanners could be large, particularly the Smart and Shipton families at Shaw and the Barkesdales of Speenhamland. The wealthiest resident at Shaw in 1522 was Maurice Smart, assessed at £60, a tanner and miller who, from the evidence of his will, also had income from lands.[115] Tanning was often associated with specific families, such as the two already mentioned, and the Walrond family at Kintbury in the early fifteenth century. They provided a wealthy and stable element in local society, unlike the millers of the corn mills.

The most common type of mill in the region was that for grain, reflecting the importance of arable farming in western Berkshire.[116] Associated with these mills were those that crushed malt, and a malt mill was operating at Shaw. The value-added element to malt would have made it a profitable commodity to trade in, particularly over distances such as to London.[117] The millers of the corn mills were not, in general, as wealthy as their tanning counterparts. For example John Hill was the miller at Buckland in the 1520s, active in the local community as tithing man and ale taster, and was assessed on goods of £1 6s. 8d. in 1522 and Patrick Mountain of Shaw was assessed at £4, both of which were significantly less than the tanner and miller Maurice Smart.

The millers of the grain mills formed a more transient element in local society as they often stayed for only a few years before moving on. For example at Shaw there was a high turnover of lessees of the mill complex; thirty different millers were recorded between 1404 and 1542, compared with nine farmers of the demesne for the same period. The millers at Shaw were often involved in violent incidents. The description of Chaucer's miller in *The Canterbury Tales* could easily have applied to those at Shaw. Nevertheless we should not underestimate the difficulties encountered when earning a living from milling, particularly in the depressed market conditions of the fifteenth century.[118] We have already seen in chapter 4 how the rents payable for the lease of the mills

---

[114] WCM, 22158.

[115] TNA, PROB11/33/22. In addition to Shaw he left lands at Woodspeen in Berkshire and Witney, Oxfordshire. Maurice Smart was succeeded by his grandson Maurice Shipton whose inventory in 1612 was appraised at £369 16s. 0d. and included £78 of leather and bark and a bark mill and other implements worth £3. BRO, D/A1/213/77.

[116] Yates, 'Watermills'.

[117] J. Galloway, 'London's Grain Supply: Changes in Production, Distribution and Consumption During the Fourteenth Century' *Franco-British Studies*, 20 (1995), 23–34. The trade in malt was mentioned in chapter 2 as one element in the rural economy of the Vale.

[118] Holt, *Mills of Medieval England*, 90–106 where he stresses our need to re-consider the business acumen of medieval millers.

were the closest to a true economic rent. In order to be a successful miller and make a profit, the lessee had to balance the payment of his rent with the repairs of the mill and the fluctuations of the market. This was the other side of the profitability equation that we have previously examined from the lords' perspective. The difficulties experienced in making the mills at Shaw pay might be one reason for the high turnover of millers there. It was the migratory past of the miller at Kintbury, William Braye, which lay behind his victimisation that was sufficiently damaging for him to bring a case to Chancery.[119] His case is useful as it illustrates the vulnerability of this sector of society. The farmer of the demesne, Bartholomew Parrock, had started a smear campaign against Braye, saying that he was a foreigner to Berkshire and charged excessive toll. Braye replied that he had been born in Abingdon and lived within a fifteen-mile radius of the town, and that as a result of this defamation people would not grind their corn at his mill to his utter impoverishment. The problem must have been resolved as Braye was still living at Kintbury ten years later when he was the lessee of both mills there. He was obviously making a relative success of it and was assessed for taxation on goods valued at £10.[120]

It would appear that the wealth and standing of the millers rose during the sixteenth century. Thomas Morne of Shaw was also assessed at £10 in 1545, the same amount as the farmer of the demesne. This had not been the case with the lessees of the corn mill in the 1520s. He was actively milling on the manor. Later in the century there is evidence that the lessees were not directly working the mills themselves. By 1570 the corn and malt mills at Shaw were leased to Henry Lynch of Newbury, a clothworker.[121] The actual men who laboured as millers remain unidentifiable. Change appears to have taken place to the social standing and wealth of millers over the course of the sixteenth century, particularly with an increase in the wealth of the lessee of the mills compared with the labourers whom he employed.

---

[119] TNA, C1/735/50.
[120] TNA, SC6/HENVIII/3739 where he was the lessee and said to be of Pusey but resident and paying tax in 1545 E179/73/171.
[121] BRO, D/EN m1/T2.

THE MIDDLING[122] OR MODAL GROUP OF TAXPAYERS[123]

This group comprised the majority of the tenant population of western Berkshire. They fell into the modal part of the distribution of wealth and landholding. They were made up of those assessed for taxation purposes in the 1520s on goods of between £2 and £20, who farmed between a half and two and a half virgates of land (15 to 75 acres of land). The wealth in their inventories when they died was less than £50, and they were active as office-holders of the parish and manor, serving as churchwardens, jurors, ale tasters and haywards. Together they formed an integral and essential element in the successful working of local society. Their cumulative impact meant they were the key players in implementing change in a locality.[124]

They were an important group who occupied the social space between the large farmer and the poor. They defined themselves in relation to the household which formed the key unit for reproduction and family life, comprised the heart of economic production whether as farm or workshop, and the household was regarded as the fiscal unit for assessment.[125] It should be noted that the incidence of this middling group varied between the regions of England, between large and small towns, especially London and local towns, in gender, age and position in the life cycle. Whether they had a sense of collective identity remains unknown, especially if we accept the arguments for individualism. Yet a sense of empathy might be observed in the increasing use of the language of 'sorts' identified by Wrightson.[126]

We need to consider their position in western Berkshire and will examine the regional differences in their distribution, the characteristic features of their wealth, and their role in the local community. Detailed examples will reveal the people behind the statistics and generalisations and illustrate these general

---

[122] The term 'middling sort' has been made famous by the work of Keith Wrightson: see, for example, 'The Social Order of Early Modern England: Three Approaches', in L. Bonfield, R. M. Smith and K. Wrightson (eds), *The World We Have Gained* (Oxford, 1986), 177–202; 'Estates, Degrees and Sorts: Changing Perceptions of Society in Tudor and Stuart England', in P. Corfield (ed.), *Language, History and Class* (Oxford, 1991), 30–52; '"Sorts of People" in Tudor and Stuart England' in J. Barry, and C. Brooks (eds), *The Middling Sort of People* (Basingstoke, 1994), 28–51; *Earthly Necessities: Economic Lives in Early Modern Britain* (New Haven, 2000).

[123] This composite form is the preferred description of this social group as opposed to Wrightson's more open definition of the 'middling sort', which also included the farmers of the demesne, merchants and professionals that have been analysed separately in this study.

[124] See chapter 1 for a general discussion of their role in the regulation of local society, and below for the examples from western Berkshire.

[125] Barry also employed the household as a unit but not these specific characteristics. J. Barry 'Introduction', in *The Middling Sort of People*, 1–27.

[126] Wrightson, '"Sorts of People" in Tudor and Stuart England', 28–51.

points. We saw in chapter 2 how the method of assessment in the fourteenth century prevented us from observing this group in any meaningful way, since those paying 12d. really did comprise the majority of the population. Instead, we had to examine the shifting proportions of those who belonged to the groups on either side, who were either poor or wealthy, as a more sensitive indicator of change.[127] Therefore, it remains difficult to quantify variations in the size and social composition of this group over time.

A study of the distribution of land among the customary tenants in Table 18 did show that their numbers declined over the course of the sixteenth century as the incidence of large landholdings increased. This would ultimately mean that the numbers in the middling or modal group would have declined as many became smaller customary tenants or successful subtenants, since only a few rose to the ranks of large farmers. Nevertheless, as the example from Kintbury will show later, a reduction in the size of landholding did not necessarily lead to a decline in wealth or impoverishment.

By the early sixteenth century, as we saw in chapter 2, the proportion of those assessed on goods of between £2 and £20 was significantly greater in the region of the Vale than elsewhere.[128] This was certainly supported by the detailed studies of individual communities. The majority of the tenants of Hanney were assessed as having goods valued at between £2 and £5. William Knight, recorded as a £2 householder, is an example of this group. He had acquired a messuage and three half-virgates of land with appurtenances in 1507, and in 1525 added another holding of a messuage and half virgate. He was a member of the manor court jury and homage at both Priors and Seymours, and held additional offices as head tithing man, ale taster and affeerer of the court. These, along with the hayward, were the main manorial officials who were active at Hanney. William Knight represents the majority of the population of Hanney who were farmers of properties that were between a half, and two and a half virgates of land. In general, their inventories reveal a comfortable standard of living and direct agricultural activity, and they frequently held manorial office.[129] As officials of the manor they were influential in the ordering of agriculture and other aspects of village life.

At Ashbury this social group also included those tenants who were said to be *nativi domini* in the manorial records, but whose customary landholdings were sizeable. The lack of personal freedom on this manor does not appear to have been an impediment to obtaining a comfortable standard of living.[130] For

---

[127] See appropriate sections in chapter 2.

[128] It should be noted that the evidence presented in Table 19 on wealth in inventories over the sixteenth century revealed a fairly uniform distribution of those assessed on less than £50.

[129] Although an inventory does not survive for William Knight.

[130] See below in the discussion of serfdom.

example Robert Horton, who in 1519 had recently obtained his manumission, was the largest customary tenant, holding 61 acres of land, was assessed in 1522 on £2 in goods, and when he died in 1544 he left a will that contained several cash bequests to his children amounting to over £7.[131] John French held a messuage and two virgates of land and additional closes of pasture and meadow, and his conditions of tenure still included the demand for carrying services of wood. Nevertheless, he was assessed as a householder with goods worth 20 marks, and in his inventory, in which his goods were valued at £32 0s. 4d., he was farming wheat and barley, producing malt, and had cattle and sheep.[132] Restrictive forms of personal status or tenure were no longer a particularly limiting or constraining force by this date.

The majority of the population at Kintbury were assessed at the lower end of the range for this middling or modal group, at under £5 in 1522, and the wealth in their inventories was valued at less than £50. Of particular interest were their probate records: these illustrate the diversified nature of this local economy and mention millers, a blacksmith, tailors, and also those associated with the cloth industry.[133] For example among the goods listed in the workshop of the 'tucker' John Silver were three pairs of great shears, four coarse handles, a shear board, certain teasels, four pairs of burling irons, a press to press cloth, and a rack to stain cloth upon. The total assessment of his inventory was £15 16s. 11d., which included agricultural items of a cow, two pigs and corn in the barn and field amounting to £2.[134] His industrial concern was pursued alongside his farming activities. He is a good example of the involvement of rural tenants in the cloth industry that dominated economic activity at Newbury and Hungerford. Although the tenants of Kintbury had smaller landholdings than those inhabitants of the other case studies, due to the additional and diversified aspects of their economic activity their wealth was sufficient for them to be included in this social category.[135]

At Shaw, however, there was a notable absence of those who belonged to the middling or modal group. The majority of the population were assessed at under £2 in 1522 and therefore fall into the sector of those liable to have earned the bulk of their income from wages and may have found employment in Newbury. And the larger farmers of customary land, such as Thomas Stanbroke and Richard Person, dominated the landholding structure by 1547.

---

[131] BRO, D/A1/2 fol. 260, 1 October 1544.

[132] BRO, D/A1/66/216 that included 4 cows, 32 sheep, 6 horses, 5 pigs, 6 acres wheat, 14 acres barley, 1 acre oats, half acre beans, in addition to 20 bushels of wheat, 2 quarters malt, and 2 quarters barley.

[133] The latter were Thomas Mathewe 1557, Robert Dolman 1558, John Woodward 1566, John Silver 1579.

[134] BRO, D/A1/115/155.

[135] Considered in more detail below.

Nevertheless, as at Kintbury, those with smaller holdings might also include other lucrative elements such as the tanhouse, mills, or the tenant who had no agricultural land but had two cottages, and one presumes sub-let the other. The polarisation of landholdings and wealth at Shaw ensured the almost total absence of this middling group and was, in part, a result of its proximity to Newbury.

The importance of this middling or modal group lay in the cumulative impact of its members. These were the men, and sometimes women, who made up the majority of the population, who together held large areas of land, and who implemented the various changes in the local economy and landholdings. Furthermore they were the key figures who were active in the regulation of local society on the manor and in the parish.[136]

TAXPAYERS ASSESSED AT LESS THAN £2 A YEAR

This category includes those who provided the chief source of labour. In general, the demand for different types of labour changed very little between the fourteenth and sixteenth centuries, although there was limited evidence for a shift in the social status of those who made up the work force.[137] By 1400 it was only on those demesnes that were still being cultivated directly that the vestiges of the older system survived whereby labour was provided by hired *famuli*, supported by the labour services of customary tenants, and augmented by additional wage labour employed at times of high demand such as harvest. By the middle of the fifteenth century, as we saw in chapter 4, the lands of most demesnes were leased, many as large farms which were worked almost entirely by hired labour. The majority of agricultural land remained in the hands of peasants and was worked by family members, supplemented by live-in servants or wage labour, who were employed to meet increased need at various times in the life-cycle and seasons of the year. By 1600, with the increase in the number of large commercial farms cultivated by servants and day labourers, and the decline in the proportion of land held in small agricultural units, this meant a rise in the number of those with a small holding, or perhaps no land, and increasingly dependent on income from wages. The act of 1589 ordered the

---

[136] Discussed below.

[137] See chapter 2, p. 52. The following survey is based on, for the medieval period, P. D. A. Harvey, *A Medieval Oxfordshire Village: Cuxham, 1240–1400* (Oxford, 1965); H. S. A. Fox, 'Servants, Cottagers and Tied Cottages During the Later Middle Ages: Towards a Regional Dimension', *Rural History*, 6 (1995), 125–54; P. R. Schofield, *Peasant and Community in Medieval England, 1200–1500* (Basingstoke, 2003). For the early modern period see A. Kussmaul, *Servants in Husbandry in Early Modern England* (Cambridge, 1981). M. Overton, *Agricultural Revolution in England* (Cambridge, 1996). Whittle, *Development of Agrarian Capitalism*.

allocation of four acres of land for every newly built cottage and was perhaps an acknowledgment of the growing numbers of those without direct access to agricultural land.[138] We now need to consider in some detail this important sector of society who provided the labour for the large farms and how their position changed in the local economy and society of western Berkshire over the course of this study.

We begin by examining the decline in the numbers of those who were compelled to provide labour for their lords as regular or occasional boon works, and in particular the end of serfdom or villeinage. In theory, because the lord owned his serf or villein as a chattel, the labour of the serf belonged to the lord. In practice the actual demands for the labour of the serf varied between lords and the different regions of the country, as did the proportion of the tenant population who were unfree. Furthermore, as the incidence of serfdom declined, so did the more general level of exactions on the peasantry.[139] Yet the survival of serfdom may still have mattered to those who were personally unfree and liable to the arbitrary exactions of their lords.

The situation in western Berkshire, in terms of the survival of personal servitude or unfreedom, rather than the tenurial obligation to perform labour services, amounted to only a very few cases identifiable after 1400. We will examine its survival before turning to consider the performance of labour services.[140] Serfdom was only found in isolated and disparate incidents, and the numbers of unfree tenants always remained very small.[141] There were occasional references to persons, usually members of the same family, who

[138] J. C. K. Cornwall, *Wealth and Society in Early Sixteenth Century England* (London, 1988), 206.

[139] R. H. Hilton, *The Decline of Serfdom in Medieval England* (London, 1970) remains the classic work on the subject. For a positive interpretation of the conditions of serfdom see J. Hatcher, 'English Serfdom and Villeinage: Towards a Reassessment', *Past and Present*, 90 (1981), 3–39. For the survival in the sixteenth century see D. MacCulloch, 'Bondmen under the Tudors', in C. Cross, D. Loades and J. J. Scarisbrick (eds), *Law and Government under the Tudors* (Cambridge, 1988), 91–109. A more recent overview of the subject can be found in Schofield, *Peasant and Community*, 12–17. For the survival of serfdom and its implications for the development of capitalism see Whittle, *Development of Agrarian Capitalism*, 37–46, 306–7; C. Dyer, 'Memories of Freedom: Attitudes Towards Serfdom in England, 1200–1350', in M. Bush (ed.), *Serfdom and Slavery. Studies in Legal Bondage* (London, 1996), 277–95.

[140] It should be noted that week work, the heaviest component of villein labour services and one that was used to define villein status, had disappeared from western Berkshire by the start of this study.

[141] This was also the conclusion reached from the larger study made by Latham. L. C. Latham, 'The Decay of the Manorial System During the First Half of the Fifteenth Century with Special Reference to Manorial Jurisdiction and the Decline of Villeinage, as Exemplified in the Records of Twenty-Six Manors in the Counties of Berkshire, Hampshire and Wiltshire.' MA thesis, London (1928), 4–5.

were styled *nativi de sanguine*. For example, at Seymours in Hanney in the first half of the fifteenth century tenants such as John Mairyet were described as *native tenentes* in 1436, and this was also the case with Richard Dyraunt in 1437, William Hall senior and Richard Payn in 1441.[142] Incidents of personal serfdom continued for rather longer at Kintbury Eaton and the last case in the court rolls was in 1478 when Richard Jolyf *nativi domini de sanguine* was reported for having a daughter Agnes who was 30 years old and lived at Newbury.[143] Glastonbury abbey was notorious for continuing to have serfdom on its manors.[144] In 1519 members of the Horton family at Ashbury; Edward, Thomas, Robert, and also Robert Bovetown, were described as *nativi domini* whereas Robert Horton senior had recently obtained his manumission.[145] As we have seen, the lack of personal freedom by this date was not necessarily an impediment to the accumulation of land and wealth at Ashbury. This was also the case at Coleshill, where a *nativi domini de sanguine* had chattels worth 100 marks at the beginning of the sixteenth century.[146]

Other incidents characteristic of the survival of serfdom included isolated payments for permission to marry, known as 'merchet'. For example, Alice the daughter of John Alwyn of Kintbury paid £2 for the freedom to marry who and where she chose in 1417.[147] More commonly recorded in the manor court rolls was the failure to obtain permission to live away from the manor and these people were fined for payments of 'chevage'.[148] Incidents can be charted which show a gradual decline on the manors studied in detail. After 1420, at Buckland, chevage payments were only exacted from members of the Keche family and these finally stopped in 1430. At Shaw they gradually ceased and had gone completely by 1429. At Kintbury they continued into the middle of century and were last recorded in 1478. Unfree tenants, *nativi domini*, were making default of court at Seymours in Hanney up to 1441. Certainly serfs were recorded as living outside the manor; for example at Buckland they were residing as far away as Gloucester and Oxford, and more locally at Bampton, Hanney and Aldworth. This reinforces the point made earlier regarding peasant mobility and migration, and the distances they were prepared to travel. The survival of serfdom by the fifteenth century may have largely been a matter of choice on the part of the peasant as the coercive power of landlords declined and

---

[142] BRO, D/EX1 m1/ 1, 4.

[143] BL, 49238 Court of 2 July 1478.

[144] MacCulloch, 'Bondmen under the Tudors', 93, and 94 where there were two serfs in Berkshire in 1560.

[145] BL, Harley MS. 3961.

[146] *VCH Berkshire*, II, 203–4. Coleshill in 21 Henry VII, and also at Sotwell in 24–25 Henry VIII.

[147] BL, Add Roll 49222.

[148] It is difficult to establish how many fines were actually paid.

there were numerous alternative opportunities available, especially the ability to leave the manor. Where it did survive, as at Ashbury, it was the combination of the continuation of landlord policy to retain serfdom on the manor, and, additionally, families choosing to remain on the manor and accept the status of unfreedom. Moreover, as we have seen, it would appear that serfdom was not an impediment to the accumulation of landholdings and wealth on this manor. These incidents of personal serfdom, although disparate, were a more lasting feature of late medieval society than demands for the performance of labour services that had declined earlier.[149]

The leasing of the demesne lands, as we have seen, was a process largely completed by the middle of the fifteenth century, and was accompanied by a decreased use of customary labour, although it had never been the mainstay of agrarian labour even in 1300. The replacement of labour services for a money rent was a gradual development and one that pre-dated the leasing of the demesne lands when tenants chose to pay a sum of money rather than perform specific duties. There were lords, however, who, during a period of labour scarcity, were reluctant to relinquish their rights to labour completely, especially at busy times such as harvest.[150] As a result some works were retained to form part of the payment with the money rent. This can be seen in the rental of Buckland in 1405, where 12 of the 52 tenancies were recorded as a money payment of rent together with *opera*, and two tenancies included the price of the commutated labour services, while the remaining rents were all stipulated in sums of money.[151] However, in the ministers' accounts commutation payments for works were far more numerous than those in the rental, implying that the performance of all the labour services was perhaps unlikely.[152] Labour services were only rarely specified as a condition of tenure in the transfer of land, but an example occurred at Shaw in 1407 when Walter Babbe took a messuage and curtilage and was ordered to pay 2s. annual rent and three days' work in autumn.[153] The more normal clause recorded in the manor court rolls of western Berkshire was the blanket phrase *secundum consuetudinem manerii per redditus servicia et consuetudines inde prius debita et consueta*. The compilation of a new rental at Kintbury Eaton in 1428 incorporated the payments for works into the rent of the tenants and was

[149] For additional examples see Faith 'Berkshire', 174–6.
[150] B. M. S. Campbell, English *Seigniorial Agriculture, 1250–1450* (Cambridge, 2000), 436.
[151] SBT, DR5/1941.
[152] Sum total of works in rental 29s. 10d. DR5/1941; compared with £8 8s. 8d. in the ministers' accounts, for example SBT, DR5/1940 for 1401–02.
[153] TNA, SC2/154/52 court of 10 September 1407.

confirmed in the minister's account of that year.[154] Nevertheless some works were still being performed, such as carrying the prioress's hay to Nuneaton in 1446.[155] As discussed in chapter 4, a fifteenth-century copy of an earlier custumal had been made for this manor, and one wonders what event had stimulated its compilation and made the effort worthwhile for the prioress.[156] At Ashbury, on the manor of Glastonbury abbey, labour services of washing and shearing the lord's sheep, and an additional carrying service of wood, were still being demanded of certain customary tenants in 1519, but whether these were performed cannot be established.[157] From the evidence of these studies, together with those by Faith, it would appear that the commutation of labour services in western Berkshire was largely complete by the middle of the fifteenth century, with only isolated instances remaining.[158]

Servants and labourers increasingly fulfilled the requirements for hired labour for agriculture and played an essential role in the rural economy. They performed a wide variety of activities involving different levels of skill. The nature of employment varied according to the type of agriculture, age and gender of the employee, and the underlying demographic and economic conditions of the period. As we saw in chapter 2 they were generally regarded as falling into two main categories: servants or servants in husbandry, and wage labourers. Alongside these categories there were also craftsmen with specialist skills who were employed for specific tasks such as in carpentry and thatching, and those involved in the rural industries such as cloth manufacture. Common to all was the fact that the majority of their income was derived from wage earnings. Together with peasants who were devoted to agricultural production, they were involved in marketing their products. As such they were influenced by the more general economic changes of the period and the fluctuations in trade discussed in chapter 1. Peasants, labourers and craftsmen were operating within a commercialised economy and had to adjust to the constraints and opportunities that were imposed by the market.[159] Difficulties arose in the second half of the sixteenth century in a period of inflation when the purchasing power of wages fell, and, as direct access to landholdings declined,

---

[154] Previously payments had been for £3 10s. od. annually and there was nothing recorded in the account of 1428–29. BL, Add Roll 49272.

[155] BL, Add Roll 49235, court 12 November 1446.

[156] BL Add MSS 36905 fols 215–18. The hand was fifteenth-century but the names of the tenants did not match those in the court rolls of the period, although many surnames were the same.

[157] BL, Harley MS. 3961. Nevertheless, they were not mentioned in first ministers' accounts after the Dissolution. TNA, SC6/HENVIII/7406, m. 2.

[158] Faith 'Berkshire' 108–9. Labour services at Coleshill were commuted between 1385 and 1421 but again we cannot establish when they were last performed.

[159] Schofield, *Peasant and Community*, 131–56.

so living conditions for those without some form of landholding deteriorated. The situation was exacerbated by government attempts to legislate on the terms of employment and enforce the Statute of Artificers.[160] Furthermore, opportunities to migrate in search of improved employment were reduced by the various statutes relating to vagrancy, settlement, and entitlement to poor relief over the sixteenth century.[161]

Establishing the true value of income from wages is fraught with difficulties, particularly in identifying any additional non-monetary methods of payment.[162] Information on wage rates in Berkshire was rather disparate and varied according to the nature of the task and length and type of employment. In general they remained at the level of the statutory rate or even below.[163] For example, the various men employed to mend the mills at Shaw were usually paid between 4d. and 6d. a day.[164] Due to the fragmentary nature of the evidence we cannot trace change over time in the wages of various craftsmen or labourers, or quantify the non-monetary payments made in addition to the wages.[165] Woodward has shown how the condition of wage labourers declined in the sixteenth century.[166] Although it is not possible to quantify this change in western Berkshire, we can accept that it might have been occurring in the region.

We saw in chapter 2 how the proportions of servants in the population of western Berkshire varied very little between 1381 and 1522. By the latter date, however, the distribution of those dependent on wage labour in western Berkshire varied between the regions and was concentrated in the Kennet area. This was not surprising given the numbers of opportunities for employment in this diversified economy and the presence of the cloth industry. Nevertheless,

---

[160] D. Woodward, 'The Background to the Statute of Artificers: The Genesis of Labour Policy, 1558–63', EcHRev, 33 (1980), 32–44. A. Everitt, 'Farm Labourers', in Thirsk, Agrarian History IV, 396–465. For a comparison of the medieval labour laws and the Statute of Artificers see Whittle, Development of Agrarian Capitalism, 287–301.

[161] P. Slack, Poverty and Policy in Tudor and Stuart England (London, 1988), 113–37. S. Hindle, The State and Social Change in Early Modern England, c.1550–1640 (Basingstoke, 2000).

[162] D. Woodward, 'Wage Rates and Living Standards in Pre-Industrial England', Past and Present, 91 (1981), 28–46. Idem, 'The Determination of Wage Rates in the Early Modern North of England', EcHRev, 47 (1994), 22–43.

[163] VCH Berkshire, II, 193–6.

[164] 1419 a sawyer 6d. a day; 1439 labourers 4d. a day, a carter and his cart 19d. a day, 1447 a tiler for the roof 5d. a day. BRO, D/ENm M24, 31, 32. For comparative material see Whittle, Development of Agrarian Capitalism, 241–7, 269–72.

[165] As was possible in the north of England see C. M. Newman, 'Work and Wages at Durham Priory, 1494–1519', Continuity and Change, 16 (2001), 357–78.

[166] D. Woodward, Men at Work (Cambridge, 1995), 212–15. Idem, 'The Background to the Statute of Artificers', 32–44. Whittle, Development of Agrarian Capitalism, 276–301.

the data from specific places in Table 17 reveals that the proportion of those assessed at under £2, and thus liable to have been assessed as wage earners, was also high at Buckland and Ashbury. By contrast, at Kintbury this category was rather smaller and was probably a result of the successful pursuit of the smallholding economy described below. Perhaps the most remarkable feature was the low incidence at Hanney, where neither the manorial or fiscal records revealed a large number of servants, or those with a low income, or landless individuals.[167]

Wage labour was particularly prevalent in the society of Shaw. There was the largest percentage shown in Table 17, and is supported by the proportion of those assessed on income from wages in the Lay Subsidies.[168] Their enumeration when following those with major landholdings would imply a working relationship, and the large customary landholdings in Table 18 would have required the employment of additional labour. Other labourers may have found employment in the minor industries of Shaw, such as the mills or brick-kiln, or the craft industries such as weaving, or else in the neighbouring town of Newbury.

It remains very difficult to quantify this sector of society; nevertheless we can augment the picture of servants with more qualitative evidence. For example, bequests to servants suggest a strong regard for the individual, such as William Slatter of Buckland who left £2 to his servant John Wykes in 1495.[169] In 1565 the wealthy yeoman sheep farmer, Richard Mills also known as Carter of Ashbury, left a sheep to each of his servants who were living with him at the time of making his will.[170] His house also had chambers reserved for his servants both 'the maynies chamber' and 'the maydens chamber'.[171] These rooms tended to be in homes of the wealthier testators and another example, this time from Kintbury, was the yeoman farmer John Elgar whose large house with ten rooms included a servants' chamber.[172] It should be noted, however, that mention of servants in the probate material was never frequent, in fewer

---

[167] The farmers of the demesne required additional labour on their farms and William Robyns had two of the four servants enumerated with him in 1522. The lack of servants is further substantiated by the probate evidence given below.

[168] In 1522 of the 34 individuals listed 14 were 'householders' holding 93 per cent of the assessed wealth and 20 were 'labourers and servants' with 7 per cent of the assessment. TNA, E315/464. In 1524 12 individuals, or 46 per cent were assessed on wages and 9 were listed after major tenants. TNA, E179/73/121.

[169] TNA, PROB11/10/15. In the description of his house in his inventory the second chamber was reserved for his servants and there were four beds there, implying that he had the potential to employ at least four resident servants. TNA, PROB2/455.

[170] BRO, D/A1/96/99. Total inventory £559 8s. 0d.

[171] This was a house with seven rooms; and there were six bedsteads in the men's chamber and two in the maiden's chamber.

[172] BRO, D/A1/65/60 dated 1577 and total inventory £220 0s. 3d.

than 10 per cent of cases.[173] Nevertheless it does strengthen our understanding of servants as an integral part of rural society.

A small landholding did not necessarily mean impoverishment for the tenant. The large proportion of persons assessed on less than £2 in the Kennet region may have been sustained by the availability of varied employment that was additional to agriculture. It was the ability to augment the produce from a smallholding or even just a garden, with additional sources of income that made this type of economy viable. The effects that the successful cloth industry of Newbury had on its hinterland, particularly on employment in the finishing of cloth, were demonstrated in chapter 3. Although large numbers of cloth workers were never identified in the documentation of the hinterland, there was enough activity to show the effects of the industry in the rural area.[174] Moreover we have already seen in previous chapters how this area of woodland pasture contained additional sources of income, particularly those obtained from the exploitation of the natural resources of the area, such as the woodland, the rivers and the extraction of clay and chalk. Tenants took commercial advantage of these opportunities and were observed fishing, making bricks, burning charcoal, digging chalk for daubing, and working as coopers. In fact, they were actively exploiting these natural advantages to a greater extent than their manorial lords who were discussed in chapter 4. In the early 1520s, a high proportion of individuals with smallholdings, or of those whose income was largely derived from wages, did not necessarily equate to impoverishment. The availability of opportunities to diversify and supplement either income from wages, or farming, made the Kennet region an attractive area, as is clear from the numbers of people who migrated to the region. In this respect there were many similarities with other areas of cloth manufacture, such as the worsted area of Norfolk,[175] or mining areas such as the coal and lead mines of County Durham or the Stannaries of Devon and Cornwall.[176] The success of the diversified smallholding economy was a feature of the fifteenth and early sixteenth centuries that was to change as the century progressed when the cost of land increased dramatically, and the value of wage income declined under the effects of inflation.

Neither the manorial nor the fiscal documents were capable of revealing a large group of low income or landless people. Their presence was discerned

---

[173] Mention of servants: Ashbury 10 per cent; Buckland 13.48 per cent; Kintbury 9.32 per cent; West Hanney 5.4 per cent.
[174] Particularly as activities such as spinning were undertaken as a secondary source of income.
[175] Whittle, *Development of Agrarian Capitalism*, 301–4.
[176] I. Blanchard, 'Labour Productivity and Work Psychology in the English Mining Industry, 1400–1600', *EcHRev*, 31 (1978), 1–24.

when considering subtenancy in the previous chapter, but it was rarely possible to establish its full extent or the cost of land to the subtenant. Nevertheless it is important to acknowledge the existence of the poor and landless in the community even if we cannot quantify their prevalence. Moreover, during the sixteenth century there was growing public concern, expressed among those who petitioned Parliament and in the legislation, about a perceived increase in the numbers of landless persons and those living in poverty. By the end of our period the legislation for the Elizabethan poor law was being finalised and implemented, and provision for the poor was becoming established at the level of the parish, although it would take some time for it to be fully enacted throughout the country.[177] One of the enduring problems for the historian is to gauge the extent of rural poverty and landlessness as the evidence is, at best, fragmentary. Contemporaries' awareness of the needs of poor people can be seen in the bequests made in wills of doles of cash, clothes and food. Provision for the poor of the parish became a feature of benefactions in wills from the middle of the sixteenth century, although there had been isolated examples, especially in Newbury, before that date.[178] Monetary contributions to the poor men's box of the parish became a regular feature after 1552 and involved many of the inhabitants of the parishes.[179] The foundation of almshouses, although on a rather larger scale, was another manifestation of these concerns, for example that created at Lambourn in 1500 by John Eastbury. Other good works included bequests towards the maintenance of highways and bridges, which were particularly a feature of Newbury. Elsewhere this type of benefaction was associated with wealthy individuals rather than as a popular response to contemporary needs.[180] The presence of the poor within the local communities was certainly visible to the testators of the second half of the sixteenth century.

Finally we need briefly to consider the commercial and craft sector of society: the butchers, brewers, bakers and blacksmiths who lived and traded

---

[177] For a review of rate of implementation see Hindle, *The State and Social Change in Early Modern England*, especially 153–4.

[178] In 1403 John Deryng left £12 to poor people, while in 1494 Richard Bedford left a tenement in Newbury for the good of the poor house. TNA, PROB11/2A/5, PROB11/10/16. Bequests to the poor in Newbury peak in their incidence between 1547 and 1559. An example from Kintbury was the £1 each given in apparel and money to ten of the poorest parishioners in Kintbury by Henry Brinklow in 1546. TNA, PROB11/31/20.

[179] The 1552 Act for the provision and relief of the poor established weekly collections of alms for the poor. Peter Marshall noted the possible association between the decline in bequests for masses for the dead and rise of bequests to the poor. P. Marshall, *Beliefs and the Dead in Reformation England* (Oxford, 2002), 102–3. Bequests to the poor men's box begin in Ashbury in 1548, Newbury in 1552, Hanney and Buckland in 1553, and Kintbury in 1559.

[180] Hanney in 1545 and 1553; Kintbury in 1558.

in the villages. These activities frequently provided a form of by-employment as an additional source of income, could involve women, and were often undertaken in addition to the cultivation of a small holding. They were repeatedly recorded in manor court rolls for infringements against the assize, either for real offences or for permission to trade. They provided invaluable elements in the commercial activities of the village, and form another element in the diversity of economic life identifiable in rural society. Moreover, their numbers could be swelled by traders from the neighbouring towns, such as the bakers from Abingdon and Gloucester who traded at Buckland, or the bakers from Hungerford who came to Kintbury.

To sum up this section, rural society in western Berkshire was characterised by the diverse nature of its composition and contained distinctive regional elements. Society was not static, but was shown to have had elements of both continuity and change. Local resident landowners formed a stable group that increased in size in the second half of the sixteenth century, but had been noticeably absent from the Kennet region before this time. As a social group they were linked together across the regions through ties of kinship, friendship and office holding, and played an important role in influencing change when acting as lords of the manor or county officials. The merchants of western Berkshire, although less numerous, were an important social group who bound the locality into wider trading networks that had an international dimension. From the end of the fourteenth century through to the sixteenth century the farmers of the demesne remained a wealthy and constant feature of local society. Millers, however, formed a more diverse social group and one with an industrial rather than agricultural focus. They were fully engaged in the market and had to make a success of the often difficult economic conditions, particularly in the fifteenth century. Change came during the sixteenth century when there was some polarisation of wealth between the lessees and the working millers. The social category of middling or modal group formed an important element in implementing change in the locality, whether as cultivators of the arable and keepers of cattle and sheep, or as officers of the manor and parish. Nevertheless, they were not a universal feature of local society as very few were identified at Shaw where the polarisation of land and wealth was apparent by the sixteenth century and where Newbury's impact was found to be greatest. Regional differences were also identified in the social group of those assessed on wealth valued at less than £2 and who might have been employed as wage labourers. The diversified nature of the local economy of the Kennet region created more opportunities for wage labour than elsewhere. Members of this social group were affected by the more general changes in the economy and landholding that resulted in a decline in their standard of living by 1600 from the optimal conditions of the middle of the fifteenth century. The need for extra-familial labour was a constant requirement of large farms whether cultivated as demesne or customary holdings. By 1400 serfdom and the use of labour services only continued in disparate areas. The rise in wage labour that others have described as a feature of early modern society and the sixteenth century could not be quantified in western Berkshire. It might have been present, but the documentation did not allow us to measure its prevalence by the end of the sixteenth century. Thus the men and women who implemented change at the local level came from diverse social groups and their presence was regionally distinctive.

The regulation of local society

Rural society in western Berkshire was neither homogenous nor harmonious. There were a variety of different forms of tension in local society that included those between neighbours, between lords and tenants, or which took the form of political and religious dissent. Our concern in this section is with the ways in which tensions in society materialised, were resolved, and had a regional dimension. We need to consider how society in western Berkshire managed local affairs, particularly conflict resolution and socially disruptive behaviour; plus the more mundane everyday activities such as the regulation of agriculture in the common fields. Pre-industrial society was highly localised and conducted on an inter-personal basis; your neighbour in the village was often your neighbour in the fields. The potential for discord was inherent within such close communities. Furthermore, episodes of conflict are seen to have escalated during periods of rapid social and economic change, and to have had regional differences, but whether these increased over the course of the sixteenth century as a result of changes within society remains a matter of some debate.[181] Conflict resolution could be carried out in a number of ways, both informal and formal. Formal regulation was achieved through a variety of institutions: seigniorial, royal, and ecclesiastical. Tenants could avail themselves of a spectrum of courts and, as will be demonstrated in the examples below, they knew the appropriate institution to which they could take their grievances.[182] We have demonstrated the importance of the middling or

---

[181] A summary of the key aspects of this large topic can be found in K. Wrightson and D. Levine, *Poverty and Piety in an English Village* (Oxford, 1995), 'Postscript' by K. Wrightson. M. McIntosh, *Controlling Misbehaviour in England, 1370–1600* (Cambridge, 1998), Introduction.

[182] The majority of cases were taken to the lord's manor court. Nevertheless, the examples of the cases of ancient demesne discussed below, and also those cases heard in the courts of Chancery, Common Pleas and later in Requests and Star Chamber, plus the archdeacon's court, all demonstrate the variety of courts attended.

modal group in local society and the differences in their distribution. These
were the men who held local positions of authority and who were active in the
regulation of local society as churchwardens and manorial officials. They were
also instrumental in the implementation of government's legislation during the
sixteenth century, especially as the parish was increasingly employed as the
unit for local administration.[183]

Regulation in the manor court

At the most local level the manor court fulfilled a long-established regulative
role which continued into the sixteenth century, albeit with a reduction in the
number of cases.[184] The courts were held by the lord's representative and a
jury consisting of prominent tenants of the manor. Here social regulation was
exercised over villagers by their friends and neighbours who acted as jurors,
and it was from among their numbers that the other manorial officials were
elected. Jurors were members of the social category of middling or modal group;
they were usually tenants of a half to two and a half virgate holdings, and they
might also include subtenants.[185] The office of juror may have been associated
with a particular holding and this would explain how, at times of increased
mortality, a woman might act as juror, as occurred at Hanney in 1511, 1520, 1545
and 1587. Furthermore there was little turnover in the personnel who acted as
jurors in the second half of the sixteenth century.[186] Thus the trend over the
sixteenth century was for an increasingly smaller section of local society to
be active both in implementing the administration of the manor and also in
social regulation. Additionally, these men were often active as churchwardens
and as such were responsible for the moral welfare of the community.

A manifestation of the different types of society that have been described is
the degree of violence and disorder that was experienced. Furthermore, quanti-
fication of the various cases of theft, violence and trespass reveals evidence for
change over time, and are presented in Appendix IV, Table 24. The reduction in
numbers in Tables 20 and 24 may reflect the rise in access to the royal courts
from the mid-sixteenth century as, in a time of inflation, more cases came

---

[183] See chapter 1 p. 17. Churchwardens' accounts do not survive for the case study
parishes and so it has not been possible to undertake an examination of the role of
churchwardens in these local communities. See B. Kümin, *The Shaping of a Community*
(Aldershot, 1996).

[184] See chapter 4 for a description of the remit of the manor court and change over
time.

[185] See the discussion of subtenancy in chapter 4.

[186] This was one element in a larger trend of stability of surnames generally, and also
of customary holdings remaining in the hands of the same family, which were both
described above.

Table 20 *Summary data of cases in the manor courts, 1401–1600.*
(Full data in Appendix IV, Table 24)

Place	Total number of courts	Violence	Theft	Trespass	Cases against the commons	Passing of Bye-laws
Priors, Hanney	54	5	1	6	0	2
Seymours, Hanney	48	0	5	5	0	4
Buckland	146	64	31	20	176	30
Shaw	71	9	13	6	1	2
Kintbury	150	41	24	38	143	11

Sources: Buckland SBT, DR5/1939–2048. Priors, Hanney NCA, 4060–4062. Seymours, Hanney BRO, D/EX1 M1–6 and Hendred House. Kintbury BL, Add Roll 49210–49284. Shaw TNA, SC2/154/52–54, 18.

within their jurisdiction.[187] Moreover, with the decline in serfdom a greater proportion of tenants were personally free, and as such also had access to the royal courts.

Some societies had a greater incidence of violence than others, and Hanney was remarkable for the *absence* of these types of cases. In general, violence, theft and trespass were more a feature of the fifteenth century than later, and may be a reflection of the broader changes in the use of manorial and royal courts already discussed. Nevertheless, there were clusters of incidents at Buckland in the 1450s and 1470s, at Priors Hanney in 1441 to 1450, at Shaw between 1471 and 1520, while at Kintbury there was a background level of 2–9 cases per decade during the fifteenth century. It was impossible to identify a specific social category as participants who dominated the violent incidents. There does, however, appear to have been a greater incidence of events in those communities that had a mobile or transient element in their society, such as at Shaw and Kintbury, which might reflect the effect of their proximity to the towns of Newbury and Hungerford. At Shaw there was a greater proportion of outsiders involved in violent events: 54 per cent of all participants.[188] Poverty may also have been a determining factor lying behind violent incidents, although this has been impossible to establish. Individuals may have been prone to involvement in acts of violence, such as the generations of the Brite family of Buckland and also, although less frequently, the Fettiplace family. Walter Fettiplace was even in prison in 1495.[189] Cases specifically against

---

[187] That is, cases over the 40 shilling threshold.

[188] Yates, thesis, 269.

[189] It was reported in the manor court that his tenement was empty because he was in prison. SBT, DR5/2015.

women were not a dominant feature of these courts.[190] It is worth noting that
the jurors themselves were not exempt from prosecutions, and as a group may
even have been vulnerable as targets.

Cases brought into the manor court could be remarkably colourful and
reveal the more extreme aspects of the breakdown of harmony within the
community. The most spectacular case at Shaw was the murder of John
Newman in 1486 as a result of having been struck by a sword.[191] At Kintbury
in 1422 Alice Godstock was arrested for the murder of her husband Richard.[192]
There appears to have been a serial rapist at Buckland; one Thomas Pole a
labourer, who raped Joan Smith in 1476 and John Bloxham's daughter in
the following year.[193] In 1456 Robert Taylour was living suspiciously and
entertaining strange men and women in his home at Buckland.[194] At Kintbury
in 1445 Thomas Cotton kept a concubine and entertained suspicious persons of
no good reputation.[195] The vicar of Kintbury, William Billesden, was accused
of violent theft when in 1468 he broke into the house of William Boney, beat
him and stole the hoard of gold that William had discovered valued at £9 16s.
8d.[196] These were all rather extraordinary cases in the general workings of the
court. However, the thefts of grain at Hanney in the 1470s that involved the
farmer of the demesne both as injured party and as thief may be a reflection
of a period of economic hardship.[197]

The more cooperative aspects of local society can be observed in the ways in
which tenants used the manor court for the regulation of open-field farming.
In this context we see the middling tenants active in the regulation of their
society and economic activity; as jurors of the manor court they drew up the
bye-laws regarding agriculture; as haywardens and constables they enforced
their implementation and brought cases to the court for prosecution. Bye-
laws determined when common grazing on the fields could begin, set the
level of stints or number of animals that could be pastured, and regulated the
pannage of pigs and their ringing to prevent damage.[198] A typical example
of a bye-law from Kintbury in 1448 ordered that no one was to enter the

---

[190] Scolds were only prosecuted at Buckland in 1453 and Kintbury in 1433. SBT, DR5/1978,
BL, Add Roll 49227 court of 16 November 1433.
[191] TNA, SC2/154/54 court of 2 August 1486.
[192] BL, Add Roll 49222.
[193] SBT, DR5/2002.
[194] SBT, DR5/1982.
[195] BL, Add Roll 49234.
[196] BL, Add Roll 49238.
[197] Yates, thesis, 190.
[198] The work of W. O. Ault on bye-laws has influenced all studies subsequently. The
Berkshire evidence is in line with that found elsewhere in central England. W. O. Ault,
Open-Field Husbandry and the Village Community (Philadelphia, 1965) and the bye-laws
were translated in his *Open Field Farming in Medieval England* (London, 1972). *Idem,*

field sown with corn until it had all been removed and carried away. They could then enter with their animals (presumably just the large beasts) for one week, after which their sheep could graze on the stubble. A penalty of 6s. 8d. in money would be imposed on each person found in default, and half was to be paid to the prioress as lord of the manor and half to the Church.[199] On the whole the system worked, and Table 20 records the incidence of the passing of bye-laws and cases against the commons. Boundaries in the open fields were administered by the community acting as a group, as occurred at Buckland where the whole village viewed the setting of the meer stones on both the east and west sides of the parish, and this activity continued into the eighteenth century.[200] Signs of stress were observed at Hanney in 1599 in a dispute between the manors of the parish over the allocation of pasture and this was the first real evidence at Hanney of a breakdown in the management of the common resources of the village.[201] At Buckland, for some unknown reason, 42 bye-laws were brought together and written down in the court book of Buckland parsonage in 1593–94.[202]

Bye-laws were enforced, and cases of infringements were reported to the manor court by locally elected officials who were prosecuting their own neighbours. Fines were levied and profits from these went to the manorial lord and, on occasion, to the repairs of the parish church, as in the example given above. Nobody was exempt. The local gentry were also fined, especially for trespass and over-stocking with animals beyond their stint. For example, Thomas Wallington of Wallingtons in Kintbury frequently over-pastured the common belonging to the manor of Kintbury Eaton in the 1430s and 1440s. Some cases of trespass, such as those against the movement and pasturing of large numbers of animals (chase and re-chase), were also a means of regulating over-commoning. This was particularly a feature of the societies in the Vale, but was also found at Kintbury when it involved tenants of neighbouring manors. There were numerous incidents of this type of activity, such as at Kintbury in 1481 when Henry Gunter made chase and re-chase with a minimum of 400 of his sheep and damaged the field at Templeton.[203] In 1545, William Fettiplace was ordered to desist giving chase and re-chase with his animals in the fields

'Manor Court and Parish Church in Fifteenth-century England: A Study of Village by-Laws' *Speculum*, 42 (1967), 53–67.

[199] BL, Add Roll 49235.

[200] BRO, D/EWE E1, M9.

[201] NCA, 1360. It also illustrates how the rights of pasture were being jealously guarded by the end of the sixteenth century.

[202] SBT, DR5/2097. These bye-laws are not included in the table as they relate to the manor of Buckland parsonage and not Buckland Dukes.

[203] BL, Add Roll 49247.

of Newenton at Buckland.[204] Thus, although tensions can be observed, local society was, on the whole, relatively successful in the self-regulatory aspects of administering and maintaining the social and agricultural features of the community and obtaining compliance from its members.

Lord–tenant relations

The relationship between a lord and his tenant was a constant feature of rural society. The degree of conflict and tension within the relationship varied over time. It is in this dynamic that historians such as Rodney Hilton discern one of the driving forces for change in society. We have already seen this relationship in operation over the conditions of tenure and take-up of landholdings which had repercussions in the shifting dynamic of the cost of land to the tenant and the level of income received by the lord. The relationship did not necessarily have to result in a clash of interests, although this was often how the evidence appears in the documentation.

Freedom from seigniorial restrictions was a recurring theme in earlier conflicts between lords and peasants and one of the contexts in which it surfaced was in claims to ancient demesne status. Kintbury was one of those communities which had been involved in the 'Great Rumour' of 1377 when the peasants applied to the Chancery for a copy of their entry in Domesday Book to establish if they had once been part of the royal demesne and were therefore free from heavy seigniorial burdens.[205] Although initially unsuccessful, the tenants of Kintbury did not give up and applied again in 1402.[206] This type of conflict recurred in 1468 when the tenants of Kintbury Eaton, who were again claiming to hold by ancient demesne, were told to show their charters and copies in the manor court or they would forfeit their tenancies.[207] Nothing more was heard of the matter. These cases are of interest as this was a manor where incidents of serfdom were still found in 1478, but where there was almost full occupancy of landholdings in the fifteenth century, unlike the prevalence of cases of empty tenements on the other manors. Perhaps demand for tenancies in this area was sufficient for individuals to accept these conditions; but if this were the case why did they pursue the claims for ancient demesne status?

Tenants also employed the royal courts to resolve disputes over tenure with their lords and among themselves. These reveal real tensions in society in addition to the ability of humble tenants to take their cases to the central

---

[204] SBT, DR5/2034.
[205] R. Faith, 'The 'Great Rumour' of 1377 and Peasant Ideology', in R. H. Hilton and T. Aston (eds), *The English Rising of 1381* (Cambridge, 1984), 43–73. *CPR* 1377–81, p. 15. For a discussion of the significance of this type of case see Dyer, 'Memories of Freedom: Attitudes Towards Serfdom in England', 277–95.
[206] *CPR* Henry IV, vol. ii, p. 107.
[207] BL, 49238, Court of 9 January 1468.

courts. For example, at a date between 1529 and 1532 Geoffrey Lane, a labourer, was using the court of Chancery to pursue his title to properties in Kintbury which he claimed were wrongfully retained by the abbess of Amesbury.[208] Similarly, Agnes Sturling was challenging the abbot of Abingdon in the Court of Requests over his claims to the lands called Sextens in Hanney.[209] Property theft was being implied in the case brought in Chancery at some point between 1537 and 1538 by John Huchyns of Shaw against the bullying tactics of Edward Fettiplace, a justice of the peace for Berkshire, and Maurice Smart 'a man of great substance'.[210] Perhaps the numerous cases relating to stolen deeds in the Court of Chancery were also cases of property theft.

Tensions between lords and their tenants are apparent in those cases of theft against the property of the lord, for example when hares were taken from the lords' warrens at Shaw and Buckland. On a larger scale was the theft of 4,000 saplings from the woods at Shaw in 1426 by William atte Burgh of Speenhamland. The attacks on the property of Alice Chaucer as Lady of the manor of Buckland in 1461 and 1462, when a cart and horses were stolen,[211] have to be viewed in the context of her vulnerability at that time, although she was specially excepted from the act of attainder in 1461.[212] There was another incident at her manor of Donnington in 1459, when £40 worth of her goods were stolen at the time of a more general attack on her son John.[213] Nevertheless, the relatively infrequent and disparate nature of these offences is significant for our understanding of lord–tenant relations.

Political and religious dissent

A rather different form in which tensions in society were expressed was in acts of political and religious dissent. In western Berkshire these types of incidents were centred on the town of Newbury and, to a lesser extent, in the surrounding region. The reasons for a popular uprising, such as that which occurred across southern England in the summer of 1450, are always varied and multi-faceted, involving a combination of political, economic and local issues.[214] Hare has convincingly argued for the correlation between the areas

---

[208] TNA, C1/651/43.

[209] TNA, REQ2/12/112, 185.

[210] TNA, C1/814/6. John Huchyns alleged that they had broken into his house and physically threatened him with eviction from his messuage and half yardland, and he was only able to avoid arrest and being sent to Oxford gaol by his ability to find sureties for his good behaviour.

[211] SBT, DR5/1988, 1989.

[212] S. Lee (ed.), *Dictionary of National Biography*, vol. xlvi (London, 1896), 55–6.

[213] TNA, CP40/795, xxxiii v. R. Griffiths, *The Reign of Henry VI* (Stroud, 1998), 825.

[214] I. M. W. Harvey, *Jack Cade's Rebellion of 1450* (1991). M. Mate, 'The Economic and Social Roots of Medieval Popular Rebellion: Sussex in 1450–1451', *EcHRev*, 45 (1992),

of disturbance in the summer of 1450 and major cloth-producing centres, especially in Wiltshire, and linked the uprising with the economic depression and disruption in foreign trade at a time when government was weak and unpopular. Newbury, however, was not as severely affected by the downturn in the economy as many other towns and there was evidence for expansion at this time.[215] Nevertheless, growth and prosperity were not a universal experience. The inhabitants of the town were inclined towards participation in political disturbances. In the aftermath of Cade's rebellion in 1450 it was felt necessary to send a quarter of the body of one of his sergeants, John Ramsey, a wine drawer, to be exhibited in the town, while his head remained in London and was placed on London bridge.[216] The selection of towns for the exhibition of the rebels' bodies was significant and so by inference something had happened at Newbury that required them to receive this gruesome warning of the fate of traitors.[217] The men of Newbury were also involved in an incident in Winchester where they extorted £100 from the abbot of Hyde, and the earlier anti-clerical rising at Crawley had been based largely on a gang of men from Newbury.[218] The stress on order made in the Reading Parliament of 1453 has to be viewed against this background.[219] Cade's rebellion is seen by some historians as presaging the Wars of the Roses and stimulated by the duke of York and his adherents.[220] York certainly held part of the manor of Newbury at this time.

The area of western Berkshire was not involved in the major skirmishes of the Wars of the Roses. Nevertheless, a number of disparate incidents reveal elements of political unrest and disturbance during the period of civil war. There was a series of uprisings in Newbury between 1458 and 1460 that may have been associated with the Wars of the Roses and the support of certain townsmen for the duke of York. The French chronicler Jean de Wavrin actually mentioned events in Newbury in 1458 when he reported that the townsmen withheld money from the earl of Wiltshire as they were keeping it for their lord the duke of York. According to Wavrin the king and his council were very unhappy, and for this reason sent lord Scales to the town to administer justice

661–76. J. N. Hare, 'The Wiltshire Risings of 1450: Political and Economic Discontent in Mid-Fifteenth-century England', *Southern History*, 4 (1982), 13–31.

[215] See chapter 3 p. 110.

[216] H. Nicolas (ed.), *Proceedings and Ordinances of the Privy Council of England Volume VI 22 Henry VI to 39 Henry VI* (Record Commission, 1837), 108.

[217] There was also a rising in the Hungerford area. Hare, 'The Wiltshire Risings of 1450', 26.

[218] Harvey, *Jack Cade's Rebellion*. Hare, 'The Wiltshire Risings of 1450', 26.

[219] Hare, 'The Wiltshire Risings of 1450', 27.

[220] Harvey, *Jack Cade's Rebellion*, 148.

to the rebels and subsequently he arrested several inhabitants who he sent as prisoners to the Tower of London.[221]

A little later, on 6 July 1459, Stephen Wyard and John Stokes alias John Clerk of Newbury husbandman rose up with 120 men armed with swords, arrows, lances, axes and spears, entered the church of St Mary of Newbury and stole the mace and opened the chest and stole money from it.[222] Later, in 1460, six other Newbury men had been accused by John Norris, sheriff of Berkshire, of various transgressions and contempts and were later outlawed at Wallingford.[223] These were not insignificant men, as Stephen Wyard and Thomas Goddard were local tax collectors of the tenth and fifteenth and John Croke was a prominent merchant in the town. Robert Croke, rather significantly, was importing hundreds of bowstaffs into Newbury in 1460 from Southampton.[224]

The link with the duke of York was most obvious in another event of 1460. According to the *English Chronicle* the earl of Wiltshire, lord Scales and lord Hungerford swept into the town, demanded to know who supported York, whereupon some of those who confessed were drawn, hanged and quartered, and 'alle other inhabitantes of the forseyde toune were spoyled of alle theyre goodes'.[225] By September of that year 70 prisoners had been delivered to Wallingford gaol, including 32 named men from Newbury.[226] Events in Newbury subsequently quietened down, perhaps also associated with the death of the duke of York at the battle of Wakefield on 30 December 1460. Meanwhile in the countryside there were attacks at Buckland and Donnington on the duchess of Suffolk which have already been mentioned. There were additional violent skirmishes in 1460 on St John's manor in Buckland.[227] Furthermore in 1462 John Fettiplace of Wolveley was violently attacked by John Eastbury and the former called on the duke of Suffolk for support.[228] Taken together, these incidents reveal the involvement of the region in the wider political unrest of the period.

Newbury and the surrounding area were involved in another flurry of political activity at the end of the fifteenth century. The town was reputed

---

[221] I would like to thank Dr Livia Visser-Fuchs for providing these references by Wavrin to events in Newbury. W. and ELCP Hardy (eds), *Recueil des Croniques et Anchiennes Istories de la Grant Bretaigne, a present nomme Engleterre par Jehan de Waurin, Seigneur du Forestel*, 5 vols (London, 1864–91), this incident is found in vol. 5, 270.

[222] TNA, KB27/798 Rex section, KB29/89. These cases were found by trawling through the documents and there may be others that a more systematic search would uncover.

[223] TNA, KB29/89.

[224] Southampton City Archives, SC5/5/12.

[225] J. S. Davies (ed.), *An English Chronicle* (Camden Society, 64 1856), 90.

[226] *CPR* 39 Henry VI, 648–9. TNA, C66/490.

[227] SBT, DR5/1986.

[228] TNA, C1/27/408.

to have been one of the headquarters of the Duke of Buckingham's revolt in 1483,[229] perhaps only as a centre for recording the names of the men involved who came from the surrounding area.[230] Nevertheless, the sessions of the peace were held in Newbury for the first time in 1483, perhaps affirming royal authority there. The Cheyneys, however, continued to be involved in various riotous events in Newbury and the hinterland.[231] Furthermore, in 1501, during Edmund de la Pole earl of Suffolk's conspiracy, there was a meeting in Speenhamland and also in Newbury at the house of Richard Marshall.[232]

Berkshire appears to have been involved in the more general unrest of 1549.[233] In July a royal order was made to repress uproars 'if any suche shall happen in the counties of Oxforde, Berkes, and Bucks', while in the same month Sir W. Paget was writing to Somerset advising him to go into Berkshire, and it was certainly one of the counties which the commissioners were especially ordered to inspect in 1549.[234] It is becoming increasingly apparent that the disenchantment of that year had a fairly widespread geographical impact.[235] This has important implications for lord–tenant relations and the confidence that lords, in particular those recent landowners, had in their abilities to bring about change in a period of more general unrest.[236] This may go some way to explaining the delay in raising the price of land to reflect the true level of economic rent that has been observed.

In addition to these varied acts of political unrest there were also cases of religious dissent and challenges to the authority of the Church. One of the responsibilities of the churchwardens was for the moral welfare of their parishioners. They had to report local cases to the archdeacon and many were active in fulfilling their responsibilities.[237] Newbury was also a centre of religious

---

[229] R. Horrox, *Richard III* (Cambridge, 1989), 153–61.

[230] *Rotuli Parliamentorum VI*, 245–6. William Noreys of Yattendon, Thomas de la Mare of Aldermaston, William Ovedale of Wickham. The Cheyneys were linked with events in Salisbury Horrox, *Richard III*, 153–61.

[231] John Cheyney of West Woodhay along with Robert and Roger Cheyney were involved in a number of events, undated case REQ2/16/25. *Calendar Close Rolls Henry VII*, vol. 1, 329 case in 1499.

[232] TNA, KB9/4.

[233] A. Fletcher, *Tudor Rebellions*, 3rd edn (London, 1983).

[234] *VCH Berkshire*, II, 207.

[235] E. H. Shagan, 'Protector Somerset and the 1549 Rebellions: New Sources and New Perspectives', *EHR*, 114 (1999), 34–63. But see the debate between Shagan, Bush and Bernard in *EHR*, 115 (2000), 103–33.

[236] R. W. Hoyle, 'Agrarian Agitation in Mid-Sixteenth Century Norfolk: A Petition of 1553', *Historical Journal*, 44 (2001), 223–38.

[237] For an example of the range of different types of cases reported by the churchwardens of western Berkshire in 1391 see T. C. B. Timmins (ed.), *The Register of John Waltham bishop of Salisbury, 1388–1395* (Canterbury and York Society, 80, 1994), 115–28.

dissent and heresy in the later middle ages and as such drew in people from the surrounding villages.[238] The men arrested and ordered to be brought before the council in 1402 are thought to have had Lollard connections.[239] By the end of the century Newbury appears to have had a strong association with Lollardy. A series of heretical trials took place in 1491 that involved a number of Newbury people, and also those from the surrounding parishes including Thatcham, Shaw, and Speen. The records of the trials provide details of their heretical beliefs.[240] For example, Thomas Tailour of Newbury, a fuller, denied the efficacy of going on pilgrimage, challenged the sacraments of baptism and penance, the authority of the pope, and had possession of a Lollard book.[241] Despite the trials and fulfilling of various penances, heretical beliefs continued into the sixteenth century.[242] Yet this heretical activity has to be balanced with the contemporary probate evidence of numerous benefactions to the church of Newbury, which resulted in its almost complete rebuilding. Moreover, as we saw in chapter 2, there were major restorations of many of the churches of western Berkshire at this time, implying support for the local church.

In reviewing the evidence concerning the manifestations of tensions and regulation of rural society it has been possible to demonstrate a regional dimension to their incidence. Through an examination of acts of violence and disorder it has been possible to show that the number of cases of this kind declined in the manor court during the sixteenth century as inflation and the greater accessibility of the royal courts to ordinary litigants expanded the choice of venue and has been supported by examples of a range of incidents and variety of different courts that involved the residents of western Berkshire. Yet what remains remarkable is the overall impression of conformity and peaceful solution to disputes. There is a sense that the cases in Table 20 were isolated examples rather than a groundswell of dissatisfaction and disillusionment, except perhaps at Kintbury. In fact, we are observing a system of regulation at the local level that was working. There were regional differences in the distribution of cases, with more cases in the Kennet valley where the effects of Newbury and Hungerford were felt. Newbury itself was shown to have been a centre for political and religious dissent in the fifteenth century that drew in inhabitants from the surrounding area. In those localities where

---

[238] J. A. F. Thomson, *The Later Lollards, 1414–1520* (Oxford, 1965), chapter 3. A. D. Brown, *Popular Piety in Late Medieval England* (Oxford, 1995). As such it conforms with the traditional view that Lollardy was found in areas associated with the cloth industry.

[239] References as before and *CPR 1401–05*, p. 198. *VCH Berkshire*, IV, 137.

[240] D. P. Wright (ed.), *The Register of Thomas Langton, Bishop of Salisbury, 1485–93* (Canterbury and York Society, 74, 1985), 69–79.

[241] Wright, *Register of Thomas Langton*, 70.

[242] Thomson, *The Later Lollards*; J. Pratt (ed.), *The Acts and Monuments of John Foxe*, vol. 4 (London, 1877).

there was a transient element such as cloth workers and labourers there were liable to be more incidents of tension, unrest and dissent in comparison with the more stable rural population of the arable Vale.

Conclusion

A recurring theme of this chapter on tenant society has been the diversified nature of rural society. We have seen the continued interaction between landscape, economy and local society and how there were very real regional differences between these societies. Regional variations were viewed in a number of different contexts including the distribution of land and wealth, the diversification of economic activity, the amounts of wage labour, and the degree of tension within local society. Nevertheless there were elements of continuity and stability, such as the wealth and agricultural activities of the farmers of the demesne and the successful operation of farming in the Vale. A crucial finding has been the identification of the cumulative impact that tenants made on the pace of change in a locality: in the take-up of customary holdings, the regulation of local society and agriculture, the expansion of sheep farming, the role of wealthy merchants in connecting the locality into a trading network that had an international dimension, and the presence and influence of county and royal officials. It was the actions of individuals, taken for a variety of different reasons, which may have involved an element of innovation and risk, which lie behind these trends. Through the detailed case studies we have been able to observe the people who were pivotal in implementing the process of change at the end of the middle ages.

CHAPTER 6

Conclusion:
The Chronology of Change

The chronological coverage of this book has been constructed to bridge the historical fault line that delineates the end of the middle ages. We have been engaged in finding answers to the questions, 'what changed, when, and why?' through a detailed examination of town and countryside in western Berkshire. The purpose of this chapter is to draw together those features of the economy and society which have a chronological significance and allow us to chart change over time and to place Berkshire in its wider context. It will have the advantage of refining our understanding of change between the fourteenth and sixteenth centuries and assessing the typicality of the experience of western Berkshire. Moreover, we must determine whether the trends that are being observed were just short-term fluctuations or are evidence for structural change which had occurred within society and the economy. The final consideration of this chapter is an evaluation of the applicability and power of our chosen influences and their success in accounting for the local variations that were such a characteristic feature of pre-industrial societies.[1]

In chapter 1 we created a framework of criteria capable of charting long-term trends between the fourteenth and sixteenth centuries. In the light of this case study we will refine the chronology now and demonstrate that the whole period from the late fourteenth to the end of the sixteenth century can be subdivided into five sections which had distinctive characteristics and within which we can identify regional variations. The distinguishing features of these smaller periods can be summarised as:

1. The late fourteenth century, from the 1380s until about 1430, which was characterised by some pressure on landholdings, and an acceleration in the decline of the characteristic medieval features of demesne farming and serfdom.

2. There was economic dislocation in the middle of the fifteenth century,

---

[1] See chapter 1, p. 19.

although this was not experienced at a universal rate or time. In addition there was a crisis in seigniorial incomes for some landlords.

3. The end of the fifteenth century and first two decades of the sixteenth century were characterised by contrasts between areas of stagnation and recovery.

4. There were more generalised signs of growth in the economy and population by the middle of the sixteenth century that were knocked back by the effects of heavy mortality, debasement and rebellions.

5. Finally, sustained rapid change characterised the period from 1570, which would continue into the seventeenth century and beyond.

This chronology is derived from examining certain features of society and the economy which have chronological significance and which play an important role in traditional explanations of change. These include demographic change, trade and urban fortunes, lord–tenant relations, changes in agriculture and its work force. This is not a comprehensive list of factors; rather, they are selected as optimal because they possess characteristics which can be measured and comparisons drawn between the Berkshire evidence and other regions. They are examined now, first in the broader context of the experiences of other areas of England, and then by comparison with the evidence from the case study to evaluate the typicality of western Berkshire.

Demographic change was one of those forces examined in chapter 1 that were credited with bringing about long-term transformations to the economy and society. There is, however, very little consensus about the size of the population before 1541. It is uncertain when population began to decline after the earlier expansion of the twelfth and thirteenth centuries and before the arrival of plague, how much it fell, when it began to rise again, and how rapidly it grew. Diversity of experience may be the key to understanding shifts in the population at this time, with migration operating as an additional and distorting agent. We saw how estimates of change in the overall size of the population between 1377 and the 1520s could differ by over a million. Periods of increased mortality do appear to have been a recurring feature. There was an increase in mortality within the populations of the monks of Canterbury and Westminster where life expectancy plummeted between 1440 and 1480 and was extended, among those at Westminster, into the first decade of the sixteenth century.[2] Continuing high levels of mortality were also found on the estates of

---

[2] J. Hatcher, 'Understanding the Population History of England, 1450–1750', *Past and Present*, 180 (2003), 83–130. B. Harvey, *Living and Dying in England, 1100–1540: The Monastic Experience* (Oxford, 1993), 114–29. J. Hatcher, 'Mortality in the Fifteenth Century: Some New Evidence', *EcHRev*, 39 (1986), 19–38.

the bishopric of Worcester in the second half of the fifteenth century, the 1520s and 1545, and were characterised by an increase in tenant deaths.[3] The fifteenth century also experienced periods of severity of illness and disease, in addition to those resulting in high mortality, such as in the 1430s and 1475–85, and a particularly bad attack of the 'sweat' in 1485. The effects of war exacerbated those of disease in the north of England in the fifteenth century where there was also evidence that the birth rate remained low.[4] Among the communities in Essex studied by Poos there was no discernible recovery of population during the 1400s and no signs of expansion before the 1530s, and at Birchanger decline in tithing members continued to about 1540.[5] This evidence is at odds with the findings of those who argue for signs of growth in the population towards the end of the fifteenth century.[6] The data from Berkshire presented in chapter 2 revealed some areas in decline before the arrival of plague, and no overall change in the totals between 1381 and 1522, which, given the difficulties of the documentation, may actually imply a fall in total numbers. In the Kennet region, where an increase was discernible, this was considered to have been due to migration and thus a redistribution of population over the whole area is suggested. Wrigley and Schofield have argued that the population of England may have been growing at a relatively rapid rate in the fifteen years before and after 1541.[7] Nevertheless, expansion would have been offset by high levels of mortality such as the possible attack of influenza in the late 1550s.[8] The Berkshire evidence revealed that where growth was discernible from 1522 the rate of population increase of the parishes studied was consistently higher

---

[3] C. Dyer, *Lords and Peasants in a Changing Society* (Cambridge, 1980), 223–5, 228.

[4] A. J. Pollard, *North-Eastern England During the Wars of the Roses* (Oxford, 1990), 44–8.

[5] L. Poos, *A Rural Society after the Back Death* (Cambridge, 1991), 109.

[6] Cornwall argued that the growth observed by the 1480s became more marked around the turn of the century: J. Cornwall, 'English Population in the Early Sixteenth Century', *EcHRev*, 23 (1970), 32–44 at 44. Postan concluded that it was not until the closing decades of the fifteenth and opening decades of the sixteenth century that indications of demographic recovery became manifest. M. M. Postan, 'Medieval Agrarian Society in its Prime: England', in *Cambridge Economic History of Europe* (Cambridge, 1966), 570. Conversely Blanchard argued for a continuation of the late medieval pattern of population decline until the 1520s. I. Blanchard, 'Population Change, Enclosure, and the Early Tudor Economy', *EcHRev*, 23 (1970), 435, 441–2.

[7] E. A. Wrigley and R. S. Schofield, *The Population History of England* (Cambridge, 1989), 569.

[8] F. J. Fisher, 'Influenza and Inflation in Tudor England', *EcHRev*, 18 (1965), 120–9 and subsequently discussed and the data expanded in J. S. Moore, 'Jack Fisher's "Flu": A Visitation Revisited', *EcHRev*, 46 (1993), 280–307, and continued with contributions by M. Zell in volume 47 (1994), 354–61. See also the comments of contemporaries on the high levels of mortality in J. Hatcher, *Plague Population and the English Economy* (Basingstoke, 1977), 66–7.

than that of the national data throughout the sixteenth century.[9] In addition, there were periods of increased mortality, at crisis level in Newbury in 1546, and the town's population may have been augmented by migration from the rural areas to maintain its size. Indirect evidence for high death rates in the countryside was observed in the increase in numbers of *post mortem* transfers, periods of rapid transfer of land, and female jurors in the manor courts.[10] To achieve the rate of population increase that was calculated, one has to assume that there was an increase in the number of births which would imply that a high-pressure demographic regime existed within western Berkshire in the sixteenth century with raised levels of mortality and fertility, the effects of which were augmented by the impact of migration.

Trade and urban fortunes could also act as forces for change, especially when considered in the wider context of their relationship with the countryside. The fortunes of towns, trade and industrial production were intertwined with those of their hinterlands through patterns of supply and demand.[11] As we have seen, the prosperity of towns varied and many, such as Newbury, were associated with the manufacture and sale of woollen cloth to such as extent that the chronology of the fortunes of towns was closely linked to that of trade, particularly the demand from overseas markets. Towns such as Colchester, Coventry, Norwich, Salisbury and York expanded in the fourteenth century in large part due to the manufacture of cloth, especially undyed broadcloth, that was stimulated by the demand for export.[12] They were affected by the disruptions in trade at the beginning of the fifteenth century, and particularly in the more general recession of the middle of the century and some older established centres, such as Colchester and Coventry, did not recover their former pre-eminence. Response to the resurgence of trade and manufacture from the 1460s came most noticeably from the 'new' areas of production, characteristically small towns, places such as Trowbridge and Bradford-on-Avon in Wiltshire, Totnes in Devon, Lavenham in Suffolk, Halifax and Leeds. These towns continued to expand through the fifteenth century and to peak

---

[9] There were peaks in 1566, 1578 and 1588; see chapter 2.
[10] Chapter 2 has the data for Newbury and chapter 5 on the rural manors.
[11] R. H. Britnell, 'The Economy of British Towns, 1300–1540', in *CUHB*, 330–2.
[12] The following draws heavily upon Britnell, 'Economy of British Towns', 313–33; *idem*, 'Urban Demand in the English Economy, 1300–1600', in J. Galloway (ed.), *Trade, Urban Hinterlands and Market Integration, c.1300–1600* (London, 2000), 9–21; E. M. Carus-Wilson, 'The Woollen Industry before 1550', in E. Crittall (ed.), *A History of the County of Wiltshire*, vol. 4 (Oxford, 1959), 115–47; D. Dymond and A. Betterton, *Lavenham: 700 Years of Textile Making* (Woodbridge, 1982); H. Heaton, *Yorkshire Woollen and Worsted Industry* (Oxford, 1920); C. Phythian-Adams, *Desolation of a City: Coventry and the Urban Crisis of the Later Middle Ages* (Cambridge, 1979); G. Ramsay, *The Wiltshire Woollen Industry in the Sixteenth and Seventeenth Centuries*, 2nd edn (London, 1965); G. Ramsay, *The English Woollen Industry, 1500–1750* (Basingstoke, 1982).

in the first half of the sixteenth century. By the 1520s there were a number of famous individual entrepreneurs who had acquired vast fortunes and who were operating in these towns, men such as Thomas Spring III of Lavenham, William Stumpe of Malmsbury, and of course John Winchecombe II of Newbury, along with earlier examples of men such as James Terumber of Bradford-on-Avon and Trowbridge (d.1488). Nevertheless, the benefits of growth were limited, and usually allied to the individual clothiers. When the market for English cloth in Antwerp collapsed from the 1560s onwards and demand shifted to the smaller and lighter 'new draperies', a corresponding adjustment in manufacture was required and those unable to respond experienced decline. This was particularly noticeable in those towns, such as Lavenham and Malmsbury, where expansion had been associated with a particular individual or family. Yet, as the case study of Newbury has shown, there were other factors that influenced the fortunes of a town, in addition to those associated with the manufacture of cloth.

The fortunes of Newbury were in line with the general experience of towns that were expanding through the production of cloth, but it should be noted that expansion in production had occurred earlier, in the 1430s, and had not been particularly adversely affected by the international disruptions in trade. One of the factors that influenced the period of growth in Newbury was the specialisation in the town on the production of kerseys. This type of cloth may have avoided the worst of the protectionism that disrupted commercial activity during the Anglo-Burgundian trade wars, and kerseys formed a growing sector of the export trade in the later fifteenth century.[13] Prior to this period, however, the town appears to have experienced economic difficulties in the second half of the fourteenth century when its place in the urban hierarchy declined, a situation that continued into the fifteenth century. Expansion was identifiable in the number of cloths exported from Southampton, imports of woad and wide-ranging credit networks. The middle years of the century were less disadvantageous for Newbury than for many larger, established towns. Following the recession, the economy of Newbury performed particularly well, largely due to the manufacture of cloth and also to the trading networks of its merchants. A short setback in the 1490s was followed by sustained growth into the sixteenth century, with boom years in the 1530s and 1540s. The particularly rapid rise in the fortunes of the town was linked to the manufacturing and trading activities of the entrepreneurial clothiers,

---

[13] J. Munro, 'Industrial Protectionism in Medieval Flanders: Urban or National?', in H. A. Miskimin (ed.), *The Medieval City* (New Haven, 1977), 240. J. Munro, 'Industrial Transformations in the North-West European Textile Trades, c.1290-c.1340: Economic Progress or Economic Crisis?', in B. M. S. Campbell (ed.), *Before the Black Death* (Manchester, 1991), 134.

especially the first two John Winchcombes. It was argued that a number of events heralded the subsequent decline of the industry, such as the death of John Winchcombe II in 1558, the absence of a new generation of enterprising entrepreneurs as illustrated in the bankruptcy of Brian Chamberlain in 1571, the instability in cloth exports from the 1550s with the eventual loss of the primacy of the Antwerp market from 1563, until gradually the heyday of the town and its manufacturing industry were over. In contrast, 1570 was the point when other towns, especially market towns, were recovering.[14] Towns and their inhabitants, such as Newbury, that did not quickly adapt to the changing conditions in the market and manufacture in the second half of the sixteenth century, were likely to decline. By comparison those, such as Norwich and Exeter, that were able to adjust, change to production of the new draperies or manufacture for other markets, prospered. The changing fortunes of Newbury did not develop in isolation and we were able to discern the, albeit limited, impact of its expansion on the symbiotic relationship between town and countryside through investment, marketing and manufacture. This was seen especially in neighbouring Shaw and more generally in the rise of population and prosperity of the Kennet region by the early sixteenth century. The fortunes of the town of Wantage, by contrast, were the mirror image of Newbury, and consequently we observed the relative absence of its impact on the surrounding area.

The examination of social forces for bringing about change usually focus on the lord–tenant relationship in which both sides were able to exert pressure on the rate of development at different times as power in the countryside altered in the changing economic and demographic conditions. One manifestation of this shift in the relationship can be quantified in the incidence of difficulties in finding tenants in the middle of the fifteenth century, a fall in the price of land, and the associated decline, or even crisis, in seigniorial income. Following a period of relative stability from the late fourteenth century, empty tenements, reduction in rents or entry fines, even incentives to attract tenants, were features of the mid-fifteenth century in areas away from London. The capital's immediate hinterland appears to have been protected from the more severe features of this type of decline, which could be a reflection of London's expanding dominance and control of exports.[15] Areas such as northern Kent and Surrey saw investment by Londoners in customary land at this time.[16] At Havering the arrival of Londoners brought an important surge in sales of land

---

[14] A. Dyer, *Decline and Growth in English Towns* (Basingstoke, 1991), 53.

[15] Britnell, *Closing of the Middle Ages?*, 232–3

[16] M. Mate, *Trade and Economic Developments, 1450–1550. The Experience of Kent, Surrey and Sussex* (Woodbridge, 2006), 197–213.

between 1455 and 1470.[17] Londoners also played a dynamic role in the changes in the Lea valley just north of the City.[18] Away from London, there were strong regional differences as the incidents of decline were more pronounced in the first half of the fifteenth century in the north of England, eastern England was affected in the 1450s and 1460s, there were rent strikes in the midlands by the 1430s, but conditions in the south were never as severe.[19] The evidence from detailed studies supports these generalisations and adds more subtle variations within the areas. Thus in Durham between 1380 and 1420 the lord could not exact his rents in full.[20] More generally conditions varied in the north-east of England as the 1440s and 1450s were difficult decades in the agrarian sector, the 1470s and 1480s were hard for the industrial and commercial sectors, yet there were some pastoral areas that were unaffected by decline.[21] In the midlands on the estates of the bishop of Worcester entry fines were at a low or nominal level between 1430 and 1470.[22] In Wiltshire the fall in rents in the middle of the century was not universal as those in the north of the county had been low at the beginning of the century and subsequently rose in 1455 and 1463, while those associated with the cloth industry fell in the mid-century.[23] The evidence from rural Berkshire also revealed marked differences between the regions as empty tenements in the Kennet region were not a feature of Kintbury in the fifteenth century, and at Shaw only in the first half of the century, both a reflection of Newbury's impact.[24] In the Vale, however, empty tenements were a feature from the 1440s that lasted on some manors into the sixteenth century as at Buckland and Seymours in Hanney.[25]

---

[17] M. K. McIntosh, *Autonomy and Community: The Royal Manor of Havering, 1200–1500* (Cambridge, 1986), 125–6, 221–2.

[18] P. Glennie, 'In Search of Agrarian Capitalism: Manorial Land Markets and the Acquisition of Land in the Lea valley c.1450–c.1560', *Continuity and Change*, 3 (1988), 11–40.

[19] Hatcher reviewed the evidence from the different regions of England and demonstrated regional characteristics and chronology. Hatcher *Plague Population*, 36–44.

[20] T. Lomas, 'South-East Durham: Late Fourteenth and Fifteenth centuries', in P. D. A. Harvey (ed.), *The Peasant Land Market in Medieval England* (Oxford, 1984), 307.

[21] Pollard, *North-Eastern England*, 78.

[22] Dyer, *Lords and Peasants*, 287–8.

[23] J. Hare, 'Growth and Recession in the Fifteenth-century Economy', *EcHRev*, 52 (1999), 7–8, 20.

[24] At Shaw entry fines were high before 1434 and then declined until 1442 with recovery thereafter.

[25] Entry fines had been high at Buckland before 1425. They then declined between 1425 and 1462 corresponding to a peak in one-way transfers from 1430–70 and followed by a period of informal recording of land transfers between 1470 and 1520. Entry fines were paid as a nominal capon at Seymours Hanney between 1438 and 1470 and one-way

One of the consequences of the lack of tenants to fill properties, negotiations over the cost of land, and reduction in rents and entry fines, was a decline in seigniorial income. Whether this trend was exacerbated by poor management strategies adopted by landlords cannot be established, and the observed reduction in income would be more suitably located in the context of a general slump in the economy.[26] Nevertheless, it is generally accepted that the fifteenth century witnessed a fall in the incomes of landlords that was fairly universal, even in commercialised areas such as East Anglia. This trend is perhaps best illustrated by the letters of the Pastons which reveal the difficulties they experienced in finding tenants, in obtaining rents, and in marketing their produce in the 1460s and 1470s.[27] Arrears were a recurring problem for landlords in north-eastern Norfolk between 1440 and 1520 which were written off in the accounts during periodic amnesties.[28] The mid-fifteenth-century depression was a significant feature for the areas furthest from London, in Kent, Surrey and Sussex.[29] In central England, on the manors of New College, income fluctuated during the fifteenth century and particularly during the years 1454–55 and 1457–58 when the lowest level of receipts was experienced for the whole period between 1390 and 1501.[30] Within Wiltshire the chronology of decline in income varied between the regions.[31] The situation in western Berkshire also revealed marked regional differences. Income from Priors in Hanney to New College fluctuated during the fifteenth century and receipts from the manor were particularly low in 1449, 1452, 1460–64, 1470 and 1472. The situation changed after 1495 to a consistent level of income from this manor. This was in contrast to Shaw in the Kennet valley, where receipts from the manor were more dependable, although there were fluctuations in income from the mills between 1439 and 1459, and thereafter these became more predictable. At Kintbury the period of economic uncertainty was rather earlier, in 1428–33, although there were no data after 1450. Income from Woolstone in the Downs was generally more dependable between 1414 and 1477, apart from 1463 when the farmer absconded with the stock of the manor. It would appear that the mid-fifteenth-century slump in the economy and decline in seigniorial incomes varied in its severity

transfers were frequent from the 1440s to a point between 1500 and 1520. Profitability stabilised at Priors Hanney after 1495.

[26] See Stone's work on the economic rationality of landlord decisions D. Stone, *Decision-Making in Medieval Agriculture* (Oxford, 2005).

[27] R. H. Britnell, 'The Pastons and their Norfolk', *AgHRev*, 36 (1988), 132–44.

[28] J. Whittle, *The Development of Agrarian Capitalism* (Oxford, 2000), 74.

[29] The effects of the mid-century depression are a recurring feature in Mate, *Trade and Economic Developments*.

[30] T. A. R Evans and R. J. Faith 'College Estates and University Finances 1350–1500', in *The History of the University of Oxford* (Oxford, 1992), 674 footnote 130.

[31] Hare, 'Growth and Recession', 1–26.

between the different regions with some variations in the chronology. Indeed, one might question whether the mid-century was just a particularly sharp downturn in a century that was more generally characterised by economic fluctuations and regional variations?

If a slump or stagnation in the economy and population are accepted for the middle of the fifteenth century then it becomes necessary to consider when recovery and an upturn are discernible. On closer examination the picture that emerges is one of a continuation of the medieval pattern of fluctuations and regional differences, rather than any strong and consistent evidence for growth before 1520, or even the 1540s in some places. We continue to employ our criteria relating to the force of social relations and look for evidence of the time when the cost of land increased, payments were able to be made, seigniorial income improved in reliability, and, by implication, there was demographic pressure on landholdings. In England generally and away from London, there were some signs of improvement, particularly in areas of pasture, from the 1470s but this was neither universal nor consistent before 1520. In the areas around London arable rents rose continuously.[32] There was an increase in demand for land at Havering from 1455 due to the arrival of Londoners. In north-eastern England there was a brief glimpse of recovery in the arable sector in the 1470s which subsequently disappeared for the rest of the century.[33] The pasture rents in Derbyshire showed marked increases from 1485 to 1520 and then stagnation thereafter.[34] Similarly, on the crown estates of the Duchy of Lancaster in the Pennines pasture rents rose from the 1470s.[35] On the midland estates of the Bishop of Worcester there was an increase in entry fines in the 1470s and 1480s but they subsequently fell in the 1510s until a rising trend was apparent by 1530.[36] In the Midland Plain of Derbyshire a similar but not identical pattern can be observed as between 1477–78 and 1498–99 rents rose and arrears decreased; in 1520–21 rents fell and arrears rose; by 1540 rents had recovered and arrears were now at zero. This was also the case on the estates in Staffordshire studied by Blanchard.[37] In north-east Norfolk manorial incomes did not increase significantly, which was in contrast to the price of land sold by tenants that fell at the end of fifteenth and early sixteenth century and then increased threefold between 1529 and 1558.[38] In Wiltshire there was evidence of

[32] Blanchard, 'Population Change', 434. Mate, *Trade and Economic Developments.*
[33] Pollard *North-Eastern England*, 53–6.
[34] I. Blanchard, *The Duchy of Lancaster's Estates in Derbyshire, 1485–1540* (Derbyshire Archaeological Society Record Series, 3, 1971), 3.
[35] Blanchard 'Population Change', 433–4.
[36] Dyer, *Lords and Peasants*, 288.
[37] Blanchard, 'Population Change', 434–5.
[38] Whittle, *Development of Agrarian Capitalism*, 74, 110–14, and Table 3.3 page 112 for data.

patchy recovery from the 1480s but it was still sensitive to fluctuations in the price of wool.[39] On lands in the south of England belonging to Oxford colleges there was no rise in rent from leases by the end of the fifteenth century; indeed they usually ended the century lower than at the beginning at New College, while at Merton there was no rise before 1521.[40]

The evidence for signs of recovery in western Berkshire continued to demonstrate regional variations whose significance could be modified by seigniorial policy. At Shaw tenements were fully occupied again from 1460 and the cost of land, as seen in the size of entry fines, began to increase gradually from 1442, and there is further evidence for increases in 1486, 1490 and 1538. Empty tenements had never been a significant problem at Kintbury, where entry fines were levied consistently on properties at fractions of a mark. Proximity to Newbury may have been having an impact. In contrast, in the Vale recovery was later and there were also differences in the lords' treatment of entry fines. There was an increase in entry fines at Buckland in 1462 followed by stability in the level of fines until 1525, and then properties were fully occupied after 1537. At Seymours in Hanney entry fines rose in 1471 to the level of a year's rent, the equivalent to Priors, and remained at this level until 1557 when they rose sharply, and one has to assume that tenements were fully occupied. At Priors in Hanney tenements were fully occupied by 1530 on a manor where there had been a consistent level of fining set at the equivalent of a year's customary rent.

If we accept that the cost of leasehold land was close to a true economic rent then there was evidence for some increases over the sixteenth century, but these were not dramatic. In the Vale the leasehold rent of the demesne at Priors in Hanney increased in 1541 from £6 to £6 13s. 8d., and then remained at that level for the rest of the century. At Seymours there was a gradual increase of a shilling in 1541, and another 3s. 3d. in 1595 making a total annual leasehold rent of £9 13s. 3d. At Buckland there was some adjustment in the level of rents but no overall gain over the sixteenth century. At Woolstone in the Downs the leasehold rent of the demesne increased in 1477, after a period of being in hand, and remained at that level until at least 1537. On the manors in the Kennet valley there were no dramatic increases. At Shaw there was little change in the rent of the farm of the demesne, but more fluctuations in the cost of the mills, which rose in 1528 and again in 1570, to £8 *per annum*. On the two large manors at Kintbury there was a fall in the rent of the demesne at Kintbury Eaton in 1450 where it remained until at least 1539, whereas the lease of the mills showed a steady increase between 1450 and 1539. At Kintbury Amesbury there was a 7 per cent rise in the leasehold rent of the demesne between 1535 and

[39] Hare 'Growth and Recession', 23–4.
[40] Evans and Faith 'College Estates', 681.

1540.[41] Taken together the evidence from the case studies of the Kennet valley reveal the limited impact that Newbury had on the cost of land as opposed to occupancy of tenancies.

It would appear that there was a continuation of the fluctuations of the medieval period into the sixteenth century with no clear evidence before 1520, at the earliest, of sustained demand, and by implication growth in the population and economy. Moreover, as we observed in previous chapters, commentators of the early sixteenth century were concerned about rack renting, enclosures and increasing poverty.[42] We need to consider the evidence for a sustained rise in the price of land and, by implication, the possibility that there was demographic pressure on resources. Nevertheless, we must be cautious as the level of rents and entry fines continued to vary between the different lords, in addition to the regional variations already considered.[43] Tawney demonstrated that the treatment of customary rent varied between lords, was modified by custom, changed over time, and yet overall remained remarkable stable.[44] He argued that a more sensitive indicator of change were those manors with variable entry fines and showed that those of the Earl of Pembroke doubled in every decade from the 1520s to 1560s.[45] Clay reviewed the evidence for the country as a whole and found that increases of four- or five-fold between the mid-sixteenth and mid-seventeenth centuries were common, while on the Wiltshire estates of the Herbert Earls of Pembroke and on some Yorkshire properties he calculated at least an eight-fold increase.[46] On certain lands belonging to the crown in Wiltshire Kerridge argued for some increase in the price of land after 1530, with a more rapid rise in the 1550s, dramatic increase in the 1560s, followed by a slow-down that lasted to the end of the century, before there was another rapid rise in 1600–09.[47] On the Herbert estates Kerridge identified a rapid rise in the 1550s, 1570s and 1590s.[48] Somewhat differently, on the manors of the Seymour estates there was a steady rise from 1510, then rapid increase in the 1560s, which was particularly steep in the 1570s, followed by a

---

[41] Table 15 chapter 4, from £15 10s. 2½d. to £16 13s. 4d.

[42] The pattern of the rate of enclosures in western Berkshire was one of a continuing process and therefore it was impossible to chart any specific features that had chronological significance.

[43] Thirsk, *Agrarian History* IV, 292, 294–5, 690–4.

[44] Tawney, *Agrarian Problem*, 115–17. See also Youings on the consistent, and often vigorous, policies of many monks in the decade before dissolution. J. Youings, 'The Church. The Last Decade, 1529–39', in Thirsk, *Agrarian History* IV, 324–32.

[45] Tawney, *Agrarian Problem*, 304–7.

[46] Clay, *Economic Expansion and Social Change*, 89.

[47] E. Kerridge, 'The Movement of Rent, 1540–1640', in E. M. Carus-Wilson (ed.), *Essays in Economic History*, vol. 2 (London, 1962), 223.

[48] Kerridge, 'The Movement of Rent', 216–17 including Table 1.

slight fall in the 1580s, and finally a rapid rise for the rest of the century.[49] In north-eastern Norfolk on the manor of Hevingham Bishops Whittle identified a dramatic rise in the price of land as sold by the tenants from 1544.[50] Bowden concluded that for many landowners a wholesale revision of rents was delayed until the 1570s and 1590s, but increased rapidly thereafter.[51] Nevertheless, it should be noted that these figures are not corrected for the effects of inflation. On the manors studied in western Berkshire there was a dramatic rise in the rate of entry fines from 1559 at Seymours in Hanney; at Buckland from 1588 after a break in the archive; and a similar increase is noticeable at Shaw by 1605. Nevertheless, there remained the consistent level of fining at Priors in Hanney and Kintbury Eaton.[52] Thus the sharp increases in the price of land were a particular feature of the second half of the sixteenth century that could be modified by landlord policy rather than regional or urban influences. The consequences would have been prohibitive for access to land for the poorer members of society. Subsequently change was sustained and marks an end to the fluctuations in the cost and access to land of the earlier period.

Associated with developments in the lord–tenant relationship and the price of land were those taking place in agriculture and its work force. Nevertheless, many were fully under way before the fifteenth century. Structural change occurred with the leasing of the demesnes, the commutation of labour services and the decline of serfdom. These had been characteristic features of a much earlier period and change was gradually taking place on some estates from at least the thirteenth century. By the close of the fourteenth century lords were leasing their demesnes wholesale and by the middle of the fifteenth century direct management had been abandoned on virtually all estates, with only a few home farms left in hand to provision the household.[53] Or, as on the estates of Westminster Abbey and the bishop of Worcester, those that were retained in the fifteenth century possessed some special feature such as sheep pastures or a profitable wool crop.[54] The pattern in Berkshire conforms to these general trends as the majority of landowners were leasing their demesne lands by 1400, especially their arable lands.[55] The process continued over approximately the

---

[49] Kerridge 'The Movement of Rent', 221.

[50] Whittle *Development of Agrarian Capitalism*, Table 3.3., page 112.

[51] P. Bowden, 'Agricultural Prices, Farm Profits, and Rents', in Thirsk, *Agrarian History* IV, 690.

[52] At Kintbury Eaton fines were consistently levied at a fraction of a mark; at Kintbury Amesbury very similarly at approx 13s. 4d. for a messuage with one virgate of land and there was no evidence of change in the level of fining before 1542.

[53] Campbell, *Seigniorial Agriculture*, 10, 29, 58–60, 234, 424, 431, 436.

[54] B. Harvey *Westminster Abbey and its Estates in the Middle Ages* (Oxford, 1977), 150–1, 269. Dyer *Lords and Peasants*, 150.

[55] Certainly on the manors studied in detail where there was evidence, that is, by 1405 at Buckland, Kintbury and Shaw.

next fifty years so that the majority of manorial demesne lands were being leased by the middle of the fifteenth century.[56] Lords did retain for longer, and for their own use, certain lucrative elements, such as pasture rights and demesne flocks at Woolstone and Kintbury, and swans and doves at Buckland. Leasing was not necessarily a straightforward process as the demesne might come back into direct management in exceptional circumstances as had happened at Woolstone in 1460.[57]

The end of direct management of demesne farms was accompanied by a decreased use of customary labour. According to Campbell the end of customary labour did not form a radical break with the past as it had faded away gradually and did not finally disappear until the last demesnes were leased in the second half of the fifteenth century.[58] Lords were reluctant in a period of increasing labour scarcity to relinquish their rights to levy important works such as at harvest time.[59] This was the case on the estates of Westminster Abbey where labour services were commuted for a money rent as a very gradual process from at least the thirteenth century, whilst some were retained to form part payment with the money rent.[60] The potential number of works that might be arbitrarily claimed by lords had the power to annoy the peasantry. In Essex it was the continuing demand for the performance of labour services by some landlords that led to numerous incidents of conflict with their tenants, the most spectacular of course being those of 1381, and demands had largely ended by 1450 on the manors studied by Poos.[61] In north-east Norfolk Whittle found the last record of labour services being performed was in the account of 1440–41, when 97 autumn works were performed on Saxthorpe Mickelhall manor.[62] By 1400 in Berkshire the majority of labour services had been commuted for a money rent and only occasional references were subsequently found for their retention, although one can never be certain whether they were ever performed. Most references to either specific labour

---

[56] Additional Berkshire examples from R. Faith 'Berkshire: Fourteenth and Fifteenth Centuries', in P. D. A. Harvey (ed.), *The Peasant Land Market in Medieval England* (Oxford, 1984), 109: Coleshill by 1422, Woolstone by 1423, Brightwalton by 1428, Sotwell Stonor by 1430, South Moreton by 1452, Mackney by 1471, and Englefield by 1486–87. Taken together the evidence supports the conclusions reached by L. C. Latham, 'The Decay of the Manorial System During the First Half of the Fifteenth Century with Special Reference to Manorial Jurisdiction and the Decline of Villeinage, as Exemplified in the Records of Twenty-Six Manors in the Counties of Berkshire, Hampshire and Wiltshire.' MA thesis, London (1928), 150–65.

[57] TNA, SC6/758/12.

[58] Campbell *Seigniorial Agriculture*, 436.

[59] *Ibid.*

[60] Harvey *Westminster Abbey*, 225–34, 256–61.

[61] Poos, *Rural Society*, 242–4.

[62] Whittle, *Development of Agrarian Capitalism*, 44.

services or payments for works had ended by 1430 in the accounts and court rolls, although the retention of the services of washing and shearing the abbot of Glastonbury's sheep in 1519 remains an anomalous burden.[63]

There has been an assumption that the decline in the use of labour services meant a corresponding increase in the employment of waged labour. Furthermore, the rise of wage labour in creating a proletariat plays a significant role in the conditions required for the transition to capitalism. Nevertheless, wage labour was an important and integral element of the work force throughout the medieval period. It is notoriously difficult to quantify and thus to chart change over time in the proportion of the population engaged in waged employment. Indeed, it may have been higher in 1300 than 1500.[64] Nevertheless, there were regional differences in its distribution, with a higher proportion dependent on income from wages in the commercialised areas of England, such as East Anglia, and also in the Kennet valley.[65] Moreover, the size of the labouring population expanded between the early sixteenth century and the end of the seventeenth century.[66] It was that sector of the population dependent on the market for essential foodstuffs who were vulnerable to the effects of inflation and dearth from the middle of the sixteenth century.

Serfdom was another characteristic medieval feature that was already in decline before the start of our period. Its significance lies in the potential power that lords had over their unfree peasants. Largely dating from the fourteenth century, and through the combined processes of manumission, migration and mortality, serfdom gradually came to an end. It is a commonplace that serfdom eventually 'withered away' by the end of Elizabeth's reign,[67] but the rate of decline varied between regions and landlords, and survival into the sixteenth century was particularly noticeable in Norfolk, Suffolk and Somerset.[68] There were accelerated spurts of decline in some areas, such as on the estates of the bishop of Worcester where the granting of manumissions increased between 1423 and 1439, and between 1450 and 1479, and a similar chronology of manumissions was found on the Ramsey abbey estate.[69] In Essex there was a gradual decline during the fourteenth century in the incidence of serfdom, such as payments of merchet and chevage, after which time orders to return serfs apparently had a whimsical quality and continued in some

[63] BL, Harley MS. 3961.
[64] See references in chapter 2 p. 50–1.
[65] A. Everitt, 'Farm Labourers', in Thirsk, *Agrarian History* IV, 396–400.
[66] *Ibid.*
[67] Hilton used the term in R. H. Hilton, *The Decline in Serfdom in Medieval England* (London, 1970), 31.
[68] D. MacCulloch, 'Bondmen Under the Tudors', in C. Cross, D. Loades and J. J. Scarisbrick (eds), *Law and Government Under the Tudors* (Cambridge, 1988), 94.
[69] Dyer *Lords and Peasants*, 272.

places until the 1460s.[70] In north-east Norfolk the number of servile families declined most rapidly between 1530 and 1560.[71] By 1400 in Berkshire serfdom had already declined and only survived in isolated pockets during the fifteenth century. Its incidence was often associated with a specific family such as that of Jolyf at Kintbury in 1478 and Horton at Ashbury in 1519. Nevertheless we also observed in previous chapters that the lack of personal freedom was not a bar to the accumulation of wealth or landholdings by the early sixteenth century. The continuing survival of serfdom by that time was not an influential force in shaping the pace of change. Thus demesne farming, labour services and serfdom, all characteristic features of the medieval period, were already coming to an end by 1400. We cannot employ these features any longer as criteria for defining the end of the middle ages. Neither can we link their decline with a corresponding rise in wage labour.

Entrepreneurs have been singled out for their role in bringing about change to an area. Nevertheless they may not have been as exceptional as previously argued; rather, they were an important and characteristic element of a general feature of enterprising individuals who accumulated capital and amassed amazing fortunes. The background economic conditions of the late fifteenth and early sixteenth centuries were conducive to entrepreneurial activity, whether in the manufacturing of cloth, or in the growing and exporting of wool. The wealthy clothiers and wool merchants of western Berkshire had their counterparts in the Springs of Lavenham and the wool merchants of Northleach. They were members of a group who had been able to manage risk during the fifteenth century to such an extent that by the 1520s many had made significant fortunes. Their impact on the locality, however, was neither very great nor long lasting. Nevertheless they bound the rural areas of England into wider trading networks. Subsequently many invested their wealth in land and removed themselves from the spheres of trade and manufacture and into the ranks of the gentry. These were the men central to the arguments for 'the rise of the gentry' as an explanation for change.[72] Although traditionally portrayed as benefiting from the massive transfer of lands at the Dissolution, we observed how they were initially not very successful in western Berkshire, in comparison with individuals who had connections with those in power in London.[73] It was

---

[70] Poos, *Rural Society*, 245–7.

[71] Whittle, *Development of Agrarian Capitalism*, 37. In 1440–60 servile families survived on six manors, in 1490–1500 on five manors, 1520–30 on four manors, and by 1560 only one manor had a servile family.

[72] Stimulated by the publication of R. H. Tawney, 'The Rise of the Gentry, 1558–1640', *EcHRev*, 11 (1941), 1–38. D. M. Palliser, '"Tawney's Century": Brave New World or Malthusian Trap?', *EcHRev*, 35 (1982), 339–53.

[73] Elsewhere in England Youings found that Tawney's conclusions were generally supported and the greater part of the lands went to established local landowning

the subsequent activities of these 'new' men as landlords that were described by contemporary commentators as influencing the pace of change when they dramatically raised the cost of their lands to their tenants.[74] Nevertheless, in western Berkshire evidence for this type of activity was not identifiable until the second half of the sixteenth century, and even then it was not a universal feature. It might be argued that the combined effects of high levels of mortality, rapid inflation, and a series of rebellions in 1549 meant that lords did not have the confidence to challenge the customary level of rent on their manors for at least another decade.

Of more impact on the sustained pace of change in a locality were the cumulative actions of the resident members of rural society, those in the middling or modal group. These were the individuals who consolidated large landholdings, held manorial and parochial office, and implemented the changes of the communal decisions made in the manor court, and those imposed on the community from outside by government legislation. They did not form a homogenous group as tenant society also changed, particularly in the possession of land and wealth. It was a gradual process that was not uniformly experienced due to the combined effects of the local economy, seigniorial attitudes to change, and the presence of individuals who wanted to develop their economic activities.

It was the decline in opportunities to acquire an affordable landholding, the reduction in the number and availability of smallholdings, and the ability to raise the initial substantial cash outlay required at the start of a new tenancy, that combined to have a prohibitive effect on direct access to land for many in the later sixteenth century. It was the combination of the reduction in the availability of both land and employment that had such a deleterious effect by the end of the sixteenth century. Changing perceptions of affluence and poverty were identifiable, particularly in the second half of the sixteenth century, in the growing recognition and acknowledgement of the poor in local society. One of its manifestations was identified in the many bequests made in wills to the poor men's box. These charitable actions were formalised and enforced by government in the various statutes relating to the poor, unemployed and vagrants. Their implementation was the responsibility of the residents of the parish, and especially the officers of the parish. Awareness of the disparities of wealth within the community was reinforced by local circumstances of access to land and employment, and by external factors, many of which can be identified in the developments that produced the Elizabethan poor law.

---

families. J. Youings, 'The Church', in C. Clay (ed.), *Rural Society: Landowners, Peasants and Labourers, 1500–1750* (Cambridge, 1990), 103–20, especially 117–20.
[74] M. Yates, 'Between Fact and Fiction: Henry Brinklow's *Complaynt* Against Rapacious Landlords', *AgHRev*, 54 (2006), 24–44.

Having completed a review of the chronology of change and placed the Berkshire evidence in its national context, our final task is to evaluate those influences that fashioned the course of developments. We have emphasised the interaction of the four factors of landscape, lordship, towns and enterprising individuals, which were operating within the more general conditions of the period, as important for bringing about change in a locality. Western Berkshire's experience was shaped by the effects of the intersection of change in the size of the population, government and the economy, which were modified by the impact of landscape, landlord policies, the proximity of an expanding town, and the presence of enterprising individuals. Regional variations in the pace of developments have been clearly demonstrated. It has been possible to substantiate the views of those historians and archaeologists who argue for a correlation between landscape, local economy and society.

The evidence from western Berkshire has revealed characteristic differences between the three regions of vale, downland and woodland pasture. In the fertile Vale of the White Horse arable farming was successfully practised by a local society of reasonably affluent farmers that included members of the gentry whose office-holding activities were influential. This society was fairly stable and there was little evidence for violence and tensions among the inhabitants until the end of the sixteenth century. The economy of the Berkshire Downs was dominated by continuity in the very profitable raising of sheep, and large flocks were owned by both lords and tenants. Social change came with the expansion of agricultural units and wealth of certain individuals over the sixteenth century. In the region of woodland pasture in the Kennet valley there was a diversified local economy where economic opportunities were expanded by the growth of the cloth industry in the towns of Newbury and Hungerford. A viable smallholding economy was possible due to the diversified nature of employment, and migration affected the composition of local society.

As the sixteenth century continued there were an increasing number of large farms and a gradual polarisation in the wealth of many of the inhabitants. Tensions in this society were more visible and there were a number of incidents that involved newcomers to the area. Yet local society was not a monolithic entity as it was also modified by the presence of enterprising individuals who could innovate and invest in the changing opportunities presented to them and establish trading networks that ranged beyond the confines of the local markets. Furthermore, we have observed the ways in which lords were able to influence the pace of change on their manors, particularly the conditions of tenure and cost of land, and hold back the tide of change in some cases. The symbiotic relationship between town and countryside formed another force for change that was particularly obvious when associated with a town that was expanding rapidly, although the manufacture of cloth was predominantly an urban phenomenon. The town's impact was felt in the surrounding countryside through migration to the area at a time of reduced population when a greater proportion of landholdings were occupied and consequently had repercussions for seigniorial income. Newbury's more direct impact on the rural economy and opportunities for employment, apart from in neighbouring Shaw, were more muted. There were opportunities for investment in the town for the wealthy and enterprising rural inhabitants. We have also observed the transitory nature of some forms of rapid growth and the role of the individual entrepreneur in bringing about change that did not necessarily create net economic growth for a town and its region, or a sustained transformation. Finally, there were exogenous factors such as the Dissolution of the Monasteries, or the debasements in the currency, whose effects could not have been predicted. The former presented increased opportunities for investment and for bringing about change in a locality after a long period of tenurial stability. But we have also seen how the effects were rarely felt immediately and often took a generation to be implemented. Until the second half of the sixteenth century the pattern of economic activity was one of fluctuations and regional variations. Furthermore, there was an absence of any unifying economic force that could drive change in this pre-modern society, neither the state, nor London as the capital, were sufficiently strong to act as an engine for national growth. Rather the forces of landscape, lordship, towns and enterprising individuals combined to influence the pace of change in a locality and account for the distinctive variations that have been observed in this study.

Documents, methodology and data relating to chapter 2

The documentary evidence

Any study of the period from the fourteenth to sixteenth centuries must employ documents which span these centuries to avoid the danger that the changes observed were archivally driven. The comparative sections of chapter 2 are based, to a large part, on an examination of documents created as part of the process of taxation. These sources were created at a national level so that comparisons can be made across a wide geographical area with reasonable confidence that the data are comparable.[1] In the late medieval and early modern periods most forms of direct taxation were granted by Parliament to provide extraordinary sources of revenue to assist the king in bearing an extraordinary burden of expenditure, normally associated with war or the preparation for war. Taxation was therefore intermittent. The types of tax varied between the fourteenth and sixteenth centuries and therefore it is essential to understand why the tax was demanded, who was liable to pay, the threshold for exemption, the basis of assessment for the particular tax, who made the assessments, and how the tax was to be collected. It is acknowledged that this type of documentary evidence contain many inconsistencies.[2] While acknowledging their limitations it is, however, acceptable to employ them as a comparative framework for a more detailed study of an area, such as this one, where they form only one category of documentary evidence among many. Totals derived from the data are analysed by their rank order to each other as the purpose is only to measure *relative* change.

[1] A general introduction to each documentary source is given in M. Jurkowski, C. L. Smith and D. Crook, *Lay Taxes in England and Wales, 1188–1688* (London, 1998). The methodological approach was developed by Roger Schofield in his thesis and certain sections were subsequently published as R. S. Schofield, 'The geographical distribution of wealth in England, 1334–1649', *EcHRev*, 18 (1965), 483–510.

[2] J. F. Hadwin, 'The Medieval Lay Subsidies and Economic History', *EcHRev*, 36 (1983), 200–17. Recently re-enforced by S. Jenks, 'The Lay Subsidies and the State of the English Economy (1275–1334)', *Vierteljahrschrift für Sozial- und Wirtschaftsgeschichte*, 85 (1998), 1–39.

Four main snapshots are taken of western Berkshire, with supplementary material for the fourteenth and sixteenth centuries: before the Black Death in 1327 and 1334, and also a comparison of 1291 and 1340–42; after the arrival of plague in 1381 and additionally landholding in 1412; in the 1520s; and finally in 1545. We begin with an examination of each of the different sources so that their potential and limitations are acknowledged. Any attempt at establishing a context of relative population and wealth before the Black Death will encounter difficulties with the data, but these are not insurmountable if their limitations are understood and they are employed indirectly as a measure of relative change. The Lay Subsidy of 1327, similar to those collected between 1290 and 1332, was largely administered at the local level and based on assessments of personal property.[3] It was granted on Edward III's accession and had been required by his desire for war with Scotland. It should be noted that there appears to have been marked variations in the way in which local men made their assessments of the individual person's taxable property. Some of these inconsistencies were still there in 1334, and it will be important to discern whether this was a true reflection of the current conditions, or the effects of the same local assessor.

The method of assessment of the subsidy changed in 1334 after complaints about the way in which the tax of 1332 had been managed. Again the stimulus was the defence of the realm against the Scots and 'other great matters'.[4] Instead of being based on an individuals' moveable property the unit of taxation was the vill. The assessment was still made on the value of moveable possessions but as a total for each vill, and these valuations remained fixed at this level until the sixteenth century. A subsidy was then granted by Parliament at a rate of a fraction of that valuation, usually a tenth for towns and a fifteenth for rural areas. These returns survive for 1334 for the whole country.[5]

Evaluating the degree of inclusiveness of these early tax lists has received attention from historians, and opinion is divided between those who expect the taxes to be an accurate guide to wealth and those who stress the inconsistencies in the assessment of the tax.[6] A quick evaluation of the Berkshire material can

---

[3] Jurkowski et al., Lay Taxes, 21–38. P. Franklin, 'Gloucestershire's Medieval Taxpayers', Local Population Studies, 54 (1995), 16–17. P. Franklin, The Taxpayers of Medieval Gloucestershire (Stroud, 1993), 4 describes the process in detail. Jenks, 'Lay Subsidies' emphases the difficulties.

[4] Jurkowski et al., Lay Taxes, 38.

[5] Published in R. E. Glasscock (ed.), The Lay Subsidy of 1334 (Oxford, 1975).

[6] The exercise was pioneered by E. Britton, The Community of the Vill (Toronto, 1977) for the manor of Broughton in Huntingdonshire. His methodology has been criticised, especially the stratification of peasant society, by Z. Razi, 'The Toronto School's Reconstruction of Medieval Peasant Society: A Critical View', Past and Present, 85 (1978). Other analyses have been undertaken subsequently by DeWindt, Harvey and Dyer, the

be made by comparing the 1327 nominal returns with a rental of 1335 for the manor of Holt in Kintbury.[7] Although the tax was levied on an assessment of moveable goods and not landholding – the concern of the rental – it should be possible to establish the type of peasant who was being taxed. There were 29 individuals taxed for the vill of which 13 could be positively identified and another three had recognisable family names. The majority held either one or half a virgate of land (eight persons), there were four cottagers and one leaseholder. Not unsurprisingly these were the wealthier tenants on this manor and the smaller landholders did not pay tax, particularly in the cottager group (a total of 33). Even allowing for change in the intervening eight years, we must conclude that these fiscal assessments are more inclusive of the wealthier tenants of this manor than the poorer inhabitants. This is an important caveat for the conclusions reached in chapter 2.

The assessments ordered by Pope Nicholas IV in 1291 and the Inquisitions of the Ninth 1340–42 were based on the unit of assessment of the parish. The Inquisition of the Ninth was a result of the grant by Parliament to Edward III of one-ninth of the value of corn, wool and lambs relating to production during 1341.[8] The reliability of the returns was to be established by a comparison with the assessments that had been made in 1291 on the order of Pope Nicholas. Although the taxation of Pope Nicholas IV was known in its own period as a true valuation, there is a considerable amount of evidence to show that its assessments were rather low.[9]

The first fiscal source to be employed in this study for the period after the Black Death is the 1381 Poll Tax that had been granted in the previous year.[10] This tax has received a very bad press both from contemporaries and from historians alike. The tax was assessed on a *per capita* basis on men and women aged fifteen years or more at a rate of one shilling per person so that the total for each vill would equal the number of taxpayers, but allowing the rich to help the poor so that everyone would be charged according to their means

---

most recent by Franklin, *Taxpayers*. For further bibliographical details see those given in Franklin, 'Gloucestershire's Medieval Taxpayers', 20.

[7] PRO, E179/73/6, BL, Add Roll 49210.

[8] Jurkowski *et al.*, *Lay Taxes*, 43–6. The published edition was examined and those places, such as Wantage, that had been omitted were obtained from the manuscript copy. *Nonarum Inquisitiones in Curia Scaccarii Temp Regis Edwardi III* (Record Commission, 1807). PRO, E179/73/16.

[9] B. Harvey, *Westminster Abbey and its Estates* (Oxford, 1977), 57–60. A. H. R. Baker, 'Evidence in the 'Nonarum Inquisitiones' of Contracting Arable Lands in England during the Early Fourteenth Century', *EcHRev*, 19 (1966), 518–32. R. Graham, *English Ecclesiastical Studies* (London, 1929), 271–301.

[10] Jurkowski *et al.*, *Lay Taxes*, 60–2.

with only the very poor being exempt.[11] This rate varied from that of the two earlier poll taxes but, unfortunately, their nominal returns do not survive for Berkshire. An evaluation of the possible degree of evasion can be obtained by comparing the total number of taxpayers for 1377 and 1381 for Berkshire of 22,723 and 15,696 respectively.[12] It is important to acknowledge this reduction in numbers in the light of the analysis in chapter 2, as it has implications for the conclusions drawn there. Nevertheless, it is presumed that evasion was universal and the relative distributions were not affected.

The grant of the subsidy based on income from lands in 1411 and collected in 1412 was assessed above the threshold of the annual value of land or rents of £20.[13] Every man or woman of whatever estate was to pay 6s. 8d. per £20 of land held. The returns of most counties are published and offer an opportunity for comparisons of landed wealth across the country.[14] There was some rounding of figures as many were in units of marks or pounds, but the assessments appear to have been relatively inclusive.

The documents employed for the analysis of the early sixteenth century include the Military Survey of 1522 and the Lay Subsidies of 1524-25. The Survey was undertaken to investigate both the military capacity of the country and also its wealth. The returns do not survive for the whole of England and those that are extant vary in their layout and detail. The Survey lists all males over the age of sixteen, with a few women, and they were assessed on the yearly value of their lands and tenements, or goods and other substances, or both where a man held freehold land in the parish where he was resident. In this study, as in Gloucestershire, a person is considered to have been resident within the parish where he had an assessment on goods, and this is confirmed by comparison with the Lay Subsidies where people were taxed in their place of residence.[15] In addition, the Military Survey recorded the lands and goods of the Church within the parish, and the stock of orphan children. The source, however, does not consistently record the social status of individuals and so we cannot refine the different categories of landowners among the laity. The fact that the fiscal nature of the Survey was not apparent to the population at the

---

[11] C. Fenwick (ed.), *The Poll Taxes of 1377, 1379 and 1381, Part 1 Bedfordshire-Leicestershire* (The British Academy, 1998), xvi.

[12] Fenwick, *Poll Taxes*, 14.

[13] Jurkowski *et al.*, *Lay Taxes*, xxxvii–xxxix, 78–9.

[14] *Inquisitions and Assessments relating to Feudal Aides*, vol. vi (Record Commission, 1920), S. Payling, *Political Society in Lancastrian England* (Oxford, 1991), Appendix 1 for Nottinghamshire. J. P. Cooper, 'The social distribution of land and men in England, 1436–1700', *EcHRev*, 20 (1967), 419–40. H. L. Gray, 'Incomes from Land in England in 1436', *English Historical Journal*, 49 (1934), 607–39.

[15] R. W. Hoyle (ed.), *The Military Survey of Gloucestershire* (Gloucester Record Series, 1993), xvii.

time of assessment may have led to the inclusion of most able-bodied men. In Berkshire the large number of assessments at nil or one pound endorses this conclusion. So too does a comparison of the manorial and fiscal documents.

This can be achieved for West Hanney in the Vale of the White Horse, where 36 men were recorded in the Military Survey and a comparison can be made with the manor court rolls of the 1520s of two manors.[16] The majority were identified in the proceedings of these courts and it is presumed that the remaining eleven were probably members of the other manor.[17] There were only three jurors recorded who should have been assessed as able-bodied men but were omitted from the 1522 assessment and whose absence cannot be accounted for. A comparison with the landholdings of the manors reveals that in the modal category of those householders assessed at £2 the majority held half a virgate of land. Those with large assessments included the farmers of the demesne who controlled the largest landholdings of the village. Thus the assessments of the men appears to have been representative and reflect the size of their landholdings. We can be reasonably confident, therefore, that the Military Survey was a fair reflection of the wealth of the majority of the male population of West Hanney.

The Tudor Lay Subsidies were a revival of the medieval practice of making individual assessments. The threshold for the subsidy granted in 1523 included those lay persons aged sixteen and over with more than £1 in lands, £2 in goods or £1 in wages.[18] A taxpayer paid only once in his place of residence on all assets within the country, and the assessment was to be made on whichever commodity would provide the most tax. The subsidy taxed the income from the capital asset of land, the capital value of goods rather than the profits generated by them, and the income from wages. The problem of under-enumeration is difficult to establish. The returns of 1524 and 1525 do not contain identical lists of names even though they were separated by only one year.[19] In the Berkshire sample the nominal lists do vary. It is possible to

[16] Priors Court manor was held by New College Oxford, NCA, 4061. Seymours Court manor was held by the Eyston family, BRO, D/EX1/M4/3, 4. See chapters 4 and 5 for details.

[17] The manorial records of Andrews Court, held by the Fettiplace family, do not survive.

[18] J. Sheail, *The Regional Distribution of Wealth in England as Indicated in the 1524/5 Lay Subsidy Returns* (List and Index Society Special Series, volume 28, 1998), 15.

[19] Campbell considered that the 1524 listing had a level of accuracy of between 71.8 per cent and 96.9 per cent, B. M. S. Campbell, 'The population of early Tudor England: a re-evaluation of the 1522 Muster Returns and 1524 and 1525 Lay Subsidies', *Journal of Historical Geography*, 7 (1981), p152. In the Towcester hundred of Northamptonshire Schofield calculated that two per cent of taxpayers had died and fifteen per cent had moved away in the course of the year between 1524 and 1525, Wrigley and Schofield, *Population History*, 567.

compare the returns of twenty-three parishes of which only four had the same number of entries, in nine the numbers of taxpayers had risen and in ten their numbers were reduced. The real problem encountered with these returns in the context of this study is the patchy survival of the nominal returns and therefore coverage of western Berkshire.

The final fiscal source to be analysed is that of the Lay Subsidy granted in 1545 and collected in 1546 and 1547, and the returns of 1546 are employed in an attempt to capture any later changes in the distribution of wealth. The subsidy was assessed on a sliding scale with the bottom threshold set at those with moveable goods of £5 and lands worth more than £1 *per annum*.[20] It was therefore only assessing the rich and moderately wealthy and was not as inclusive as the earlier subsidies. It was, however, the last of the subsidies to have been rigorously assessed and useful for this type of study.[21]

Methodological approach

The documents' chronological coverage of more than two hundred years, combined with the fact that they were derived from different forms of taxation and compiled under separate circumstances as a result of changing fiscal demands, meant that a methodological approach had to be devised which would standardise their use. The data derived from the 1327 Lay Subsidy, 1334 Lay Subsidy and the 1381 Poll Tax were compiled at the level of the vill as were the Tudor Lay Subsidies and the Military Survey. The Tax of Pope Nicholas IV 1291 and the Inquisitions of the Ninth 1340–42 were based on the unit of the parish. Significant change had occurred in the intervening years between the different assessments as some vills were either very much smaller or had entirely disappeared from the sources between the various dates. In fact, some vills were severely reduced such as Barcote, Carswell and Newton in Buckland parish.[22] In order to standardise the material in a way that enabled comparisons between the sources to be made the data were entered into a relational database as they appeared in the original documentation and the individual vills were coded by giving each a unique number. The vills were identified either by reference to Glasscock, or from the manorial registers held at the National Register of Archives, London. The vills were then grouped into parishes. The parishes were also coded with a unique number and standardised as some change had occurred to the ecclesiastical map of Berkshire. The parochial

[20] Jurkowski *et al.*, *Lay Taxes*, 146–7.
[21] R. W. Hoyle, *Tudor Taxation Records A Guide for Users* (London, 1994), 26–9.
[22] See chapter 4 for additional examples of shrunken or deserted settlements.

structure employed was that used in the nineteenth-century census returns and the acreages refer to these parishes.[23]

The area of western Berkshire chosen for analysis was determined by the combined chance survival of the nominal returns of the 1381 Poll Tax and the 1522 Military Survey. These form the core parishes of this study. Furthermore, uneven survival of the documentary evidence accounts for differences in the acreages in the composite tables. In the examination of changes to the size of the population only data from males were employed due to the inconsistent recording of women in all the sources.

Coded vills were therefore grouped together into coded parishes as the unit of analysis and, because of the system of coding, a greater degree of flexibility could be employed to ensure a standard unit of comparison. Changes in the acreages at the level of the regional analysis are due to the survival of data. This has been, of necessity, an artificial methodology but, as the original data were entered as they appeared in the documents, and the coding of the vills into parishes has been double checked for consistency, we can be reasonably confident that the somewhat arbitrary parishes are standardised sufficiently to enable comparisons to be drawn between the fourteenth and sixteenth centuries.

For the discussions of economic change within the county the parishes were combined into their three main ecological areas described in chapter 2, with the addition of a fourth group of mixed landscapes for the broader analysis. The areas for analysis were thus the Vale of the Kennet in the south, the Berkshire Downs, the area of mixed economies, and finally the Vale of the White Horse in the north of the county. Furthermore, the data for the towns were removed for separate analysis. In this manner we could ensure that the rural and urban analyses were discrete.

[23] VCH Berks II, 234–43.

Table 21 *Composite data of population and assessed wealth, 1327–1546*

Parish	*Acres*	*Men in 1327*	*Total tax paid by men in 1327 in d.*	*Total assessment in 1334 in d.*	*Men in 1381*	*Total tax paid by men in 1381 in d.*	*Resident men in 1522*	*Total assessment on resident men in 1522 in d.*	*All taxpayers in 1546*	*Total assessment in 1546 in d.*
Berkshire Downs										
Aldworth	1806	6	337¾	660			24	45360	6	892
Beedon	2012	15	461	809¼	3	36	27	40160	5	448
Boxford	2819	19	1132½	1649½			44	35752		
Brightwalton	2054	18	699¾	1232¼			44	59016	4	434
Catmore	710	4	241	360						
Chaddelworth	3400	21	520¼	1006¾			39	25960	9	1349
Chievley	5328	23	1420¾	1734¾	10	112	78	65712	12	676
Compton	3863	14	724½	1043½			48	54308	11	1112
East Garston	4409	30	1073¾	1656¾	94	1034	52	66304	10	808
Farnborough	1886	8	386½	619½			30	31888	6	536
Fawley	2190	14	500	722			28	18720		
Frilsham	978	6	339	592¼	7	86	14	13320	2	128
Hampstead Norris	6046	23	1344¾	2794¾	36	436	55	85141	10	1818
Ilsley, East	3017	16	520¼	640			55	131973	11	1808
Ilsley, West	3037	14	1563	843½			25	32320	4	1448
Lambourn	14873	69	3815¼	5926¼	235	2718½	179	316175½	43	7452
Leckhampstead	1777	9	498¼	786¼	16	178	28	47520	5	543
Peasemore	2049	10	787½	1128	20	236	22	22120	3	440

Parish	*Acres*	*Men in 1327*	*Total tax paid by men in 1327 in d.*	*Total assessment in 1334 in d.*	*Men in 1381*	*Total tax paid by men in 1381 in d.*	*Resident men in 1522*	*Total assessment on resident men in 1522 in d.*	*All taxpayers in 1546*	*Total assessment in 1546 in d.*
Shefford, East	1069	7	338½	553			12	11480		
Shefford, West	2243	16	496¾	797½			29	30524	8	536
Stanford Dingley	927	6	438¾	672			21	26783¼	8	1832
Welford	5228	27	1408½	1909¼	23	264	85	70160	12	536
Winterbourne	2112	23	962¾	1187½			31	35720	3	316
Yattendon	1400	14	481¾	780¾	22	270	34	27360	4	164
Total	**75233**	**412**	**20492¾**	**30105¼**	**466**	**5370½**	**1004**	**1293776¾**	**176**	**23276**
Kennet Valley										
Avington	1185	9	331¼	1092	9	108	11	26960	2	696
Brimpton	1705	8	390½							
Enborne	2501	15	886¾	1324	39	478	29	33200	8	488
Greenham	2564	6	228¼	843¾			30	28080		
Hamstead Marshall	1852	11	611¼	742¼	13	156	40	56152	6	326
Inkpen	2886	16	682	1121½	32	366	34	43120	7	498
Kintbury	7778	60	2395¼	3481¼	99	812	91	111600	34	5216
Shalbourne	3675	28	1078½	912	37	436	66	46560	8	556
Shaw Cum Donnington	1996	12	512¼	1013	15	176	62	75800	9	1168
Speen	3862	58	2346¾	3829	113	1209	162	184887¾	24	1708
Wasing	690	2	20½							

Parish	*Acres*	*Men in 1327*	*Total tax paid by men in 1327 in d.*	*Total assessment in 1334 in d.*	*Men in 1381*	*Total tax paid by men in 1381 in d.*	*Resident men in 1522*	*Total assessment on resident men in 1522 in d.*	*All taxpayers in 1546*	*Total assessment in 1546 in d.*
West Woodhay	1432	11	412¾	540	17	268	23	14308	2	80
Total	**32126**	**236**	**9896**	**14898¾**	**374**	**4009**	**548**	**620667¾**	**100**	**10736**
Mixed Parishes										
Ardington	1820	57	1584¼	1935¾	80	954½	51	72136	9	2590
Ashbury	5609	34	1114¼	2320½	38	413	66	100439¾		
Childrey	2861	25	1231½	1829¾	57	687½	61	69920	9	3175
Chilton	1448	14	475¾	712			28	37688	7	402
Compton Beauchamp	1466	8	273¼	445½			7	4560	2	88
Hendred, East	3117	32	934¾	1364	79	953	30	40200	11	1468
Hendred, West	2007	38	695¼	868	94	1120½	38	79824		
Kingston Lisle	2147	30	579½	1141	33	402	23	21000	7	312
Letcombe Bassett	1662	13	1081	904			39	39081	6	460
Letcombe Regis	2459	39	1732¾	2314			34	39320		
Lockinge, East & West	3742			643¾	50	577	34	37336	9	1448
Lockinge, East	2878	42	1138	287			11	11480		
Sparsholt	3698	36	1756¼	2967¼	72	707	40	76544	11	1560
Uffington	3205	30	610¾	975¼			42	58872	12	1384
Woolstone	2012	14	349	561½			30	36656	7	1064
Total	**40131**	**412**	**13556¼**	**19269¼**	**503**	**5814½**	**534**	**725056¾**	**90**	**13951**

Parish	*Acres*	*Men in 1327*	*Total tax paid by men in 1327 in d.*	*Total assessment in 1334 in d.*	*Men in 1381*	*Total tax paid by men in 1381 in d.*	*Resident men in 1522*	*Total assessment on resident men in 1522 in d.*	*All taxpayers in 1546*	*Total assessment in 1546 in d.*
Vale Of The White Horse										
Balking	1473	14	488¼	1099	10	116	19	30520	5	968
Buckland	4505	64	3418	2560	122	1521½	69	71563	8	912
Buscot	2887	30	852	1288¼			23	86480		
Challow, East & West	2092	15	665½	1223½	50	278	18	11052	11	528
Charney Bassett	1209	13	611¼	611¼	24	288	38	37178	6	552
Coleshill	2014	16	517¾	1142¼			14	11760	7	544
Coxwell, Great	1435	17	619	1281	29	346	29	87480		
Coxwell, Little	887	6	320	990			27	64792		
Denchworth	1041	8	367	1295	22	261	23	34588	2	588
Eaton Hastings	1570	25	597	1014¾			27	47408		
Farringdon	5897	131	4829½	12799¼	250	2982	8	13120		
Fernham	1016	12	328	821			175	178039½	3	408
Goosey	968	14	391½	307¼	15	180	12	18760		
Grove	1791	35	805¾	1331¾	63	763	36	30968		
Hanney, East	2120	52	1929	1859¾	75	907	24	21240	5	344
Hanney, West	1383	34	1259½	1522	42	480	36	40584	6	1532
Hatford	993	9	249	356½	17	197	14	19520	2	384
Hinton Waldrist	2016	25	1138¼	1124¾	41	484	36	27320	5	288
Longworth	2291	27	665¼	1039½	63	709	25	30608	10	1488

Parish	Acres	Men in 1327	Total tax paid by men in 1327 in d.	Total assessment in 1334 in d.	Men in 1381	Total tax paid by men in 1381 in d.	Resident men in 1522	Total assessment on resident men in 1522 in d.	All taxpayers in 1546	Total assessment in 1546 in d.
Lyford	773				16	192			18	1535
Pusey	1040	10	454	600	14	168	13	11200	4	1472
Shellingford	1761	33	921¼	1172	44	508	21	24504	7	590
Shrivenham	7366	102	2829	4560	41	474½	121	191423½	28	2988
Stanford In The Vale	2927	75	2145½	1917¼	88	891	57	132982		
Total	51455	767	26401¼	4916	1026	11746	865	1223090	127	15121

Note: Blank cells indicate no surviving data.

Sources: 1291 *Taxatio Ecclesiastica Angliae et Walliae Auctoritate Pope Nicholai IV circa AD 1291* (Record Commission, 1831). 1327 TNA, E179/73/6. 1334 R. Glasscock (ed.), *The Lay Subsidy of 1334* (London, 1975), 6–14. 1340–42 *Nonarum Inquisitiones in Curia Scaccarii Temp Regis Edwardi III* (Record Commission, 1807). Additional data from TNA, E179/73/16. 1381 TNA, E179/73/41, 42, 43, 46, 48, 49, 50, 51, 52, 53, 54, 55, 62. 1412 *Inquisitions and Assessments relating to Feudal Aides*, vol. vi (Record Commission, 1920), 399–404. 1522 TNA, E315/464. 1546 TNA, E179/74/178, 181.

Table 22 *Comparative data for imports of woad and wine through Southampton from 1439–40 to 1491–92*

1439–40		1443–44		1448–49		1460–61	
Woad, in ballets and descending order of quantities taken.							
London	1680	Salisbury	2087	Salisbury	765	London	2485
Salisbury	919	Coventry	631	Winchester	336	Salisbury	900
Winchester	636	Winchester	474	Coventry	151	Coventry	695
Coventry	333	Romsey	197	London	114	Reading	402
Romsey	285	Gloucester	128	Romsey	113	Chesterfield	167
Gloucester	85	London	124	Gloucester	83	Winchester	137
Frome	79	Ringwood	66	Ringwood	56	Romsey	115
Ringwood	52	Frome	59	Frome	38	Langport	74
Newbury	11	Reading	55	**Newbury**	8	Northampton	48
		Newbury	13			**Newbury**	17
Wine, in pipes and descending order of quantities taken							
Winchester	171	Salisbury	229	Salisbury	297	Salisbury	195
Salisbury	125	Winchester	194	Winchester	284	Bristol	45
Oxford	44	London	65	Romsey	42	Winchester	42
Gloucester	22	Oxford	61	Bristol	29	Gloucester	32
Newbury	14	Romsey	36	Oxford	27	Oxford	24
		Newbury	21 (27)	**Newbury**	21	Romsey	21
				London	20	**Newbury**	11

Comparative data from O. Coleman (ed.), *The Brokage Book of Southampton, 1443–44*, vol. ii (Southampton Records Series, 1961), pp. 322–7.

My figures in parenthesis when different from Coleman's.

Bunyard, *The Brokage Book of Southampton from 1439–40*; Coleman, *The Brokage Book of Southampton, 1443–44* vols I and II; E. A. Lewis (ed.), *The Southampton Port and Brokage Books, 1448–49* (Southampton Records Series 36, 1993); Stevens, *The Brokage Books of Southampton for 1477–78 and 1527–28*; Southampton City Archives, SC5/5/12 Brokage Book for 1460–61; SC5/5/19 for 1469–70; SC5/5/28 for 1491–92; SC5/5/31 for 1494–95; SC5/5/32 for 1505; SC5/5/34 for 1534–35; SC5/5/35 for 1537–38.

1465–66		1469–70		1477–78		1488–89		1491–92	
London	3100	Salisbury	327	London	385	Alton	14	Winchester	139
Salisbury	678	Coventry	135	Coventry	214	Romsey	13	Salisbury	95
Coventry	641	Shepton Mallet	79	Salisbury	165	**Newbury**	0	Farnham	35
Winchester	251	Winchester	63	Winchester	156			Romsey	30
Langport	131	**Newbury**	55 (38)	Northampton	65			Alton	24
Shepton Mallet	125	Ringwood	52	**Newbury**	41			**Newbury**	0
Northampton	94								
Newbury	88								
Leigh on Mendip	46								
Bradford on Avon	40								

1465–66		1469–70		1477–78		1488–89		1491–92	
Salisbury	283	Salisbury	226	Salisbury	139	Salisbury	168	Salisbury	192
London	94	Winchester	98	London	127	Winchester	163	London	187
Winchester	46	Oxford	71	Winchester	125	London	40	Winchester	84
Newbury	18	London	70	**Newbury**	22	Oxford	36	Bristol	50
		Andover	33			**Newbury**	33 (29.5)	Gloucester	32
		Newbury	20			Abingdon	24	Oxford	23
						Reading	24	**Newbury**	3

Methodology and documentation
for the case studies of chapter 4

Community case studies are the optimal method for reconstructing village life
in the late medieval and early modern periods. They are, however, demanding
of both time and the quality of the documentary sources. They require, particularly in the context of this study, documentary series which span the late
fourteenth to sixteenth centuries in order to provide archival consistency.
Records of the manor are ideal, as they cover the whole period in question
and avoid the hazard that the changes observed between the medieval and
early modern periods might be archivally driven and a product of the different
types of documentary evidence.[1] The manor court rolls provide information
on important aspects of village life such as land and tenure, the management
of the open fields, cases of violence, trespass and debt. Furthermore, they
record all males over the age of 12 and are therefore an important source for
calculating the size of the manor's population. The information from court
rolls is augmented by that found in the ministers' accounts, particularly on
the income-generating aspects of the manor. Surveys and rentals provide
'snapshots' of the tenurial structure of the manor at a specific moment. The
quantitative use of manorial records for studies of rural society has been refined
and developed over the last thirty years[2]. The use of computer-aided analysis
has revolutionised the speed with which communities can be reconstructed,
it remains however a very time-consuming process, particularly if a variety of
documentary sources are employed.

The number of case studies that could be undertaken for western Berkshire
was constrained by the paucity of sites with good documentary coverage.[3]
Furthermore, places were selected for examination on the basis that they had

---

[1] For detailed discussions of the different types of manorial records, their usefulness and
drawbacks, see M. Bailey, *The English Manor c.1200–c.1500* (Manchester, 2002). M. Ellis,
Using Manorial Records (London, 1997). P. D. A. Harvey, *Manorial Records* (British
Records Association 5, 1984).

[2] For a detailed discussion of the historiography of the use of manor court rolls
see Z. Razi and R. Smith, *Medieval Society and the Manor Court* (Oxford, 1996),
Introduction.

[3] With the exception of Woolstone, the manors studied by Faith were not investigated
again in detail, rather her work is employed to extend this study. R. Faith, 'Berkshire:

different types of landlords and additionally, came from the different regions of the area. The number of suitable sites was therefore small and the result has had to be, of necessity, a compromise.

There were no manors in western Berkshire that had continuous series of documents of any single type, such as manor court rolls or ministers' accounts, which covered the whole period. They all had gaps of several years in the survival of their archives.[4] To overcome this deficiency a range of sources was employed to augment the manorial records, although these remained the core basis of the documentary evidence. Thus fiscal records were employed as these covered both the fourteenth and sixteenth centuries. Probate materials were also used, although they had a strong bias towards the sixteenth century. A variety of other sources such as charters, *inquisitions post mortem*, plea rolls from the courts of Chancery and Common Pleas were employed to strengthen the more detailed and continuous records. Moreover, by combining a variety of different types of documentary sources it has been possible to overcome many of the deficiencies in the manorial archive.[5]

As a result of the fragmentary nature of the archive it has not been feasible to attempt a full reconstruction of any community, or to perform the type of demographic analysis that Razi used at Halesowen[6]. By employing a system of coding it was possible to bridge some of the breaks in the documentary series. Properties and persons were given unique numbers that were linked in the relational databases across the different types of documentary sources. This allowed a high level of flexibility to be undertaken in the analysis and faster checking for accuracy. This system of coding was essential for maintaining continuity where there were gaps in the archive.[7]

Fourteenth and Fifteenth Centuries', in P. D. A. Harvey (ed.), *The Peasant Land Market in Medieval England* (Oxford, 1984).

[4] See below where itemised.

[5] For a discussion of the limitations of manorial records and how a more comprehensive investigation of different documentary sources can reduce the inherent weaknesses of those relating to the manor see J. Whittle and M. Yates, *'Pays reel or pays legal'*? Contrasting patterns of land tenure and social structure in eastern Norfolk and western Berkshire, 1450–1600', *AgHRev*, 48 (2000), 1–26.

[6] Z. Razi, *Life, Marriage and Death in a Medieval Parish: Economy, Society and Demography in Halesowen, 1270–1400* (Cambridge, 1980). Although this method has not been without its critics as is seen in the debate in *Law and History Review* (1984–87) between Razi and Poos and Smith and reprinted in *Medieval Society and the Manor Court*. Nevertheless, Razi remains confident and an advocate of the potential of manor court rolls. Z. Razi, 'Manorial court rolls and local population: An East Anglian case study', *EcHRev*, 49 (1996).

[7] The databases are now deposited with the ESRC Data Archive 'Town and Countryside in West Berkshire, c.1400–1600 (Study Number 4339)'.

As a result, it has been possible to examine the records of manors belonging to landlords from different social groupings – aristocratic, gentry, monastic, and collegiate – and, additionally, to study manors from the different regions of western Berkshire. This was very successful for the Vale and Kennet regions where there was good documentary survival; but was disappointing due to the fragmentary nature of the archive for a study of the Downs region which was consequently less intensively investigated. The potential weakness of the manorial archive is acknowledged and all conclusions drawn are subject to this caveat. Nevertheless, by employing similar archival sources and the same methodological approach for their analysis, a comparison can be made between several communities within western Berkshire. These studies form the basis of the generalisations made in chapter 4 and 5.

Chronological coverage of the manorial documentation

Buckland

Manor courts 1406–1413, 1419–1423, 1424–1432, 1438, 1440–1449, 1451–1470, 1472–1487, 1493–1496, 1509–1512, 1522, 1524, 1526, 1529, 1535–1537, 1545, 1547, 1586–1595, 1601.[8]
Ministers' accounts 1535–6.[9]
Rental 1405.[10]

West Hanney

PRIORS COURT

Manor courts 1444–48, 1486–1495, 1498–1510, 1513–1528, 1532, 1554–1558, 1588, 1591, 1599, 1600, 1602.[11]
Accounts 1442–1492, 1494–1498, 1500–1518, 1521–1544, 1546–1589, 1591, 1595–1596.[12]
Rentals 1490, 1605.[13]

SEYMOURS COURT

Manor courts 1433, 1435–1439, 1441, 1445, 1471, 1473, 1475, 1479–1480, 1491–1494, 1499, 1501–1502, 1506, 1509, 1511–1512, 1514, 1534–1536, 1541–1542, 1545, 1547, 1555, 1557, 1559–1560, 1562, 1567, 1572, 1576–1577, 1582, 1587, 1594, 1607.[14]
Rental 1492.[15]

[8] SBT, DR5/1943–2048.
[9] PRO, SC6/HENVIII/6900.
[10] SBT, DR5/1941.
[11] NCA, 4060–4062.
[12] N.C.A., Ministers' Accounts, 7190–7225. Bailiffs' Accounts, 2569–2571, 1733–1845, 1962–1977, 1980–1989. College Receipts, 2109–2125, 2578. College Accounts, 7407–7419, 7439–7516, 7713–7738.
[13] NCA, 4075, 4076.
[14] BRO, D/EX1/M1/1–5, M2/1–6, M3/1–8, M4/1–9, M5/1–2, M6; Hendred House for 1433, 1536, 1541–2.
[15] BRO, D/EX1/M7.

Kintbury
KINTBURY EATON
Manor courts 1413–1422, 1424, 1427–1438, 1441–1457, 1464–1482, 1493–1500.[16]
Ministers' accounts 1406, 1413–1422, 1425–1435, 1437–1446, 1449–1451, 1539.[17]

KINTBURY AMESBURY
Ministers' account 1540.[18]

Shaw
Manor courts 1405–1412, 1426–1436, 1441–1442, 1444, 1447, 1449–1452, 1457–1458, 1461, 1464–1465, 1468–1469, 1473–1484, 1486, 1490, 1496, 1499, 1505–1509, 1512, 1514, 1517, 1543–1546, 1605.[19]
Accounts 1404–1462, 1464–1502, 1505, 1507–1543.[20]
Rental 1450, Survey 1547.[21]

Ashbury
Terrier 1519.[22]

Woolstone
Manor courts 1412, 1510, 1532–3.[23]
Ministers' accounts 1414, 1416–1417, 1424, 1430, 1434–1436, 1458, 1460, 1463–1469, 1536.[24]
Survey 1547–48.[25]

---

[16] BL, Add Roll 49210–49284.
[17] BL, Add Roll 49266–49284, 49236. PRO, SC6/HENVIII/3739.
[18] PRO, SC6/HENVIII/3986.
[19] PRO, SC2/154/52–54, 18; BRO D/ENm1/M1.
[20] W.C.M., Bursars' Accounts, 22100–22200. Ministers' Accounts, BRO, D/ENmM12–55 and Newbury Museum for 1461–62 and 1466–67.
[21] PRO, SC2/154/53, LR2/187.
[22] BL, Harley MS. 3961.
[23] PRO, SC2/154/82, 83.
[24] PRO, SC6/758/2–12, 14–25, SC6/HENVIII/104.
[25] PRO, LR2/187, ff.166–9.

Table 23 *The transfer of land, 1401–1600*

Dates	1401 -10	1411 -20	1421 -30	1431 -40	1441 -50	1451 -60	1461 -70	1471 -80	1481 -90
Priors, Hanney									
Total number of courts	0	0	0	0	9	0	0	0	4
Total number of transfers					6				8
One way					1				5
Transfer to family					2				2
Transfer no relationship					3				1
Reversions					0				0
Seymours, Hanney									
Total number of courts	0	0	0	6	2	0	0	6	0
Total number of transfers				10	9			16	
One way				6	8			13	
Transfer to family				4	1			1	
Transfer no relationship				0	0			2	
Reversions				0	0			0	
Buckland [a]		a Break 1547–86, returns 1586–95, 1601 ff.							
Total number of courts	8	8	11	6	13	18	15	17	11
Total number of transfers	25	16	28	14	16	42	31	28	16
One way	19	7	24	11	12	39	28	17	11
Transfer to family	5	7	2	0	2	1	2	4	0
Transfer no relationship	1	2	2	3	2	2	1	7	5
Reversions	0	0	0	0	0	0	0	0	0
Shaw [b]		b Courts resume 1605							
Total number of courts	10	2	6	4	7	4	6	8	6
Total number of transfers	20	7	8	17	18	7	5	8	14
One way	12	6	4	8	13	4	2	0	1
Transfer to family	2	0	0	5	2	2	1	1	4
Transfer no relationship	6	1	3	4	3	1	2	7	9
Reversions	0	0	0	0	0	0	0	0	0
Kintbury									
Total number of courts	0	19	23	22	23	16	7	21	5
Total number of transfers		17	24	16	14	14	5	13	5
One way		7	7	9	5	5	2	6	3
Transfer to family		4	10	4	5	9	1	7	2
Transfer no relationship		6	7	3	4	0	2	0	0
Reversions		3	7	2	2	0	0	0	0

Sources as Table 16.

1491 -1500	1501 -10	1511 -20	1521 -30	1531 -40	1541 -50	1551 -60	1561 -70	1571 -80	1581 -90	1591 -1600	Totals	Later
												1602
7	9	8	7	1	0	5	0	0	1	3	54	1
2	18	6	18	0		5			0	5	68	1
1	13	1	10	0		0			0	1	32	0
1	2	2	8	0		1			0	2	20	0
0	3	3	0	0		4			0	2	16	1
0	0	0	0	0		0			0	1	1	1
5	4	4	0	5	4	4	2	3	2	1	48	
16	3	6		3	0	5	3	4	3	2	80	
15	3	5		2	0	3	0	1	0	0	56	
0	0	0		0	0	1	3	1	0	0	11	
1	0	1		1	0	1	0	2	3	2	13	
0	0	0		0	0	0	0	1	0	1	2	
												1601
8	0	2	5	5	3	0	0	0	9	7	146	1
8		1	8	11	0				16	17	277	7
3		1	4	7	0				0	8	191	2
4		0	0	1	0				14	6	48	3
1		0	4	3	0				2	3	38	2
0		0	0	0	0				7	1	8	0
												1605
2	5	3	0	1	7	0	0	0	0	0	71	1
0	6	0		0	1						111	4
0	0	0		0	0						50	0
0	4	0		0	1						22	4
0	2	0		0	0						38	0
0	0	0		0	0						0	4
12	2	0	0	0	0	0	0	0	0	0	150	
6	2										116	
4	2										50	
2	0										44	
0	0										22	
0	0										14	

Table 24 *Cases in the manor courts, 1401–1600*

Dates	1401 –10	1411 –20	1421 –30	1431 –40	1441 –50	1451 –60	1461 –70	1471 –80	1481 –90
Priors, Hanney									
Courts	0	0	0	0	9	0	0	0	4
Violence					5				
Theft					1				
Trespass					6				
Commons					0				
Bye-laws					0				
Seymours, Hanney									
Courts	0	0	0	6	2	0	0	6	0
Violence				0	0			0	
Theft				3	0			2	
Trespass				1	0			2	
Commons				0	0			0	
Bye-laws				2	0			0	
Buckland [a]	*a Break 1547–86, returns 1586–95, 1601 ff.*								
Courts	8	8	11	6	13	18	15	17	11
Violence	0	2	0	3	4	18	7	12	6
Theft	1	1	2	2	0	10	5	6	0
Trespass	0	10	5	0	2	0	0	2	0
Commons	0	0	34	1	37	19	7	22	3
Bye-laws	2	1	4	0	3	3	1	3	1
Shaw [b]	*b View of Frankpledge granted in 1461.*								
Courts	10	2	6	4	7	4	6	8	6
Violence	0	0	0	0	0	0	0	1	1
Theft	2	0	5	0	0	0	1	0	1
Trespass	0	0	2	1	0	0	2	0	0
Commons	0	0	0	0	0	0	0	0	1
Bye-laws	0	0	0	0	0	0	0	1	0
Kintbury									
Courts	0	19	23	22	23	16	7	21	5
Violence		7	9	5	4	4	2	2	0
Theft		8	0	2	6	2	1	1	0
Trespass		16	6	14	1	0	0	0	0
Commons		8	21	40	36	6	7	12	6
Bye-laws		0	0	1	4	0	0	0	0

Sources as Table 16.

1491 -1500	1501 -10	1511 -20	1521 -30	1531 -40	1541 -50	1551 -60	1561 -70	1571 -80	1581 -90	1591 -1600	Totals
7	9	8	7	1	0	5	0	0	1	3	54
0	0	0	0	0		0			0	0	5
0	0	0	0	0		0			0	0	1
0	0	0	0	0		0			0	0	6
0	0	0	0	0		0			0	0	0
0	2	0	0	0		0			0	0	2
5	4	4	0	5	4	4	2	3	2	1	48
0	0	0		0	0	0	0	0	0	0	0
0	0	0		0	0	0	0	0	0	0	5
0	1	0		0	0	0	0	0	0	1	5
0	0	0		0	0	0	0	0	0	0	0
0	0	0		1	0	0	0	1	0	0	4
8	0	2	5	5	3	0	0	0	9	7	146
7	0	0	2	1	1				0	1	64
2	0	2	0	0	0				0	0	31
0	0	0	0	0	1				0	0	20
5	0	2	7	13	14				6	6	176
1	0	1	0	2	0				6	2	30
2	5	3	0	1	7	0	0	0	0	0	71
1	3	2		0	1						9
1	0	1		0	2						13
0	1	0		0	0						6
0	0	0		0	0						1
0	0	1		0	0						2
12	2	0	0	0	0	0	0	0	0	0	150
6	2										41
4	0										24
1	0										38
7	0										143
6	0										11

Bibliography

(A) Manuscript sources

Berkshire Record Office (BRO)

Parish registers

D/P46/1/1	Denchworth
D/P65/1/1	Hatford
D/P117/1/1	Stanford Dingley
D/P62/1/1	Hampstead Norris
D/P106/1/1	East Hendred
D/P92/1/1	Peasemore
D/P32/1/1	Chaddelworth
D/P81/1/1	Letcombe Regis
D/P82/1/1	Lockinge
D/P55/1/1	Fawley
D/P63/1/1	Hanney
D/P106/1/1	Shaw
D/P89/1/1	Newbury

Manorial documents

WEST HANNEY, SEYMOURS COURT

D/EX1/M1/1–5	1435–45	Court Rolls.
D/EX1/M2/1–6	1471–80	Court Rolls.
D/EX1/M3/1–8	1491–06	Court Rolls.
D/EX1/M4/1–9	1510–57	Court Rolls.
D/EX1/M6	1555–94	Court Book.
D/EX1/M5/1–2	1582&1607	Court Rolls.
D/EX1/M9	1499	Homage Presentment.
D/EX1/M7	1492	Rental
D/EX1/M8	c.1470	Instructions to the steward.

SHAW

D/ENm1 M1–M9	1605–1638	Court Rolls
D/ENm1 M12–M55	1404–05 to 1542–43	Ministers' Accounts.
D/ENm1 E5	1630	Rental
D/ENm1 T2	1570–1	Lease of Shaw mills.
D/ENm1 T4	1592	Lease of messuage called Cornecrofte.

D/ENm1 T5	1594–1606	Lease of nine acres arable land.
D/ENm1 T11	1592–1865	Various leases.

Maps surveys and awards

D/EFe/P3	1809	Plan of Estate in West Hanney
D/P63/27 A & B	1844	Tithe Award and Map of West Hanney.
D/D1 106/1	1840	Tithe Award and Map of Shaw.
D/D1 27/1	1842	Tithe map and award Buckland.
D/ENm1 E8	c.1730	References to the map of Shaw
D/A2 c185	1634	Glebe Terriers of Berkshire
D/EZ 80/7	1721	Survey of Holt
D/EZ 80/9/1	1784	Plan of Miss Hoadleys Estate at Kintbury
D/EZ 80/9/3	1784	Survey of estate belonging to Miss E. Hoadley
D/EC/E11/1	1775	Survey of Holt in Kintbury Eaton
D/EC/ E13, P12, 13		Surveys of Craven Estate.
D/EW E/E3	1748	Reference to the plan of Buckland
D/EW E/E17	1748	Terrier of the East and West side fields in Buckland

Probate wills and inventories of the Archdeacon of Berkshire's court
D/A1

ASHBURY
82 wills and 59 inventories 1533–1600

BUCKLAND
60 wills and 51 inventories 1545–1600.

KINTBURY
83 wills and 83 inventories 1522–1600.

NEWBURY
207 wills and 104 inventories 1510–1580.

SHAW
17 wills and 19 inventories 1528–1600.

WEST HANNEY
66 wills and 44 inventories 1521–1600.

Charters

H/RTa 1–41	1275–1465	Hungerford charters which refer to lands both there and in Newbury.

Miscellaneous

D/ED c/T5	1574	Writ of possession John Cheyney.
D/EWE E1	1688, 1711, 1741	Boundaries of fields at Buckland.
D/EPT/uncat.		Newbury Clothier's Book.

Hampshire Record Office

Winchester College documents

SHAW
22100–22200	1418–9 to 1542–3	Bursars' Accounts.

NEWBURY
22158–22212	1493–4 to 1556–7	Bursars' Accounts.

Hendred House, Berkshire

Manorial documents of Seymours court
21 Mart 7 H.V AD 1419	1419	Court Roll
1 Oct 1433 12 H.VI	1433	Court Roll
18 June 33 H.VIII 1541	1541	Court Roll
21 Apr 33 H.VIII 1542	1542	Court Roll
24 Oct 28 H.VIII 1536	1536	Court Roll

London, British Library (BL)
Lansdowne MSS 5, no 9	c.1561	Names of Berkshire Freeholders
Lansdowne MSS 13, no 13		Cases of Bankruptcy

ASHBURY
Harley MS. 3961	Terrier of Glastonbury Abbey.

NEWBURY
Additional Charters: Add Ch 56725–7, 72664–5
                    1476–1536 Charters, Newbury.
Harley Charters: Harl Ch 52.I.16, 48.E.4, 47.E.42, 56.C.37–8.
                    1369–1465 Charters
Additional: ADD 46400, 5485 fol. 138, 6041 fol. 13, 6693 fol. 59.
                    Various lands in Newbury

KINTBURY
Add Roll 49210–49284	1335–1500	Manor Court Rolls and Ministers' Accounts of Kintbury Eaton
Add Ch 47439–47448	1436–1520	Various covenants of leases.
Add Ch 56051–2	1566, 1597	Templeton in Kintbury
Add Mss 36905	15th century	Customs, services etc. due to Nuneaton priory.
Maps 136.a.1	1875	Plan of Barton Court Estate.

London, Corporation of London Records Office, Guildhall
MC1/3/44	1441	Mayor's Court, case of debt between John Benet of Newbury & German merchant.

London, Mercers' Company Archive
Thomas Gresham's Day Book

London, The National Archives (TNA) (formerly the Public Record Office)

Chancery
C1/

NEWBURY
10/46, 10/334, 11/464, 12/152, 12/244, 12/245, 16/350, 17/85, 27/408, 28/530, 29/54, 33/241, 45/288, 69/381, 74/98, 158/76, 199/12, 224/74, 284/64, 296/77, 360/49, 371/78, 435/4, 435/6, 446/33, 474/11, 485/46, 504/12, 604/3, 604/4, 611/15, 621/31, 640/6, 755/23, 809/12, 911/1, 965/30, 965/31, 1115/62, 1115/64, 1115/65, 1183/20, 1276/75, 1276/76, 1276/77, 1385/1, 1385/2, 1419/42, 1419/43, 1419/44, 1456/51.

BUCKLAND
7/231, 9/126, 27/421, 74/84, 289/16, 457/15, 1171/7.

WEST HANNEY
100/51, 259/44, 717/42, 1096/54, 1298/27–9, 1428/41.

KINTBURY
144/39, 651/43, 735/51, 820/27–8, 1050/23, 1250/1–3.

SHAW
15/344, 44/70, 814/6, 1220/35, 1517/30.
C131/

NEWBURY
101 m.18, 224 m.18, 226 m.32.

Common Pleas

CP40/715	Mich. 1439
CP40/755	Mich. 1449
CP40/759	Mich. 1450
CP40/795	Mich. 1459
CP40/798	June 1460
CP40/799	Mich. 1460
CP40/800	Feb. 1461
CP40/833	Mich. 1469
CP40/864	Mich. 1478
CP40/910	Mich. 1489
CP40/954	Mich. 1500
CP40/993	Mich. 1510
CP40/1030	Mich. 1520.

Exchequer

E101/343/23	1354	Particulars of account of aulnage
E101/343/24	1394–95	Particulars of account of aulnage
E101/343/26	1471	Particulars of account of aulnage
E101/346/23	1468	Particulars of account of aulnage
E101/347/8	1471–72	Particulars of account of aulnage
E101/347/9	1472–73	Particulars of account of aulnage
E101/347/10	1474–76	Particulars of account of aulnage
E101/347/11	1476–78	Particulars of account of aulnage

E101/347/17	Temp Henry VIII to Edward VI	Names of clothiers.
E179/73/91	1439–40	Alien Subsidy
E179/73/109	1483–84	Alien Subsidy
E179/236/113	1468–69	Alien Subsidy
E179/73/47	1379–80	Subsidy 15th and 10th County
E179/73/56	1382–83	Subsidy 15th and 10th County
E179/73/58	1387–88	Subsidy 15th and 10th County
E179/73/59	1388	Subsidy 15th and 10th County
E179/73/60	1392–93	Subsidy 15th and 10th County
E179/73/71	1410	Subsidy 15th and 10th County
E179/73/97a	1449–50	Subsidy 15th and 10th County
E179/73/100	1453	Subsidy 15th and 10th County
E179/73/6	1327–28	Subsidy 20th County
E/179/73/62	1379	Poll Tax Eagle Hundred.
E179/73/48	1381	Poll Tax Faringdon Hundred
E179/73/49	1381	Poll Tax Ganfield Hundred
E179/73/55	1381	Poll Tax Kintbury Hundred
E179/73/50	1381	Poll Tax Lambourn Hundred
E179/73/41	1381	Poll Tax Ock Hundred (Part)
E179/73/51	1381	Poll Tax Ock Hundred (Part)
E179/73/52	1381	Poll Tax Ock Hundred (Part)
E179/73/53	1381	Poll Tax Ock Hundred (Part)
E179/73/42	1381	Poll Tax Reading Hundred
E179/73/43	1381	Poll Tax Shrivenham Hundred
E179/73/43A	1381	Poll Tax Bucklebury, Cottsettlesford and Roeburg Hundreds.
E179/73/46	1381	Poll Tax Wantage Hundred.
E179/73/132	1523–24	Anticipation Berkshire.
E179/73/121	1524	Lay Subsidy Faircross, Kintbury, Eagle and Compton Hundreds.
E179/73/124	1525	Lay Subsidy Faircross and Compton Hundreds.
E179/73/125	1525	Lay Subsidy Eagle, Faircross and Kintbury Hundreds.
E179/73/126	1525	Lay Subsidy Ganfield Hundred.
E179/73/165	1545	Lay Subsidy Berkshire.
E179/73/171	1545	Lay Subsidy Berkshire.
E179/74/178	1546	Lay Subsidy Berkshire.
E179/74/181	1546	Lay Subsidy Berkshire.
E159/350, m. 329–332	1565	Memoranda Roll.
E159/355 m. 206	1567	Memoranda Roll.
E315/464	1522	Military Survey West Berkshire
E315/465	temp Henry VIII	Book containing sums of money prested to the King.
E315/83/2	1–3 Edward VI	View of accounts.
E315/81/11	Henry VIII	Lands at Coleshill
E315/414/8 m. 107	1519	Renewal of rental Coleshill.
E315/185		Crown leases
E315/121 fols 22–26	1540 and earlier	Evidence of Church Commissioners on

		Hospital St Bartholomew.
E118/1/46	1516	Conventual lease, Coleshill
E118/1/73		Conventual lease, Coleshill
E303/1 m.8,9		Court of Augmentations, conventual leases.
E134/36&37Eliz/Mich39	1594	Depositions Benham Valence
E321/43/116, 129		Depositions regarding St Bartholomew's Hospital Newbury.
E301/3, 7, 51	1546	Chantry Certificates, Berkshire

Inquisitions Post Mortem

C135/101/3	1349	Inquisition at Benham with reference to pestilence in Newbury re town's tanning mill.
C135/103/46	1349	John de Lenham, Buckland
C139/18/32, 19/32	1416	Edmund late earl of March (rents, market, court profits etc. in Newbury).
C140/54/45	1474	Thomas Herbert (third of rents etc. with details of dates of fairs).
C142/111/10	1558	John Winchcombe.
E150/822/6	1558	John Winchcombe (Exchequer series II).
C/139/115 folio 24	1443	Peter Fettiplace for Andrews Court.
C/142/8 folio 32	1491	Henry Doget of West Hanney.
C/142/10 folio 141	1495	William Eyston of West Hanney

Kings Bench

KB27/798	Mich term 39 Hen VI
KB29/89	Hilary term 38 Hen VI

Manorial Documents

BUCKLAND

SC2/154/3, 4,18	1505, 1538–39	Court rolls.
SC6/HENVIII/6899	1535	Ministers' accounts.
SC6/HENVIII/6900	1535	Ministers' accounts.

KINTBURY

SC2/208/65–68	1514–23	Court Rolls Hungerford Engleford
SC2/201/5	1551–53	Court Rolls Balsdon
SC6/1122/26	1311–12	Ministers Account Templeton
SC6/HenVIII/3914	1539–41	Ministers' Accounts Hungerford Engleford
SC11/3	Richard II	Rental of Templeton
SC12/1/1	1394	Rental Inglewood and Templeton

NEWBURY

SC2/154/49	1527	Court Roll
SC6/750/3–7, 1115/1–2, Hen VII/1226, Hen VIII/6066, Hen VIII/6909		
		Ministers' accounts of 15th and 16th century.
SC11/47, 62	Hen VI	Rentals
SC12/4/41	1608	Rental
LR2/187	Ed VI	Survey of free tenants

LR2/197, 198, 209	1608	Surveys.

SHAW MANOR

SC2/154/52	1405–1412	Court Rolls
SC2/154/53	1426–1469	Court Rolls and includes Rental.
SC2/154/54	1473–1517	Court Rolls
SC2/154/18	1543–1546	Court Rolls
LR2/187	1547	Manorial Survey

WOOLSTONE

LR2/187 ff.166–9	1547–8	Survey of Woolstone.
SC6/HENVIII/3343, fols 53–4		Account of Woolstone.
SC6/HENVIII/103,104	1530, 1536	Ministers' accounts.
SC6/758/2–12, 14–25	1413–60, 1463–78	Ministers' accounts.
SC2/154/82, 83	1412, 1510, 1532–33	Court rolls, Woolstone. First Ministers' Accounts after the Dissolution

SC6/HENVIII/109	Abingdon Monastery
SC6/HENVIII/2402	Priory or Hospital of St John of Jerusalem
SC6/HENVIII/3739	Nuneaton
SC6/HENVIII/3986	Amesbury

Miscellaneous

C66/490 m. 22, 23	1460	Patent Roll. Individuals delivered to Wallingford gaol.
JUST1/36	1224–25	Berkshire Assize and Gaol Delivery Roll.
SP1/238, 265		State Papers.

P.C.C. Wills and Inventories

PROB2/455, 95, 523, 345, 374	Inventories for Buckland and Newbury.
PROB 11	Wills from Ashbury, Buckland, Hanney, Kintbury, Shaw, Woolstone, Newbury.

Requests

REQ 2/4/52		Newbury.
REQ 2/4/68	undated	Buckland.
REQ 2/7/67	undated	Buckland.
REQ 2/8/264	1542	Buckland.
REQ 2/10/230	1539–40	Newbury.
REQ 2/12/112, 185	undated	Hanney.
REQ 2/16/14	1547–49	Kintbury.
REQ 2/16/25	c.1499–1503	Newbury.
REQ 2/17/16	1551	Newbury.
REQ 2/30/103	1541	Newbury.
REQ 2/35/2	1568	Kintbury.
REQ 2/35/20	1576	Kintbury.
REQ 2/35/22	1586	Kintbury.
REQ 2/89/29	c.1535	Newbury.
REQ 2/127/31	1601	Newbury.
REQ 2/173/18	1572	Shaw.

Star Chamber

STAC2/2 fol. 95	undated 1509–47	
STAC 2/15 fol. 15, 95	undated 1509–47	
STAC 2/17/283	undated 1509–47	
STAC 2/17/374	undated 1509–47	
STAC 2/24/202	undated	Eaton Hastings

Newbury Museum

Manorial documents of Shaw

1461–62	Ministers' Account
1466–67	Ministers' Account
1542–42	Ministers' Account.

Map

c.1730   'An accurate survey of Speen Mannour in the County of Barks belonging to his Grace Duke Chandos'.

Oxford, Bodleian Library

Leases MS.ch.Berks a.10–11   1443–1604

Oxford, New College Archive (NCA)

Manorial documents

WEST HANNEY, PRIORS COURT

NCA 7190–7225	1442–82	Ministers' Accounts.
NCA 2569–2571 and 1733–1845	1481–1544	Bailiffs' Accounts.
NCA 4060	1444–1508	Court Roll.
NCA 4061	1510–32	Court Roll
NCA 4062	1554–1602	Court Roll.
NCA various	1442–1549	College Receipts.
NCA 4075	1490	Rental
NCA 4076	1605	Rental
NCA 1360	1599	'Concerning the commons of the tenants of the three manors of Hanney' Contains list of tenants of all manors (3 documents).
NCA 4455	1634	Terrier of Priors Farm
NCA 3578	1664	Survey of West Hanney.
NCA 9181	1476	Valor of manor.
NCA 9134	1477	Valor of manor.
NCA 9135	1502–3	Valor of manor.
NCA 9136	1512	Draft valor of manor.
NCA 9757	1480–1528	Leases
NCA 9758	1535	Lease.

Shakespeare Birthplace Trust (SBT)

BUCKLAND

DR5/ 1925, 1932–2047 1315, 1348–1595, Court Rolls, Ministers' Accounts, Rentals, Writs, Grants that relate to manors of Dukes and St Johns.

DR5/2097, 2100   1588–1609, 1544–1712   Court Book and Rent Rolls of Bishops Manor

Southampton City Archive

SC5/5/12	1460–61	Brokage Book
SC5/5/16	1465–66	do
SC5/5/19	1469–70.	do
SC5/5/27	1488–89	do
SC5/5/28	1491–92	do
SC5/5/31	1494–95	do
SC5/5/32	1505	do
SC5/5/34	1534–35	do
SC5/5/35	1537–38	do.
SC5/6/1	1552–57	Cloth Hall Account.

Surrey History Centre (SHC)

LM/317/3	1549	Rough presentments and officers elected.
LM/317/4	1549	Notes of suits and complaints for the court.
LM/835/2	mid-16th century	Complaints and suits at Newbury
LM/345/52/1–2	1528	Deed of Newbury Town Mills
LM/1739/1–2	1552	Petition to King for Letters Patent
LM/1954	16th century	List of towns near Newbury

Winchester College Muniments (WCM)

SHAW

11471	c.1540	Rental
11471A	1405	Copy of writ of si fecerit.
8183	1543	Valor
11444&3	1404	Grant of Shaw manor to Winchester College.
22992 'Liber Albus'		Contains leases.
22993 Reg G.		Contains leases of properties.
14641–2, 14587, 14618–20		Relate to tenements in Newbury.
20033, 20035–6, 20084		Obligationes.

NEWBURY

14558–14598, 14600–14603, 14606–14633, 14641–14645 14th–16th century
Grants, quitclaims etc. relating to properties in Newbury.

14599	1478	Will of Richard Wyard.
14634	1438	Copy of will of John Chelrey of Newbury
14635–14640	1452–53	Declarations relating to Chelrey's will.
14646	1464	Estreats of View with court held at Newbury
14647–8	16th century	Acquittance and Bond

14649–14659   15th & 16th century Accounts
27592 –3, 27613–5, 27631–3, 27641–3   Leases to properties in Newbury.

Windsor, St George's Chapel, Windsor Castle

NEWBURY
XV.61.75, XV.61.94–6, XV.53.1–5, XV.29.46, XV.31.62
              14th–16th century   Rentals, terriers, quit rents.
XV.5.4, XV.5.39, XV.29.1–3, XV.29.21, XV.29.26–7, XV.29.35, XV.30.25–33, XV.54.57–8, XV.54.80–94.
              14th–16th century   Leases.
XV.2.63, XV.2.66–7, XV.2.85, XV.2.109, XV.2.111, XV.2.129, XV.2.146, XV.2.150.
              16th century   Bonds and releases.
XV.3.21, XV.61.76–93 15th and 16th century   Ministers' accounts.
XV.48.42–68, XV.49.1–41, XV.42.2–8.
              15th and 16th century   Stewards' accounts.
IV.B.4   1620   Frith's Old Register, or Liber Collegii.
CC120349   Mr Wilson's Book.
27/3 120050/2 1367–68   Rental of Sandleford Priory for lands in
                                       Newbury, from Church Commissioners.

(B) Printed Primary Sources

Calendar of Charter Rolls, I–V, 1226–1417 (HMSO, London, 1903–).
Calendar of Close Rolls (HMSO, London, 1892–).
Calendar of Fine Rolls (HMSO, London, 1962).
Calendar of Inquisitions (HMSO, London, 1954).
Calendar of Patent Rolls (HMSO, London, 1891–).
Calendar of State Papers Domestic (HMSO, London, 1992).
Historical Manuscripts Commission; National Register of Archives Eyston (East Hendred) MSS vols I and II.
Inquisitions and Assessments relating to Feudal Aids vols I, VI (Record Commission, 1899, 1920).
Letters and Papers Foreign and Domestic, of the Reign of Henry VIII (London, 1862–).
List of Early Chancery Proceedings, 10 vols (PRO List and Indexes, HMSO, London, 1901–).
Nonarum Inquisitiones in Curia Scaccarii Temp Regis Edwardi III (Record Commission, 1807).
Parliamentary Writs, 4 vols (Record Commission, 1827–34).
Placita de Quo Warranto (Record Commission, 1818).
Proceedings and Ordinances of the Privy Council of England Vol. VI (Record Commission, 1837).
Records of the Honourable Society of Lincoln's Inn. Volume I Admissions from 1420 to 1799 (London: Lincoln's Inn, 1896).
Rotuli Hundredorum, 2 vols (Record Commission, 1812, 1818).
Rotuli Litterarum Clausarum, 2 vols (Record Commission, 1833, 1844).
Rotuli Parliamentorum, 6 vols (Record Commission, 1783).
Statutes of the Realm from Original Records and Authentic Manuscripts, 11 vols (Record Commission, 1810–28).

Taxatio Ecclesiastica Angliae et Walliae Auctoritate Pope Nicholai IV circa AD 1291 (Record Commission 1831).
Valor Ecclesiasticus Temp. Henr' VIII, vol. 2 (Record Commission, 1814).

Ashmole, E., *The Antiquities of Berkshire* (London, 1723).
Bunyard B. D. M. (ed.), *The Brokage Book of Southampton from 1439–40* (Southampton Records Series 40, 1941)
Chibnall A. C. (ed.), *The Certificate of Musters for Buckinghamshire in 1522* (Royal Commission on Historical Manuscripts, vol. 18, 1973).
Chibnall A. C., and A. V. Woodman (eds), *Subsidy Roll for the County of Buckingham* (Buckingham, 1950).
Clanchy M. T. (ed.), *The Roll and Writ File of the Berkshire Eyre of 1248* (Selden Society, 90, 1973).
Coleman O. (ed.), *The Brokage Book of Southampton, 1443–44*, 2 vols (Southampton Records Series iv, 1960 and vi, 1961).
Cowper J. M. (ed.), *Henry Brinklow's Complaynt of Roderyck Mors* (Early English Text Society, Extra Series, 22, 1874).
Davies J. S. (ed.), *An English Chronicle* (Camden Society, 64, 1856).
Deloney, Thomas, *The pleasant historie of John Winchcomb in his yonguer* [sic] *ye Jack of Newbery, the famous and worthy clothier of England* STC (2nd ed.)/6560 (London, 1626)
Dugdale, W. *Monasticon Anglicanum*, 8 vols (London, 1849).
Edelen, G. (ed.), *The Description of England by William Harrison* (New York, 1968).
Fenwick, C. C. (ed.), *The Poll Taxes of 1377, 1379 and 1381*, 3 vols (The British Academy, 1998, 2001, 2005).
Flower, C. T. (ed.), *Public Works in Medieval Law*, 2 vols (Selden Society, 32, 40, 1915).
Franklin, P. (ed.), *The Taxpayers of Medieval Gloucestershire* (Stroud, 1993).
Glasscock R. (ed.), *The Lay Subsidy of 1334* (London, 1975).
Guilding, J. M. (ed.), *Reading Records. Diary of the Corporation; Vol. I. Henry VI to Elizabeth, 1431–1602*, 3 vols (London, 1892).
Hanham, A. (ed.), *The Cely Letters, 1472–1488* (Early English Text Society, Original Series, 273, 1975).
Hardy W. and E.L.C.P. (eds), *Recueil des Croniques et Anchiennes Istories de la Grant Bretaigne, a present nomme Engleterre par Jehan de Waurin, Seigneur de Forestel*, 5 vols (London, 1864–91).
Harvey, P. D. A. (ed.), *Manorial Records of Cuxham Oxfordshire c.1200–1359.* (Oxfordshire Record Society, 50, 1976).
Hockey, S. F. (ed.), *The Account Book of Beaulieu Abbey* (Camden Society, Fourth Series, 16, 1975).
Horn, J. M. (ed.), *The register of Robert Hallum, Bishop of Salisbury, 1407–17* (Canterbury and York Society, 72, 1982).
Hoyle R. W. (ed.), *The Military Survey of Gloucestershire* (Gloucester Record Series, 6, 1993).
Jackson, C. (ed.), *Newbury Kendrick Workhouse Records, 1627–1641* (Berkshire Record Society, 8, 2004).
Kemp, B. R. (ed.), *Reading Abbey Cartularies* (Camden Fourth Series, 31 and 33, 1986).
Kirk, R. E. G. (ed.), *Accounts of the Obedientiars of Abingdon Abbey* (Camden Society, New, 51, 1892).
Kitchin, G. W. (ed.), *Compotus Rolls of the Obedientiaries of St Swithun's Priory, Winchester*

(Hampshire Record Society, 1892).

Lambrick, G., and C. F. Slade (eds), *The Cartularies of Abingdon Abbey*, 2 vols (Oxford Historical Society, New Series 32, 33, 1990, 1992).

Larking, L. B., and J. M. Kemble (eds), *The Knights Hospitallers in England: Being the Report of Prior Philip De Thame to the Grand Master Elyan De Villanova for A.D. 1338* (Camden Society, 65, 1857).

Leadam I. S. (ed.), *The Domesday of Inclosures, 1517–1518*, vol. 2 (London, 1897).

Lewis E. A. (ed.), *The Southampton Port and Brokage Books, 1448–49* (Southampton Records Series 36, 1993).

Lysons, D. and S., *Magna Britannia Berkshire* (Wakefield, 1806; 1978 edn).

Malthus, T. *An Essay on the Principle of Population* (Penguin, 1970).

Mann F. O. (ed.), *The Works of Thomas Deloney* (Oxford, 1912).

Marx, Karl. *Capital*, vols 1–3 (Harmondsworth, 1990).

Merson A. L. (ed.), *The Third Book of Remembrance of Southampton, 1514–1602* (Southampton Records Series 2, 1952).

Money, W. *The History of the Ancient Town and Borough of Newbury in the County of Berks* (London, 1887).

Mortimer I. (ed.), *Berkshire Glebe Terriers* (Berkshire Record Society, 2, 1995).

Mortimer, I. (ed.), *Berkshire Probate Accounts, 1583–1712* (Berkshire Record Society, 4, 1999).

Nicolas H. (ed.), *Proceedings and Ordinances of the Privy Council of England, Volume VII, 1540–1542* (Record Commission, 1837).

Oschinsky, D. (ed.), *Walter of Henley and Other Treatises on Estate Management and Accounting.* (Oxford, 1971).

Page, M. (ed.), *The Pipe Roll of the Bishopric of Winchester, 1301–2* (Winchester, 1996).

— (ed.), *The Pipe Roll of the Bishopric of Winchester, 1409–10* (Winchester, 1999).

Poos, L. R. (ed.), *Lower Ecclesiastical Jurisdiction in Late-Medieval England. The Courts of The Dean and Chapter of Lincoln, 1336–1349, and the Deanery of Wisbech, 1458–1484* (The British Academy, 2001).

Poos, L. R., and L. Bonfield (eds), *Select Cases in Manorial Courts, 1250–1550* (Selden Society, 114, 1998).

Pound, J. (ed.), *The Military Survey of 1522 for Babergh Hundred* (Suffolk Records Society, 28, 1986).

Pratt, J. (ed.), *The Acts and Monuments of John Foxe* (London, 1868, 1877).

Ramsey, G. D. (ed.), *John Isham Mercer and Merchant Adventurer. Two Account Books of a London Merchant in the Reign of Elizabeth I* (Northamptonshire Record Society, 21, 1962).

Roulx, J. Delaville le (ed.), *Cartulaire Générad de l'Ordre des Hospitaliers de S. Jean de Jerusalem*, vol. 2 (Paris, 1897).

Rylands W. H. (ed.), *The Four Visitations of Berkshire* (Harleian Society, 56, 1907).

Sheail, J. *The Regional Distribution of Wealth in England as Indicated in the 1524/5 Lay Subsidy Returns* (List and Index Society Special Series, vol. 28, 1998).

Slade C. (ed.), *Reading Gild Accounts, 1357–1516* (Berkshire Record Society, vols 6 and 7, 2002).

Smith, Adam, *The Wealth of Nations, Books I–III* (Harmondsworth, 1997).

—, *The Wealth of Nations, Books IV–V* (Harmondsworth, 1999).

Smith L. T. (ed.), *Leland's Itinerary in England and Wales*, 5 vols (London, 1964).

Stevens K. F. (ed.), *The Brokage Books of Southampton for 1477–78 and 1527–28* (Southampton Records Series 28, 1985).

Tawney, R. H. and E. Power (eds), *Tudor Economic Documents*, 3 vols (London, 1924).

Timmins, T. C. B. (ed.), *The register of John Waltham, Bishop of Salisbury, 1388–1395* (Canterbury and York Society, 80, 1994).

Wallis Chapman A. B. (ed.), *The Black Book of Southampton, 1388–1414* (Southampton Records Series, 13, 1912)

Weber, Max. *The Protestant Ethic and the Spirit of Capitalism* (London, 1930).

Wordie J. R. (ed.), *Enclosure in Berkshire, 1485–1885* (Berkshire Record Society, 5, 2000).

Wright, D. P. (ed.), *The register of Thomas Langton, Bishop of Salisbury, 1485–93* (Canterbury and York Society, 74, 1985).

(C) Secondary Sources

Allen, M., 'The Volume of the English Currency, 1158–1470', *EcHRev*, 54 (2001), 595–611.

Allen, R. C., *Enclosure and the Yeoman* (Oxford, 1992).

——, 'Progress and Poverty in Early Modern Europe', *EcHRev*, 56 (2003), 403–43.

Almond, R. and A. J. Pollard, 'The Yeomanry of Robin Hood and Social Terminology in Fifteenth-century England', *Past and Present*, 170 (2001), 52–77.

Archer, R. E. and S. Walker (eds), *Rulers and Ruled in Late Medieval England* (London, 1995).

Ashley, W. J., *An Introduction to English Economic History and Theory. Part II, The End of the Middle Ages* (London, 1893, 8th impression, 1914).

Ashmole, E., *The Antiquities of Berkshire.* (London, 1719).

Astill, G., *Historic Towns in Berkshire: An Archaeological Appraisal* (Reading, 1978).

——, 'The Towns of Berkshire', in J. Haslam (ed.), *Anglo-Saxon Towns in Southern England* (Chichester, 1984), 53–86.

——, 'Archaeology and the Smaller Medieval Town', *Urban History Yearbook* (1985), 46–53.

——, 'Towns and Town Hierarchies in Saxon England', *Oxford Journal of Archaeology*, 10 (1991), 95–116.

——, 'Archaeology and the Late-Medieval Urban Decline', in T. R. Slater (ed.), *Towns in Decline, AD 100–1600* (Aldershot, 2000), 214–34.

—— and A. Grant (eds), *The Countryside of Medieval England* (Oxford, 1988).

Aston, M., *Lollards and Reformers* (London, 1984).

——, 'Corpus Christi and Corpus Regni: Heresy and the Peasants' Revolt', *Past and Present*, 143 (1994), 3–47.

Aston, T. H. and C. H. E. Philpin (eds), *The Brenner Debate: Agrarian Class Structure and Economic Development in Pre-industrial Europe* (Cambridge, 1985).

Ault, W. O., *Open-field Husbandry and the Village Community* (Philadelphia, 1965).

——, 'Manor Court and Parish Church in Fifteenth-century England: A Study of Village By-laws', *Speculum*, 42 (1967), 53–67.

——, 'The Village Church and the Village Community in Medieval England', *Speculum*, 45 (1970), 197–215.

——, *Open Field Farming in Medieval England* (London, 1972).

Aylmer, G. E., 'The Economics and Finances of the Colleges and University, c.1530–1640', in J. McConica (ed.), *The History of the University of Oxford*, III (Oxford, 1986).

Bailey, M., 'The Concept of the Margin in the Medieval English Economy', *EcHRev*, 42 (1989), 1–17.

——, *A Marginal Economy? East Anglian Breckland in the Later Middle Ages* (Cambridge, 1989).

——, '*Per Impetum Maris*: Natural Disaster and Economic Decline in Eastern England, 1275–1350', in B. M. S. Campbell (ed.), *Before the Black Death* (Manchester, 1991).

——, 'A Tale of Two Towns: Buntingford and Standon in the Later Middle Ages', *Journal of Medieval History*, 19 (1993), 351–71.

——, 'Rural Society', in R. Horrox (ed.), *Fifteenth-century Attitudes* (Cambridge, 1994).

——, 'Demographic Decline in Late Medieval England: Some Thoughts on Recent Research', *EcHRev*, 49 (1996), 1–19.

——, 'Historiographical Essay. The Commercialisation of the English Economy, 1086–1500', *Medieval History*, 24 (1998), 297–311.

——, 'Peasant Welfare in England, 1290–1348', *EcHRev*, 51 (1998), 223–51.

——, 'Trade and Towns in Medieval England: New Insights from Familiar Sources', *The Local Historian*, 29 (1999), 194–211.

——, *The English Manor, c.1200–c.1500* (Manchester, 2002).

Baillie, M. G. L., *A Slice Through Time: Dendrochronology and Precision Dating* (London, 1995).

Bainbridge, V., *Gilds in the Medieval Countryside.* (Woodbridge, 1996).

Baker, J. H., *An Introduction to English Legal History* (3rd edn, London, 1990).

Baker, R. H., 'Evidence in the 'Nonarum Inquisitiones' of Contracting Arable Lands in England during the Early Fourteenth Century', *EcHRev*, 19 (1966), 518–32.

Bardsley, S., 'Women's Work Reconsidered: Gender and Wage Differentiation in Late Medieval England', *Past and Present*, 165 (1999), 3–29.

Barron, C. M., *London in the Later Middle Ages* (Oxford, 2004).

Barron, C. M. and A. F. Sutton (eds), *Medieval London Widows, 1300–1500* (London, 1994).

Barry, J. and C. Brooks (eds), *The Middling Sort of People* (Basingstoke, 1994).

van Bavel, B. J. P., 'Land, Lease and Agriculture: The Transition of the Rural Economy in the Dutch River Area from the Fourteenth to the Sixteenth Century', *Past and Present*, 172 (2001), 3–43.

——, 'Rural Population Developments in the Low Countries, c.1300–c.1600', *Continuity and Change*, 17 (2002), 9–37.

Bean, J. M. W., 'Plague, Population and Economic Decline in England in the Later Middle Ages', *EcHRev*, 15 (1962/3), 423–37.

Beckerman, J. S., 'The Articles of Presentment of a Court Leet and Court Baron, in English, c.1400', *BIHR,*, 47 (1974), 230–4.

——, 'Procedural Innovation and Institutional Change in Medieval English Manorial Courts', *Law and History Review*, 10 (1992), 197–252.

——, 'Towards a Theory of Medieval Manorial Adjudication: The Nature of Communal Judgments in a System of Customary Law', *Law and History Review*, 13 (1995), 1–22.

Beckett, J. V., *The Agricultural Revolution* (Oxford, 1990).

Beier, A. L., *The Problem of the Poor in Tudor and Early Stuart England* (London, 1983).

Bennett, H. S., *Life on the English Manor: A Study of Peasant Conditions, 1150–1400* (3rd impression, Cambridge, 1948).

Bennett, J. M. *Women in the Medieval English Countryside* (Oxford, 1987).

——, 'The Tie that Binds: Peasant Marriages and Families in Late Medieval England', *Journal of Interdisciplinary History*, 15 (1984), 111–29.

——, 'Conviviality and Charity in Medieval and Early Modern England', *Past and Present*, 134 (1992), 19–41.

——, *Ale, Beer and Brewsters in England* (Oxford, 1996).

——, 'Writing Fornication: Medieval Leyrwite and Its Historians', *TRHS*, 6 (2003), 131–62.

Beresford, M.W., *Lay Subsidies and Poll Taxes* (Bridge Place near Canterbury, 1963).

——, *The Lost Villages of England* (Stroud, 1983).

——, and Hurst, J.G., 'Introduction to a First List of Deserted Medieval Village Sites in Berkshire', *Berkshire Archaeological Journal*, 60 (1962), 92–7.

Berg, M., and P. Hudson, 'Rehabilitating the Industrial Revolution', *EcHRev*, 45 (1992), 24–50.

Bernard, G.W. and R.W. Hoyle, 'The Instructions for the Levying of the Amicable Grant, March 1525', *Historical Research*, 68 (1994), 190–202.

Biddick, K., 'Medieval English Peasants and Market Involvement', *JEH*, 45 (1985), 823–31.

——, 'Missing Links: Taxable Wealth, Markets, and Stratification among Medieval English Peasants', *Journal of Interdisciplinary History*, 18 (1987), 277–98.

Bindoff, S.T. (ed.), *The History of Parliament: The House of Commons, 1509–1558*, 3 vols (London, 1982).

Binski, P. *Medieval Death: Ritual and Representation* (New York, 1996).

Bisson, T.N., 'The "Feudal Revolution"', *Past and Present*, 142 (1994), 6–42.

Blair J. (ed.), *Minsters and Parish Churches* (Oxford, 1988).

——, *Early Medieval Surrey* (Stroud, 1991).

——, *Anglo-Saxon Oxfordshire* (Stroud, 1994).

——, and N. Ramsay (eds), *English Medieval Industries: Craftsmen, Techniques, Products* (London, 1991).

Blanchard, I., 'Population Change, Enclosure, and the Early Tudor Economy', *EcHRev*, 23 (1970), 427–45.

—— (ed.), *The Duchy of Lancaster's Estates in Derbyshire, 1485–1540* (Derbyshire Archaeological Society Record Series, vol. 3 for 1967, 1971).

——, 'Labour Productivity and Work Psychology in the English Mining Industry, 1400–1600', *EcHRev*, 31 (1978), 1–24.

Bloch, M., *Feudal Society*, 2 vols (London, 1961).

——, 'The Advent and Triumph of the Watermill', in M. Bloch (ed.), *Land and Work in Medieval Europe* (London, 1967).

Bois, G., *The Transformation of the Year One Thousand: The Village of Lournand from Antiquity, to Feudalism* (Manchester, 1989).

Bolton, J.L., *The Medieval English Economy, 1150–1500* (London, 1980).

——, '"The World Turned Upside Down". Plague as an Agent of Economic and Social Change', in M. Ormrod and P. Lindley (eds), *The Black Death in England* (Stamford, 1996).

——, and M.M. Maslen (eds), *Calendar of the Court Books of the Borough of Witney, 1538–1610* (Oxfordshire Record Society, 54, 1985).

Bond, C.J., 'The Reconstruction of the Medieval Landscape; The Estates of Abingdon Abbey', *Landscape History*, 1 (1979), 59–75.

Bonfield, L., 'Normative Rules and Property Transmission: Reflections on the Link between Marriage and Inheritance in Early Modern England', in L. Bonfield, R. Smith, and K. Wrightson (eds), *The World We Have Gained* (Oxford, 1986).

——, 'The Nature of Customary Law in the Manor Courts of Medieval England',

Comparative Studies In Society and History, 31 (1989), 514–34.

——, 'Introduction: The Dimensions of Customary Law', *Continuity and Change*, 10 (1995), 331–6.

Bonney, M., *Lordship and the Urban Community: Durham and Its Overlords, 1250–1540* (Cambridge, 1990).

Boserup, E., *The Conditions of Agricultural Growth* (London, 1965).

Bothwell, J., P. J. P. Goldberg, and M. Ormrod (eds), *The Problem of Labour in Fourteenth-century England* (York, 2000).

Bowden, P., 'Agricultural Prices, Farm Profits and Rents', in J. Thirsk (ed.), *The Agrarian History of England and Wales, IV, 1500–1640* (Cambridge, 1967), 593–695 and Appendix, 814–70.

Bowden, P. J., *The Wool Trade in Tudor and Stuart England* (London, 1971).

Brenner, R., 'Agrarian Class Structure and Economic Development in Pre-Industrial Europe', *Past and Present*, 70 (1976), 30–75.

Brenner, R., *Merchants and Revolution: Commercial Change, Political Conflict, and London's Overseas Traders, 1550–1653* (Cambridge, 1993).

Bridbury, A. R., *Economic Growth: England in the Later Middle Ages* (London, 1962).

——, 'The Black Death', *EcHRev*, 26 (1973), 577–92.

——, 'The Hundred Years' War: Costs and Profits', in D. C. Coleman and A. H. John (eds), *Trade Government and Economy in Pre-industrial England: Essays presented to F. J. Fisher* (London, 1976).

——, 'Before the Black Death', *EcHRev*, 30 (1977), 393–410.

——, 'English Provincial Towns in the Later Middle Ages', *EcHRev*, 34 (1981), 1–24.

——, *Medieval English Clothmaking: An Economic Survey* (London, 1982).

Briggs, C., 'Creditors and Debtors and Their Relationships at Oakington, Cottenham and Dry Drayton (Cambridgeshire), 1291–1350', in P. R. Schofield and N. J. Mayhew (eds), *Credit and Debt in Medieval England c.1180–c.1350* (Oxford, 2002), 127–48.

Briggs, J., C. Harrison, A. McInnes, and D. Vincent (eds), *Crime and Punishment in England* (London, 1996).

Britnell, R. H., 'Minor Landlords in England and Medieval Agrarian Capitalism', *Past and Present*, 89 (1980), 3–22.

——, 'The Proliferation of Markets in England, 1200–1349', *EcHRev*, 24 (1981), 209–21.

——, *Growth and Decline in Colchester, 1300–1525* (Cambridge, 1986).

——, 'The Pastons and their Norfolk', *AgHRev*, 36 (1988), 132–44.

——, 'Feudal Reaction after the Black Death in the Palatinate of Durham', *Past and Present*, 128 (1990), 28–47.

——, 'Commerce and Capitalism in Late Medieval England: Problems of Description and Theory', *Journal of Historical Sociology*, 6 (1993), 359–76.

——, *The Commercialisation of English Society, 1000–1500* (Cambridge, 1993).

——, 'The Black Death in English Towns', *Urban History*, 21 (1994), 195–210.

——, 'The Economic Context', in A. J. Pollard (ed.), *The Wars of the Roses* (Basingstoke, 1995).

——, 'Price-Setting in English Borough Markets, 1349–1500', *Canadian Journal of History*, 31 (1996), 1–15.

——, *The Closing of the Middle Ages? England, 1471–1529* (Oxford, 1997).

——, 'The English Economy and the Government, 1450–1550', in J. L. Watts (ed.), *The End of the Middle Ages? England in the Fifteenth and Sixteenth Centuries* (Stroud, 1998), 89–116.

—— (ed.), *Daily Life in the Late Middle Ages* (Stroud, 1998).

——, 'Specialization of Work in England, 1100–1300', *EcHRev*, 54 (2001), 1–16.

——, *Britain and Ireland, 1050–1530 Economy and Society* (Oxford, 2004).

——, and B. M. S. Campbell (eds), *A Commercialising Economy: England, 1086 to c.1300* (Manchester, 1995).

——, and J. Hatcher (eds), *Progress and Problems in Medieval England* (Cambridge, 1996).

Brooks, C. W., *Pettyfoggers and Vipers of the Commonwealth: The 'Lower Branch' of the Legal Profession in Early Modern England* (Cambridge, 1986).

——, *Lawyers, Litigation and English Society Since 1450* (London, 1998).

Brooks, J., 'The Deserted Medieval Villages of North Berkshire', Ph.D. thesis, Reading (1982).

Brown, A. D., *Popular Piety in Late Medieval England: The Diocese of Salisbury, 1250–1550* (Oxford, 1995).

Brown, A. L., *The Governance of Late Medieval England, 1272–1461* (London, 1989).

Brown, D., *Pottery in Medieval Southampton, c.1066–1510* (CBA, 2002).

Burgess, C., 'Pre-Reformation Churchwardens' Accounts and Parish Government: Lessons from London and Bristol', *EHR*, 117 (2002), 306–32.

Bush, M., 'Tax Reform and Rebellion in early Tudor England', *History*, 76 (1991), 379–400.

——, *The Language of Orders in Early Modern Europe* (London, 1992).

—— (ed.), *Serfdom and Slavery: Studies in Legal Bondage* (London, 1996).

Butcher, A. F., 'The Origins of Romney Freemen, 1433–1523', *EcHRev*, 27 (1974), 16–27.

——, 'Rent and the Urban Economy: Oxford and Canterbury in the Later Middle Ages', *Southern History*, 1 (1979), 11–43.

Campbell, B. M. S., 'The Population of Early Tudor England: A Re-Evaluation of the 1522 Muster Returns and 1524 and 1525 Lay Subsidies', *Journal of Historical Geography*, 7 (1981), 145–54.

——, 'Towards an Agricultural Geography of Medieval England', *AgHRev*, 36 (1988), 87–98.

——, 'People and Land in the Middle Ages, 1066–1500', in R. A. Dodgshon and R. A. Butlin (eds), *An Historical Geography of England and Wales* (London, 1990).

—— (ed.), *Before the Black Death* (Manchester, 1991).

——, 'A Fair Field Once Full of Folk: Agrarian Change in an Era of Population Decline, 1348–1500', *AgHRev*, 41 (1993), 60–70.

——, 'Matching Supply to Demand. Crop Production and Disposal by English Demesnes in the Century of the Black Death', *JEH*, 57 (1997), 827–58.

——, *English Seigniorial Agriculture, 1250–1450* (Cambridge, 2000).

——, 'The Agrarian Problem in the Early Fourteenth Century', *Past and Present*, 188 (2005), 3–70.

——, and M. Overton (eds), *Land, Labour and Livestock: Historical Studies in European Agricultural Productivity* (Manchester, 1991).

——, J. A. Galloway, D. Keene, and M. Murphy, *A Medieval Capital and its Grain Supply: Agrarian Production and Distribution in the London Region, c.1300* (Historical Geography Research Series, 30, 1993).

——, J. A. Galloway, and M. Murphy, 'Rural Land Use in the Metropolitan Hinterland, 1270–1339: the Evidence of Inquisitiones Post Mortem', *AgHRev*, 40 (1992), 1–22.

——, and M. Overton., 'A New Perspective on Medieval and Early Modern Agriculture: Six Centuries of Norfolk Farming, c.1250–c.1850', *Past and Present*, 141 (1993), 38–105.

Campbell, E. M. J., 'Berkshire', in H. C. Darby and E. M. J. Campbell (eds), *The Domesday Geography of South-East England* (Cambridge, 1962).

Cannadine, D., 'The Present and the Past in the English Industrial Revolution, 1880–1980', *Past and Present*, 103 (1984), 131–72.

——, *Class in Britain* (London, 1998).

Cantor, N. F., *Inventing the Middle Ages: The Lives, Works, and Ideas of the Great Medievalists of the Twentieth Century* (Cambridge, 1991).

Carlin, M. *Medieval Southwark* (London, 1996).

——, 'Fast Food and Urban Living Standards in Medieval England', in M. Carlin and J. T. Rosenthal Carlin (eds), *Food and Eating in Medieval Europe* (London, 1998), 27–52.

Carpenter, C., *Locality and Polity: A Study of Warwickshire Landed Society, 1401–1499* (Cambridge, 1992).

——, 'Gentry and Community in Medieval England', *JBS*, 33 (1994), 340–80.

—— (ed.), *Kingsford's Stonor Letters and Papers, 1290–1483* (Cambridge, 1996).

Carter, H., *An Introduction to Urban Historical Geography* (London, 1983).

——, *The Study of Urban Geography* (London, 1995).

Carus-Wilson, E. M., 'An Industrial Revolution of the Thirteenth Century', *EcHRev*, 11 (1941), 39–60.

——, *Medieval Merchant Venturers* (London, 1954).

——, 'The Woollen Industry before 1550', in E. Crittall (ed.), *A History of the County of Wiltshire*, vol. 4 (Oxford, 1959), 115–47.

——, 'Evidences of Industrial Growth on some Fifteenth-century Manors', *EcHRev*, 12 (1959–60), 190–205.

——, and O. Coleman, *England's Export Trade, 1275–1547* (Oxford, 1963).

Challis, C. E., *A New History of the Royal Mint* (Cambridge, 1992).

Childs, W. R., 'England's Iron Trade in the Fifteenth Century', *EcHRev*, 34 (1981), 25–47.

——, 'The Commercial Shipping of South-Western England in the Later Fifteenth Century', *The Mariner's Mirror*, 83 (1997), 272–92.

Chrimes, S. B., Ross, C. D., and Griffiths, R. A. (eds), *Fifteenth-century England, 1399–1509* (Stroud, 1995).

Clanchy, M. T., *From Memory to Written Record*, 2nd edn (Oxford, 1993).

Clapham, J., *A Concise Economic History of Britain. From the Earliest Times to 1750* (Cambridge, 1949; reprinted 1966).

Clark, E., 'Social Welfare and Mutual Aid in the Medieval Countryside', *JBS*, 33 (1994), 381–406.

Clark, L. and C. Carpenter (eds), *The Fifteenth Century IV. Political Culture in Late Medieval Britain* (Woodbridge, 2004).

Clark, P., *Small Towns in Early Modern Europe* (Cambridge, 1995).

—— and P. Slack, *Crisis and Order in English Towns, 1500–1700* (London, 1972).

——, *English Towns in Transition* (Oxford, 1976).

Clarke, W. N., *Parochial Topography of the Hundred of Wanting* (Oxford, 1824).

Clay, C. G. A., *Economic Expansion and Social Change: England, 1500–1700*, 2 vols (Cambridge, 1984).

Cobb, H. S., 'Cloth Exports from London and Southampton in the Later Fifteenth and Early Sixteenth Centuries: A Revision', *EcHRev*, 31 (1978), 601–9.

——, 'Textile Imports in the Fifteenth Century: The Evidence of the Customs Accounts', *Costume*, 29 (1995), 1–11.

Cobban, A., *English University Life in the Middle Ages* (London, 1999).

Cockburn, A. E., *The Corporations of England and Wales, Collected and Abridged from the Reports of the Commissioners for Inquiring into Municipal Corporations* (London, 1835).

Coleman, D. C., *Industry in Tudor and Stuart England* (London, 1975).

——, *The Economy of England, 1450–1750* (Oxford, 1977).

Coleman, J., *English Literature in History* (London, 1981).

Coleman, O., 'Trade and Prosperity in the Fifteenth Century: Some Aspects of the Trade of Southampton', *EcHRev*, 16 (1963), 9–22.

Collinson, P., *The Birthpangs of Protestant England: Religious and Cultural Change in the Sixteenth and Seventeenth Centuries* (Basingstoke, 1988).

—— (ed.), *The Sixteenth Century: The Short Oxford History of the British Isles* (Oxford, 2002).

——, and J. Craig (eds), *The Reformation in English Towns* (Basingstoke, 1998).

Cooper, J. P., 'The Social Distribution of Land and Men, 1436–1700', *EcHRev*, 20 (1967), 419–40.

Corfield, P. J., N. B. Harte, and F. J. Fisher (eds), *London and the English Economy, 1500–1700* (London, 1990).

Cornwall, J. C. K., 'English County Towns in the Fifteen Twenties', *EcHRev*, 15 (1962), 54–69.

——, 'English Population in the Early Sixteenth Century', *EcHRev*, 23 (1970), 32–44.

——, *Wealth and Society in Early Sixteenth Century England* (London, 1988).

Coss, P. R., 'Bastard Feudalism Revised', *Past and Present*, 125 (1989), 27–64.

——, 'Debate: Bastard Feudalism Revised', *Past and Present*, 131 (1991), 190–203.

——, *The Knight in Medieval England, 1000–1400* (Stroud, 1993).

——, 'Knights, Esquires and the Origins of Social Gradation in England', *TRHS*, 5 (1995), 155–78.

——, 'The Formation of the English Gentry', *Past and Present*, 147 (1995), 38–64.

——, *The Lady in Medieval England, 1000–1500* (Stroud, 1998).

——, *The Origins of the English Gentry* (Cambridge, 2003).

Cottis, J., 'Agrarian Change in the Vale of the White Horse, 1660–1760', Ph.D. thesis, Reading (1984).

Cressy, D., *Birth, Marriage and Death* (Oxford, 1997).

Crittall E. (ed.), *A History of the County of Wiltshire*, IV (Oxford, 1959).

Crone, P., *Pre-Industrial Societies* (Oxford, 1989).

Crowley, D. A., 'The Later History of Frankpledge', *BIHR*, 48 (1975), 1–15.

Cunningham, W., *The Growth of English Industry and Commerce During the Early and Middle Ages* (Cambridge, 1882; 4th edn 1905).

Currie, C. R. J., 'Smaller Domestic Architecture in Society in North Berkshire c.1300–c.1650 with special reference to Steventon', D.Phil. thesis, Oxford (1976).

——, 'Larger Medieval Houses in the Vale of the White Horse', *Oxoniensia*, 57 (1992), 81–244.

Curry, A., and E. Matthew (eds), *Concepts and Patterns of Service in the Later Middle Ages* (Woodbridge, 2000).

Dalton, J. N. (ed.), *The Manuscripts of St George's Chapel, Windsor Castle* (Windsor, 1957).

Darby, H. C., R. E. Glasscock, J. Sheail, and G. R. Versey, 'The Changing Geographical Distribution of Wealth in England: 1086–1334–1525', *Journal of Historical Geography*, 5 (1979), 247–62.

Davenport, F. G., *The Economic Development of a Norfolk Manor, 1086–1565* (Cambridge, 1906).

Davie, N., 'Chalk and Cheese? "Fielden" and "Forest" Communities in Early Modern England', *Journal of Historical Sociology*, 4 (1991), 1–31.

Davies, C. S. L., 'Provisions for Armies, 1509–50: a Study in the Effectiveness of Early Tudor Government', *EcHRev*, 17 (1964), 234–48.

——, *Peace, Print and Protestantism, 1450–1558* (London, 1988).

Davies, R. R., 'Baronial Accounts, Incomes, and Arrears in the Later Middle Ages', *EcHRev*, 21 (1968), 211–29.

Day, J., 'The Great Bullion Famine of the Fifteenth Century', *Past and Present*, 79 (1978), 3–54.

——, *The Medieval Market Economy* (Oxford, 1987).

Dell, R. F, 'The Decline of the Clothing Industry in Berkshire', *Newbury District Field Club*, 10 (1954), 50–64.

Denholm-Young, N., *Seignorial Administration in England* (Oxford, 1937).

Denton, J., *Orders and Hierarchies in Late Medieval and Renaissance Europe* (Basingstoke, 1999).

Dewindt, E. B., *Land and People in Holywell-cum-Needingworth* (Toronto, 1972).

Dickens, A. G., *The English Reformation*, 2nd edn (London, 1989).

Digby, A., and C. Feinstein, *New Directions in Economic and Social History* (Basingstoke, 1989).

Dils, J. *Redding, 1540–1640. A Portrait of a Community* (Reading, 1980).

——, 'Epidemics, Mortality and the Civil War in Berkshire, 1642–46', *Southern History*, 11 (1989), 40–52.

——, 'Comings and Goings in Tudor Berkshire', *Berkshire Old and New*, 8 (1991), 12–19.

—— (ed.), *An Historical Atlas of Berkshire* (Reading, 1998).

Dimmock, S., 'Class and the Social Transformation of a Late Medieval Small Town: Lydd c.1450–1550', Ph.D. thesis, Canterbury (1998).

Ditchfield, P. H., and W. Page (eds), *The Victoria History of the Counties of England: Berkshire*, 4 vols (London, 1907).

Dobb, M., *Studies in the Development of Capitalism* (London, 1946).

Dobson, R. B. (ed.), *The Peasants' Revolt of 1381* (Basingstoke, 1983).

Dodds, B., 'Workers on the Pittington Demesne in the Late Middle Ages', *Archaeologia Aeliana*, 28 (2000), 147–61.

Dodwell, B., 'Reading Records', *Berkshire Archaeological Journal*, 60 (1962), 101–13.

Doughty, R. A., 'Industrial Prices and Inflation in Southern England, 1401–1640', *Exploration in Economic History*, 12 (1975), 177–92.

Drew, J. S., 'Manorial Accounts of St Swithun's Priory, Winchester', *EHR*, 62 (1947), 20–41.

DuBoulay, F. R. H., *The Lordship of Canterbury: An Essay on Medieval Society* (London, 1966).

——, 'The Fifteenth Century', in C. H. Lawrence (ed.), *The English Church and the Papacy in the Middle Ages* (London, 1965).

——, 'Who Were Farming the English Demesnes at the End of the Middle Ages?' *EcHRev*, 17 (1965), 443–55.

——, *An Age of Ambition: English Society in the Late Middle Ages* (London, 1970).

Duby, G. *Rural Economy and Country Life in the Medieval West* (London, 1968).

Duffy, E., *The Stripping of the Altars. Traditional Religion in England, c.1400–c.1580* (New

Haven, 1992).

——, *The Voices of Morebath. Reformation and Rebellion in an English Village* (New Haven, 2001).

Dunlop, J. R., 'The Fettiplace Family', *Newbury District Field Club*, 5 (1895–1911), 1–16.

Dunsford, H. M. and Harris, S. J. 'Colonization of the Wasteland of County Durham, 1100–1400', *EcHRev*, 56 (2003), 34–56.

Durston, C. G., 'Berkshire and Its County Gentry, 1625–1649', Ph.D. thesis, Reading (1977).

——, 'London and the Provinces: The Association between the Capital and the Berkshire County Gentry of the Early Seventeenth Century', *Southern History*, 3 (1981), 38–53.

——, '"Wild as Colts Untamed": Radicalism in the Newbury Area during the Early Modern Period', *Southern History*, 6 (1984), 36–52.

Duvosquel, J.-M., and E. Thoen (eds), *Peasants and Townsmen in Medieval Europe* (Gent, 1995).

Dyer, A., 'The Market Towns of Southern England, 1500–1700', *Southern History*, 1 (1979), 123–34.

——, *Decline and Growth in English Towns, 1400–1640* (Basingstoke, 1991).

——, '"Urban Decline" in England, 1377–1525', in T. R. Slater (ed.), *Towns in Decline, AD 100–1600* (Aldershot, 2000), 266–88.

Dyer, C., 'A Redistribution of Incomes in Fifteenth-century England?' *Past and Present*, 39 (1968), 11–33.

——, *Lords and Peasants in a Changing Society. The Estates of the Bishopric of Worcester, 680–1540* (Cambridge, 1980).

——, 'Warwickshire Farming, 1349–c.1520', *Dugdale Society Occasional Papers*, 27 (1981), 1–35.

——, 'Deserted Medieval Villages in the West Midlands', *EcHRev*, 35 (1982), 19–34.

——, 'English Diet in the Later Middle Ages', in T. H. Aston, P. R. Coss, C. Dyer and J. Thirsk (eds), *Social Relations and Ideas* (Cambridge, 1983).

——, 'Changes in the Size of Peasant Holdings in Some West Midland Villages, 1400–1540', in R. M. Smith (ed.), *Land, Kinship and Life-Cycle* (Cambridge, 1984).

——, 'The Social and Economic Background to the Rural Revolt of 1381', in R. H. Hilton and T. Aston (eds), *The English Rising of 1381* (Cambridge, 1984), 9–42.

——, 'Power and Conflict in the Medieval English Village', in D. Hooke (ed.), *Medieval Villages* (Oxford, 1985), 27–32.

——, 'English Peasant Buildings in the Later Middle Ages (1200–1500)', *Medieval Archaeology*, 30 (1986), 19–45.

——, '"The Retreat from Marginal Land": The Growth and Decline of Medieval Rural Settlements', in M. Aston, D. Austin, and C. Dyer (eds), *The Rural Settlements of Medieval England* (Oxford, 1989).

——, *Standards of Living in the Later Middle Ages* (Cambridge, 1990).

——, *Hanbury: Settlement and Society in a Woodland Landscape* (Leicester, 1991).

——, 'Were There Any Capitalists in Fifteenth-century England?', in J. Kermode (ed.), *Enterprise and Individuals in Fifteenth-century England* (Stroud, 1991).

——, 'The Hidden Trade of the Middle Ages: Evidence from the West Midlands of England', *Journal of Historical Geography*, 18 (1992), 141–57.

——, 'Small-Town Conflict in the Later Middle Ages: Events at Shipston-on-Stour', *Urban History*, 19 (1992), 183–210.

——, *Everyday Life in Medieval England* (London, 1994).

——, 'The English Medieval Village Community and its Decline', *JBS*, 33 (1994), 407–29.

——, 'Piers Plowman and Plowmen: A Historical Perspective', *Yearbook of Langland Studies*, 8 (1994), 155–76.

——, 'Sheepcotes: Evidence for Medieval Sheepfarming', *Medieval Archaeology*, 39 (1995), 136–64.

——, 'Taxation and Communities in Late Medieval England', in R. Britnell and J. Hatcher (eds), *Progress and Problems in Medieval England* (Cambridge, 1996).

——, 'Market Towns and the Countryside in Late Medieval England', *Canadian Journal of History*, 31 (1996), 17–35.

——, 'Memories of Freedom: Attitudes Towards Serfdom in England, 1200–1350', in M. Bush (ed.), *Serfdom and Slavery: Studies in Legal Bondage* (London, 1996), 277–95.

——, 'How Urban Was Medieval England?' *History Today*, 47 (1997), 37–43.

——, 'Medieval Stratford: A Successful Small Town', in R. Bearman (ed.), *The History of an English Borough: Stratford-Upon-Avon, 1196–1996* (Stroud, 1997).

——, 'Peasants and Coins: The Use of Money in the Middle Ages', *British Numismatic Journal*, 67 (1997), 30–47.

——, 'Peasants and Farmers: Rural Settlements and Landscapes in an Age of Transition', in D. Gaimster and P. Stamper (eds), *The Age of Transition: The Archaeology of English Culture, 1400–1600* (Oxford, 1997).

——, 'Did the Peasants Really Starve in Medieval England?" in M. Carlin and J. T. Rosenthal (eds), *Food and Eating in Medieval Europe* (London, 1998), 53–72.

——, *Bromsgrove: A Small Town in Worcestershire in the Middle Ages* (Worcester, 2000).

——, 'Work Ethics in the Fourteenth Century', in J. Bothwell, P. J. P. Goldberg and M. Ormrod (eds), *The Problem of Labour in Fourteenth-century England* (York, 2000), 21–41.

——, *Making a Living in the Middle Ages: The People of Britain, 850–1520* (New Haven, 2002).

——, *An Age of Transition?* (Oxford, 2005).

——, and J. Laughton, 'Small Towns in the East and West Midlands in the Later Middle Ages: A Comparison', *Midland History*, 5 (1999), 24–52.

Dymond, D., and A. Betterton, *Lavenham: 700 Years of Textile Making* (Woodbridge, 1982).

Edler, F., 'Winchcombe Kerseys in Antwerp (1538–44)', *EcHRev*, first series 7 (1936), 57–62.

Edmonds, J., *The History of Woad and the Medieval Woad Vat* (Chalfont St Giles, 1998).

Edwards, J. F., and B. P. Hindle, 'The Transportation System of Medieval England and Wales', *Journal of Historical Geography*, 17 (1991), 123–34.

Ellis, M. *Using Manorial Records* (London, 1997).

Elton, G. R., *Reform and Reformation: England, 1509–1558* (London, 1977).

——, 'Reform and the 'Commonwealth-Men' of Edward VI's Reign', in his *Studies in Tudor and Stuart Politics and Government*, vol. 3 (Cambridge, 1983), 234–53.

——, *England Under the Tudors*, 3rd edn (London, 1991).

Emden, A. B., *A Biographical Register of the University of Oxford to AD 1500* (Oxford, 1957).

Epstein, S. R., 'Regional Fairs, Institutional Innovation, and Economic Growth in Late

Medieval Europe', *EcHRev*, 47 (1994), 459–82.

——, *Freedom and Growth* (London, 2000).

—— (ed.), *Town and Country in Europe, 1300–1800* (Cambridge, 2001).

Erickson, A. L., *Women and Property in Early Modern England* (London, 1993).

Evans, R., 'Merton College's Control of its Tenants at Thorncroft, 1270–1349', in Z. Razi and R. M. Smith (eds), *Medieval Society and the Manor Court* (Oxford, 1996).

Evans, T. A. R. and R. J. Faith, 'College Estates and University Finances, 1350–1500', in J. I. Catto and T. A. R. Evans (eds), *The History of the University of Oxford*, vol. 2 (Oxford, 1992).

Everitt, A., 'Farm Labourers', in J. Thirsk (ed.), *The Agrarian History of England and Wales, IV, 1500–1640* (Cambridge, 1967), 396–465.

——, 'The Marketing of Agricultural Produce', in J. Thirsk (ed.), *The Agrarian History of England and Wales, IV, 1500–1640* (Cambridge, 1967), 466–592.

——, 'Country, County and Town: Patterns of Regional Evolution in England', *TRHS*, 29 (1979), 79–108.

Faith, R. J., 'The Peasant Land Market in Berkshire', Ph.D. thesis, Leicester (1962).

——, 'Peasant Families and Inheritance Customs in Medieval England', *AgHRev*, 14 (1966), 77–95.

——, 'Berkshire: Fourteenth and Fifteenth Centuries', in P. D. A. Harvey (ed.), *The Peasant Land Market in Medieval England* (Oxford, 1984).

——, 'The "Great Rumour" of 1377 and Peasant Ideology', in R. Hilton and T. Aston (eds), *The English Rising of 1381* (Cambridge, 1984).

——, 'Demesne Resources and Labour Rent on the Manors of St Paul's Cathedral, 1066–1222', *EcHRev*, 47 (1994), 657–78.

——, *The English Peasantry and the Growth of Lordship* (London, 1997).

Farmer, D. L., 'Two Wiltshire Manors and Their Markets', *AgHRev*, 37 (1989), 1–11.

——, 'Prices and Wages, 1350–1500', in E. Miller (ed.), *The Agrarian History of England and Wales, III, 1348–1500* (Cambridge, 1991).

——, 'Millstones for Medieval Manors', *AgHRev*, 40 (1992), 97–111.

——, 'The Famuli in the Later Middle Ages', in R. H. Britnell and J. Hatcher (eds), *Progress and Problems in Medieval England* (Cambridge, 1996).

Feinstein, C., and M. Thomas, *Making History Count* (Cambridge, 2002).

Fenwick, C. C., 'The English Poll Taxes of 1377, 1379 and 1381: A Critical Examination of the Returns', Ph.D. thesis, London School of Economics (1983).

Ferguson, W. K. *The Renaissance in Historical Thought* (Cambridge, Massachusetts, 1948).

Field, R. K., 'Worcestershire Peasant Buildings, Household Goods and Farming Equipment in the Later Middle Ages', *Medieval Archaeology*, 9 (1965), 105–25.

——, 'Migration in the Later Middle Ages: The Case of the Hampton Lovett Villeins', *Midland History*, 9 (1983), 29–48.

Fisher, F. J., 'Influenza and Inflation in Tudor England', *EcHRev*, 18 (1965), 120–9.

——, 'The Development of London as a Centre of Conspicuous Consumption in the Sixteenth and Seventeenth Centuries', in P. Corfield *et al.* (eds), *London and the English Economy, 1500–1700* (London, 1990).

——, 'London as an "Engine of Economic Growth"', in P. Corfield *et al.* (eds), *London and the English Economy, 1500–1700* (London, 1990).

——, 'Tawney's Century', in P. Corfield *et al.* (eds), *London and the English Economy, 1500–1700* (London, 1990).

Fleming, P., *Family and Household in Medieval England* (Basingstoke, 2001).

Fletcher, A., *Tudor Rebellions* (London, 3rd edn, 1983).

Flinn, M. W., 'The Population History of England, 1541–1871', *EcHRev,* 35 (1982), 443–57.

Floud, R., *An Introduction to Quantitative Methods for Historians* (London, 1973).

Ford, S. D., 'Excavations, Newbury Town Centre, 1971–74, Part I', *Transactions of the Newbury District Field Club,* 12 (4) (1976), 21–41.

——, 'Excavations, Newbury Town Centre, 1971–74, Part II', *Transactions of the Newbury District Field Club,* 12 (5) (1979), 19–40.

——, 'Excavations, Newbury Town Centre, 1971–74, Part III', *Transactions of the Newbury District Field Club,* 12 (6) (1980), 42.53.

——, 'Excavations, Newbury Town Centre, 1971–74, Addendum & Corrigendum', *Transactions of the Newbury District Field Club,* 13 (4) (1989), 21–30.

——, *Charnham Lane Hungerford Berkshire Archaeological Investigations, 1988–1997* (Reading, 2002).

Fox, H. S. A., 'The Chronology of Enclosure and Economic Development in Medieval Devon', *EcHRev,* 28 (1975), 181–202.

——, 'Servants, Cottagers and Tied Cottages During the Later Middle Ages: Towards a Regional Dimension', *Rural History,* 6 (1995), 125–54.

——, *The Evolution of the Fishing Village. Landscape and Society Along the South Devon Coast, 1086–1550* (Oxford, 2001).

Frank, R., 'A Theory of Moral Sentiments', in J. Mansbridge (ed.), *Beyond Self-Interest* (Chicago, 1990).

Franklin, P., 'Gloucestershire's Medieval Taxpayers', *Local Population Studies,* 54 (1995), 16–27.

Freedman, P., *Images of the Medieval Peasant* (Stanford, California, 1999).

French, K. L., 'Maidens' Lights and Wives' Stores: Women's Parish Guilds in Late Medieval England', *Sixteenth Century Journal,* 29 (1998), 399–425.

Fryde, E. B., *Studies in Medieval Trade and Finance* (London, 1983).

——, *Peasants and Landlords in Later Medieval England* (Stroud, 1996).

Gaimster, D., and P. Stamper (eds), *The Age of Transition: The Archaeology of English Culture, 1400–1600* (Oxford, 1997).

Galloway, J. A., 'London's Grain Supply: Changes in Production, Distribution and Consumption During the Fourteenth Century', *Franco-British Studies,* 20 (1995), 23–34.

——, 'Driven by Drink? Ale Consumption and the Agrarian Economy of the London Region, c.1300–1400', in M. Carlin and J. T. Rosenthal (eds), *Food and Eating in Medieval Europe* (London, 1998), 87–100.

——, *Trade, Urban Hinterlands and Market Integration c.1300–1600* (London, 2000).

——, 'Town and Country in England, 1300–1570', in S. R. Epstein (ed.), *Town and Country in Europe, 1300–1800* (Cambridge, 2001), 106–31

——, and M. Murphy, 'Feeding the City: Medieval London and Its Agrarian Hinterland', *London Journal,* 16 (1991), 3–14.

——, D. Keene, and M. Murphy, 'Fuelling the City: Production and Distribution of Firewood and Fuel in London's Region, 1290–1400', *EcHRev,* 49 (1996), 447–72.

Gatrell, P., 'Historians and Peasants: Studies of Medieval English Society in a Russian Context', *Past and Present,* 96 (1982), 22–50.

Gee, E. A., 'Oxford Carpenters, 1370–1530', *Oxoniensia,* 17–18 (1952–53), 112–84.

Gelling, M., *The Place-Names of Berkshire* (English Place-Name Society, 49–50, 1973–74).

——, *The Early Charters of the Thames Valley* (Leicester, 1979).

Gerth, H. H., and C. W. Mills, *From Max Weber: Essays in Sociology* (London, 1948).

Gervers, M., 'Pro Defensione Terre Sancte: The Development and Exploitation of the Hospitallers' Landed Estate in Essex', in M. Barber (ed.), *The Military Orders. Fighting for the Faith and Caring for the Sick* (Aldershot, 1994), 3–20.

Giddens, A. *Sociology* (Cambridge, 1993).

Giles, K., *An Archaeology of Social Identity. Guildhalls in York, c.1350–1630* (Oxford, 2000).

——, 'Framing Labour: The Archaeology of York's Medieval Guildhalls', in J. Bothwell, P. J. P. Goldberg and M. Ormrod (eds), *The Problem of Labour in Fourteenth-century England* (York, 2000), 65–83.

Giner, S., *Sociology* (London, 1972).

Glennie, P., 'In Search of Agrarian Capitalism: Manorial Land Markets and the Acquisition of Land in the Lea valley, c.1450–c.1560', *Continuity and Change*, 3 (1988), 11–40.

Goheen, R. B., 'Peasant Politics? Village Community and the Crown in Fifteenth-century England', *American Historical Review*, 96 (1991), 42–62.

Goldberg, P. J. P., 'Mortality and Economic Change in the Diocese of York, 1390–1514', *Northern History*, 24 (1988), 38–55.

——, 'Women in Fifteenth-century Town Life', in J. A. F. Thomson (ed.), *Towns and Townspeople in the Fifteenth Century* (Stroud, 1988), 107–28.

——, 'Urban Identity and the Poll Taxes of 1377, 1379 and 1381', *EcHRev*, 43 (1990), 194–216.

——, *Women, Work, and Life Cycle in a Medieval Economy: Women in York and Yorkshire c.1300–1520* (Oxford, 1992).

—— (ed.), *Woman is a Worthy Wight* (Stroud, 1992).

—— (ed.), *Women in England, c.1275–1525* (Manchester, 1995).

Gollancz, M., 'The System of Goal Delivery as Illustrated in the Extant Gaol Delivery Rolls of the Fifteenth Century', *BIHR*, 16 (1939), 191–3.

Goodacre, J., *The Transformation of a Peasant Economy, Townspeople and Villagers in the Lutterworth Area, 1500–1700* (Aldershot, 1994).

Goose, N. R., 'Decay and Regeneration in Seventeenth Century Reading: A study in a changing economy', *Southern History*, 6 (1984), 53–74.

——, 'In Search of the Urban Variable: Towns and the English Economy, 1500–1650', *EcHRev*, 39 (1986), 165–85

——, 'Local Population Studies: History, Demography and Locality', *The Local Historian*, 34 (2004), 37–44.

Goring, J. J., 'The General Proscription of 1522', *EHR*, 86 (1971), 681–705.

Gradon, P., 'Langland and the Ideology of Dissent', *Proceedings of the British Academy*, 66 (1980), 179–205.

Graham, A. H., 'The Old Malthouse, Abbotsbury, Dorset: The Medieval Watermill of the Benedictine Abbey', *Proceedings of the Dorset Natural History and Archaeology Society*, 108 (1986), 103–25.

Graham, R., *English Ecclesiastical Studies* (London, 1929).

Gray, H. L., *English Field Systems* (Oxford, 1915).

——, 'The Production and Exportation of English Woollens in the Fourteenth Century', *EHR*, 39 (1924), 13–35.

——, 'Incomes from Land in England in 1436', *English Historical Journal*, 49 (1934), 607–39.

Green, J. R., *Town Life in the Fifteenth Century*, 2 vols (London, 1894).

Gregson, N., 'Tawney Revisited: Custom and the Emergence of Capitalist Class Relations in North-East Cumbria, 1600–1830', *EcHRev*, 42 (1989), 18–42.

Greig, W, *General Report on the Gosford Estates in County Armagh, 1821* (Belfast, 1976).

Griffiths, P., A. Fox, and S. Hindle (eds), *The Experience of Authority in Early Modern England* (Basingstoke, 1996).

Griffiths, R., *The Fourteenth and Fifteenth Centuries* (Oxford, 2003).

Gritt, A. J., 'The 'Survival' of Service in the English Agricultural Labour Force: Lessons from Lancashire, c.1650–1851', *AgHRev*, 50 (2002), 25–50.

Gunn, S. J., *Early Tudor Government, 1485–1558* (Basingstoke, 1995).

Guy, J., *Tudor England* (Oxford, 1988).

Habakkuk, H. J., 'The Market for Monastic Property, 1539–1603', *EcHRev*, 10 (1958), 362–80.

Haigh, C. (ed.), *The Reign of Elizabeth I* (Basingstoke, 1984).

—— (ed.), *The English Reformation Revised* (Cambridge, 1987).

——, *Elizabeth I* (London, 1988).

——, *English Reformations* (Oxford, 1993).

——, 'Success and Failure in the English Reformation', *Past and Present*, 173 (2001), 28–49.

Hajnal, J., 'Two Kinds of Pre-industrial Household Formation System', in R. Wall, J. Robin, and P. Laslett (eds), *Family Forms in Historic Europe* (Cambridge, 1983).

Hallam, H. E. (ed.), *The Agrarian History of England and Wales Volume, II, 1042–1350* (Cambridge, 1988).

Hanawalt, B., *The Ties that Bound* (Oxford, 1986).

——, *Chaucer's England: Literature in Historical Context* (Minneapolis, 1992).

——, *Of Good and Ill Repute: Gender and Social Control in Medieval England* (Oxford, 1998).

——, ed. *Medieval Crime and Social Control* (Minneapolis, 1999).

Hanham, A., 'Profits on English Wool Exports, 1472–1544', *BIHR*, 55 (1982), 139–47.

——, *The Celys and their World: An English Merchant Family of the Fifteenth Century* (Cambridge, 1985).

Hare, J. N., 'The Demesne Lessees of Fifteenth-century Wiltshire', *AgHRev*, 29 (1981), 1–15.

——, 'The Wiltshire Risings of 1450: Political and Economic Discontent in Mid-Fifteenth-century England', *Southern History*, 4 (1982), 13–31.

——, 'The Monks as Landlords: The Leasing of the Monastic Demesnes in Southern England', in C. Barron and C. Harper-Bill (eds), *The Church in Pre-Reformation Society* (Woodbridge, 1985), 82–94.

——, 'The Growth of the Roof-Tile Industry in Later Medieval Wessex', *Medieval Archaeology*, 35 (1991), 86–103.

——, 'The Lords and their Tenants: Conflict and Stability in Fifteenth-century Wiltshire', in B. Stapleton (ed.), *Conflict and Community in Southern England* (Stroud, 1992).

——, 'Agricultural and Rural Settlement in the Chalklands of Wiltshire and Hampshire from c.1200 to c.1500', in M. Aston and C. Lewis (eds), *The Medieval Landscape of Wessex* (Oxford, 1994), 159–69.

——, 'Growth and Recession in the Fifteenth-century Economy: The Wiltshire Textile Industry and the Countryside', *EcHRev*, 52 (1999), 1–26.

——, Recycling the Monastic Buildings: The Dissolution in Southern England', *The*

Historian, 79 (2003), 22-7.

Hargreaves, P. V., 'Seignorial Reaction and Peasant Responses: Worcester Priory and Its Peasants after the Black Death', *Midland History*, 24 (1999), 53-78.

C. Harper-Bill, *The Pre-Reformation Church in England, 1400-1530* (London, 1989).

——, 'Who Wanted the English Reformation?' *Medieval History*, 2 (1992), 66-77.

Harris, B. J., 'Landlords and Tenants in England in the Later Middle Ages', *Past and Present*, 43 (1969), 146-50.

Harrison, C., 'Elizabethan Village Surveys: A Comment', *AgHRev*, 27 (1979), 82-9.

Harrison, D. F. 'Bridges and Economic Development, 1300-1800', *EcHRev*, 45 (1992), 240-61.

Harriss, G. L., 'Political Society and the Growth of Government in Late Medieval England', *Past and Present*, 138 (1993), 28-57.

——, 'Medieval Government and Statecraft', *Past and Present*, 25 (1963), 8-39.

Harte, N. B. (ed.), *The Study of Economic History: Collected Inaugural Lectures* (London, 1971).

——, 'State Control of Dress and Social Change in Pre-Industrial England', in D. C. Coleman and A. H. John (eds), *Trade Government and Economy in Pre-Industrial England* (London, 1976), 132-65.

Harvey, B. F., 'Draft Letters Patent of Manumission and Pardon for the Men of Somerset in 1381', *EHR*, 80 (1965), 89-91.

——, 'The Population Trend in England between 1300 and 1348', *TRHS*, 16 (1966), 23-42.

——, 'Work and *Festa Ferianda* in Medieval England', *Journal of Ecclesiastical History*, 23 (1972), 289-308.

——, *Westminster Abbey and its Estates in the Middle Ages* (Oxford, 1977).

——, 'The Leasing of the Abbot of Westminster's Demesnes in the Later Middle Ages', *EcHRev*, 35 (1982), 17-27.

——, 'Introduction: the 'Crisis' of the Early Fourteenth Century', in B. M. S. Campbell (ed.), *Before the Black Death* (Manchester, 1991).

——, *Living and Dying in England, 1100-1540: The Monastic Experience* (Oxford, 1993).

——, and J. Oeppen, 'Patterns of Morbidity in Late Medieval England: A Sample from Westminster Abbey', *EcHRev*, 54 (2001), 215-39.

Harvey, P. D. A., *A Medieval Oxfordshire Village: Cuxham, 1240-1400* (Oxford, 1965).

——, 'Agricultural Treatises and Manorial Accounting in Medieval England', *AgHRev*, 20 (1972), 170-82.

—— (ed.), *The Peasant Land Market in Medieval England* (Oxford, 1984).

——, *Manorial Records* (British Records Association 5, 1984).

Harvey, I., *Jack Cade's Rebellion of 1450* (Oxford, 1991).

Harwood, W. A., 'The Customs System in Southampton in the Mid-Fifteenth Century', *Proceedings Hampshire Field Club Archaeological Society*, 53 (1998), 191-200.

L. Haskins, and K. Jeffrey, *Understanding Quantitative History* (Cambridge, Massachusetts, 1990).

Hasler, P. W. (ed.), *The History of Parliament: The House of Commons, 1558-1603*, 3 vols (London, 1981).

Hassell Smith, A., 'Labourers in Late Sixteenth-century England: A Case Study from North Norfolk', *Continuity and Change*, 4 (1989), 11-52 and 367-94.

Hastings, M., *The Court of Common Pleas in Fifteenth-century England* (New York, 1947).

Hatcher, J., *Rural Economy and Society in the Duchy of Cornwall, 1300-1500* (Cambridge,

1970).

——, *English Tin Production and Trade Before 1550* (Oxford, 1973).

——, *Plague, Population and the English Economy, 1348–1530* (Basingstoke, 1977).

——, 'English Serfdom and Villeinage: Towards a Reassessment', *Past and Present*, 90 (1981), 3–39.

——, 'Mortality in the Fifteenth Century: Some New Evidence', *EcHRev*, 39 (1986), 19–38.

——, *The History of the British Coal Industry, Volume I, Before 1700: Towards the Age of Coal* (Oxford, 1993).

——, 'England in the Aftermath of the Black Death', *Past and Present*, 144 (1994), 3–35.

——, 'The Great Slump of the Mid-fifteenth Century', in R. H. Britnell and J. Hatcher (eds), *Progress and Problems in Medieval England* (Cambridge, 1996).

——, 'Labour, Leisure and Economic Thought before the Nineteenth Century', *Past and Present*, 160 (1998), 64–115.

——, 'Women's Work Reconsidered: Gender and Wage Differentiation in Late Medieval England', *Past and Present*, 173 (2001), 191–202.

——, 'Understanding the Population History of England, 1450–1750', *Past and Present*, 180 (2003), 83–130.

——, and M. Bailey, *Modelling the Middle Ages: The History and Theory of England's Economic Development* (Oxford, 2001).

Hatherly, J. M., and L. M. Cantor, 'The Medieval Parks of Berkshire', *Berkshire Archaeological Journal*, 70 (1979), 67–80.

Hawkins, D., 'The Black Death and the New London Cemeteries of 1348', *Antiquity*, 64 (1990), 637–42.

Heal, F., *Reformation in Britain and Ireland* (Oxford, 2003).

——, and C. Holmes, *The Gentry in England and Wales, 1500–1700* (Basingstoke, 1994).

Heaton, H., *Yorkshire Woollen and Worsted Industries* (Oxford, 1920).

Henderson, J., and R. Wall (eds), *Poor Women and Children in the European Past* (London, 1994).

Herbert, N. M., 'The Borough of Wallingford, 1155–1400', Ph.D. thesis, Reading (1971).

Hicks, J., *A Theory of Economic History* (Oxford, 1969).

Hicks, M., 'Chantries, Obits and Almshouses: The Hungerford Foundations, 1325–1478', in C. Barron and C. Harper-Bill (eds), *The Church in Pre-Reformation Society* (Woodbridge, 1985), 123–42.

Higgott, A., *The Story of Newbury* (Newbury, 2001).

Hilton, R. H., *The Economic Development of Some Leicestershire Estates in the Fourteenth and Fifteenth Centuries* (Oxford, 1947).

——, *The Decline of Serfdom in Medieval England* (London, 1970).

——, *Bond Men Made Free* (London, 1973).

——, *The English Peasantry in the Later Middle Ages* (Oxford, 1975).

—— (ed.), *The Transition from Feudalism to Capitalism* (London, 1976).

——, 'Medieval Market Towns and Simple Commodity Production', *Past and Present*, 109 (1985), 3–23.

——, *Class Conflict and the Crisis of Feudalism* (London, 1985).

——, *English and French Towns in Feudal Society* (Cambridge, 1992).

——, and T. Aston (eds), *The English Rising of 1381* (Cambridge, 1984).

Hindle, S., *The State and Social Change in Early Modern England, c.1550–1640* (Basingstoke, 2000).

——, 'A Sense of Place? Becoming and Belonging in the Rural Parish, 1550–1650', in A. Shepard and P. Withington (eds), *Communities in Early Modern England* (Manchester, 2000), 96–114.

——, 'Dearth, Fasting and Alms: The Campaign for General Hospitality in Late Elizabethan England', *Past and Present*, 172 (2001), 44–86.

——, 'Exhortation and Entitlement: Negotiating Inequality in English Rural Communities, 1550–1650', in M. J. Braddick and J. Walter (eds), *Negotiating Power in Early Modern Society* (Cambridge, 2001), 102–22, 268–72.

Holmes, G., *The Later Middle Ages, 1272–1485* (Edinburgh, 1962).

Holt, R., 'Whose Were the Profits of Corn Milling? An Aspect of the Changing Relationship Between the Abbots of Glastonbury and Their Tenants, 1086–1350', *Past and Present*, 116 (1987), 3–23.

——, *The Mills of Medieval England* (Oxford, 1988).

——, and G. Rosser (eds), *The English Medieval Town: A Reader in English Urban History, 1200–1540* (London, 1990).

Holton, R. J., *The Transition from Feudalism to Capitalism* (Basingstoke, 1985).

Homans, G. C., *English Villagers of the Thirteenth Century* (Harvard, 1942).

——, 'The Explanation of English Regional Differences', *Past and Present*, 42 (1969), 18–34.

Hooke, D., 'Anglo-Saxon Estates in the Vale of the White Horse', *Oxoniensia*, 52 (1987), 129–43.

——, 'The Administrative and Settlement Framework of Early Medieval Wessex', in M. Aston and C. Lewis (eds), *The Medieval Landscape of Wessex* (Oxford, 1994), 83–94.

Hopcroft, R., 'The Social Origins of Agrarian Change in Late Medieval England', *American Journal of Sociology*, 99 (1994), 1559–95.

Horrox, R., 'Urban Patronage and Patrons in the Fifteenth Century', in R. A. Griffiths (ed.), *Patronage, the Crown and the Provinces* (Stroud, 1981), 145–66.

——, 'The Urban Gentry in the Fifteenth Century', in J. A. F. Thomson (ed.), *Towns and Townspeople in the Fifteenth Century* (Stroud, 1988), 22–44.

——, *Richard III* (Cambridge, 1989).

——ed., *The Black Death* (Manchester, 1994).

——, 'Service', in R. Horrox (ed.), *Fifteenth-century Attitudes* (Cambridge, 1994), 61–78.

Hoskins, W. G., *The Making of the English Landscape* (Penguin Books, 1955).

——, 'Harvest Fluctuations and English Economic History, 1480–1619', *AgHRev*, 12 (1964), 28–46.

——, *The Age of Plunder* (London, 1976).

Houlbrooke, R., *The English Family, 1450–1700* (London, 1984).

Houston, R. A., *The Population History of Britain and Ireland, 1500–1750* (Basingstoke, 1992).

Howell, C., 'Peasant Inheritance Customs in the Midlands, 1280–1700', in J. Goody, J. Thirsk, and E. P. Thompson (eds), *Family and Inheritance* (Cambridge, 1976).

——, *Land Family and Inheritance in Transition: Kibworth Harcourt, 1280–1700* (Cambridge, 1983).

Howell, M., and M. Boone, 'Becoming Early Modern in the Late Medieval Low Countries', *Urban History*, 23 (1996), 300–24.

Hoyle, R. W., 'Land and Landed Relations in Craven, Yorkshire c.1520–1600', D.Phil. thesis, Oxford (1986).

——, 'An Ancient and Laudable Custom: The Definition and Development of Tenant

Right in North-Western England in the Sixteenth Century', *Past and Present*, 116 (1987), 24–55.

——, 'Monastic Leasing before the Dissolution: The Evidence of Bolton Priory and Fountains Abbey', *Yorkshire Archaeological Journal*, 61 (1989), 111–37.

——, 'Tenure and the Land Market in Early Modern England: or a Late Contribution to the Brenner Debate', *EcHRev*, 43 (1990), 1–20.

—— (ed.), *The Estates of the English Crown, 1558–1640* (Cambridge, 1992).

——, 'Resistance and Manipulation in Early Tudor Taxation: Some Evidence From the North', *Archives*, 90 (1993), 158–76.

——, *Tudor Taxation Records: A Guide for Users* (London, 1994).

——, 'Crown, Parliament and Taxation in Sixteenth-century England', *EHR*, 109 (1994), 1174–1196.

——, 'Taxation and the Mid-Tudor Crisis', *EcHRev*, 51 (1998), 649–75.

——, 'Agrarian Agitation in Mid-Sixteenth Century Norfolk: A Petition of 1553', *Historical Journal*, 44 (2001), 223–38.

——, *The Pilgrimage of Grace and the Politics of the 1530s* (Oxford, 2001).

——, and G. Sreenivasan, 'The Land-Family Bond in England', *Past and Present*, 146 (1995), 151–87.

Hudson, A., *The Premature Reformation: Wycliffite Texts and Lollard History* (Oxford, 1988).

Hudson, P., *History by Numbers: An Introduction to Quantitative Approaches* (London, 2000).

Huizinga, J., *The Waning of the Middle Ages* (London, 1927).

Humphrey, C., *The Politics of Carnival: Festive Misrule in Medieval England* (Manchester, 2001).

Hunt, E. S., and J. M. Murray, *A History of Business in Medieval Europe, 1200–1550* (Cambridge, 1999).

Hutton, R., 'The English Reformation and the Evidence of Folklore', *Past and Present*, 148 (1995), 89–116.

——, *The Rise and Fall of Merry England* (Oxford, 1996).

Hyams, P. R., 'The Origins of a Peasant Land Market in England', *EcHRev*, 23 (1970), 18–31.

——, *Kings, Lords and Peasants in Medieval England: The Common Law of Villeinage in the Twelfth and Thirteenth Centuries* (Oxford, 1980).

Hybel, N., *Crisis or Change: The Concept of Crisis in the Light of Agrarian Structural Reorganisation in Late Medieval England* (Aarhus, Denmark, 1989).

Ingram, M., 'Religion, Communities and Moral Discipline in Late Sixteenth- and Early Seventeenth-century England: Case Studies', in K. Greyerz (ed.), *Religion and Society in Early Modern Europe, 1500–1800* (London, 1984), 177–93.

——, *Church Courts, Sex and Marriage in England, 1570–1640* (Cambridge, 1987).

Jackson, C. A., 'The Berkshire Woollen Industry, 1500–1650', Ph.D. thesis, Reading (1993).

——, 'The Kendrick Bequests: An Experiment in Municipal Enterprise in the Woollen Industry in Reading and Newbury in the Early Seventeenth Century', *Southern History*, 16 (1994), 44–66.

——, 'Clothmaking and the Economy in Sixteenth-century Abingdon', *Oxoniensia*, 67 (2002), 59–78.

Jarvis, M. G., *Soils of the Wantage and Abingdon District* (Harpenden, 1973).

——, J. Hazelden, and D. Mackney, *Soils of Berkshire* (Soil Survey Bulletin No. 8,

Harpenden, 1979).

Jefferies, P., 'A Consideration of Some Aspects of Landholding in Medieval Berkshire', Ph.D. thesis, Reading (1972).

——, 'Social Mobility in the Fourteenth Century: The Example of the Chelreys of Berkshire', *Oxoniensia*, 41 (1976), 324–36.

——, 'The Medieval Use as Family Law and Custom: the Berkshire Gentry in the fourteenth and fifteenth centuries', *Southern History*, 1 (1979), 45–69.

Jenkins, J. G. (ed.), *The Wool and Textile Industry in Great Britain* (London, 1972).

Jenks, S., 'The Lay Subsidies and the State of the English Economy (1275–1334)', *Vierteljahrschrift fur Sozial-und Wirtschaftsgeschichte*, 85 (1998), 1–39.

Johnson, C., 'The Collectors of Lay Taxes', in W. A. Morris and J. R. Strayer (eds), *The English Government at Work, 1327–1336* (Cambridge, Massachusetts, 1947), 201–26.

Johnson, M., *An Archaeology of Capitalism* (Oxford, 1996).

Johnson, P. A., *Duke Richard of York, 1411–1460* (Oxford, 1988).

Jones, A. C., 'Land and People at Leighton Buzzard in the Later Fifteenth Century', *EcHRev*, 25 (1972), 18–27.

——, 'Bedfordshire: Fifteenth Century', in P. D. A. Harvey (ed.), *The Peasant Land Market in Medieval England* (Oxford, 1984).

Jones, B. C., 'Westmorland Pack-Horse Men in Southampton', *Transactions of the Cumberland and Westmorland Antiquarian and Archaeological Society*, 59 (1960), 65–84.

Jones, E. D., 'Medieval Merchets as Demographic Data: Some Evidence from the Spalding Priors Estates, Lincolnshire', *Continuity and Change*, 11 (1996), 459–70.

Jones, K., and M. Zell., 'Gender and Social Control in a Kentish Borough, c.1450–c.1570', *Continuity and Change*, 13 (1998), 11–32.

Jones, W. R. D., *The Tudor Commonwealth, 1529–1559* (London, 1970).

Jope, E. M., 'Medieval Pottery in Berkshire', *Berkshire Archaeological Journal*, 50 (1947), 49–76.

Jordan, W. C., *The Great Famine: Northern Europe in the Early Fourteenth Century* (Princeton, 1996).

Jordan, W. K., *The Charities of Rural England, 1480–1660* (London, 1961).

Jurkowski, M., C. L. Smith, and D. Crook., *Lay Taxes in England and Wales, 1188–1688* (London, 1998).

Justice, S., *Writing and Rebellion: England in 1381* (Berkeley, 1994).

Kanzaka, J., 'Villein Rents in Thirteenth-century England: An Analysis of the Hundred Rolls of 1279–1280', *EcHRev*, 55 (2002), 593–618.

Kaye, J. *Economy and Nature in the Fourteenth Century. Money, Market Exchange and the Emergence of Scientific Thought* (Cambridge, 1998).

Keen, M. H., *England in the Later Middle Ages* (London, 1988).

——, *English Society in the Later Middle Ages, 1348–1500* (Penguin, 1990).

——, *Origins of the English Gentleman: Heraldry, Chivalry and Gentility in Medieval England, c.1300–1500* (Stroud, 2002).

Keene, D., *Survey of Medieval Winchester* (London, 1985).

——, 'Medieval London and its Region', *London Journal*, 14 (1989), 99–111.

——, 'Small Towns and the Metropolis: The Experience of Medieval England', in J.-M. Duvosquel and E. Thoen (eds), *Peasants and Townsmen in Medieval Europe* (Gent, 1995), 223–38.

Kemp, B. R. *Reading Abbey: An Introduction to the History of the Abbey* (Reading, 1968).

Kenyon, N., 'Labour Conditions in Essex in the Reign of Richard II', *EcHRev*, 14 (1932/34), 429–43.

Kermode, J., 'Merchants, Overseas Trade, and Urban Decline: York, Beverley and Hull, c.1380–1500', *Northern History*, 23 (1987), 51–73.

—— (ed.), *Enterprise and Individuals in Fifteenth-century England* (Stroud, 1991).

——, 'Money and Credit in the Fifteenth Century: Some Lessons from Yorkshire', *Business History Review*, 65 (1991), 475–501.

——, 'Medieval Indebtedness: The Regions Versus London', in N. Rogers (ed.), *England in the Fifteenth Century* (Stamford, 1994), 72–88.

——, *Medieval Merchants. York, Beverley and Hull in the Later Middle Ages* (Cambridge, 1998).

——, and G. Walker (eds), *Women, Crime and the Courts in Early Modern England* (London, 1994).

Kerr, B., *Religious Life for Women, c.1100–c.1350: Fontevraud in England* (Oxford, 1999).

Kerridge, E., 'The Movement of Rent, 1540–1640', *EcHRev*, 6 (1953), 16–34. Reprinted in E. M. Carus-Wilson (ed.), *Essays in Economic History*, vol. 2 (London, 1962).

——, 'The Returns of the Inquisitions of Depopulation', *EHR*, 70 (1955), 212–28.

——, *Agrarian Problems in the Sixteenth Century and After* (London, 1969).

——, 'Wool Growing and Wool Textiles in Medieval and Early Modern Times', in J. G. Jenkins (ed.), *The Wool and Textile Industry in Great Britain* (London, 1972).

Kershaw, I., 'The Great Famine and Agrarian Crisis in England, 1315–1322', *Past and Present*, 59 (1973), 3–50.

Kimball, E. G., *Serjeanty Tenure in Medieval England* (New Haven, 1936).

King, E. *Peterborough Abbey, 1086–1310: A Study in the Land Market* (Cambridge, 1973).

——, *Medieval England* (London, 1988).

Kingsford, C. L., *Prejudice and Promise in Fifteenth-century England* (London, 1962).

Kirby, T. F., *Winchester Scholars* (London, 1888).

Knowles, D. and R. Neville Hadcock, *Medieval Religious Houses England and Wales* (London, 1971).

Kosminsky, E. A., *Studies in the Agrarian History of England in the Thirteenth Century* (Oxford, 1956).

Kowaleski, M., *Local Markets and Regional Trade in Medieval Exeter* (Cambridge, 1995).

——, 'The Expansion of the South-Western Fisheries in Late Medieval England', *EcHRev*, 53 (2000), 429–54.

Kriedte, P., *Peasants, Landlords and Merchant Capitalists: Europe and the World Economy, 1500–1800* (Leamington Spa, 1983).

Kümin, B., *The Shaping of a Community* (Aldershot, 1996).

Kussmaul, A., *Servants in Husbandry in early modern England* (Cambridge, 1981).

——, *A General View of the Rural Economy of England, 1538–1840* (Cambridge, 1990).

Ladd, R. A., 'Thomas Deloney and the London Weavers' Company', *Sixteenth Century Journal*, 32 (2001), 981–1001.

Lamb, H. H., *Climate History and the Modern World*, 2nd edn (London, 1995).

Lambert, M., *Medieval Heresy: Popular Movements from the Gregorian Reform to the Reformation*, 2nd edn (Oxford, 1992).

Lambrick, G., 'Abingdon and the Riots of 1327', *Oxoniensia*, 29–30 (1964), 129–41.

Lander, J. R., *Conflict and Stability in Fifteenth-century England* (London, 1969).

——, *Crown and Nobility, 1450–1509* (London, 1976).

——, *Government and Community: England, 1450–1509* (London, 1980).

Langdon, J., 'Horse Hauling: A Revolution in Vehicle Transport in Twelfth- and Thirteenth-century England', in T. H. Aston (ed.), *Landlords, Peasants and Politics in Medieval England* (Cambridge, 1987), 33–64.

——, 'Water-Mills and Windmills in the West Midlands, 1086–1500', *EcHRev*, 44 (1991), 424–44.

——, 'Inland Water Transport in Medieval England', *Journal of Historical Geography*, 19 (1993), 1–11.

——, 'Lordship and Peasant Consumerism in the Milling Industry of Early Fourteenth Century England', *Past and Present*, 145 (1994), 3–46.

——, 'The Mobilisation of Labour in the Milling Industry of Thirteenth- and Early Fourteenth-century England', *Canadian Journal of History*, 31 (1996), 37–58.

——, *Mills in the Medieval Economy: England, 1300–1540* (Oxford, 2004).

Laslett, P. (ed.), *Household and Family in Past Time* (Cambridge, 1972).

——, *Family Life and Illicit Love in Earlier Generations* (Cambridge, 1977).

——, 'Family, Kinship and Collectivity as Systems of Support in Pre-industrial Europe: A Consideration of the 'Nuclear-Hardship' Hypothesis', *Continuity and Change*, 3 (1988), 153–75.

Latham, L. C., 'The Decay of the Manorial System During the First Half of the Fifteenth Century with Special Reference to Manorial Jurisdiction and the Decline of Villeinage, as Exemplified in the Records of Twenty-Six Manors in the Counties of Berkshire, Hampshire and Wiltshire', MA thesis, London (1928).

——, 'A Berkshire Manor at the Close of the Middle Ages', *Transactions of the Newbury District Field Club*, 6 (1931), 70–80.

——, 'Accounts of Shaw Manor', *Transactions of the Newbury District Field Club*, 8 (1939), 129–35.

Latimer, P., 'The English Inflation of 1180–1220 Reconsidered', *Past and Present*, 171 (2001), 3–29.

Lawrence, C. H., *Medieval Monasticism* (London, 1984).

Leadam, I. S., 'The Security of Copyholders in the Fifteenth and Sixteenth Centuries', *EHR*, 8 (1893), 684–96.

Leamon, R., *Historic Landscape of Shaw, A West Berks Manor* (Reading, 1991).

Lee, J. S., 'Feeding the Colleges: Cambridge's Food and Fuel Supplies, 1450–1560', *EcHRev*, 56 (2003), 243–64.

——, *Cambridge and its Economic Region, 1450–1560* (Hatfield, 2005).

Lee, S. (ed.), *Dictionary of National Biography*, vol. xlvi (London, 1896)

Levett, E., 'The Black Death on the Estates of the See of Winchester', in P. Vinogradoff (ed.), *Studies in Social and Legal History* (Oxford, 1916).

——, *Studies in Manorial History* (Oxford, 1938).

Levine, D. and K. Wrightson, *The Making of an Industrial Society: Whickham, 1560–1765* (Oxford, 1991).

Leyser, H., *Medieval Women* (London, 1995).

Lipson, E., *The Economic History of England, Volume I, The Middle Ages* (London, 1915; 11th edn, 1956).

——, *The History of the Woollen and Worsted Industries* (London, 1921).

Little, L. K., and B. H. Rosenwein, *Debating the Middle Ages: Issues and Readings* (Oxford, 1998).

Lloyd, T. H., *The Movement of Wool Prices in Medieval England* (Cambridge, 1973).

——, *The English Wool Trade in the Middle Ages* (Cambridge, 1977).

——, *Alien Merchants in England in the High Middle Ages* (Sussex, 1982).

——, *England and the German Hanse, 1157–1611* (Cambridge, 1991).

Loades, D., *The Mid-Tudor Crisis, 1545–1565* (Basingstoke, 1992).

——, *Tudor Government* (Oxford, 1997).

Lobb, S. J., and P. G. Rose, *Archaeological Survey of the Lower Kennet Valley, Berkshire* (Salisbury, 1996).

Lobel, M. D. (ed.), *The Victoria History of the Counties of England: Oxfordshire* VII (London, 1962).

Lock, R., 'The Black Death in Walsham-Le-Willows', *Proceedings of the Suffolk Institute of Archaeology and History*, 37 (1992), 316–37.

Lomas, T., 'South-East Durham: Late Fourteenth and Fifteenth Centuries', in P. D. A. Harvey (ed.), *The Peasant Land Market in Medieval England* (Oxford, 1984).

Lyle, H. M. *The Rebellion of Jack Cade, 1450* (London, 1950).

Lytle, G. F., 'The Social Origins of Oxford Students in the Late Middle Ages: New College, c.1380–c.1510', in J. Ijsewijn and J. Paquet (eds), *The Universities in the Late Middle Ages* (Leuven, 1978).

MacCulloch, D., 'Kett's Rebellion in Context', *Past and Present*, 84 (1979), 36–59.

——, *Suffolk under the Tudors: Politics and Religion in an English County, 1500–1600* (Oxford, 1986).

——, 'Bondmen under the Tudors', in C. Cross, D. Loades, and J. J. Scarisbrick (eds), *Law and Government under the Tudors* (Cambridge, 1986), 91–109.

—— (ed.), *The Reign of Henry VIII: Politics, Policy and Piety* (Basingstoke, 1995).

——, *Tudor Church Militant: Edward VI and the Protestant Reformation* (London, 1999).

Macfarlane, A., *Reconstructing English Historical Communities* (Cambridge, 1977).

——, *The Origins of English Individualism* (Oxford, 1978).

Maddicott, J., *The English Peasantry and the Demands of the Crown, 1294–1341* (Past and Present, Supplement I, 1975).

Manning, R. B., 'Violence and Social Conflict in Mid-Tudor Rebellions', *JBS*, 16 (1977), 18–40.

Marsh, C., *Popular Religion in Sixteenth-century England* (Basingstoke, 1998).

——, '"Common Prayer" in England, 1560–1640: The View from the Pew', *Past and Present*, 171 (2001), 66–94.

——, and Ryrie, A. (eds), *The Beginnings of English Protestantism* (Cambridge, 2002).

Marshall, P., *Reformation England, 1480–1642* (London, 2003).

——, Marshall, P., *Beliefs and the Dead in Reformation England* (Oxford, 2002).

Martin, J., 'Leadership and Priorities in Reading During the Reformation', in J. Craig and P. Collinson (eds), *The Reformation in English Towns, 1500–1640* (Basingstoke, 1998).

Martin, J. E., *Feudalism to Capitalism: Peasant and Landlord in English Agrarian Development* (Basingstoke, 1983).

Marwick, A., *The Nature of History*, 3rd edn (Basingstoke, 1989).

Mason, E., 'The Role of the English Parishioner, 1100–1500', *Journal of Ecclesiastical History*, 27 (1976), 17–29.

Masschaele, J., 'The Multiplicity of Medieval Markets Reconsidered', *Journal of Historical Geography*, 20 (1994), 255–71.

——, *Peasants, Merchants and Markets. Inland Trade in Medieval England, 1150–1350* (Basingstoke, 1997).

Mate, M., 'Labour and Labour Services on the Estates of Canterbury Cathedral Priory in the Fourteenth Century', *Southern History*, 7 (1985), 55–67.

——, 'The Economic and Social Roots of Medieval Popular Rebellion: Sussex in 1450–1451', *EcHRev*, 45 (1992), 661–76.

——, 'The East Sussex Land Market and Agrarian Class Structure in the Late Middle Ages', *Past and Present*, 139 (1993), 46–65.

——, 'The Rise and Fall of Markets in Southeast England', *Canadian Journal of History*, 31 (1996), 59–86.

——, *Daughters, Wives and Widows after the Black Death* (Woodbridge, 1998).

——, *Women in Medieval English Society* (Cambridge, 1999).

——, *Trade and economic developments, 1450–1550: The Experience of Kent, Surrey and Sussex* (Woodbridge, 2006).

Mattingly, J. M., 'Cookham, Bray and Isleworth Hundreds: A Study in Changing Local Relations in the Middle Thames Valley, 1422–1558', Ph.D. thesis, London (1994).

Mavor, W., *General View of the Agriculture of Berkshire* (London, 1809).

Mawdsley, E. and T. Munck, *Computing for Historians* (Manchester, 1993).

Mayhew, N. J., 'The Monetary Background to the Yorkist Recoinage of 1464–1471', *British Numismatic Journal*, 44 (1974), 62–73.

——, 'Numismatic Evidence and Falling Prices in the Fourteenth Century', *EcHRev*, 27 (1974), 1–15.

——, 'Money and Prices in England from Henry II to Edward III', *AgHRev*, 35 (1987), 121–32.

——, 'Population, Money Supply, and the Velocity of Circulation in England, 1300–1700', *EcHRev*, 48 (1995), 238–57.

McFarlane, K. B., *The Nobility of Later Medieval England* (Oxford, 1973).

——, *England in the Fifteenth Century* (London, 1981).

McIntosh, M. K., *Autonomy and Community: The Royal Manor of Havering, 1200–1500* (Cambridge, 1986).

——, 'Local Change and Community Control in England, 1465–1500', *The Huntington Library Quarterly*, 49 (1986), 219–42.

——, 'Local Responses to the Poor in Late Medieval and Tudor England', *Continuity and Change*, 3 (1988), 209–45.

——, *A Community Transformed: The Manor and Liberty of Havering, 1500–1620* (Cambridge, 1991).

——, *Controlling Misbehaviour in England, 1370–1600* (Cambridge, 1998).

——, 'Symposium: Controlling (Mis)Behavior', *JBS*, 37 (1998), 231–305.

McKisack, M., *The Fourteenth Century, 1307–1399* (Oxford, 1959).

McNiven, P., *Heresy and Politics in the Reign of Henry V* (Woodbridge, 1987).

McRae, A., *God Speed the Plough: The Representation of Agrarian England, 1500–1660* (Cambridge, 1996).

McRee, B. R., 'Religious Gilds and Civic Order: The Case of Norwich in the Late Middle Ages', *Speculum*, 67 (1992), 69–97.

Medick, H., 'The Proto-Industrial Family Economy', in P. Kriedte, H. Medick, and J. Schlumbohm (eds), *Industrialization Before Industrialization* (Cambridge, 1981).

Meekings, C. A. F., 'Thomas Kerver's Case, 1444', *EHR*, 90 (1975), 331–46.

Mendels, F., 'Proto-Industrialization: The First Phase of the Industrial Process', *JEH*, 32 (1972), 241–61.

Miles, D.; Rowley, T., 'Tusmore Deserted Village', *Oxoniensia*, 41 (1976), 309–15.

Miller, E., *The Abbey and Bishopric of Ely. The Social History of an Ecclesiastical Estate from the Tenth Century to the Early Fourteenth Century* (Cambridge, 1951).

——, 'The Fortunes of the English Textile Industry During the Thirteenth Century', *EcHRev*, 18 (1965), 64–82.

—— (ed.), *The Agrarian History of England and Wales, III, 1348–1500* (Cambridge, 1991).

——, and J. Hatcher, *Medieval England: Rural Society and Economic Change, 1086–1348* (London, 1978).

——, and J. Hatcher. *Medieval England: Towns, Commerce and Crafts, 1086–1348* (London, 1995).

Mills, D. R., *Lord and Peasant in Nineteenth-century Britain* (London, 1980).

Mollat, M., and R. Wolff., *The Popular Revolutions of the Late Middle Ages* (London, 1973).

Money, W., *The History of the Ancient Town and Borough of Newbury in the County of Berks* (London, 1887).

Moore, E. W., *The Fairs of Medieval England: An Introductory Study* (Toronto, 1985).

Moore, J. S., 'Jack Fisher's "flu": a Visitation Revisited', *EcHRev*, 46 (1993), 280–307.

——, 'Jack Fisher's 'flu: a Virus still Virulent', *EcHRev*, 47 (1994), 359–61.

Moreton, C. E., *The Townsends and Their World: Gentry, Law and Land in Norfolk, c.1450–1551* (Oxford, 1992).

Morgan, M., *The English Lands of the Abbey of Bec* (Oxford, 1946).

Morrill, J., 'The Ecology of Allegiance in the English Revolution', *JBS*, 26 (1987), 451–67.

Morris, W. A., *The Frankpledge System* (London, 1910).

Morriss, R. K., *The Archaeology of Buildings* (Stroud, 2000).

Muldrew, C., 'Interpreting the Market: the Ethics of Credit and Community Relations in Early Modern England', *Social History*, 18 (1993), 163–83.

——, *The Economy of Obligation: the Culture of Credit and Social Relations in Early Modern England* (Basingstoke, 1998).

——, '"Hard Food for Midas": Cash and Its Social Value in Early Modern England', *Past and Present*, 170 (2001), 78–120.

Muller, M., 'The Function and Evasion of Marriage Fines on a Fourteenth-century English Manor', *Continuity and Change*, 14 (1999), 169–90.

Munro, J. H., *Wool, Cloth and Gold: The Struggle for Bullion in Anglo-Burgundian Trade, 1340–1478* (Toronto, 1972).

——, 'Industrial Protectionism in Medieval Flanders: Urban or National?', in H. A. Miskimin (ed.), *The Medieval City* (Yale, 1977), 229–67.

——, 'Wool-Price Schedules and the Qualities of English Wools in the Later Middle Ages c.1270–1499', *Textile History*, 9 (1978), 118–69.

——, 'Industrial Transformations in the North-West European Textile Trades, c.1290–c.1340: Economic Progress or Economic Crisis?', in B. M. S. Campbell (ed.), *Before the Black Death* (Manchester, 1991), 110–48.

——, *Textiles, Towns and Trade: Essays on the Economic History of Late-Medieval England and the Low Countries* (Aldershot, 1994).

——, 'The Origins of the English 'New Draperies': The Resurrection of an Old Flemish Industry, 1270–1570', in N. B. Harte (ed.), *The New Draperies in the Low Countries and England, 1300–1800* (Oxford, 1997), 35–127.

——, 'The Symbiosis of Towns and Textiles', *Journal of Early Modern History*, 3 (1999), 1–74.

——, 'The 'New Institutional Economics' and the Changing Fortunes of Fairs in Medieval and Early Modern Europe: the Textile Trades, Warfare and Transaction Costs',

Vierteljahrschrift fur Sozial-und Wirtschaftsgerschichte, 88 (2001), 1–47.

Musson, A., 'New Labour Laws, New Remedies? Legal Reaction to the Black Death 'Crisis'', in N. Saul (ed.), *Fourteenth-century England, 1* (Woodbridge, 2000), 73–88.

——, 'Sub-Keepers and Constables: The Role of Local Officials in Keeping the Peace in Fourteenth-century England', *EHR*, 117 (2002), 1–24.

——, and W. M. Ormrod. *The Evolution of English Justice. Law Politics and Society in the Fourteenth Century* (Basingstoke, 1999).

Neeson, J. M., *Commoners: Common Right, Enclosure and Social Change in England, 1700–1820* (Cambridge, 1993).

Nef, J. U., 'The Progress of Technology and the Growth of Large-Scale Industry in Great Britain, 1540–1640', *EcHRev*, 5 (1934), 3–24.

Neilson, N., *Customary Rents* (Oxford Studies in Social and Legal History, edited by P. Vinogradoff, II. Oxford, 1910).

Neville, C. J. 'Common Knowledge and the Common Law in Later Medieval England', *Canadian Journal of History*, 29 (1994), 461–78.

Newman, C. M. *Late Medieval Northallerton: A Small Market Town and Its Hinterland, c.1470–1540* (Stamford, 1999).

——, 'Work and Wages at Durham Priory, 1494–1519', *Continuity and Change*, 16 (2001), 357–78.

Newman, E. I., 'Medieval Sheep-Corn Farming: How Much Grain Yield Could Each Sheep Support?' *AgHRev*, 50 (2002), 164–80.

——, and P. D. A. Harvey, 'Did Soil Fertility Decline in Medieval English Farms? Evidence from Cuxham, Oxfordshire, 1320–1340', *AgHRev*, 45 (1997), 119–36.

Nicholas, D. *The Transformation of Europe, 1300–1600* (London, 1999).

Nielsen, R., 'Storage and English Government Intervention in Early Modern Grain Markets', *JEH*, 57 (1997), 1–33.

Nightingale, P., 'Capitalists, Crafts and Constitutional Change in Late Fourteenth-century London', *Past and Present*, 124 (1989), 3–35.

——, 'Monetary Contraction and Mercantile Credit in Later Medieval England', *EcHRev*, 43 (1990), 560–75.

——, *A Medieval Mercantile Community: The Grocers' Company and the Politics and Trade of London, 1000–1485* (New Haven, 1995).

——, 'The Growth of London in the Medieval English Economy', in R. Britenell and J. Hatcher (eds), *Progress and Problems in Medieval England* (Cambridge, 1996).

——, 'England and the European Depression of the Mid-Fifteenth Century', *The Journal of European Economic History*, 26 (1997), 631–56.

——, 'Knights and Merchants: Trade, Politics and the Gentry in Late Medieval England', *Past and Present*, 169 (2000), 36–62.

——, 'Some New Evidence of Crises and Trends in Mortality in Late Medieval England', *Past and Present*, 187 (2005), 33–68.

North, D. C., and R. P. Thomas, 'An Economic Theory of the Growth of the Western World', *EcHRev*, 23 (1970), 1–17.

——, *The Rise of the Western World. A New Economic History* (Cambridge, 1973).

Norton, E. C., 'The Medieval Pavingtiles of Winchester College', *Proceedings of the Hampshire Field Club and Archaeological Society*, 31 (1974), 23–41.

O'Brien, P. K., and P. A. Hunt, 'The Rise of a Fiscal State in England, 1485–1815', *Historical Research*, 66 (1993), 129–76.

O'Day, R., *The Professions in Early Modern England, 1450–1800: Servants of the Commonweal* (London, 2000).

Olson, S., 'Jurors of the Village Court', *JBS*, 30 (1991), 237–56.

——, 'Family Linkages and the Structure of the Local Elite in the Medieval and Early Modern Village', *Medieval Prosopography*, 13 (1992), 53–82.

Orme, N., 'The Culture of Children in Medieval England', *Past and Present*, 148 (1995), 48–88.

——, *Medieval Children* (New Haven, 2001).

Ormrod, W. M., 'The Peasants' Revolt and the Government of England', *JBS*, 29 (1990), 1–30.

——, 'The Crown and the English Economy, 1290–1348', in B. M. S. Campbell (ed.), *Before the Black Death* (Manchester, 1991).

——, *Political Life in Medieval England, 1300–1450* (Basingstoke, 1995).

——, and P. Lindley (eds), *The Black Death in England* (Stamford, 1996).

Ostrom, E., *Governing the Commons* (Cambridge, 1990).

Outhwaite, R. B., *Inflation in Tudor and Early Stuart England* (Basingstoke, 1969).

——, 'Progress and Backwardness in English Agriculture, 1500–1650', *EcHRev*, 39 (1986), 1–18.

——, *Dearth, Public Policy and Social Disturbance in England, 1550–1800* (Cambridge, 1991).

Overton, M., *Agricultural Revolution in England* (Cambridge, 1996).

——, and B. M. S. Campbell, 'Norfolk Livestock Farming, 1250–1740: A Comparative Study of Manorial Accounts and Probate Inventories', *Journal of Historical Geography*, 18 (1992), 377–96.

Owst, G. R., *Literature and Pulpit in Medieval England* (Cambridge, 1933).

Page, F. M., 'The Customary Poor-Law of Three Cambridgeshire Manors', *Cambridge Historical Journal,*, 3 (1930), 125–33.

Page, M., 'The Technology of Medieval Sheep Farming: Some Evidence from Crawley, Hampshire, 1208–1349', *AgHRev*, 51 (2003), 137–54.

Palliser, D. M., 'Tawney's Century: Brave New World or Malthusian Trap?' *EcHRev*, 35 (1982), 339–53.

——, *The Age of Elizabeth* (London, 1983).

——, 'Urban Decay Revisited', in J. A. F. Thomson (ed.), *Towns and Townspeople in the Fifteenth Century* (Stroud, 1988).

—— (ed.), *The Cambridge Urban History, of Britain, Volume I, 600–1540* (Cambridge, 2000).

Parker, G., 'Success and Failure During the First Century of the Reformation', *Past and Present*, 136 (1992).

Payling, S., *Political Society in Lancastrian England: The Greater Gentry of Nottinghamshire* (Oxford, 1991).

——, 'Social Mobility, Demographic Change, and Landed Society in Late Medieval England', *EcHRev*, 45 (1992), 51–73.

——, 'The Economies of Marriage in Late Medieval England: The Marriage of Heiresses', *EcHRev*, 54 (2001), 413–29.

Peacock, D. M., 'The Winchcombe Family and the Woollen Industry in Sixteenth-century Newbury', Ph.D. thesis, Reading (2003).

Pearson, S., *The Medieval Houses of Kent: An Historical Analysis* (London, 1994).

Peberdy, R. B., 'Navigation on the River Thames between London and Oxford in the Late Middle Ages: A Reconsideration', *Oxoniensia*, 61 (1997), 311–40.

Pedersen, F., 'Demography in the Archives: Social and Geographical Factors in Fourteenth-century York Cause Paper Marriage Litigation', *Continuity and Change*,

10 (1995), 405–36.

Penn, S., 'Female Wage-Earners in Late Fourteenth-century England', *AgHRev*, 35 (1987), 1–14.

——, and C. Dyer, 'Wages and Earnings in Late Medieval England: Evidence from the Enforcement of the Labour Laws', *EcHRev*, 43 (1990), 356–76.

Pennell, S., 'Consumption and Consumerism in Early Modern England', *Historical Journal*, 42 (1999), 549–64.

Perkins, C., 'The Knights Templars in the British Isles', *EHR*, 25 (1910), 209–30.

——, 'The Knights Hospitallers in England after the Fall of the Order of the Temple', *EHR*, 45 (1930), 285–9.

Perring, D., *Town and Country in England: Frameworks for Archaeological Research* (York, 2002).

Peters, C., 'Gender, Sacrament and Ritual: The Making and Meaning of Marriage in Late Medieval and Early Modern England', *Past and Present*, 169 (2000), 63–96.

Phelps Brown, E. H. and S. V. Hopkins, 'Seven Centuries of the Prices of Consumables, compared with Builders Wage-rates', *Economica*, 23 (1956). Reprinted in E. H. Phelps Brown and S. V. Hopkins, *A Perspective of Wages and Prices* (London, 1981), 13–59.

Phillips, R., 'Grassroots Change in an Early Modern Economy: The Emergence of a Rural Consumer Society in Berkshire', *Southern History*, 11 (1989), 23–39.

Phythian-Adams, C., 'Ceremony and the Citizen: The Communal Year at Coventry, 1450–1550', in P. Clark and P. Slack (eds), *Crisis and Order in English Towns, 1500–1700: Essays in Urban History* (London, 1972).

——, 'Urban Decay in Late Medieval England', in P. Abrams and E. A. Wrigley (eds), *Towns in Societies* (Cambridge, 1978).

——, *Desolation of a City: Coventry and the Urban Crisis of the Late Middle Ages* (Cambridge, 1979).

Pirenne, H., *Economic and Social History of Medieval Europe* (London, 1936).

Platt, C., *Medieval Southampton: The Port and Trading Community, A.D. 1000–1600* (London, 1973).

——, *The Great Rebuildings of Tudor and Stuart England* (London, 1994).

——, *King Death* (London, 1996).

Pollard, A. J., 'Estate Management in the Later Middle Ages: The Talbots and Whitchurch, 1383–1525', *EcHRev*, 25 (1972), 553–66.

——, 'The North-Eastern Economy and the Agrarian Crisis of 1438–1440', *Northern History*, 25 (1989), 88–105.

——, *North-Eastern England During the Wars of the Roses* (Oxford, 1990).

—— (ed.), *The Wars of the Roses* (Basingstoke, 1995).

——, *Late Medieval England, 1399–1509* (London, 2000).

Poos, L. R., 'The Social Context of Statute of Labourers Enforcement', *Law and History Review*, 1 (1983), 28–52.

——, 'The Rural Population of Essex in the Later Middle Ages', *EcHRev*, 38 (1985), 515–30.

——, *A Rural Society After the Black Death: Essex, 1350–1525* (Cambridge, 1991).

——, 'Sex, Lies and the Church Courts of Pre-Reformation England', *Journal of Interdisciplinary History*, 25 (1995), 585–607.

——, and R. M. Smith, '"Legal Windows onto Historical Populations"? Recent Research on Demography and the Manor Court in Medieval England', *Law and History Review*, 2 (1984), 128–52.

——, '"Shades Still on the Window": A Reply to Zvi Razi', *Law and History Review*, 3

(1985), 409–29.

Postan, M. M., 'Credit in Medieval Trade', *EcHRev*, 1 (1928), 234–61.

——, 'Some Economic Evidence of Declining Population in the Later Middle Ages', *EcHRev*, 2 (1950), 221–46.

——, *The Famulus. The Estate Labourer in the Twelfth and Thirteenth Centuries* (Cambridge, 1954).

——, 'Medieval Agrarian Society in its Prime: England', in M. M. Postan (ed.), *The Cambridge Economic History of Europe* (Cambridge, 1966).

——, 'A Plague of Economists?', in M. M. Postan (ed.), *Fact and Relevance: Essays on Historical Method* (Cambridge, 1971).

——, *The Medieval Economy and Society* (London, 1972).

——, *Essays on Medieval Agriculture and General Problems of the Medieval Economy* (Cambridge, 1973).

Postles, D., 'The Perception of Profit before the Leasing of the Demesnes', *AgHRev*, 34 (1986), 12–28.

——, 'Personal Naming Patterns of Peasants and Burgesses in Late Medieval England', *Medieval Prosopography*, 12 (1991), 29–56.

——, 'Some Differences between Seignorial Demesnes in Medieval Oxfordshire', *Oxoniensia*, 58 (1993), 219–32.

——, 'An English Small Town in the Later Middle Ages: Loughborough', *Urban History*, 20 (1993), 7–29.

——, 'Notions of the Family, Lordship and the Evolution of Naming Processes in Medieval English Rural Society: a Regional Example', *Continuity and Change*, 10 (1995), 169–198.

Pounds, N. J. G., *An Economic History of Medieval Europe*, 2nd edn (London, 1994).

Power, E., *Medieval People* (London, 1924).

——, *The Wool Trade in English Medieval History* (Oxford, 1941).

——, *Medieval Women* (Cambridge, 1975).

——, and M. M. Postan (eds), *Studies in English Trade in the Fifteenth Century* (London, 1933).

Prescott, A., 'Writing About Rebellion: Using the Records of the Peasants' Revolt of 1381', *History Workshop*, 45 (1998), 1–27.

Prestwich, M., *English Politics in the Thirteenth Century* (Basingstoke, 1990).

Prior, M., 'Wives and Wills, 1558–1700', in J. Chartres and D. Hey (eds), *English Rural Society, 1500–1800* (Cambridge, 1990).

Pugh, T. B., 'The Magnates, Knights and Gentry', in S. B. Chrimes *et al.* (eds), *Fifteenth-century England, 1399–1509* (Stroud, 1995).

Putnam, B. H., *The Enforcement of the Statute of Labourers* (London, 1908).

Raftis, J. A., *The Estates of Ramsey Abbey: A Study of Economic Growth and Organisation* (Toronto, 1957).

——, *Tenure and Mobility* (Toronto, 1964).

——. *Warboys* (Toronto, 1974).

——, *Peasant Economic Development Within the English Manorial System* (Stroud, 1996).

Ramsay, G. D., 'The Distribution of the Cloth Industry in 1561–62', *EHR*, 57 (1942), 361–9.

——, *The Wiltshire Woollen Industry in the Sixteenth and Seventeenth Centuries* (London, 1943).

——, *English Overseas Trade During the Centuries of Emergence* (London, 1957).

——, *The English Woollen Industry, 1500–1750* (Basingstoke, 1982).

Rawcliffe, C., 'The Profits of Practice: The Wealth and Status of Medical Men in Later Medieval England', *Social History of Medicine*, 1 (1988), 61–78.

——, *Medicine and Society in Later Medieval England* (Stroud, 1995).

——, *Medicine for the Soul: The Life, Death and Resurrection of an English Medieval Hospital* (Stroud, 1999).

Razi, Z., 'The Toronto School's Reconstitution of Medieval Peasant Society: A Critical View', *Past and Present*, 85 (1979), 141–57.

——, *Life, Marriage and Death in a Medieval Parish* (Cambridge, 1980).

——, 'Family, Land and the Village Community in Later Medieval England', *Past and Present*, 93 (1981), 3–36.

——, 'The Struggles between the Abbots of Halesowen and Their Tenants in the Thirteenth and Fourteenth Centuries', in T. H. Aston (ed.), *Social Relations and Ideas* (Cambridge, 1983), 151–67.

——, 'The Use of Manorial Court Rolls in Demographic Analysis: A Reconsideration', *Law and History Review*, 3 (1985), 191–200.

——, 'The Demographic Transparency of Manorial Court Rolls', *Law and History Review*, 5 (1987), 523–35.

——, 'The Myth of the Immutable English Family', *Past and Present*, 140 (1993), 3–44.

——, 'Manorial Court Rolls and Local Population: an East Anglian Case Study', *EcHRev*, 49 (1996), 758–63.

——, and R. M. Smith (eds), *Medieval Society and the Manor Court* (Oxford, 1996).

Reynolds, S. *An Introduction to the History of English Medieval Towns* (Oxford, 1977).

——, 'Medieval Urban History, and the History of Political Thought', *Urban History Yearbook* (1982), 14–23.

——, *Fiefs and Vassals* (Oxford, 1994).

——, *Kingdoms and Communities in Western Europe, 900–1300*, 2nd edn (Oxford, 1997).

Richardson, H. G., 'Business Training in Medieval Oxford', *The American Historical Review*, 46 (1941), 259–80.

Richardson, W. C., *History of the Court of Augmentations, 1536–1554* (Baton Rouge, Louisiana, 1961).

Richmond, C., *The Paston Family in the Fifteenth Century* (Cambridge, 1990).

——, 'An Outlaw and Some Peasants: The Possible Significance of Robin Hood', *Nottingham Medieval Studies*, 27 (1993), 90–101.

——, 'The Transition from Feudalism to Capitalism in the Archives of Magdalen College, Oxford: A Note', *History Workshop*, 37 (1994), 165–9.

——, and E. Scarff (eds), *St George's Chapel, Windsor, in the Late Middle Ages* (Windsor, 2001).

Rigby, S., '"Sore Decay" and "Fair Dwellings": Boston and Urban Decline in the Later Middle Ages', *Midland History*, 10 (1985), 47–61.

——, 'Urban 'Oligarchy', in Late Medieval England', in J. A. F. Thomson (ed.), *Towns and Townspeople in the Fifteenth Century* (Gloucester, 1988), 62–86.

——, *Medieval Grimsby: Growth and Decline* (Hull, 1993).

——, 'Historical Causation: Is One Thing More Important Than Another?' *History*, 80 (1995), 227–42.

——, *English Society in the Later Middle Ages: Class, Status and Gender* (Basingstoke, 1995).

——, *Chaucer in Context. Society, Allegory and Gender* (Manchester, 1996).

——, 'Approaches to Pre-Industrial Social Structure', in J. Denton (ed.), *Orders and Hierarchies in Late Medeival and Renaissance Europe* (Basingstoke, 1999).

——, ed. *A Companion to Britain in the Later Middle Ages* (Oxford, 2003).

Roberts, B. K., *The Making of the English Village: A Study in Historical Geography* (London, 1987).

——, and S. Wrathmell, *An Atlas of Rural Settlement in England* (London, 2000).

——, and S. Wrathmell, *Region and Place a Study of English Rural Settlement* (London, 2002).

Rogers, J. E. Thorold, *A History of Agriculture and Prices in England, 1259–1793*, 8 vols (Oxford, 1866–1902).

——, *Six Centuries of Work and Wages: The History of English Labour*, 2 vols (London, 1884; 11th edn, 1912).

Rogers, N. *England in the Fifteenth Century* (Stamford, 1994).

Rollison, D., *The Local Origins of Modern Society: Gloucestershire, 1500–1800* (London, 1992).

——, 'Discourse and Class Struggle: The Politics of Industry in Early Modern England', *Social History*, 26 (2001), 166–89.

Rosener, W., *Peasants in the Middle Ages* (Oxford, 1992).

Roskell, J. S., *The Commons and Their Speakers in English Parliaments, 1376–1523* (Manchester, 1965).

——, L. Clark, and C. Rawcliffe (eds), *The History of Parliament: The House of Commons, 1386–1421*, 4 vols (Stroud, 1992).

Rosser, G., 'The Essence of Medieval Urban Communities: The Vill of Westminster, 1200–1540', *Transcripts of the Royal Historical Society*, 34 (1984), 91–112.

——, 'Communities of Parish and Guild in the Late Middle Ages', in S. Wright (ed.), *Parish Church and People* (London, 1988).

——, *Medieval Westminster, 1200–1540* (Oxford, 1989).

——, 'Crafts, Guilds and the Negotiation of Work in the Medieval Town', *Past and Present*, 154 (1997), 3–31.

Rubin, M., *Charity and Community in Medieval Cambridge* (Cambridge, 1987).

——, *Corpus Christi. The Eucharist in Late Medieval Culture* (Cambridge, 1991).

Ruddock, A. A., *Italian Merchants and Shipping in Southampton, 1270–1600* (Southampton, 1951).

Runciman, W. G., *A Treatise on Social Theory*, vol. 2 (Cambridge, 1989).

Rush, I., 'The Impact of Commercialisation in Early Fourteenth-century England: Some Evidence from the Manors of Glastonbury Abbey', *AgHRev*, 49 (2001), 123–39.

Rushton, N. S., 'Monastic Charitable Provision in Tudor England', *Continuity and Change*, 16 (2001), 9–44.

——, and Currie, C. K., 'Land Management and Custumal Diversity on the Estate of Mottisfont Priory in the 1340s', *Hampshire Studies*, 45 (2001), 202–18.

Russell, J. C., *British Medieval Population* (Albuquerque, 1948).

Salzman, L. F., *England in Tudor Times: An Account of Its Social Life and Industries* (London, 1926).

Saul, N., *Knights and Esquires: The Gloucestershire Gentry in the Fourteenth Century* (Oxford, 1981).

——, *Scenes from Provincial Life: Knightly Families in Sussex, 1280–1400* (Oxford, 1986).

——, 'The Social Status of Chaucer's Franklin: A Reconsideration', *Medium Aevum*, 52 (1983), 10–23.

—— (ed.), *The Oxford Illustrated History of Medieval England* (Oxford, 1997).

——, *Richard II* (New Haven, 1997).

Savine, A., 'Bondmen under the Tudors', *TRHS*, new series, 17 (1903), 235–89.

——, *English Monasteries on the Eve of the Dissolution* (Oxford, 1909).

Scarisbrick, J. J., *Henry VIII* (London, 1969).

——, *The Reformation and the English People* (Oxford, 1984).

Scattergood, V. J., *Politics and Poetry in the Fifteenth Century* (London, 1971).

——, 'Pierce the Ploughman's Crede: Lollardy and Texts', in M. Aston and C. Richmond (eds), *Lollardy and the Gentry in the Later Middle Ages* (Stroud, 1997), 77–94.

Schofield, J. and A. Vince, *Medieval Towns: The Archaeology of Medieval Europe, 1100–1600* (London, 2003).

Schofield, P. R., 'Land, Family and Inheritance in a Later Medieval Community: Birdbrook, 1292–1412', D.Phil. thesis, Oxford (1992).

——, 'Tenurial Developments and the Availability of Customary Land in a Later Medieval Community', *EcHRev*, 49 (1996), 250–67.

——, 'Dearth, Debt and the Local Land Market in a Late Thirteenth-century Village Community', *AgHRev*, 45 (1997), 1–17.

——, 'Peasants and the Manor Court: Gossip and Litigation in a Suffolk Village at the Close of the Thirteenth Century', *Past and Present*, 159 (1998), 3–42.

——, '*Extranei* and the Market for Customary Land on a Westminster Abbey Manor in the Fifteenth Century', *AgHRev*, 49 (2001), 1–16.

——, *Peasant and Community in Medieval England, 1200–1500* (Basingstoke, 2003).

——, and N. J. Mayhew (eds), *Credit and Debt in Medieval England, c.1180–c.1350* (Oxford, 2002).

Schofield, R., 'The Geographical Distribution of Wealth in England, 1334–1649', *EcHRev*, 18 (1965), 483–510.

——, 'English Marriage Patterns Revisited', *Journal of Family History*, 10 (1985), 2–20.

——, 'Taxation and the Political Limits of the Tudor State', in C. Cross, D. Loades, and J. Scarisbrick (eds), *Law and Government under the Tudors* (Cambridge, 1988).

——, 'Family Structure, Demographic Behaviour, and Economic Growth', in J. Walter and R. Schofield (eds), *Famine, Disease and the Social Order in Early Modern Society* (Cambridge, 1989).

——, and E. A. Wrigley, 'Infant and Child Mortality in England in the late Tudor and early Stuart period', in C. Webster (ed.), *Health, Medicine and Mortality in the Sixteenth Century* (Cambridge, 1979).

Scott, S., S. R. Duncan, and C. J. Duncan, 'The Origins, Interactions and Causes of the Cycles in Grain Prices in England, 1450–1812', *AgHRev*, 46 (1998), 1–14.

Scott, T. *The Peasantries of Europe* (London, 1998).

Scott, V. G., and E. McLaughlin, *County Maps and Histories Berkshire* (London, 1984).

Searle, E., 'Seigneurial Control of Women's Marriage: The Antecedents and Function of Merchet in England', *Past and Present*, 82 (1979), 3–43.

Shagan, E. H., 'Protector Somerset and the 1549 Rebellions: New Sources and New Perspectives', *EHR*, 114 (1999), 34–63.

Sharpe, J., *Crime in Early Modern England, 1550–1750* (London, 1984).

——, *Instruments of Darkness: Witchcraft in England, 1550–1750* (London, 1996).

——, *Witchcraft in Early Modern England* (London, 2001).

Shaw, D., *The Creation of a Community: The City of Wells in the Middle Ages* (Oxford, 1993).

Shaw-Taylor, L., 'Labourers, Cows, Common Rights and Parliamentary Enclosure: The

Evidence of Contemporary Comment c.1760–1810', *Past and Present*, 171 (2001), 95–126.

Sheail, J., 'The Regional Distribution of Wealth in England as indicated in the 1524/25 Lay Subsidy Returns', Ph.D. thesis, London (1968). Reprinted in *List and Index Society Special Series*, 29 (1998).

——, 'The Distribution of Taxable Population and Wealth in England during the Early Sixteenth Century', *Transactions of the Institute of British Geographers*, 55 (1972), 111–26.

Sheehan, M. M., 'English Wills and the Records of the Ecclesiastical and Civil Jurisdictions', *Journal of Medieval History*, 14 (1988), 3–12.

Shepard, A., and P. Withington (eds), *Communities in Early Modern England* (Manchester, 2000).

Shepherd, G., 'Poverty in Piers Plowman', in T. H. Aston, P. Coss, C. Dyer and J. Thirsk (eds), *Social Relations and Ideas* (Cambridge, 1983), 169–89.

Short, B., 'The Evolution of Contrasting Communities Within Rural England', in B. Short (ed.), *The English Rural Community* (Cambridge, 1992).

Shrewsbury, J. F. D., *A History of Bubonic Plague in the British Isles* (Cambridge, 1970).

Slack, P., 'Mortality Crises and Epidemic Disease in England, 1485–1610', in C. Webster (ed.), *Health, Medicine and Mortality in the Sixteenth Century* (Cambridge, 1979).

——, *The Impact of Plague in Tudor and Stuart England* (Oxford, 1985).

——, *Poverty and Policy in Tudor and Stuart England* (London, 1988).

——, *From Reformation to Improvement. Public Welfare in Early Modern England* (Oxford, 1999).

Slade, C. F. 'Reading', in M. D. Lobel (ed.), *Historic Towns* (London, 1969), 1–9 and maps.

——, *The Town of Reading and Its Abbey* (Reading, 2001).

Slater, T. R., and G. Rosser (eds), *The Church in the Medieval Town* (Aldershot, 1998).

Smith, L. B., 'The "Taste for Tudors" since 1940', in E. C. Furber (ed.), *Changing Views on British History* (Cambridge, Massachusetts, 1966).

Smith, R. B., *Land and Politics in the England of Henry VIII: The West Riding of Yorkshire, 1530–1546* (Oxford, 1970).

Smith, R. M., 'Fertility, Economy, and Household Formation in England Over Three Centuries', *Population and Development Review*, 7 (1981), 595–622.

——, 'Some Thoughts on 'Hereditary' and 'Proprietary' Rights in Land under Customary Law in Thirteenth and Fourteenth Century England', *Law and History Review*, 1 (1983), 95–128.

——, 'Hypotheses sur la Nuptualite en Angleterre aux XIII–XIV Siecles', *Annales Economies Societes Civilisations*, 38 (1983), 107–36.

——, '"Modernization" and the Corporate Medieval Village Community in England: Some Sceptical Reflections', in A. R. H. Baker and D. Gregory (eds), *Explorations in Historical Geography* (Cambridge, 1984).

—— (ed.), *Land, Kinship and Life-cycle* (Cambridge, 1984).

——, 'Marriage Processes in the English Past: Some Continuities', in L. Bonfield, R. M. Smith, and K. Wrightson (eds), *The World We Have Gained* (Oxford, 1986).

——, 'Human Resources', in G. Astill and A. Grant (eds), *The Countryside in Medieval England* (Oxford, 1988).

——, 'Coping with Uncertainty: Women's Tenure of Customary Land in England, c.1370–1430', in J. Kermode (ed.), *Enterprise and Individuals in Fifteenth-century England* (Stroud, 1991).

——, 'Demographic Developments in Rural England, 1300–48: A Survey', in B. M. S. Campbell (ed.), *Before the Black Death* (Manchester, 1991).

——, 'The Manorial Court and the Elderly Tenant in Late Medieval England', in M. Pelling and R. M. Smith (eds), *Life, Death and the Elderly* (London, 1991).

——, 'Geographical Diversity in the Resort to Marriage in Late Medieval Europe: Work, Reputation, and Unmarried Females in the Household Formation Systems of Northern and Southern Europe', in P. J. P. Goldberg (ed.), *Woman is a Worthy Wight: Women in English Society, c.1200–1500* (Stroud, 1992).

——, 'Charity, Self-Interest and Welfare: Reflections from Demographic and Family History', in M. Daunton (ed.), *Charity, Self-Interest and Welfare in the English Past* (London, 1996).

——, 'Plagues and Peoples. The Long Demographic Cycle, 1250–1670', in P. Slack and R. Ward (eds), *The Peopling of Britain: The Shaping of a Human Landscape* (Oxford, 2002).

Sorokin, P. A., 'What is a Social Class?', in R. Bendix and S. M. Lipset (eds), *Class Status and Power: A Reader in Social Stratification* (Glencoe, Illinois, 1953), 87–92.

Spring, E., *Law, Land, and Family. Aristocratic Inheritance in England, 1300 to 1800* (Chapel Hill, 1993).

Spufford, M., *Contrasting Communities, English Villagers in the Sixteenth and Seventeenth Centuries* (Cambridge, 1974).

——, 'Peasant Inheritance Customs and Land Distribution in Cambridgeshire from the sixteenth to the eighteenth centuries', in J. Goody, J. Thirsk, and E. P. Thompson (eds), *Family and Inheritance* (Cambridge, 1976).

——, *Small Books and Pleasant Histories* (Cambridge, 1981).

——, 'Puritanism and Social Control?', in A. Fletcher and J. Stevenson (eds), *Order and Disorder in Early Modern England* (Cambridge, 1985), 41–57.

——, 'The Limitations of the Probate Inventory', in J. Chartres and D. Hey (eds), *English Rural Society, 1500–1800* (Cambridge, 1990), 139–74.

—— (ed.), *The World of Rural Dissenters, 1520–1725* (Cambridge, 1995).

Spufford, P., *Money and its Use in Medieval Europe* (Cambridge, 1988).

——, *Power and Profit the Merchant in Medieval Europe* (London, 2002).

Sreenivasan, G., 'The Land-family Bond at Earls Colne (Essex), 1550–1650', *Past and Present*, 131 (1991), 3–37.

Stapleton B. (ed.), *Conflict and Community in Southern England* (Stroud, 1992).

Steane, J., *The Archaeology of Power* (Stroud, 2001).

——, 'Medieval Oxfordshire, 1100–1540', *Oxoniensia*, 66 (2001), 1–12.

Stein, P., 'Custom in Roman and Medieval Civil Law', *Continuity and Change*, 10 (1995), 337–44.

Stenton, F. M., *The Early History of the Abbey of Abingdon* (Stamford, reprinted 1989).

Stephenson, J., *The Land of Britain: The Report of the Land Utilisation Survey of Britain. Part 78, Berkshire* (London, 1936).

Stephenson, M. J., 'Wool Yields in the Medieval Economy', *EcHRev*, 41 (1988), 368–91.

Stone, D., 'The Productivity of Hired and Customary Labour: Evidence from Wisbech Barton in the Fourteenth Century', *EcHRev*, 50 (1997), 640–56.

——, 'Medieval Farm Management and Technological Mentalities: Hinderclay before the Black Death', *EcHRev*, 54 (2001), 612–38.

——, 'The Productivity and Management of Sheep in Late Medieval England', *AgHRev*, 51 (2003), 1–22.

——, *Decision-Making in Medieval Agriculture* (Oxford, 2005).

Stone, E., 'Profit-and-Loss Accountancy at Norwich Cathedral Priory', *TRHS*, 5th series, 12 (1962), 25–48.

Strohm, P., *Hochon's Arrow: The Social Imagination of Fourteenth-century Texts* (Princeton, 1992).

Stuart, D., *Manorial Records: An Introduction to Their Transcription and Translation* (Chichester, 1992).

Stubbs, W., *Seventeen Lectures on the Study of Medieval and Modern History and Kindred Subjects*, 3rd edn (Oxford, 1900).

Sussman, N., 'The Late Medieval Bullion Famine Reconsidered', *JEH*, 58 (1998), 126–54.

Sutton, A. F., 'Caxton Was a Mercer: His Social Milieu and Friends', in N. Rogers (ed.), *England in the Fifteenth Century* (Stamford, 1994), 118–48.

——, 'Mercery through Four Centuries, 1130s–c.1500', *Nottingham Medieval Studies*, XLI (1997), 100–25.

——, *A Merchant Family of Coventry, London and Calais: The Tates, c.1450–1515* (London, 1998).

——, 'The Silent Years of London Guild History before 1300: The Case of the Mercers', *Historical Research*, 71 (1998), 121–41.

——, 'Some Aspects of the Linen Trade c.1130s to 1500, and the Part Played by the Mercers of London', *Textile History*, 30 (1999), 155–75.

——, 'The Shop-Floor of the London Mercery Trade, c.1200–c.1500: The Marginalisation of the Artisan, the Itinerant Mercer and the Shopholder', *Nottingham Medieval Studies*, 45 (2001), 12–50.

——, *The Mercery of London: Trade, Goods and People, 1130–1578* (Aldershot, 2005).

Sutton, J., 'Ridge and Furrow in Berkshire and Oxfordshire', *Oxoniensia*, 29–30 (1964–65), 99–115.

Swabey, F., 'The Household of Alice De Bryene, 1412–13', in M. Carlin and J. T. Rosenthal (eds), *Food and Eating in Medieval Europe* (London, 1998), 133–44.

——, *Medieval Gentlewoman: Life in a Widow's Household in the Later Middle Ages* (Stroud, 1999).

Swanson, H., 'The Illusion of Economic Structure: Craft Guilds in Late Medieval English Towns', *Past and Present*, 121 (1988), 29–48.

——, *Medieval Artisans: An Urban Class in Late Medieval England* (Oxford, 1989).

——, *Medieval British Towns* (Basingstoke, 1999).

Swanson, R. N., *Church and Society in Late Medieval England* (Oxford, 1989).

——, *Religion and Devotion in Europe, c.1215–c.1515* (Cambridge, 1995).

Swedberg, R., *Max Weber Essays in Economic Sociology* (Princeton, 1999).

Tann, J., 'Multiple Mills', *Medieval Archaeology*, 11 (1967), 253–5.

Tanner, N. (ed.), *Heresy Trials in the Diocese of Norwich, 1428–31* (Camden Society, fourth series, 20, 1977).

Tawney, R. H., *The Agrarian Problem in the Sixteenth Century* (London, 1912).

——, *Religion and the Rise of Capitalism: A Historical Study* (London, 1926).

——, 'The Rise of the Gentry, 1558–1640', *EcHRev*, 11 (1941), 1–38.

Taylor, M. M., 'Justices of Assize', in J. F. Willard, W. A. Morris and W. H. Dunham (eds), *The English Government at Work, 1327–1336* (Cambridge, Massachusetts, 1950), 219–57.

Taylor, J., *English Historical Literature in the Fourteenth Century* (Oxford, 1987).

Thirsk, J., *Tudor Enclosures* (London, 1959).

——, 'Industries in the Countryside', in F. J. Fisher (ed.), *Essays in the Economic and*

Social History of Tudor and Stuart England (Cambridge, 1961).

—— (ed.), *The Agrarian History of England and Wales, Volume IV, 1500–1640* (Cambridge, 1967).

——, *England's Agricultural Regions and Agrarian History, 1500–1750* (Basingstoke, 1987).

——, 'English Rural Communities: Structures, Regularities, and Change in the Sixteenth and Seventeenth Centuries', in B. Short (ed.), *The English Rural Community* (Cambridge, 1992), 44–61.

——, *Alternative Agriculture: A History from the Black Death to the Present Day* (Oxford, 1997).

—— (ed.), *The English Rural Landscape* (Oxford, 2000).

Thoen, E., 'A 'Commercial Survival Economy', in Evolution. The Flemish Countryside and the Transition to Capitalism (Middle Ages–19th Century)', in P. Hoppenbrouwers and J. L. van Zanden (eds), *Peasants into Farmers? The Transformation of Rural Economy and Society in the Low Countries (Middle Ages–19th Century) in Light of the Brenner Debate* (Turnhout, 2000), 102–57.

Thomas, K., *Religion and the Decline of Magic: Studies in Popular Beliefs in Sixteenth- and Seventeenth-century England* (London, 1971).

Thomas, K., 'Age and Authority in Early Modern England', *Proceedings of the British Academy*, 62 (1976), 205–48.

Thompson, B. (ed.), *The Reign of Henry VII* (Stamford, 1995).

Thompson, E. P., 'The Grid of Inheritance: A Comment', in J. Goody, J. Thirsk, and E. P. Thompson (eds), *Family and Inheritance: Rural Society in Western Europe, 1200–1800* (Cambridge, 1976).

——, *Customs in Common* (London, 1991).

Thomson, J. A. F., *The Later Lollards, 1414–1520* (Oxford, 1965).

——, *The Transformation of Medieval England* (London, 1983).

——, *The Early Tudor Church and Society* (London, 1993).

Thorner, D., B. Kerblay, and R. E. F. Smith (eds), *A. V. Chayanov on The Theory of Peasant Economy* (Manchester, 1966).

Thornton, T. (ed.), *Social Attitudes and Political Structures in the Fifteenth Century* (Stroud, 2000).

Thrupp, S., *The Merchant Class of Medieval London* (Michigan, 1948).

——, 'The Problem of Replacement-Rates in Late Medieval English Population', *EcHRev*, 18 (1965), 101–19.

——, 'Aliens In and Around London in the Fifteenth Century', in A. E. J. Hollaender and W. Kellaway (eds), *Studies in London History* (London, 1969), 251–72.

Titow, J. Z., *English Rural Society, 1200–1350* (London, 1969).

——, *Winchester Yields: A Study in Medieval Agricultural Productivity* (Cambridge, 1972).

——, 'Lost Rents, Vacant Holdings and the Contraction of Peasant Cultivation after the Black Death', *AgHRev*, 42 (1994), 97–114.

Tittler, R., 'The End of the Middle Ages in the English Country Town', *Sixteenth Century Journal*, 18 (1987), 471–87.

——, *Architecture and Power: The Town Hall and the English Urban Community, c.1500–1640* (Oxford, 1991).

—— and N. Jones (eds), *A Companion to Tudor Britain* (Oxford, 2004).

Todd, B. J., 'Widowhood in a Market Town, Abingdon, 1540–1720', D.Phil. thesis, Oxford (1982).

——, 'Freebench and Free Enterprise: Widows and Their Property in Two Berkshire Villages', in J. Chartres and D. Hey (eds), *English Rural Society, 1500–1800* (Cambridge, 1990), 175–200.

Trenholme, N. M., 'The Risings in the English Monastic Towns in 1327', *American Historical Review*, 6 (1900), 650–70.

Tuck, J. A., 'Nobles, Commons and the Great Revolt of 1381', in R. H. Hilton and T. Aston (eds), *The English Rising of 1381* (Cambridge, 1984), 194–212.

Turner, M. E., J. V. Beckett, and B. Afton, *Agricultural Rent in England, 1690–1914* (Cambridge, 1997).

Underdown, D., *Revel, Riot, and Rebellion: Popular Politics and Culture in England, 1603–1660* (Oxford, 1985).

——, 'A Reply to John Morrill', *JBS*, 26 (1987), 468–79.

Unwin, G., *Industrial Organization in the Sixteenth and Seventeenth Centuries* (London, 1904, new impression 1963).

van Zanden, J. L., 'The "Revolt of the Early Modernists" and the "First Modern Economy": An Assessment', *EcHRev*, 55 (2002), 619–41.

VCH Berkshire, see Ditchfield above.

Vince, A. G., S. J. Lobb, J. C. Richards, and L. Mepham, *Excavations in Newbury, Berkshire, 1979–1990* (Salisbury, 1997).

Vinogradoff, P., *Villainage in England* (Oxford, 1892).

Virgoe, R., 'The Parliamentary Subsidy of 1450', *BIHR*, 55 (1982), 125–38.

——, 'Inheritance and Litigation in the Fifteenth Century: The Buckenham Disputes', *Journal of Legal History*, 15 (1994), 23–40.

Walker, S., *The Lancastrian Affinity, 1361–1399* (Oxford, 1990).

——, 'Sir Richard Abberbury (c.1330–1399) and His Kinsmen: The Rise and Fall of a Gentry Family', *Nottingham Medieval Studies*, 34 (1990), 113–40.

——, 'Rumour, Sedition and Popular Protest in the Reign of Henry IV', *Past and Present*, 166 (2000), 31–65.

Wall, A., *Power and Protest in England, 1525–1640* (London, 2000).

Wallace, D. (ed.), *The Cambridge History of Medieval English Literature* (Cambridge, 1999).

Wallerstein, I., *The Modern World System I: Capitalist Agriculture and the Origins of the European World-Economy in the Sixteenth Century* (London, 1974).

Walter, J., 'A "Rising of the People"? The Oxfordshire Rising of 1596', *Past and Present*, 107 (1985), 90–143.

——, and K. Wrightson, 'Dearth and the Social Order in Early Modern England', *Past and Present*, 71 (1976), 22–42.

——, and R. Schofield (eds), *Famine, Disease and the Social Order in Early Modern Society* (Cambridge, 1989).

Watkins, A., 'Small Towns in the Forest of Arden in the Fifteenth Century', *Dugdale Society Occasional Papers*, 38 (1998), 1–29.

——, 'Landowners and Their Estates in the Forest of Arden in the Fifteenth Century', *AgHRev*, 45 (1997), 18–33.

Watt, T., *Cheap Print and Popular Piety, 1550–1640* (Cambridge, 1991).

Watts, D. G., 'A Model for the Early Fourteenth Century', *EcHRev*, 20 (1967), 543–7.

——, 'Peasant Discontent on the Manors of Titchfield Abbey, 1245–1405', *Proceedings Hampshire Field Club Archaeological Society*, 39 (1983), 121–35.

Watts, J. L. (ed.), *The End of the Middle Ages? England in the Fifteenth and Sixteenth Centuries* (Stroud, 1998).

Weatherill, L., 'Consumer Behaviour and Social Status in England, 1660-1750', *Continuity and Change*, 1 (1986), 191-216.

——, *Consumer Behaviour and Material Culture in Britain, 1660-1760*, 2nd edn (London, 1996).

Westlake, H. F., *The Parish Guilds of Medieval England* (London, 1919).

White, L., *Medieval Technology and Social Change* (Oxford, 1964).

Whiting, R., *The Blind Devotion of the People* (Cambridge, 1989).

Whittington, G., 'The Common Lands of Berkshire', *Transactions of the Institute of British Geographers*, 35 (1964), 129-48.

Whittle, J., 'The Development of Agrarian Capitalism in England from c.1450 to c.1580', D.Phil. thesis, Oxford (1995).

——, 'Individualism and the Family-Land Bond: A Reassessment of Land Transfer Patterns among the English Peasantry', *Past and Present*, 160 (1998), 25-63.

——, 'Inheritance, Marriage, Widowhood and Remarriage: A Comparative Perspective on Women and Landholding in North-East Norfolk, 1440-1580', *Continuity and Change*, 13 (1998), 33-72.

——, *The Development of Agrarian Capitalism. Land and Labour in Norfolk, 1440-1580* (Oxford, 2000).

——, and M. Yates, '"Pays Réel or Pays Légal"? Contrasting Patterns of Land Tenure and Social Structure in Eastern Norfolk and Western Berkshire, 1450-1600', *AgHRev*, 48 (2000), 1-26.

Wickham, C., 'The Other Transition: From the Ancient World to Feudalism', *Past and Present*, 103 (1984), 3-36.

——, 'Gossip and Resistance among the Medieval Peasantry', *Past and Present*, 160 (1998), 3-24.

Willard, J. F., *Parliamentary Taxes on Personal Property, 1290-1334* (Cambridge, Massachusetts, 1934).

Williams, P., 'The Tudor State', *Past and Present*, 25 (1963), 39-58.

——, *The Tudor Regime* (Oxford, 1979).

Williamson, T., *Shaping Medieval Landscapes: Settlement, Society, Environment* (Macclesfield, 2003).

——, 'Understanding Fields', *The Local Historian*, 33 (2003), 12-29.

Wilson, S., 'The Myth of Motherhood a Myth: The Historical View of European Child-Rearing', *Social History*, 9 (1984).

Winchester, B., *Tudor Family Portrait* (London, 1955).

Woodman, A. V., 'The Buckinghamshire and Oxfordshire Rising of 1549', *Oxoniensia*, 22 (1957), 78-84.

Woods, R., *The Population of Britain in the Nineteenth Century* (Basingstoke, 1992).

——, and N. Williams, 'Must the Gap Widen Before It Can Be Narrowed? Long-Term Trends in Social Class Mortality Differentials', *Continuity and Change*, 10 (1995), 105-37.

Woodward, D., 'The Background to the Statute of Artificers: The Genesis of Labour Policy, 1558-63', *EcHRev*, 33 (1980), 32-44.

——, 'Wage Rates and Living Standards in Pre-Industrial England', *Past and Present*, 91 (1981), 28-46.

——, 'The Determination of Wage Rates in the Early Modern North of England', *EcHRev*, 47 (1994), 22-43.

——, *Men at Work: Labourers and Building Craftsmen in the Towns of Northern England, 1450-1750* (Cambridge, 1995).

——, 'Early Modern Servants in Husbandry Revisited', *AgHRev*, 48 (2000), 141–50.

Wordie, J. R., 'Deflationary factors in the Tudor price rise', *Past and Present*, 154 (1997), 32–70.

Workman, K. J., 'Manorial Estate Officials and Opportunity in Late Medieval English Society', *Viator*, 26 (1995), 223–40.

Wrightson, K., 'Villages, Villagers and Village Studies', *Historical Journal*, 18 (1975), 632–9.

——, 'Medieval Villagers in Perspective', *Peasant Studies*, 7 (1978), 203–17.

——, *English Society, 1580–1680* (London, 1982).

——, 'The Social Order of Early Modern England: Three Approaches', in L. Bonfield, R. M. Smith, and K. Wrightson (eds), *The World We Have Gained* (Oxford, 1986), 177–202.

——, 'Estates, Degrees and Sorts: Changing Perceptions of Society in Tudor and Stuart England', in P. Corfield (ed.), *Language, History and Class* (Oxford, 1991), 30–52.

——, '"Sorts of People" in Tudor and Stuart England', in J. Barry and C. Brooks (eds), *The Middling Sort of People* (Basingstoke, 1994), 28–51.

——, 'The Politics of the Parish in Early Modern England', in P. Griffiths (ed.), *The Experience of Authority in Early Modern England* (Basingstoke, 1996).

——, *Earthly Necessities: Economic Lives in Early Modern Britain* (New Haven, 2000).

——, and D. Levine, *Poverty and Piety in an English Village* (Oxford, 1995).

Wrigley, E. A., 'A Simple Model of London's Importance in Changing English Society and Economy, 1650–1750', *Past and Present*, 37 (1967), 44–70.

——, 'Urban Growth and Agricultural Change: England and the Continent in the Early Modern Period', *Journal of Interdisciplinary History*, 15 (1985), 683–728.

——, *Continuity, Chance and Change* (Cambridge, 1988).

——, 'Explaining the Rise in Marital Fertility in England in the 'Long' Eighteenth Century', *EcHRev*, 51 (1998), 435–64.

——, 'The Transition to an Advanced Organic Economy: Half a Millennium of English Agriculture', *EcHRev*, 59 (2006), 435–80.

——, and R. S. Schofield, *The Population History of England, 1541–1871* (Paperback edn, Cambridge, 1989).

——, R. S. Davies, J. E. Oeppen, and R. S. Schofield, *English Population History from Family Reconstitution* (Cambridge, 1997).

Yates, M., 'Continuity and Change, in Rural Society, c.1400–1600: West Hanney and Shaw (Berkshire) and their Region', D.Phil. thesis, Oxford (1997).

——, 'Change and Continuities in Rural Society from the Later Middle Ages to the Sixteenth Century: The Contribution of West Berkshire', *EcHRev*, 52 (1999), 617–37.

——, 'Watermills in the Local Economy of a Late Medieval Manor in Berkshire', in T. Thornton (ed.), *Social Attitudes and Political Structures in the Fifteenth Century* (Stroud, 2000), 184–201.

——, 'Between Fact and Fiction: Henry Brinklow's *Complaynt* Against Rapacious Landlords', *AgHRev*, 54 (2006), 24–44

Yelling, J. A., 'Agriculture, 1500–1730', in R. A. Dodgshon and R. A. Butlin (eds), *An Historical Geography of England and Wales* (London, 1978), 151–72.

Youings, J., 'The Terms of the Disposal of the Devon Monastic Lands, 1536–58', *EHR*, 69 (1954), 18–38.

——, *The Dissolution of the Monasteries* (London, 1971).

——, 'The Church', in C. Clay (ed.), *Rural Society: Landowners, Peasants and Labourers, 1500–1750* (Cambridge, 1990), 71–121.

Young, N. D., *Seignorial Administration in England* (Oxford, 1937).

Youngs, D., 'Servants and Labourers on a Late Medieval Demesne: The Case of Newton, Cheshire, 1498–1520', *AgHRev*, 47 (1999), 145–60.

Zell, M., 'Accounts of a Sheep and Corn Farm, 1558–60', *AgHRev*, 27 (1979), 122–82.

——, *Industry in the Countryside. Wealden Society in the Sixteenth Century* (Cambridge, 1994).

——, 'Fisher's 'flu and Moore's Probates: Quantifying the Mortality Crisis of 1556–1560', *EcHRev*, 47 (1994), 354–8.

——, 'Credit in the Pre-Industrial English Woollen Industry', *EcHRev*, 49 (1996), 667–91.

Ziegler, P., *The Black Death* (London, 1969).

Index

All places in county of Berkshire (pre-1974) unless otherwise indicated.